STUDIES IN IMPERIALISM

general editor John M. MacKenzie

When the 'Studies in Imperialism' series was founded more than twenty-five years ago, emphasis was laid upon the conviction that 'imperialism as a cultural phenomenon had as significant an effect on the dominant as on the subordinate societies'. With more than eighty books published, this remains the prime concern of the series. Cross-disciplinary work has indeed appeared covering the full spectrum of cultural phenomena, as well as examining aspects of gender and sex, frontiers and law, science and the environment, language and literature, migration and patriotic societies, and much else. Moreover, the series has always wished to present comparative work on European and American imperialism, and particularly welcomes the submission of books in these areas. The fascination with imperialism, in all its aspects, shows no sign of abating, and this series will continue to lead the way in encouraging the widest possible range of studies in the field. 'Studies in Imperialism' is fully organic in its development, always seeking to be at the cutting edge, responding to the latest interests of scholars and the needs of this ever-expanding area of scholarship.

Imperial spaces

Manchester University Press

Imperial spaces

PLACING THE IRISH AND SCOTS IN COLONIAL AUSTRALIA

Lindsay Proudfoot and Dianne Hall

MANCHESTER
UNIVERSITY PRESS
Manchester and New York

distributed in the United States exclusively by
PALGRAVE MACMILLAN

Published by MANCHESTER UNIVERSITY PRESS
OXFORD ROAD, MANCHESTER M13 9NR, UK
and ROOM 400, 175 FIFTH AVENUE, NEW YORK, NY 10010, USA
www.manchesteruniversitypress.co.uk

Distributed in the United States exclusively by
PALGRAVE MACMILLAN, 175 FIFTH AVENUE, NEW YORK, NY 10010, USA

Distributed in Canada exclusively by
UBC PRESS, UNIVERSITY OF BRITISH COLUMBIA,
2029 WEST MALL, VANCOUVER, BC, CANADA V6T 1Z2

British Library Cataloguing-in-Publication Data
A catalogue record for this book is available from the British Library

Library of Congress Cataloging-in-Publication Data applied for

ISBN   978 0 7190 7837 8 hardback

First published 2011

Typeset in Trump Medieval
by Servis Filmsetting Ltd, Stockport, Cheshire
Printed in Great Britain
by the MPG Books Group

For
Jennifer, Gillian and Robin
Louise, Rowan and Jack

CONTENTS

FIGURES AND TABLES

Figures

Tables

GENERAL EDITOR'S INTRODUCTION

In modern times it has become increasingly obvious that to understand the larger issues of imperialism/colonialism, it is necessary to
understand the local. The older 'macro' approaches often floated free
of real places and specific people, concentrating as they did on the
'official mind' or on economic or demographic flows which were often
divorced from what actually happened 'on the ground'. So far as the
British experience is concerned, it has become increasingly obvious
that we need to abandon the portmanteau 'Briton' and examine the
varied and sometimes contrasting specific ethnicities of the British and
Hibernian Isles – Irish, Scottish, Welsh and English. Moreover, we have
increasingly seen the welcome development of insights being shared
across the disciplines. The complexities of imperialism can indeed only
be understood when ideas are pooled from anthropology, art history,
environmental issues, the history of science, economics and, as in
this case, historical geography. Moreover, the breaking down of imperial history into the national 'stories' of individual territories has also
run its course. We have to examine comparative themes and interactions, notably between the so-called (and very diverse) 'metropole' and
colonial territories.

The authors of this book offer some very valuable insights into the
stage currently reached in the historiography and historical geography
of the British Empire, not least in their critical appraisal of the writ-
ings of 'postcolonial' scholars, as well as in their analysis of different
approaches to the concept of 'diaspora'. They also present new interpretations of the now long-standing theme of European settlement
history by considering both Irish and Scots migrants and the manner in
which they imaginatively re-conceptualised the cultural and religious,
familial and economic, environmental and meteorological characteristics of place both in their origins and in their destinations. In doing
so, they constructed family backgrounds in terms of home villages,
towns and landscapes while adopting new colonial identities in the
unfamiliar spaces in which they located themselves. Key components
of such imaginative linkages included religion, literature (oral and
written), genealogies and a whole variety of cultural forms, including
dance, music and sports. The authors examine the spatial manifestations of these processes (including architecture and various iconic and
visual memorials) in the vast pastoral landscapes of southern Australia,
mainly in Victoria, as well as in towns and smaller communities where

settlers often attempted to impose familiar forms – or the semblance of such forms – on highly unfamiliar places.

But the development of such multi-layered identities did not take place suddenly in the colonial setting. As the authors demonstrate, the developing transformation of such identities took place on ship-board voyages as well as in initial contacts with indigenous peoples. If that constitutes one end of the experience, the other is to be found in graveyards, where death acted as something more than the 'great level-ler', offering opportunities for commemoration (through gravestones, for example) which sometimes continued to express myths of ethnic origin. To arrive at their stimulating conclusions, Proudfoot and Hall make innovative use of a wide variety of valuable sources, including diaries, letters, the local press and much else, the analysis of which offers insights into ways in which such studies can press forward.

They conclude that the emergence of fresh colonial identities was a complex and multi-layered process, contingent on a whole variety of experiences. Some of these contained echoes of the past mixed with new forms stimulated by the present. These developments were also highly interactive, as between different peoples, places, experiences and environments. Although it is no place of this book to do so, it is interesting and important to carry such developments forward into the era of swifter travel, when people who continued to cling to ethnic origins often sought cultural reinvigoration from returns to 'home' while never abandoning their new diasporic personas. As these ways of 'replugging' into past identities continued, we see the 'jigsaw' of ethnic attributes and affiliations beginning to form and re-form through successive generations. While far from universal, there are indeed con-tinuing processes here that require to be understood. To use a culinary metaphor, the 'melting pot' contains many elements that are far from 'liquidised' into the whole. We are, in other words, dealing with con-stantly changing and developing phenomena. This book points the way to the manner in which further comparative studies can be developed, as well as constituting a foundation for these continuing generational studies.

John M. MacKenzie

ACKNOWLEDGEMENTS

In writing *Imperial spaces* the authors have incurred numerous debts to colleagues and institutions in both the Northern and Southern hemispheres. Our primary debt is to the Leverhulme Trust in London, who between 2001 and 2004 generously funded the original research project ('Memory, place, and symbol: Irish identities and landscape in colonial Australia') on which this book is based. In Australia, we are indebted to the staff of the following institutions for their unfailingly courteous and helpful response to our frequently arcane enquiries: the National Library of Australia, Canberra; the Mitchell Library, Sydney; the State Library of Victoria, Melbourne; the New South Wales State Archives; and the Royal Historical Society of Victoria. We happily acknowledge the permission granted by these institutions to quote from archives held in their care.

The School of Historical Studies at the University of Melbourne provided a congenial base for much of the time spent researching this book, not least during the sabbatical year Lindsay Proudfoot spent as an Honorary Visiting Fellow there in 2004–5. We are grateful to Professor Elizabeth Malcolm, Gerry Higgins Professor of Irish Studies at the University, for facilitating this. Without her encouragement, friendship and support the project would have been much more difficult to complete. Also in the School of History, Professor Joy Damousi, Professor Patricia Grimshaw, Professor Stuart McIntyre, the late Associate Professor David Philips, Professor Charles Sowerwine as well as Dr Dolly McKinnon, Dr Pamela O'Neill, Dr Kier Reeves, Dr Peter Sherlock and Dr Clare Wright all contributed at various times to the intellectually stimulating and collegiate environment in which we worked. The quiet efficiency of the School's management team, especially Erica Mehrtens, ensured that things ran as smoothly as possible.

We have benefited from discussions with an active and engaged community of scholars of Irish studies in various parts of Australia and New Zealand, including the late Professor Patrick O'Farrell in Sydney; Dr Philip Bull, Associate Professor Frances Devlin-Glass, Mary Doyle, Dr Liz Rushen and Dr Val Noone in Melbourne; Dr Jennifer Harrison in Brisbane; and Dr Gordon Forth in Warrnambool. In Melbourne, Professor Joe Powell and his wife, Suzie, command our especial thanks for their unstinting hospitality to the Proudfoot family during their visits to Australia, and for Joe's insights into Australian geography. In New Zealand, Dr Brad Patterson, Professor Michael Roche, Dr Lyndon

Fraser, Professor Peter Kuch and Professor Malcolm Campbell have all provided useful correctives to the hegemonic Australian view of the Antipodean Irish. Lindsay Proudfoot owes Brad and Kathryn Patterson and Mike Roche particular thanks for their generous hospitality in Wellington and Palmerston North respectively.

Elsewhere, we wish to thank Dorothy King, Wendy Melbourne and all at the Stawell Historical Society; all the dedicated volunteers at the Kilmore District Hospital and Kilmore Historical Society, particularly Heather Knight; Rachel Naughton of the Melbourne Diocesan Historical Commission; Mrs Chris Palmer, Church Records Manager, Presbyterian Church of Victoria; Fr Peter Rankin, Parish Priest, St Patrick's Catholic Church, Kilmore and Ray Thorburn of the Kiama Family History Centre.

Successive Irish Australian (subsequently Irish Australasian) Studies conferences in Melbourne and Wellington in 2004, 2007 and 2009, the AHRC Nations and Diasporas conferences in Aberdeen and Wellington in 2008 and meetings of the Melbourne Irish Studies Seminar between 2002 and 2008 provided congenial forums for frequently challenging debates which have helped to shape this book. We are grateful to all those – alas now anonymous – contributors who took part. An earlier version of a small portion of the material in Chapter 6 appeared as 'Imagining the Frontier: Environment, Memory and Settlement: Narratives from Victoria, Australia, 1850–1890', in the *Journal of Irish and Scottish Studies* (3, 2010).

In Ireland, the early formulation of the research owed much to the constructive advice and criticism of Professor David Fitzpatrick, whose own work on Irish emigration to Australia has been of foundational importance to it. In Belfast, we greatly benefited from the professionalism of the staff at the Public Record Office of Northern Ireland. Much of the book was written while Lindsay Proudfoot was Reader in Irish Historical Geography at Queen's University, Belfast. We acknowledge the interest shown in the project by his colleagues there, particularly Professor Bruce Campbell, who was unstinting in his support. We owe particular thanks to Maura Pringle, Senior Cartographer in the School of Geography, Archaeology, and Palaeoecology at Queen's for her professionalism in turning our scrappy drawings into the polished figures that appear here.

Our final debts are more personal. To Jennifer, Gillian and Robin in Belfast; and Louise, Rowan and Jack in Melbourne, our greatest debt is due.

Belfast and Melbourne

ABBREVIATIONS

APCA	*Ararat and Pleasant Creek Advertiser*
ML	*Mitchell Library*
NLA	*National Library of Australia*
PCN	*Pleasant Creek News*
RHSV	*Royal Historical Society of Victoria*
SLV	*State Library of Victoria*
SN	*Stawell News*
UOWA	*University of Wollongong Archives*

CHAPTER 1

Introduction

You folks have queer ideas of this country. (James Parkinson, Bendigo, 1857)

The country around is thoroughly English like ... quite different from any other colony out here. (Alex Kerr, Hobart Town, 1858)

We do not know whether James Parkinson and Alex Kerr ever met while they were in Australia. It is unlikely that they did. Both hailed from Ireland. Both came from families who inhabited that uncertain social terrain between undoubted gentry status, on the one hand, and professional respectability, on the other. Parkinson was born into a minor land-owning family in County Down, where his father was also a Church of Ireland clergyman. Kerr, who was of partly Scottish ancestry, came from a naval family who had lived first in Dublin and, latterly, in Cork. After failing to enter Trinity College Dublin to read medicine in 1848, Parkinson embarked on a merchant maritime career that took him to India, China and Australia. In 1854 he abandoned this to try his luck on the Victorian goldfields, where he stayed for five generally unsuccessful years. In 1859 he returned to sea, before settling in Hobart Town in 1863.[1] Alex Kerr also went to sea, as an officer in the Royal Navy. His first commission was as a midshipman on the frigate HMS *Iris*, which was sent to join the Australian squadron in 1857. She arrived in Sydney harbour in July of that year, at much the same time as James Parkinson was commenting on his family's misapprehensions about Australia in his letter to his mother from Bendigo. Over the next two years, while James continued to try to wrest a living from the unpromising surrounds of Phillip's Reef and New Chum Gulley, Alex enjoyed the life of a well-connected young naval officer on the Sydney station. His letters home speak of picnics, balls and riding parties with the Governor, as well as of periodically showing the flag in Aotearoa/ New Zealand and suppressing unrest in New Caledonia.[2]

[1]

Although Parkinson and Kerr were both Irishmen by birth, they hardly accord with conventional representations of Irish emigrants in colonial Australia as predominantly Catholic, rural, poorly skilled and impoverished.[3] Rather, their stories remind us of the numerous ambiguities which attended Ireland's place within the British Empire and the role of her people as its subjects, servants and, occasionally, protagonists. Thus Kerr, who was equally scrupulous in enquiring after his Scottish relatives as he was in declaring his Irish origins to the 'decent Irishmen' he encountered in Sydney, also lambasted and patronised the 'ungrateful colonials' for their political hubris and social *gaucherie*.[4] This suggests some consciousness of his own ambiguous identity. As an Irishman of mixed ancestry who held a commission in the service of the British sovereign, he was active in the pursuit of empire and espoused a socially exclusive and distinctly metropolitan world-view.

In comparison, Parkinson's career was decidedly opportunistic and driven by circumstance. Yet he, too, occupied a variety of liminal spaces that testify to the complexity of empire and of the Irish presence within it. Parkinson's land-owning background, although comparatively modest, was still sufficient to separate him by reason of wealth and colonial history from the majority of his fellow countrymen.[5] His seafaring career, forced upon him by his failure to enter that bastion of Anglo-Irish privilege, Trinity College, involved him in a complex web of trade and communications that bound the Empire together and articulated its meanings for its agents and subjects. Finally, his fruitless search for gold exposed him to the egalitarianism of life on the diggings and sustained his mocking self-image as 'a poor sunburnt digger with his swag on his back', moulded by the exigencies of colonial life.[6]

The experience of empire thus told very differently on each of these men. But for both of them, that experience was constructed through material encounters with people and localities that were necessarily framed by the sense of translocation and difference that lay at the heart of empire. This was both spatial and temporal. Discursive flows of information, beliefs, capital, goods and labour, the mutually transformative encounter between European selfhood and the indigenous other – now recognised for what it always was, diverse and complex – and the continual re-imagining of empire, all combined to destabilise singular, bounded understandings of the white colonial presence. Neither the white self nor the colonised other were inherent or stable: both had to be actively defined and maintained.[7] Past experience played a particular role in this. Kerr's picnics on the shores of Sydney Harbour, or the claims Parkinson staked at Bendigo, were not only imagined and material places in the colonial 'here and now', they were also enacted in the light of the 'there and then' of memory. Just as Kerr admired the out-of-place 'Englishness' of Hobart Town, so he welcomed the temporary waterside emplacement of familiar social codes and practices that were otherwise troublingly absent from his general social *milieu* in Sydney.[8] Parkinson acknowledged his want of 'good society' as a digger.[9] For both men, the colonial present held meanings which were only intelligible in terms of a past that was construed as much in terms of space as of time.

The complex interplay between settler identities, colonial practice, time and space that these episodes call attention to, forms the subject of this book. Eschewing grand narratives of empire, be they formulated in terms of a Eurocentric modernist epistemology or a postcolonial critique, we offer a place-centred analysis of settler colonialism as ethnicised 'white' experience of the discursive and the local. Taking the spatiality of the human condition – the idea that people create, consume and contest a multiplicity of material and imagined spaces in the quotidian pursuit of their everyday lives – as axiomatic, we argue that settler experience needs to be understood in terms of the 'local worlds' settlers created, inhabited and imagined. In this way we may hope to recover something of the intimate textures of colonial life and their meaning for these settlers' sense of identity and purpose within the spaces of empire. We argue that these 'local worlds' were not simply constructed from presentist colonial experience, but were also inflected by memory. Accordingly, they reflected, among other things, the diverse ethnic origins of the British and Irish migration stream, but in ambiguous and hybrid ways which have not always been recognised hitherto. This was a question not merely of nationality, but rather of the extent to which individuals negotiated their colonial present in terms which consciously invoked – or ignored – their diasporic past.

We argue our case in the context of the so-called Second British Empire, specifically the settler colonies that were created in Australia, as they were in Canada, Aotearoa/New Zealand and South Africa, during the nineteenth century. Following Mcleod, we envisage imperialism in discursive terms, as a metropolitan-centred (though not one-way), transnational network or field of trade and commerce, articulated by, and under the protection of, political, legal and military controls. Colonialism represented the historically specific instances where this system was enacted through various modes of territorial acquisition or aggrandisement, with consequences that were as much cultural and epistemological as economic and political. In each case, the effects were local and transnational, with 'fractured and ambiguous meanings' which, in Mitchell's phrase, 'varied with the specificities of places, peoples, and historical moments'.[10] These semiotic or symbolic meanings were ascribed, negotiated and exchanged through the signify-ing processes of social group formation which we designate as 'culture'. In this way, colonising and colonised subjects alike made sense of their world and of their position (and that of others) in it. Thus, following Lester, we envisage culture not as a 'residual category left unaccounted for by more powerful economic analysis' but as 'the very medium through which [colonial] social relations [were] expressed, experienced and contested'.[11]

We focus on the experience of Irish and, for comparison, Scottish emigrants in south-east Australia – particularly Victoria – during the period between the 1840s, when widespread assisted emigration from Britain to Australia began, and the Federation of the Australian colo-nies in 1901. This was a period of profound social, political, economic and environmental change within Australia, and of equally profound changes in the relationship between the Australian colonies and Britain.[12] Caught up in these were the Irish and Scots, who constituted the two largest and culturally most influential European minorities in Australia at this time. Many among them embodied a culturally complex and ambiguous role in the Australian colonies as agents either of British imperialism or of colonial nationalism, and sometimes of both. This colonial hybridity variously mirrored and/or belied their sense of their origins in ethnically marked, culturally subaltern and constitutionally subordinate parts of the United Kingdom. In either case, it speaks of the diversity of the British and Irish migrant stream and of the complexity of the imagined worlds created in the colonies by subaltern elements within it.

Our perspectives are critical, material and geographical. We pursue our claims regarding the defining heterogeneity, spatiality and local-ism of white settler experience by interrogating various narratives of place that were constructed as part of this. We argue that these place narratives were fundamental to the ongoing (re)negotiation of both indigenous and non-indigenous identities in the Australian colonies, as elsewhere. Here, we conceive of places as subjectively constructed sites of memory, agency and meaning, loosely bounded within the material world, which, in differing though interacting ways for indigenous and non-indigenous people, were framed and articulated by the material and informational flows and networks which knit empire together. In other words, colonial places existed in the settlers' imagination as a set of interpretations that they attached to the social behaviours, economic activity and cultural inscriptions that they believed were enacted at particular locales in the material landscape. The meanings of place that attached to a particular locale for a given individual were inter-subjective. That is, they were informed by that person's accumulating experience of other place meanings elsewhere. Accordingly, we may envisage each settler's 'imagined world' as a nexus of constantly 'emerging' places that were continuously [re]performed as these inter-subjective contexts changed, but which still connected the settler's past with their present.[13]

To the extent that our primary concern is with Irish and Scottish settlers, our focus is unfashionably Eurocentric, but we believe there are sound reasons for this. While heeding Coombes's claim that settler societies were shaped by the nature of their encounter with the indigenous other,[14] we argue that most critical scholarship has failed to acknowledge sufficiently the implications of the ethnic heterogeneity of the English, Scots and Irish migrant stream for the constructions of whiteness that were fundamental to the colonial experience. Following Fraser, we envisage ethnicity as shared cultural consciousness that is *actively constructed* rather than primordial. Consequently, though it gives rise to a sense of common selfhood that is derived from shared cultural traditions, language, religion (possibly) and experience, this is variably expressed in ways that are contingent on circumstance.[15] Moreover, although ethnic consciousness may well support claims to nationhood, it is not itself synonymous with nationality, still less race. Accordingly, nineteenth-century migration from the British Isles (itself an invented term) to Australia encompassed ethnic solidarities whose diversity and potential for change were not always easily accommodated by straightforward national labels, still less by representations of the settler presence in the Australian colonies as a 'white hegemonic other'.

Recent scholarship on the so-called British World has begun to address aspects of the social and cultural production of settler identities. Similarly, some Australian historians have acknowledged ethnic differences within the Anglo-Celtic migrant stream, albeit from a largely essentialist perspective that has privileged certain cultural traditions as being more 'authentically' Irish than others. Despite this, these developments are welcome. Initial postcolonial representations of empire have long been criticised for their espousal of black/white, self/other, European/indigenous binaries, which the ongoing debate over cultural hybridity has, paradoxically, reinforced.[16] The fundamental postcolonial critique of the racialising Eurocentric epistemologies underpinning ideas of empire – and the ability of these to 'colonise' the indigenous self – remains a powerful one. But it has little to say about the ethnic and cultural heterogeneity of the British colonial presence at different moments of empire. Or, specifically, about its diverse materiality in colonies of settlement as varied as New South Wales, Aotearoa/New Zealand or Canada, or in any other of the various Crown colonies, dependencies, mandated territories, administrative colonies or colonies of trade that comprised the British Empire.[17]

Representations of Irish participation in the British Empire provide a case in point. Although Irish historians have long debated the relevance of colonialism and imperialism as explanative categories to describe Ireland's constitutional relationship to England (later, Britain) from the sixteenth century onwards and the social and economic structures and practices which developed there, until recently they have paid relatively little attention to Irish involvement in the empire overseas.[18] By contrast, comparatively extensive local literatures exist relating to Irish experience in the settler colonies, particularly Australia, Canada and Aotearoa/New Zealand, but in Australia at least, this tends towards ethnic essentialism and rarely uses an explicitly imperial frame.[19] An even larger migration literature relates to Irish settlement in Britain and the United States during the nineteenth century and after, and this provides a point of comparison with the Australasian material.[20] Scotland has been better served by recent empirical analyses of the global extent of Scottish participation in empire.[21] Comparatively little of this material offers a critical perspective, however. In the Irish academy, this is to be found in the work of the literary and cultural theorists who, since the 1980s, have engaged in a sometimes polemical debate concerning Ireland's postcolonial condition. Originally grounded in a re-evaluation of the Irish literary canon, which was concerned to expose the continuing linguistic colonial legacy of the British presence in Ireland, this debate has been held to invoke an essentialist nationalism in its reading of Ireland before and after Partition. It has also remained, quite literally, insular in focus, notwithstanding its claim to draw parallels with the postcoloniality of other ex-colonies.[22]

Because this literature either has been primarily concerned with the condition of Ireland *within* the Empire or else has treated the Irish colonial presence overseas as an essentialist, autonomous subject, it has failed to challenge postcolonial representations of the non-indigenous colonial subject as a Manichaean white other. It has also failed to adequately acknowledge the conditional, multi-layered and unstable nature of all forms of self-identification, be the individual white, indigenous, Scots or Irish. More than this, much the greater part of the literature also fails to acknowledge the complicity of perceptual and material forms of space within this process of identity formation. Our concern with the narratives of place constructed by Scots and Irish emigrants in Victoria and New South Wales focuses precisely on the contested meanings of these as they were imagined by settlers and others. We consider the evidence for the ways in which individuals and communities among the migrants grounded their sense of selfhood within a narrative of material colonial belonging; whether and in what ways this relied for its construction on memory; and the extent to which these imagined material places were susceptible to re-imagination as a result of the continuing dislocation of the self that lay at the heart of empire.

In developing these themes, we make no claim to panoptic universalism. Our book is not another history of the Irish and Scots in Australia. In our attempt to uncover the lives that were imagined and performed as place by Irish and Scots emigrants, and to locate these within the broader discursive spaces of empire, we narrate the experience of a relatively limited number of individuals and communities. These were selected on the basis of the nature and extent of their representation in the archival record and their residual material presence in the cultural landscape. By definition, therefore, the individuals thus represented were self-identifying Scots and Irish men and women who were sufficiently literate and, by implication, materially well placed to leave a historically traceable record of their existence and subjective positionality within the colonies. Not everyone was so fortunate. Accordingly, we supplement the correspondence, journals and diaries of the Irish and Scottish squatters, selectors, clergymen and others whose individual imaginings of place form the subject of much of our enquiry with evidence relating to the collective 'voice' of those who, as individuals, were effectively silenced within colonial society: the poor, labouring men and women and the marginalised generally. By its nature, this evidence derives from collective activities and the communal expression of identity: membership of or participation in religious and other representative institutions; public debate in newspapers; and material inscriptions in the landscape.

We use this evidence to recover collective expressions of Scots and Irish migrant selfhood in four small towns, chosen for their diverse histories and varied Irish and Scots presence: Kilmore, Port Fairy and Stawell in Victoria, and Kiama in New South Wales (Figure 1.1). All four towns were locally or regionally important agricultural or pastoral market centres. Kiama and Port Fairy (renamed Belfast between 1843 and 1887) were also ports, while Kilmore and Port Fairy were founded as part of Special Surveys, the legislative device used by the government of New South Wales in the early 1840s to attract well-capitalised land investment.[23] Stawell was established in the late 1850s as a gold-rush town, under the name of Pleasant Creek.[24] Although these towns are all located in or near what were, in the nineteenth century, regions of relatively dense Scots and Irish settlement, we do not claim that the place narratives enacted in them were necessarily widely representative of Irish and Scots experience in Australia at that time.[25] Nor do we

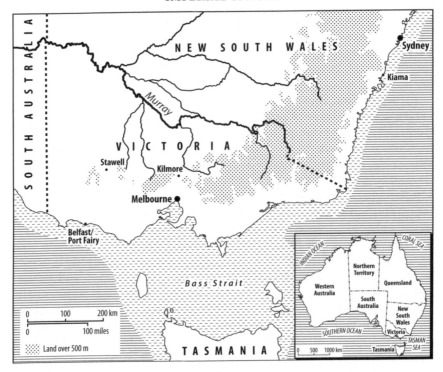

1.1 Location of the study towns

claim that the individual lives we have recovered were typical of the socio-economic classes and religious groups from which the subjects came. Rather, we explore these particular instances of individual and collective place making as examples of the ways in which the singular and 'messy' imagined geographies of the colonial margins of empire might be constructed. While acknowledging the subjectivities inherent in our evidence,[26] we believe that these narratives of place, constructed and imagined at specific moments of empire, demonstrate the inherent spatiality of white settler identities and prompt further consideration of their heterogeneity, cultural ambiguity and discursively framed localism.

The structure of the book

We begin by considering the historiographical contexts for our place-based approach to settler identities. Chapter 2 examines recent historical and geographical literature on empire and colonialism and pays particular attention to its engagement with postcolonial theory. We argue that, although this has led productively to deeper understanding of the hybrid cultural identities created by imperial practice, the historical literature has remained largely immune to the idea that different social and cultural constructions of space and place might play an instrumental role in colonial identity formation. Modern historical geographies of colonialism, on the other hand, have long acknowledged this, but have yet to consider its implications for settler colonies in light of the ethnic diversity exhibited by British and Irish emigrants. Chapter 3 develops this theme of Irish and Scottish migrant ethnic consciousness in the context of recent critical approaches to emigration. The Irish and Scottish settlers in Australia formed part of a much wider, global migration which took their fellow countrymen and women to numerous countries both within and beyond the British Empire. Recent representations have construed these wider movements in terms of diaspora, in which the individual migrant is variously argued either to have retained a sense of home and its loss, or else to have become place-less, inhabiting 'in-between' space, characterised by a transnational sense of identity. Chapter 3 considers how these competing ideas of diaspora might inform our understanding of Irish and Scottish overseas settlement within the Empire and elsewhere and, in light of this, explores recent representations of Irish and Scottish settlement in Australia and Aotearoa/New Zealand.

The remaining chapters work within these contexts to examine evidence for ethnicity and other markers of identity within place narratives performed by Scots and Irish settlers en route to and within colonial south-east Australia. Chapter 4 discusses the ways Scots and Irish migrant *mentalités* were constructed on board ship during the outward voyage to Australia. The migrants' negotiation of these unfamiliar shipboard worlds was an essential step in the formation of their identity as migrants – people in the process of leaving the familiar and known, to enter an imagined future. The long sea voyage to Australia required confinement within the intimately bounded material social spaces of shipboard life, and these constituted unstable and changing places in which migrants explored feelings of anticipation for their new lives and memories of home, and negotiated changing circumstances of class and culture through their associations with other passengers.

Once migrants arrived in Australia they progressively inscribed the landscape with the discursive signatures of settler capitalism. Chapter 5 examines the extent of Scottish and Irish involvement in the pastoral geographies that were the mainstay of the Australian economy until the gold rushes of the 1850s and which remained of considerable importance thereafter. It compares the legislative framework that provided the basis for this pastoral exploitation with contemporary Scottish and Irish land legislation and considers whether, together, these prompted particular expressions of cultural memory by Irish and Scots settlers in Australia. Chapter 6 continues the rural theme and explores four narratives of place which exemplify the complex and ambiguous environmental, racial, social and ethnic semiotics that inflected the pastoral cartographies created by Scots and Irish squatters in Victoria and New South Wales.

The erection of an effective urban network was central to the discourse of settler capitalism, and chapter 7 examines aspects of the contested place meanings that attached to Belfast, Kiama, Kilmore and Stawell as part of the urban process of colonial foundation. The variety of 'voices' and social positionalities that characterised even the smallest towns in colonial Australia ensured that hegemonic . urban narratives rarely remained uncontested. After surveying the characteristics of colonial urbanism in general, the chapter explores the idea of conflicting urban semiotics via an analysis of the interpretation different Scots and Irish interest groups placed on civic improvement and urban associational space in Melbourne and the four study towns. The chapter concludes by considering examples of gendered ethnic space in Stawell and other towns and the diverse subjectivities this entailed.

Irish and Scottish religious performance and its grounding in ethnic memory provides the theme for chapter 8, which explores the ways in which Irish and Scots place identities were mediated through discursive religious practice. The chapter considers the nature of the religious networks which linked the major Irish and Scots denominations throughout the Empire, setting these as context for the local meanings of self and other embodied by these Churches in Victoria and New South Wales. The chapter challenges essentialist readings of denominational affiliation and reads allegedly 'ethnic' religious institutions such as the Presbyterian and Roman Catholic churches as arenas of developing social and theological conflict as much as sites of essentialist selfhood.

The final chapter returns to the objectives laid out in this introduction. It argues for increasing recognition of the diversity of the white presence during modern Australia's foundational narrative and for the complex place narratives created by subaltern settler groups as they imbued the landscape with their own sense of self. Drawing on the substantive argument that runs through the book, the conclusion argues that the existence of these unstable and polyvocal landscapes constitutes a powerful corrective to any master narrative of Australian history which construes this in binary and racialised terms.

Notes

1   James C. Parkinson, Bendigo, to Anne Parkinson, Killough, 10 July 1857, 'The James Cumine Parkinson Letters', www.lecalehistory.co.uk/parkinson.

2   'Alex Kerr. Letters to his family in Ireland while a midshipman on the Australian station, 1856–1862', NLA Ms 7257.

3   D. Fitzpatrick, *Oceans of Consolation. Personal Accounts of Irish Migration to Australia* (Cork, 1994), p. 13. See also, L. Proudfoot, 'Landscape, Place, and Memory: Towards a Geography of Irish Identities in Colonial Australia', in O. Walsh (ed.), *Ireland Abroad. Politics and Professions in the Nineteenth Century* (Dublin, 2003), pp. 172–85.

4   Alex Kerr, Farm Cove, Sydney, to Mrs Kerr, 18 May 1858, 'Alex Kerr. Letters to his family in Ireland while a midshipman on the Australian station, 1856–1862', NLA Ms 7257, Folder 4, 41–2; Alex Kerr, Sydney, to Mrs Kerr, 28 September 1858, *ibid.*, Folder 4, 58; Alex Kerr, Sydney, to Mrs Kerr, 20 May 1859, *ibid.*, Folder 5, 69–71; Alex Kerr, Sydney, to Robert Kerr, 2 July 1859, *ibid.*, Folder 5, 75.

5   In 1876, Anne Parkinson, James's mother, was recorded as owning 294 acres, valued at £360, at Killough, Co. Down. See: *Return of Owners of Land of One Acre and Upwards in the Several Counties, Counties of Cities, and Counties of Towns in Ireland* (Dublin, 1876, repr., Baltimore, 1988), p. 244. This would have placed the family among the lower *echelons* of landowners in Co. Down. See: L. Proudfoot, 'Land Ownership and Improvement, 1700–1845', in *Idem* (ed.), *Down: History and Society. Interdisciplinary Essays on the History of an Irish County* (Dublin, 1997), pp. 203–37.

6   James C. Parkinson, Bendigo, to Anne Parkinson, 14 March 1858, 'The James Cumine Parkinson Letters', www.lecalehistory.co.uk/parkinson.

7   E. Buettner, *Empire Families. Britons and Late Imperial India* (Oxford, 2004), pp. 1–15; F. Cooper and A. L. Stoler (eds), *Tensions of Empire. Colonial Cultures in a Bourgeois World* (Berkeley, 1997), pp. 6–7; M. A. Procida, *Married to the Empire. Gender, Politics and Imperialism in India, 1883–1947* (Manchester, 2002), p. 7.

8   Alex Kerr, Sydney, to Mrs Kerr, 4 May 1858, 'Alex Kerr. Letters to his family in Ireland while a midshipman on the Australian station, 1856–1862', NLA Ms 7257, Folder 4, 38; Alex Kerr, Hobartown, to Mrs Kerr, 28 December 1858, *ibid.*, Folder 4, 61.

9   James C. Parkinson, Bendigo, to Anne Parkinson, 12 July 1858, 'The James Cumine Parkinson Letters', www.lecalehistory.co.uk/parkinson.

10   J. McLeod, *Beginning Postcolonialism* (Manchester, 2000), pp. 7–8; W. J. T. Mitchell (ed.), *Landscape and Power. Space, Place and Landscape* (Chicago, 2nd edn, 2002), pp. 9–10; L. Proudfoot and M. Roche, 'Introduction: Place, Network, and the Geographies of Empire', chapter 1 in *Eidem* (eds), *(Dis)Placing Empire. Renegotiating British Colonial Geographies* (London, 2005), p. 1.

11   C. Hall, *Cultures of Empire. A Reader* (Manchester, 2000), pp. 10–12; A. Lester, *Imperial Networks. Creating Identities in Nineteenth-century South Africa and Britain* (London, 2001), p. 3; McLeod, *Beginning Postcolonialism*, pp. 7–8.

12   See especially L. Trainor, *British Imperialism and Australian Nationalism. Manipulation, Conflict and Compromise in the Late Nineteenth Century* (Cambridge, 1994). J. M. Powell's *An Historical Geography of Modern Australia. The Restive Fringe* (Cambridge, 1988) still provides the best account of the geographical dimension to these developments. S. Macintyre's *A Concise History of Australia* (Cambridge, 2nd edn, 2004) offers an accessible summary of the main developments in Australia. For broader contextual accounts of the wider governance and socio-economic practice of empire at this period, see A. Porter (ed.), *The Oxford History of the British Empire, Volume III, The Nineteenth Century* (Oxford, 1999), especially Part I.

13   The geographical literature on place is extensive. Works which have particularly informed our thinking include: J. Agnew and J. Duncan (eds), *The Power of Place*

(Boston, 1990); S. Daniels, 'Place and the Geographical Imagination', *Geography*, Vol. 77 (1992), pp. 310–22; J. Duncan and D. Ley (eds), *Place/Culture/Representation* (New York, 1993); A. Pred, 'Place as Historically Contingent Process: Structuration and the Time-Geography of Becoming Places', *Annals of the Association of American Geographers*, Vol. 74, No. 2 (1984), pp. 279–97; Yi-Fu Tuan, 'Space and Place: Humanistic Perspective', *Progress in Human Geography*, Vol. 6 (1974), pp. 211–52.

14 A. Coombes (ed.), 'Introduction. Memory and History in Settler Colonialism', in *Idem, Rethinking settler colonialism. History and Memory in Australia, Canada, Aotearoa New Zealand and South Africa* (Manchester, 2006), pp. 1–3.

15 L. Fraser, *Castles of Gold. A History of New Zealand's West Coast Irish* (Dunedin, 2007).

16 C. Bridge and K. Fedorowich (eds), 'The British World: Diaspora, Culture and Identity', *The Journal of Imperial and Commonwealth History*, Special Issue, Vol. 31, No. 2 (May 2003); Cooper and Stoler, *Tensions of Empire*, pp. 34 ff; A. Curthoys, 'History and Identity', in W. Hudson and G. Bolton (eds), *Creating Australia. Changing Australian History* (St Leonards, 1997), pp. 23–38; *Idem*, 'Mythologies', in R. Nile (ed.), *The Australian Legend and its Discontents* (St Lucia, 2000), pp. 11–41; M. Dixson, *The Imaginary Australian. Anglo-Celts and Identity – 1788 to the Present* (Sydney, 1999); R. White, '*Inventing Australia* Revisited', in Hudson and Bolton, *Creating Australia*, pp. 12–22. Important recent contributions to the debate over the necessarily 'bounded' nature of Homi Bhabha's concept of cultural hybridity include: L. Benton and J. Muth, 'On Cultural Hybridity: Interpreting Colonial Authority and Performance', *Journal of Colonialism and Colonial History*, Vol. 1, No. 1 (2000), n.p.; F. Anthias, 'New Hybridities, Old Concepts: The Limits of "Culture"', *Ethnic and Racial Studies*, Vol. 24, No. 4, July 2001, pp. 619–41; J. Nederveen Pieterse, 'Hybridity, So What? The Anti-hybridity Backlash and the Riddles of Recognition', *Theory, Culture & Society*, Vol. 18, Nos 2–3 (2001), pp. 219–45; and N. Papastergiardis, 'Hybridity and Ambivalence. Places and Flows in Contemporary Art and Culture', *Theory, Culture & Society*, Vol. 22, No. 4 (2005), pp. 39–64.

17 Which, in non-critical terms, has of course been the stuff of the conventional imperial history discussed below. The *Oxford History*'s historiography remains useful in this respect. See R. Winks (ed.), *The Oxford History of the British Empire, Volume V, Historiography* (Oxford, 1999).

18 Recent important general studies of Ireland and empire include: D. Fitzpatrick, 'Ireland and the Empire', chapter 22 in Porter (ed.), *Nineteenth Century*, pp. 495–521; S. Howe, *Ireland and Empire. Colonial Legacies in Irish History and Culture* (Oxford, 2000); K. Jeffery (ed.), '*An Irish Empire?' Aspects of Ireland and the British Empire* (Manchester, 1996); K. Kenny (ed.), *Oxford History of the British Empire, Companion Series, Ireland and the British Empire* (Oxford, 2004).

19 Useful summaries of this literature may be found in: D. H. Akenson, *The Irish Diaspora. A Primer* (Belfast, 1996); A. Bielenberg (ed.), *The Irish Diaspora* (London, 2000); L. Fraser, *A Distant Shore. Irish Migration and New Zealand Settlement* (Otago, 2000); C. J. Houston and W. J. Smyth, 'The Irish Diaspora: Emigration to the New World, 1720–1920', in B. J. Graham and L. J. Proudfoot (eds), *An Historical Geography of Ireland* (London, 1993), pp. 338–65; *Eidem, Irish Emigration and Canadian Settlement. Patterns, Links and Letters* (Toronto, 1990); P. O'Farrell, *The Irish in Australia. 1788 to the present* (3rd edn, Sydney, 2000); B. Patterson (ed.), *The Irish in New Zealand. Historical Contexts and Perspectives* (Wellington, 2002).

20 For summaries, see: Akenson, *Irish Diaspora*; Bielenberg (ed.), *Irish Diaspora*; B. Collins, 'The Irish in Britain, 1780–1921', in Graham and Proudfoot (eds), *Historical Geography*, pp. 366–98; G. Davis, *The Irish in Britain 1815–1914* (Dublin, 1991); M. Dezell, *Irish America. Coming into Clover: The Evolution of a People and a Culture* (London, 2001); D. N. Doyle and O. D. Edwards (eds), *America and Ireland 1776–1976. The American Identity and the Irish Connection* (London, 1980); P. J. Drudy (ed.), *The Irish in America: Emigration, Assimilation, Impact* (Cambridge,

1985); J. J. Lee and M. R. Casey, *Making the Irish American. History and Heritage of the Irish in the United States* (New York, 2006); D. M. MacRaild, *Irish Migrants in Modern Britain 1750–1922* (London, 1999); R. Swift and S. Gilley (eds), *The Irish in Britain 1815–1939* (London, 1989).

21 J. Brock, *The Mobile Scot: A Study of Emigration and Migration, 1861–1911* (Edinburgh, 1999); T. M. Devine, *Scottish Emigration and Scottish Society* (Edinburgh, 1992); *Idem, Scotland's Empire 1600–1815* (London, 2004); M. Harper, *Adventurers and Exiles. The Great Scottish Exodus* (London, 2003).

22 J. Cleary, 'Postcolonial Ireland', chapter 9 in Kenny (ed.), *Ireland*, pp. 251–88.

23 J. W. Powling, *Port Fairy. The First Fifty Years 1837–1887. A Social History* (Melbourne, 1980), pp. 24–61; A. G. L. Shaw, *A History of the Port Phillip District. Victoria before Separation* (Melbourne, 1996), pp. 157–62; M. V. Tucker, *Kilmore on the Sydney road* (Kilmore, 1988), pp. 31–53.

24 R. Murray and K. White, *The Golden Years of Stawell* (Stawell, 1983), pp. 8–35.

25 The essentialist problems inherent in conventional interpretations of the 'Irish' population distributions recorded by late nineteenth-century Australian censuses are discussed in Proudfoot, 'Landscape, Place, and Memory', pp. 176–82.

26 Buettner, *Empire Families*, pp. 75 ff.

CHAPTER 2

(Re)presenting empire

It must be clear therefore as daylight that Great Britain has been specially called, in the good Providence of God, to the heroic work of colonisation. (John Dunmore Lang, Sydney, 1857[1])

Despite the Reverend Dr Lang's characteristically trenchant views on the subject, modern historical scholarship has grown increasingly wary of suggesting that 'the Bible and Flag' enjoyed any form of consistent relationship during the process of British imperial expansion.[2] Still less would scholars claim that the global assertion of Britain's economic, military and political interests between the seventeenth and nineteenth centuries was an act of Providence, in however Seeley-esque a fit of absent-mindedness. Rather, Anglophone historians of empire have increasingly engaged in a debate about the nature of their craft: about what can and cannot be known about empire, and about the ways in which post-imperial western scholarship has imposed its own forms of knowledge and understanding on the postcolonial world. Much of this has been a response to the challenge posed by postcolonial scholars since the 1970s to what were once considered to be some of the verities of European imperial history in general: its narratives of modernity and economic expansion; the metropolitan *locus* of ideas of governance and civil society; and the encounter with indigenous peoples, who were perceived as possessing none of these things.

These debates inform our present concern with place-based settler narratives in Australia and we explore the issues they raise from two perspectives. First, we examine the encounter between postcolonial theory and British imperial history per se. We conclude that, despite the growing awareness of cultural boundaries and boundary crossing and of cultural hybridities that transgress essentialist representations of identity, the 'new' imperial history remains as resolutely aspatial as the 'old'. Retaining a similar focus on the 'non-white' Empire, it remains

Offaly County Library	Date of Application	*For office use*	
		Branch	
Author			
Title/Subject		Class No.	
		Acc. No.	
Place & Publisher		Loc.	
Date	Price	ISBN	ILL	S.S.

Very EXPENSIVE Book.

immune to the idea that the performance of socially and culturally valorised place is an inherent part of identity formation, whether of Europeans or indigenes – past or present – in the colonies or elsewhere. We then explore recent historical geographies of colonialism. While acknowledging the diversity of tropes within this field, and the shared concern of many of them with the spatialised construction of identity, we argue that this has not extended to critical recognition of the ethnic diversity of the British and Irish settler stream. Consequently, there has been serious engagement neither with the individual subaltern white place narratives this created nor with their general contribution to the semiotic landscapes of settler colonialism.

New imperial histories?

In his review of the final volume in *The Oxford History of the British Empire*, on the historiography of the Empire (1999), Stephen Howe offered a cautionary assessment of the magnitude of the task the contributors faced and noted the inevitable unevenness of the results of their labour. Eschewing an earlier reviewer's polemic that it was 'bizarre' to attempt to separate historiography from historical revision, Howe nevertheless identified both significant absences (identity, migration, race and intellectual history) and a general unease in the book over the intellectual challenges imperial history was then thought to be facing, particularly from postcolonial theory.[3] Other dissonances in the collection had longer antecedents. In asserting the importance of neo-Britons and the British World as subjects of imperial history, Bridge and Fedorowich suggest that the limited coverage given in *The Oxford History* to colonies of white settlement reflects the overwhelming concern among recent historians of the British Empire with the non-white empire, its acquisition, administration, exploitation and decolonisation. Perhaps not surprisingly, they claim that some of the dominant tropes within this, for example Robinson and Gallagher's ideas of informal empire, with its implied continuities of indigenous collaboration and colonial influence, and emphasis on peripheral crises as the main driver of empire, did not really apply to settler colonies, especially after they gained dominion status.[4]

In this view, by the turn of the millennium, settler colonies had been more or less sidelined from the major thrust of historical imperial scholarship, a perspective which led to the subsequent attempt to reposition the dominions at the heart of a reinvigorated British imperial history.[5] Insofar, as Robin Winks notes, as all history – including imperial history – is embedded in its context and time and serves current purposes, we might adduce various reasons for this.[6] As the

Empire/Commonwealth connection moved from the mainstream to the margins of life in the ex-dominions, so too, imperial history was marginalised within academic discourse there. In Canada, traditionally pro-imperialist sentiments in historical scholarship were swamped by the growing engagement with the 'new American Empire' and its cultural hegemony.[7] In Australia, Macintyre ascribed the neglect of the imperial dimension of Australian history to what he saw as contemporary Australian society's failure to identify 'new points of reference' when it discarded the old British colonial frame of (self-)understanding. Until the last vestiges of the colonial condition were shrugged off, he saw little future for imperial history in the collective narrative of the country's imagined past. Accordingly, the subject was likely to remain stranded in the Whiggish discourse of 'filial growth' which had characterised it until the late 1960s, and which had long been abandoned by generations of historians intent on a critical re-appraisal of their country's contested past, in line with the re-invention of Australia as a multicultural state.[8]

As such, this seemingly final *floreat* of Australian imperial history, even in its late guise of nationalist imperialism, exhibited many of the characteristics that Louis and Winks both identified in 1999 as defining the old imperial history. Of particular account among these were: a belief in the civilising mission of empire and in its moral legitimacy as the unfolding story of humanitarian progress and liberty; its representation from Eurocentric and male-gendered perspectives; a primary concern with politics, constitutional affairs and the economic basis of empire; and finally, the assumption of normalcy in the uneven distribution of social power and authority between the coloniser and colonised.[9] It was precisely on these grounds that the postcolonial challenge to the European epistemologies underpinning empire was mounted. The encounter between colonial discourse theory and old imperial history has been represented in various ways, but perhaps most cogently in terms, ironically enough, of a colonising metaphor. Thus Dane Kennedy speaks of the 'invasion' of the professional 'domain' of British imperial historians by literary critics and other post-structuralists, and of their claiming 'squatter's rights over imperial history's unclaimed provinces'.[10] Howe notes the apparently widespread feeling among historians that this represented a 'threat' to their discipline, mounted by 'invading hordes ... [of] discourse analytical, poststructuralist and 'postmodernist' ideas, [as well as] postcolonial theorists [and] the influence of literary theory and cultural studies. . .'.[11]

The territorial analogy is apt. For if the study of British imperial history, under its widely acknowledged foundational figure J. R. Seeley, was initially undertaken as much for the *purposes* of empire and the instruction of politicians and statesmen, as for the didactic pursuit of knowledge for its own sake, the postcolonial turn was equally politicised. Situated initially in a variety of literary and cultural academies from the late 1970s onwards, it was a reaction to the continuing, covert influence of western colonial forms of knowledge and understanding in framing and subverting seemingly autonomous ideas of self-representation in the ex-colonies.[12] But to describe postcolonialism in this way is to under-represent its heterogeneity of purpose and practice. The term itself is debated. The presence of the signifying hyphen (post-colonialism) is widely understood to denote a particular historical epoch, field of study or subject position, after independence or after the end of empire. Postcolonialism, on the other hand, acknowledges no such bounding periodisation. It refers to the critical analysis of the cultural effects of colonialism as these are represented in various textual forms both during and after the colonial period.[13] Ashcroft *et al.* identify a variety of fields of enquiry within this broader meaning: the analysis of (early modern and later) European territorial conquests and their constituent colonial institutions; the discursive operations of empire; subject construction and resistance within colonial discourse; and the cultural legacies of such colonial incursions in pre- and post-independence nations and communities.[14]

The seminal figure in establishing this paradigm was Edward Said, whose foundational text, *Orientalism*, was published in 1978.[15] This work provided the point of departure for the wider body of work that subsequently became known as colonial discourse theory. Central to this broader field is Foucault's concept of discourse. He defines this as a socially bounded area of knowledge which prescribes the ontological status of claims to truth and falsehood within it according to self-referential rules of admissibility.[16] Holding that all knowledge is socially constructed and linguistically framed, colonial discourse theory challenges the fundamental Enlightenment epistemological presumption that universal and objective truths about the human condition are discoverable through rational enquiry. Thus, denying the possibility of there being an 'objective' history *to* recover, colonial discourse theory has sought to expose the cultural conditions under which Western colonial knowledge has been produced and, crucially, imposed on the colonial subjects' own forms of understanding. The key issue, therefore, is not merely what is known but the way it is known, and the implications of this for the continued relations of dominance between the colonising power and its colonised subjects.[17] In *Orientalism*, Said broached these ideas in connection with Western, specifically French and British, representations of North Africa and the Middle East from the eighteenth century onwards. He argued that Western thought constructed and othered these regions as 'the Orient' in an ongoing process of epistemological domination which set its own terms for what was true and false and for what could and could not be known about the East. Represented as the antithesis of what the West thought itself to be – irrational rather than rational, despotic not democratic, timeless rather than progressive, 'feminine' rather than 'masculine', the Orient played an essential role in enabling the West's assertion of its own hegemonic modernity.[18]

Robert Young claims that 'it was above all the idea of Orientalism as discourse in a general sense that allowed the creation of a general conceptual paradigm through which the cultural forms of colonial and imperial ideologies could be analysed, and enabled *Orientalism* to be so outstandingly successful'.[19] Yet Said's arguments were deemed to be problematic from the start, not least among his own adherents. His view that the West's construction of the Orient was a form of late nineteenth-century Modernism offers little acknowledgement of earlier, Romantic understandings of the East or of non-male perspectives upon it generally. His overwhelming emphasis on the importance of literary representations – in itself much more narrowly conceived than Foucault's original conception of a range of socially constructed knowledges – has led to doubts about the significance and representative status of these texts and the historicity of their use. By assigning equal discursive status to diverse literary texts selected from widely different time/space moments within empire, *Orientalism* – like colonial discourse theory in general – has been accused of flattening the lumpiness of history and of ignoring the importance of the material and locational specificities of colonial experience. Finally, and perhaps most importantly, by emphasising the centrality of *Western* constructions of the non-Western other, Said stands accused of being complicit in reproducing the very Western knowledge hegemony he claims to have been trying to subvert.[20]

The entrenched nature of the initial encounters between colonial discourse theorists and imperial historians is hard to exaggerate. For historians, issues of inattention to economic and social contexts, and the consequent leadening effect on historical understanding, run deep.[21] In one sense, this is inevitable. As Robert Young has argued, the postcolonial critique is, in *essence*, ahistorical insofar as it racialises and mythologises the totalising claims of Western History and seeks to decentre these from the frame of postcolonial self-understanding.[22] Yet dialogue has proved possible. Just as some colonial discourse analysts have recognised the need to ground their work more securely in specific historical and material contexts, so too some imperial historians have acknowledged the insights that postcolonial scholarship offers into the epistemological relationship between knowledge, power and representation, the cultural foundations of group identity and the mutually constructive relationship between metropolitan and colonial societies.[23] The upshot, Dane Kennedy claims, has been the 'reinvigoration' of British imperial history or, as Marshall aptly terms it, the emergence of a 'new' imperial history in which the traditional focus on political and economic domination, civil administration and systems of power, and the eventual transfer of rule, has been supplemented by a new focus on the nature and effects of the cultural domination that was implicit in all of these.[24] Central to this, Midgley suggests, is the recognition 'that the production of dominant forms of knowledge about the colonised provided an important basis for the exercise of imperial power', in which Seeley's notion of imperial history as practice was implicated.[25] The consequent concern, in Ballantyne's words, 'with the complex cultural traffic that connected colonies to the metropole, and [with] the role of these exchanges in constituting domestic culture', has, in his view, 'reconfigured understandings of the very basis of imperialism; no longer [can] the imperial past be imagined purely in terms of economic and elite politics, but instead [this must also be] through cultural struggles of various kinds. . .'.[26]

Central to the recovery of these cultural struggles have been issues of race, ethnicity and gender, a concern with difference, and the constitutive effects of the external other on the construction and representation of the self. As such, these works exhibit the same essentially postmodern understanding of culture as this book: namely, as a signifying system endowing meaning to individuals and groups within particular life-worlds. In a perceptive assessment of the new imperial history, Kathleen Wilson summarises its primary concerns as: the impact of the Empire on metropolitan social and cultural practice; the transgressive role of imperial networks, not merely in sustaining flows of goods, ideas and people, but in destabilising different public and private spheres as they did so; and the role of (epistemological) representation in 'enabling, multiplying and contesting British imperial power'.[27] As Wilson recognises, however, this diversity poses a further problem. Quoting C. A. Bayley, she asks whether this 'attempt to recover "the decentred narrative, the local discourse and the particular experience of the oppressed and marginalised is not in danger of foundering in its own particularism and of becoming a form of post modern [sic] antiquarianism?"'[28]

Where, in short, is this new imperial history to be centred? *Can* it be centred without losing its claim to write for non-elite and non-western pasts? In emphasising the effects of empire on metropolitan British society, does it re-inscribe Britain as the inevitable, inescapable referent for postcolonial imperial history? As Cooper and Stoler note, both colonies and metropole(s) 'shared in the dialectics of inclusion and exclusion', though these were materially inscribed in significantly different ways.[29] The challenge, according to Midgley, is for the new imperial history to be constructed in a way which recognises the mutually constructive relationship between *subjective* inquiry and *objective* externality. In doing so, it should combine the postcolonial focus on culture with analyses of the 'economic, social, political, administrative and military facets of imperialism' that are sensitive to 'regional difference and chronological shifts'.[30]

What does seem to be clear, currently, is that despite (or perhaps because of) its emphasis on race, gender and ethnicity, its concern with new forms of textual evidence and its engagement with the complex exchanges between metropolitan and colonial societies, for the most part the new imperial history is just as preferentially engaged with the non-white parts of empire as was the old. With some notable exceptions, for example Lynette Russell's *Colonial Frontiers*, Annie Coombes' *Rethinking Settler Colonialism* and Stasiulis and Yuval-Davis's *Unsettling Settler Societies*,[31] white settler societies have not figured largely in this trope, other than as the focus of attention of the so-called British World school. Here, the emphasis has been on what Bridge and Fedorowich describe as 'the heart of the imperial enterprise, the expansion of Britain and the peopling and building of the trans-oceanic British world'.[32] Thus, its concern has been with notions of Britishness, the allegedly diasporic character of 'Greater Britain' – though this term is sometimes used as a straightforward synonym for migration[33] – and the diverse expressions and longevity of the imperial link in popular and official imagination in the dominions.[34] More recently, however, scholars working in this field have also engaged with critical racial and gendered approaches to dominion history. Recent research has explored the connectivities between masculine/feminine identities and representations of race, nationhood and empire, as well as the contested legacies of the encounter between indigeneity and the European self in Canada and Aotearoa/New Zealand.[35]

But, as already noted, the complex intimacies between race, gender and representation, both at the metropolitan 'heart of empire' and in the colonies, have long been common currency in the new imperial history of the non-white empire. In 1998, Clare Midgley identified six main 'connections' with gender in historical imperial scholarship: white Western women and imperialism; the effect of empire on women in Britain; the experience of colonised women; masculinity and empire; sexuality and empire; and gender and colonial discourse.[36] While these perspectives are variously situated within the metropole

and non-white colonies, all continue to provide a powerful corrective to the hegemonic male-gendered and Eurocentric perspectives
of traditional imperial history. Among studies of white women and
empire, the emphasis on India remains, and mirrors the continuing
mesmeric effect of the Raj on the post-imperial popular British historical imagination, well exemplified by so-called 'Raj revival' of the 1970s
and 1980s.[37] For example, Alison Blunt has explored the feminised
constructions of India and England 'as home' among Anglo-Indian
women travelling to post-war Britain, highlighting the liminal nature
of these.[38] Elizabeth Buettner finds this sense of being in-between also
to have characterised the selfhood exhibited by 'British Indians', those
Britons whose work in India left them in a state of 'permanent imper-
manence'. Careful to differentiate themselves from the (undifferenti-
ated) Indian majority and mixed-race Anglo-Indians alike through a
variety of racialised social and cultural practices, British Indians found
that they occupied marginal, hybridised cultural spaces on their return
to Britain. Thus, as Catherine Hall notes, 'the making of these colonising subjects, their racialised and gendered selves, took place in both
empire and at home'.[39]

A concern with gendered representations of empire and the role of
men and women within it also permeates Mary Procida's analysis of the
informal penetration by British women into the official political world
of the Raj. Highlighting the multiple and – for the male hegemony –
frequently subversive character of white feminine self-understanding
in India, Procida challenges representations of empire as a masculine
public sphere.[40] The idea of empire as a homosocial male arena, where
white masculine virtues might be displayed in the presence of a feminised male native other – and in the absence of a constraining white
female presence – has proved to be tenacious.[41] Procida argues that its
corollary, the representation of those European women who did pen-
etrate the colonial spaces of the Raj, in essentialist terms, as 'sexual
and domestic creatures . . . inhabiting a feminine private realm', fails
to recognise the extent to which they were 'active agents' in imperial
politics. She concludes that, in terms of gender relations, there was a
'partnership' in India between British men and women as imperialists
in a masculine mould in which domestic ideas about femininity were
reconfigured as women adopted traditionally male roles and traits.[42]
Other studies of European women in empire have considered their
experience as travellers and missionaries in West Africa and South-
East Asia,[43] as well as the ways in which, in the metropole, differently
situated groups of women appropriated official male discourses of
imperial knowledge or power[44] to sustain their own social position or
existence.[45]

Underpinning all these discussions is the so-called second-generation postcolonial concern with cultural boundaries, their instability, transgression, and the liminal and hybrid spaces of identity this creates.[46] These ideas were originally enunciated in linguistic terms by Mikhail Bakhtin, but have subsequently been associated with Homi Bhabha's analysis of the tensions and contradictions inherent in colonial discourse.[47] The idea of hybridity, particularly in the cultural formulation proposed by Bhabha, remains one of the most widely appropriated but contested concepts in colonial discourse theory. Bhabha's central concern is to demonstrate the mutually formative relationship between the colonisers and the peoples they colonise, and the consequent creation of transcultural forms and processes which transgressed or displaced the intellectual, cultural and material boundaries between them. These forms and processes created 'third space', which invoked both the ambivalence of the coloniser and the mimicry of the colonised and pointed to the necessarily partial and incomplete exercise of hegemonic colonial authority. Thus, colonial authority attempted to legitimise itself by othering the colonised subject as an uncivilised inferior, but at the same time drew him or her into the colonial embrace through nurturing processes designed to create compliancy. This ambivalent relationship of repulsion and attraction created – and depended upon – a state of intermediacy in the colonised, who were encouraged to adopt the colonisers' cultural habits, institutions and values in a process of mimicry. This mimicry was itself ambivalent, however, insofar as it was always questioning – and thus potentially subversive of – colonial authority. Thus the coloniser and the colonised engaged in a mutually formative, dialogical relationship, but one which contained the seeds of its own destruction.[48]

Critics of hybridity theory have argued that, far from blurring the Saidian distinction between self and other, the idea of hybridity has meaning only when set against the continuing, essentialised 'anterior pure', fetishising the boundaries that define this.[49] Thus Benton and Muth, in their analysis of colonial legal and military discourses in India, the Cape Colony and Ethiopia, conclude that recognition by metropolitan observers of Western traits in indigenous elites was too dangerous a strategy to be pursued too far. It had always to be countered by the ascription of an essentialist otherness which confirmed the indigenes' inferiority. In this way, acknowledging the unstable and hybrid spaces of the 'contact zone' merely served to confirm the continuing asymmetry and dualism of the relationship between both groups and to 'sharpen the difference' between them.[50] Perhaps this was inevitable. In his analysis of contemporary cultural hybridities and diasporas, Papastergiardis suggests that cultural exchanges are never universal, never all embracing. Social and other barriers and filters operate to ensure that they are only ever partial and incomplete, creating ambivalent spaces of identity which invoke multiple attachments driven by the dual desire for connection and separation. These multiple attachments denote the hybrid subject's multiple positionality within two or more cultural locations, and the consequent destabilisation of their singular, essentialist self.[51]

A similar concern with boundary crossing, hybridity and resistance has inflected those relatively few studies of settler societies which have appeared as part of the new imperial history outside the British World project. Once again, the emphasis has been on the settlers' interaction with the indigenous communities they displaced, rather than their own white heterogeneity. The ambiguous location of settler societies within the practice of empire has previously been noted by imperial historians, old and new. For example, in an important early analysis of settler societies in Australia, Aotearoa/New Zealand and South America, Donald Denoon noted the anti-imperialism of some settlers. He also noted that this did not undermine the specialised production for metropolitan markets that underpinned these colonies' 'wide autonomy and considerable prosperity'.[52] Central to this success was the early creation of settler capitalism, unhindered by the presence of a densely settled indigenous population. Indeed, Denoon argues that settler societies came into existence only when and where indigenous societies were 'too fragile' to 'carry the burden' of European settlers and merchants 'as an additional imposition'.[53] Denoon's perspectives are essentially those of class formation and political economy, and are more redolent of the old imperial history than the new. A subsequent feminist analysis by Davia Stasiulis and Nira Yuval-Davis, *Unsettling Settler Societies*, broadened these perspectives to consider the interactions between race, class, ethnicity and especially gender in the articulation of settler societies. Stasiulis and Yuval-Davis claim that settler societies 'complicated the neat dichotomy between Europe and the rest of the world', insofar as they supported large 'fragment societies' derived from Europe which, while economically dependent on the metropole, 'sought *de facto* or *de jure* political independence from it'.[54]

Unsettling Settler Societies challenges homogenising representations of settler society through its exploration of the complex ways in which gender and ethnicity inflected constructions of colonisation, nation and citizenship. In so doing, it foreshadows some of the concerns of this book. Two other studies of settler societies alluded to earlier, *Colonial Frontiers* and *Rethinking Settler Colonialism*, place particular emphasis on racialised and ethnic constructions of place, identity and the 'border crossings' that transgressed these. Coombes's rationale for this in *Rethinking Settler Colonialism* has already been noted. Despite similar structures and developmental trajectories (created, as Denoon noted, through the search for solutions to similar problems), individually, settler societies were shaped historically by their encounter with aboriginal people and the processes of 'resistance, containment, appropriation, assimilation, miscegenation and attempted destruction' that this involved.[55] These processes continue to resonate throughout the ex-dominions, troubling non-indigenous conceptions of belonging and legitimacy. In Australia, this has been manifest in the highly politicised and frequently polemical debate among historians, politicians and others, referred to as 'The History Wars'.[56] At issue is the nature of the European historical encounter with Aboriginal society, the ways this has subsequently been represented, and the implications of both of these things for contemporary non-indigenous Australians, their sense of belonging and nationhood, and the legitimacy of their presence in Australia.

Anne Curthoys explains 'The History Wars'' vehemence as a function of the sense of victimhood that she alleges is fundamental to the Anglo-Celtic Australian national imaginary. Accordingly, the contest has been between those who see non-indigenous Australians as historical aggressors and those who see them as victims – of imperial coercion (convicts), indigenous hostility (white captivity narratives), environmental hardship (battlers), rival claims to nationhood (the Irish), international competition and economic predation (by big business and the middle classes).[57] In this imaginary, white settler suffering conferred ownership of the land, their labour in transforming a distant 'hell on earth' into 'the lucky country' constituting its own moral legitimacy. But in constructing this national myth of triumph through expulsion, exodus, exile and suffering, non-indigenous Australians denied themselves the possibility of empathising with the aboriginal peoples they displaced. When Aborigine claims to land ownership and of past genocide challenged this collective imaginary in the 1980s and after, they were perceived as a sustained attack on the legitimacy of non-indigenous Australia and raised atavistic fears of real or symbolic dispossession and displacement – again.[58] In contrast, Miriam Dixson has asserted the need for the 'self confident' survival of what she terms Australia's 'Anglo-Celtic core culture', crucially enabled by a mutuality of understanding with, and reparation towards, indigenous Australians. Acknowledging 'white' Australia's historical defects and ambiguities, she argues that only in this way can the social cohesion required to maintain a sense of national identity be created in the face of the broader challenge of the 'unhoused emptiness of internationalism'.[59]

But as *Colonial Frontiers* and *Rethinking Settler Colonialism* both demonstrate, this unsettling of settler societies has not been unique to Australia. First Nations and Maori activism in Canada and Aotearoa/ New Zealand, let alone the tortuous and sometimes violent paths by which post-apartheid South Africa has emerged, all speak of a postcolonial rejection of the asymmetrical relations of cultural domination that characterised these dominions during and after empire. *Colonial Frontiers* demonstrates the complexity of the material and intellectual boundaries that marked these encounters, arguing that they were never neutral, but always dialogic, sometimes contested and fixed neither in space nor in time.[60] The very character of these boundaries might themselves change. In his analysis of models of aboriginal resistance to white settlement in Australia, Nathan Wolski emphasises the ubiquity, localism and hybridity of the 'border spaces' which were negotiated between indigenous and non-indigenous Australians in Western Victoria. He concludes that these spaces acted as frequently to connect as to divide communities and individuals.[61] *Rethinking Settler Colonialism* shares this concern with the mutually formative nature of the encounter between indigenous and settler societies. In contrast to the racialised self/other polemicism of 'The History Wars', it argues for the contingency and mutability of the ethnic and cultural identities created by the indigenous/settler encounter in Australia, as in Canada, South Africa and Aotearoa/New Zealand during and after empire. But in the long term, these hybridised identities too have proved to be subversive of the hegemonic legacies of settler society and have provided one focus for the continuing struggle over 'ownership' of the national histories of the ex-dominions.[62]

Similar representational issues inflect the current debate concerning Ireland's place within the British Empire. At stake is the island's modern historical status as, variously, a British colony and/or a part of the British imperial metropole, and the uniqueness or otherwise of this condition within the British Empire. Although less polemical than Australia's 'History Wars' – accusations of racism haven't surfaced with quite the same frequency – the debate is no less entrenched and hardly less politicised. As we have already noted, contributions by literary and cultural theorists which have stressed Ireland's past colonial status and present postcolonial condition have in turn been criticised for their unexplicated nationalism and ahistorical tone. Thus Stephen Howe, in his contribution to the *Companion* volume on Ireland in the *Oxford History of the British Empire*, claims that behind the theoretical sophistication of major contributions by three of Ireland's leading postcolonial critics, Seamus Deane, Declan Kiberd and David Lloyd, lies the same 'highly traditional nationalist world view', questionable command of historical evidence and 'unduly homogenising' conception of colonialism.[63] Recent contributions by postcolonial-minded historians have sought to address at least some of these issues. In *Was Ireland a Colony?*, which takes as its premise Joseph Ruane's 1992 observation that nineteenth-century Irish history has rarely been framed in colonial terms, Terence McDonough marshals a collection of essays which seek to demonstrate that Ireland's history at that period can be fully understood only from a colonial perspective.[64] The development of Ireland's textile industries, and the country's class relations generally, are explained in terms of Marxist-influenced dependency theory. The failure of British relief policy during the Potato Famine is read as evidence of a British attempt to 'anglicise' the structure of Irish rural society. Notions of settler colonialism are invoked to explain both the concentrated presence in Ulster of Irishmen of Scottish ancestry and their particular claim to imperial loyalty. The structures and practices of governance, literary and other cultural representations, and the social *milieux* of the landed elite, are all found to be imbued with a sense of colonial difference; the latter, indeed, reaching out to other colonial sites within the Empire.[65]

But in taking nineteenth-century Ireland's colonial status as a given, *Was Ireland a Colony?* presupposes the answer to its own titular question and neatly illustrates the conundrum which lies at the heart of the contested representations of Ireland's place in the British Empire. Following the Act of Union of 1801, Ireland supposedly became an equal constitutional partner in the newly enlarged United Kingdom. Yet, as David Fitzpatrick, Alvin Jackson, Keith Jeffery and others have pointed out, Irish men and women remained subject to discriminatory racialised stereotyping; and the country was governed via a curious medley of instruments and institutions which were variously metropolitan or colonial in character. Moreover, following the abolition of tariffs in 1824, its economy was opened up to British competition on very uneven terms of trade, and when famine struck in 1848, the fiscal burden was very quickly placed squarely on the shoulders of Irish landlords, rather than being borne by the Treasury of the *United* Kingdom.[66] Nevertheless, Irish men and women of all creeds and classes remained active in their pursuit of Britain's imperial interest, as settlers, soldiers, policemen, administrators, missionaries and entrepreneurs, while aspects of Ireland's governance were adopted elsewhere in the Empire.[67] Between 1815 and 1910, upwards of 1.4 million Irish men and women sought their identity and future in the Empire overseas.[68]

Hence the uniquely ambiguous and contradictory position claimed for Ireland within Britain's nineteenth-century Empire, which Kevin Kenny, in his introduction to the *Oxford History's Companion* volume on Ireland, so robustly denies.[69] Constitutionally equal, as part of the imperial metropolitan heartland, with England, Scotland and Wales, yet commonly viewed and frequently governed as a subaltern other, Ireland was nevertheless equally complicit in providing the agents and subjects who administered and peopled the mutable and contingent hegemonic spaces of empire. Kenny argues that Ireland's self-evident dualism as both subject and agent of imperialism was not exceptional, and hardly paradoxical: 'There is nothing anomalous in members of one colonised people helping to govern their homeland, or to conquer and govern another country elsewhere in the same Empire.'[70] But, as Fitzpatrick notes, this misses the point. Claims to Ireland's exceptional status within Britain's nineteenth-century empire stand because, *in addition* to these things, Ireland was part of the imperial metropole.[71] Not surprisingly, historians have consequently found the effects of empire on nineteenth-century Ireland to be complex, not least because of the diverse nature of Britain's overseas possessions and the continuously changing imperial attitude towards these. Just as no one colonial model existed against which Ireland's putative colonial status might be measured, so too the framing influence of empire on Irish society and culture, now belatedly recognised for its importance, constantly evolved.[72]

Echoing Keith Jeffrey, Kevin Kenny suggests that although the immediate effects of empire on Irish men and women would have varied according to individual circumstance, they are likely nevertheless to have exhibited some commonalities among those sharing a similar position in society.[73] In Kenny's view, Ascendancy Anglicans and Presbyterian Dissenters shared in the same deep attachment, 'like colonial settlers in many other places, to the land where they settled', but can be differentiated in terms of their imperial positionality in other ways. The Anglican social elite formed a 'distinctively Irish ... settler nationalist group' who, though they belonged to 'the British social and imperial ruling classes, never did so on equal terms. They were, in the end, Irishmen of a particular sort.' Ulster Presbyterians, on the hand, though subject to disabling legislation during the eighteenth century, and perceived to be a threat to the Empire's security during the revolutionary decade of the 1790s, nevertheless occupied a liminal space between the Ascendancy and the Catholic majority, forming a 'buffer ... between civilisation and barbarism'. And not only in Ireland. Kenny argues that they also played a similarly protective role on the frontiers of Britain's North American colonies.[74]

Representations such as these speak more to the seventeenth and eighteenth centuries than to post-Union Ireland. During the nineteenth century, the defensiveness apparent in earlier Protestant Irish identities – argued by Pamela Clayton to be an atavism inherent in all

settler mentalities – gave way to more modern forms of self-identification, as class differentials deriving from regionally uneven processes
of economic and social modernisation cross-cut older religious and
ethnic divides.[75] Within these more nuanced social spaces, themselves
framed by empire, Irishmen of all denominations and political persua-
sions found different levels of accommodation within imperialism,
even though, individually, their attitudes might change over time.
Unionists might find succour for their loyalism in the outright assertion of a British imperial identity. Redmondites and other moderate
Nationalists might see in dominion status a means of securing Ireland's
independence while maintaining the advantages of an imperial link.

But all depended on circumstance. Following the suppression of
the 1916 Dublin rebellion, attitudes hardened both in Ireland and the
dominions, as a more extreme form of nationalism made its ultimately
successful bid for Irish independence, providing a role model for future
anti-colonialist movements in India, Palestine and elsewhere in the
Empire as it did so.[76] As Jackson notes, empire was not only fundamentally important to Ireland's political culture in the nineteenth
century, it was also fundamentally complex in its effects. Acting both
as 'an agent of liberation and oppression', it provided opportunities for
individual advancement within the imperial establishment, on the one
hand, and colonial political support for the Irish nationalist cause, on
the other. 'By the end of the nineteenth century the Empire harnessed
much Irish talent . . . yet many Irish people saw the Empire (which their
kinsmen had helped to shape) as alien and menacing . . . '.[77] Clearly, no
one reading of Ireland's place within the Empire is possible.

The question remains, however, as to how far any of these new imperial histories, whether of settler colonialism in the white dominions or
of Ireland's position in empire, address the complicities of place and
self-identification which lie at the heart of this book. In one sense, of
course, as Blunt and McEwan have noted, the entire postcolonial critique of empire is inherently geographical, and thus, to an extent, so too
is the new imperial history.[78] Postcolonialism's abiding emphasis on
the way representations of cultural difference sustained Western imperial epistemologies inevitably implies consideration of individual and
collective positionalities which were differently located in space and
time. Hence the spatiality inherent in the conundrum, already noted,
of whether – and how – the new imperial history might be centred, in
light of its concern with local and subaltern, as much as transnational
and hegemonic, narratives of difference. Yet for all this, notions of the
complicity of material and imagined place in constructions of self and
other remain implicit rather than explicit in the texts considered here.
Despite their emphasis on the way self and other might be represented

in racialised and gendered terms, and the frequency with which they invoke liminality, hybrid space and border crossings, most recent analyses of settler societies in the new imperial history rarely make explicit the connection between these abstract spaces and the valorised geographical intimacies of place. The same is equally true of the recent histories of Ireland and empire. The inherent spatiality of the imperial enterprise is taken for granted. As particularised sites of agency, memory and identity, where the materiality of human existence prompts and supports multiple and unstable meanings for those whose lives are bound up in them, geographies of place have, seemingly, yet to enter the lexicon of the new imperial history.

Modern historical geographies of colonialism

Current geographical representations of empire and its colonial legacies, on the other hand, have used ideas of both place and, more widely, semiotic landscapes, to address the ways in which the material and imagined geographies of colonialism were constructed. But, as Daniel Clayton has pointed out, this concern with what he describes as 'colonialism's geographies' represents only one of a number of tropes which have characterised recent geographical engagements with empire. Equally evident has been a concern, first, with geography's own disciplinary complicity in the practice of empire and the racialising epistemologies that supported it; and, second, with the ways in which different forms of imperial knowledge and identity were spatialised. Clayton identifies a number of recurrent themes within these tropes which echo those noted earlier by Cheryl McEwan and Alison Blunt: the imaginative geographies and spaces of knowledge that shaped empire; the spatial construction of the subjective experience of empire; imperial and colonial urbanism; the gendered, racialised and sexualised imprinting of colonial landscapes; cartography and other visual forms of representing empire; imperial networks and their links with local colonial practice; and the construction of regional colonial geographies.[79]

Eclecticism of this sort almost defies Clayton's own synthesis, but a number of general points may be made. First, the concern, in Jonathan Crush's words, to 'decolonise Geography' and expose its complicity in the asymmetrical power relations inherent in empire and its postcolonial aftermath, would appear to position the discipline at the heart of the broader postcolonial critique of European epistemologies that have consistently disabled the non-Western other.[80] This complicity has been well attested by geographers influenced by the postcolonial turn in the Western academy. In *Geography and Empire*, Anne Godlewska and Neil Smith offered an early survey of geography's revival of interest in its own colonial encounter, which drew attention to the foundational importance to this of the geographical sensibilities displayed by Said in both *Orientalism* and his subsequent *Culture and Imperialism*.[81] Quoting Said's famous aphorism that 'None of us is completely free from the struggle over geography', they detect in his work a concern with 'geographical difference, the movement of people and ideas, and the rootedness of place'. Together, these fashioned geography as a 'vital lens' on empire, albeit one which failed, in Said's hands, to focus on the materiality of the geographical differences it purported to espouse.[82] Subsequent commentaries, for example by McEwan and Blunt in *Postcolonial Geographies* and by James Ryan, also acknowledge the contextual influence of Said's geographical sensibility, as well as that of later work by Homi Bhabha and Gayatri Spivak, in framing geography's current postcolonial concern with its own imperial legacies.[83] Studies, among others, by Maddrell and Ploszajska on the intimate links between British geography education and the promotion of imperial world views;[84] by Ryan and Etherington on the cartographic fashioning of imperial space;[85] and by Cameron, Grove and Mackenzie on the role of metropolitan geographical societies in promoting exploration and discovery, and mapping and surveying,[86] all point to the intimacies between geography, as *the* uniquely panoptic nineteenth-century science, and imperialism.[87]

Yet we may wonder whether even those geographers fully sensitised to their discipline's inherent colonialism will ever be completely able to escape its consequences. Sidaway, for example, argues that geography is 'inescapably marked (both philosophically and institutionally) by its location and development as a western-colonial science ... its norms, definitions inclusions, exclusions and structure cannot be disassociated from certain European philosophical concepts of presence, order and intelligibility ... that have rooted geography amongst the advance-guard of a wider "Western" epistemology, deeply implicated in colonial-imperial power'.[88] Exploring the implications of this for the practice of historical and cultural geography, Duncan concludes that these areas continue to rely upon and promulgate the same asymmetrical power–knowledge relationships that underpinned the imperial archive, thus supplanting indigenous histories and forms of knowledge and objectifying the non-Western self as a category of study.[89] Clayton makes the same point succinctly. Echoing Spivak, he notes the difficulty of bringing 'western and native evidence together in ways that bridge the inter-subjective spaces of contact', without subordinating these '"other voices" to the secular codes of western academic discourse'.[90] Geographers, in short, may be no more capable of decoupling themselves from their subject's colonial imaginings and disciplines, past and present, than new imperial historians are capable of writing about non-elite and non-Western pasts without re-inscribing European imperial powers as their inescapable referent.

But if historical geographers and new imperial historians share a critical awareness of their own inescapably colonial positionality in the study of empire, we may note, secondly, that recent work by geographers has also been characterised by a particular concern with the material aspects of colonialism, the physicality of transnational movement and the diverse localism of colonialism's footprints. In this way, geographers have begun to move beyond the merely textual in their analyses. In their emphasis on the material diversity of the structures, practices and spaces of the numerous colonialisms that constituted empire, they can be seen to have responded to earlier criticism of the ahistoricity of much postcolonial theory.[91] But a note of caution is in order. Cole Harris's dictum that 'colonialism spoke with many voices' calls attention to this material diversity, but reminds us too that these local colonial geographies were precisely that: the product of *colonialism*.[92] Unstable, contingent and polyvocal in their cultural meanings these places and landscapes may have been, but, as we recognise in this study, they were still in major part the product of externally derived processes of European subjugation, appropriation and exploitation. Although these processes were themselves spatially and temporally diverse and, in Thomas's phrase, occasionally displayed a far from uniform 'will to rule',[93] they nevertheless all ultimately derived from the same fundamentally uneven relationships of epistemological authority and material power, predicated on the exercise of European military and economic supremacy. However diverse and occasionally tentative their expression, the asymmetry of these relationships is undeniable.

Geographical studies of the spatial construction of imperial knowledge and identities – Clayton's second trope – have been particularly varied in their treatment of these foundational power relations within empire. And here we may make our third point. Running through these diverse engagements is a central conception of empire as *discourse*, as a set of spatialised practices, knowledges and institutions which between them shaped the spaces of encounter between the colonising power and the colonised indigenes. Clayton's own account of the early European exploration of Vancouver Island, *Islands of Truth*, stresses how the construction of imperial knowledge was itself part of the ongoing process of colonialism. In marginalising some locally evident identities and forms of knowledge and privileging and authenticating others, precolonial and colonial contacts created an imaginary which represented the island both as 'the product of the west' and also as a place with its

own 'specific and irreducible identities'.[94] In effect, imperial epistemological discourse created the very things it claimed to discover, and in
doing so informed its own future practice. Consequently, such knowledge was not immutable. As colonial encounters widened, so these
truth claims changed, along with the power relations they supported.
Imperialism continuously recreated the truths which underpinned its
own claims to moral purpose.

Other studies of the production of imperial knowledge in different
places and moments of empire underscore Clayton's claim that different types and phases of colonial encounter produced different histories,
geographies and truths.[95] For example, Livingstone's examination
of the moral basis for the scientific truth claims that underpinned
European exploration and expropriation in the tropics finds these to be
grounded in an evolutionary discourse of racial superiority that privileged the temperate world over the tropical as a favourable site of social
development.[96] Feminist geographers, including Alison Blunt, Cheryl
McEwan, Sara Mills and Gillian Rose, have shared the perspectives of
Catherine Hall and other new imperial historians in emphasising the
liminality of the spaces inhabited by women travellers and colonists
within what was an overwhelmingly masculine discourse of empire.
They have shown, too, the subversive quality of female representations of these.[97] The truths produced by colonial encounters were no
less gendered because they were the complex outcome of the West's
diverse engagement with varied forms of indigeneity. Moreover, the
discursive spaces of empire were gendered in other ways as well.
Howell, Kumar and Phillips have represented the sexualised landscapes
of colonial prostitution in Singapore, India and Gibraltar as evidence
of the bounded spaces created by contagious disease legislation. This
particular form of governance connected the metropolis with the colonies in a complex web of regulatory practice, serving to remind us of
the mutually constitutive relationship between empire and the imperial homeland.[98] Thus, in Clayton's phrase, colonial places 'cannot be
studied in isolation from the translocational discourses and western
projects of encroachment that framed them'.[99]

Various studies have pointed to the power and tenacity of the subjective colonial geographies created and sustained by different imperial
claims to truth. Brayshaw, Selwood and Tonts have shown how, in
Western Australia, the government's promotion of group settlement
and yeoman farming in the late nineteenth and early twentieth centuries continued to be supported by sophisticated imperial propaganda
long after the environmental limitations to both schemes had become
apparent.[100] Imperial knowledge might deceive as well as inform.
Exploring the imagined geographies of the mid-nineteenth-century

Australian gold rush, Keith Lilley argues that the accounts of these which circulated in the metropolis and other parts of the Empire were fundamental not only in promoting emigration and sustaining exploration for gold, but also in fictionalising the ideal emigrant.[101] In this way, these imaginary geographies became a central part of the discursive networks of empire, framing – but also being informed by – the specific and irreducible identities of local colonial life.

Perhaps the most sustained account of how these discursive networks may have functioned transnationally is offered by Alan Lester. His work on the Cape Colony and, latterly, Australia and Aotearoa/ New Zealand, is grounded in an understanding of culture as a naturalising medium of social exchange and empowerment.[102] He represents nineteenth-century European settlement at the Cape and its engagement with the local Xhosa people in terms of the interplay between three competing yet overlapping colonial discourses: settler capitalism, governmentality and (evangelical) humanitarianism. These connected the metropolis with the Cape and other colonies, and the colonies with each other. Each represented 'a particular ensemble of regulated practices that were sufficiently coherent to be considered a separate imperial project . . . and which were devised and promoted by different British interests'.[103] Beyond this, each discourse was subject to continuous remaking as colonial agendas in the colonies and the metropolis changed, and imperial agents and subjects variously appropriated the rhetoric of competing discourses as time and place demanded. These discursive networks, with their associated circuits and flows of capital, commodities, labour and knowledge were fixed in neither space nor time, but in their remaking, continuously reconnected and reformed colonial and metropolitan places alike within new epistemological and relational spaces.[104]

Lester's emphasis on this discursive remodelling of colonial place echoes the importance Clayton places on 'western projects of encroachment' in determining the local character of colonialism. Studies of colonial places re-connected and re-formed in this way, and of the semiotic colonial landscapes of which they formed part, constitute the final trope in Clayton's account of geography's engagement with empire, and the one which resonates most strongly with *Imperial Spaces*.[105] The emphasis in these studies on 'colonialism's geographies' and the materialities of white settler experience has not gone unchallenged, however. Brenda Yeoh has argued, rather, for greater engagement with what she describes as the 'geographies of the colonised world', in which particular attention should be paid to indigenous resistance and the hybridised spaces of the contact zone.[106] In this, of course, she follows Bhabha and Spivak, but as we have already noted (p. 22), their emphasis

on such third spaces of resistance has been argued to depend on the continuing existence of the very frontiers and bounded spaces of identity
they purport to subvert. Accordingly, we may wonder whether, in the
white dominions just as much as in colonies where the white presence
was a minority one, the geographies of the colonised can be truly distinguished from colonialism's geographies? Each was defined in terms
of the other. The places and landscapes which embodied white settler
experience and aspiration were polyvocal, and spoke not only of the
heterogeneity and contingency of the colonists' collective memory and
identity, but also of the, sometimes resistant, presence – and memory –
of indigeneity, no matter what the attempts to erase it.[107]

Ultimately, the question is one of academic positionality. What
is clear is that, in addressing the material places and imagined landscapes embodied in the colonial presence in the 'white dominions',
studies of colonialism's geographies have invariably also been alert to
indigenous identities and spaces. What has been at issue, however, is
precisely how far these were (and are) truly knowable within the frame
of colonialism, whatever the degree of accommodation and hybridity
they may have exhibited. The predominant emphasis has been on the
possibility of formative, though not necessarily always acquiescent,
exchanges between settlers and indigenous peoples. Here, two texts
have been particularly influential in locating these as a subaltern aspect
of colonial power relations: W. J. T. Mitchell's *Landscape and Power*
and Nicholas Thomas's *Colonialism's Culture: Anthropology, Travel
and Government*, both of which were published in 1994.[108] Thomas's
emphasis on the variable, complex and ambivalent nature of colonial
ideologies, the fragmented nature of colonialism as a cultural system
and the consequently fractured construction of individual colonial
projects, does not deny the extent to which these were also shaped by
indigenous resistance and accommodation. But he also emphasises the
asymmetry of these relationships as well as the fundamentally invasive
and destructive nature of colonialism.[109] To paraphrase Cole Harris
once more: colonialism may have spoken in different ways in different
places, but it was still colonialism.

Thomas's claims for the heterogeneous nature of colonialism provide
one foundational context for this study. Mitchell's work on the semiotics of imperial landscapes provides another. He represents landscape
as a dynamic cultural production that, in effacing the signs of its own
creation, naturalises the ideological conditions and relations of power
that brought it into being. As such, it provides a seemingly neutral
medium of exchange between self and other, humanity and nature,
but one that, in reality and despite the spaces it provides for subaltern
identities, is geared towards the prolongation of prevailing hegemonic

power structures. Furthermore, as a cultural production of this kind, landscape is 'not only a matter of internal politics and national or class ideology, but also an international phenomenon, intimately bound up with the discourse of imperialism'.[110] In encoding the cultural meanings and values of the hegemonic white presence, expanding colonial landscapes invited understanding as an inevitable, progressive historical development which civilised and transformed the exotic barbarous spaces of the non-West. But in embodying the semiotics of the fractured and ambiguous colonial self, these landscapes necessarily contrasted them against an equally contingent and changing indigenous other. Consequently, in reading specific colonial landscapes, we may find evidence of indigenous resistance as well as accommodation within the 'complicated process of exchange, mutual transformation and ambivalence' that constituted imperialism. 'Conducted simultaneously at concrete levels of violence, expropriation, collaboration and coercion, and at a variety of symbolic or representational levels whose relation to the concrete was rarely mimetic or transparent',[111] imperialism was made manifest in landscapes that were equally fractured and ambiguous in meaning.

Subsequent studies have drawn on these perspectives to emphasise the diversity of colonialism's places, as well as the importance of land as a medium of cultural exchange within colonial discourse. In *Edge of Empire: Postcolonialism and the City*, Jane Jacob stresses not only the global nature of the 'imperial project' but also the 'messy' nature of its local effects, due in part to the 'unanticipated trajectories of identity and power' created by its negotiation of indigeneity. This involved complicity and co-operation as much as resistance: the idea that 'the colonised always resisted' she views as a revisionist form of imperial nostalgia.[112] In short, although imperialism 'may have been energised by apparently quite rigid ideologies which centred on the west and legitimated certain social relations of domination ... these ideologies tumbled into the fractured and erratic everyday practices of the personalities (colonised and coloniser) who were forced together in the making of the colonies'.[113] Here, the unknowable other is made familiar by the inevitable boundary-crossing intimacies that constituted everyday life in the embodied places of colonialism.

Other writers have followed Mitchell more closely in placing greater emphasis on the ways the meanings of the places and landscapes created by settler colonialism were contested. In their study of the relationship between land and cultural identity in South Africa and Australia, Kate Darian-Smith *et al.* argue that place and landscape are produced by culturally specific processes of 'imagining, seeing, historicising and remembering', which ascribe meaning to what would otherwise be, for the groups concerned, meaning*less* space and territory.[114] But *terra nullius*, or 'empty land', has always been a European fiction.[115] Whether in eighteenth-century Australia or postcolonial South Africa or elsewhere, prior claims to land and to the narratives of identity inscribed within it have always existed. Accordingly, the semiotic places and landscapes inscribed by settlers within the newly created spaces of empire were inevitably contested, giving rise to complex, multiple and possibly contradictory meanings. Trigger and Griffiths suggest that, in settler societies, this amounted to a struggle over the 'imaginative possession of land', as Europeans tried to establish an ideological basis for their presence by incorporating the land within their own intellectual and aesthetic understanding. Existing indigenous inscriptions of identity might find some accommodation within this, but were more likely to form the basis of a 'hidden dialogue' with the settlers' understanding, which exposed sharp differences with it.[116] Thus, in Australia, Hills argues that the aboriginal landscape 'can never be white'. As ever developing 'liturgies of creation', inscribed with traditional rites and knowledge, the aboriginal understanding of landscape places this entirely outside 'static, fragmentary and externalised' European perception.[117] Accordingly, aboriginal symbolism co-exists with white semiotics in an Australian cultural landscape that Taylor describes as a palimpsest of conflicting meaning, in which these indigenous knowledges are susceptible to erasure rather than recognition.[118]

But if, *pace* Clayton, the varied forms of colonialism that constituted empire created their own, different geographies, histories and truths, then clearly, conflict and complicity will have played varying roles within these. The spaces of empire accommodated both boundary crossing and boundary reification. As Cole Harris makes clear in *Making Native Space*, his study of the Indian reserve system in British Columbia, such boundaries might be very material indeed. Arguing that colonial encounters did not necessarily create cultural hybridity, Cole Harris envisages these, rather, as the succession of 'one human geography by another', with all their implicit ideological and value-laden assumptions.[119] Stressing the internal contradictions within colonialism as to how natives (*sic*) should be treated, he narrates the Native Land Question in Canada as the protracted and tortuous negotiation of provision for the dispossessed. Contested as much by different imperial and colonial agencies as by the indigenous people themselves, the unevenness of this particular relationship was self-evident from the start. The progressive bounding and shaping of ever more restricted native space destroyed traditional geographies, along with the indigenous ideologies and social relations of power inherent within them.[120]

Summary

Nevertheless, we may still wonder whether, in the bounded spaces of surveillance described by Cole Harris in nineteenth-century British Columbia, or in the intimacies of postcolonial urban place recovered by Jane Jacobs, or in the re-empowered spaces of indigeneity in post-colonial Australia or New Zealand, the indigenous other can ever be truly known within the frame of colonialism and its legacies. The modern historical geographies of colonialism discussed here offer few certainties. Grounded in their own (post)colonial positionality, they, like the new imperial history, can only ever be other to the indigenous self. But to reiterate, herein lies our present purpose. We claim that, encompassed within the white colonial other were equally ambiguous and contradictory subaltern identities, including those of the subjects of this study, the Scots and the Irish. These, we argue, were embodied within the semiotics of colonial place and landscape in ways that neither the new imperial history nor modern historical geographies of colonialism have adequately addressed. The new imperial history, for all its critical concern with the diversity of imperial subject positions, their boundaries and liminality, remains remarkably immune to the seductive charms of geography's irredentist claims concerning the inherent spatiality of the human condition. Increasing critical engagement with the construction of colonial identities there may have been, but these continue to be narrated against inert and passive colonial landscapes that do little more than provide a backdrop for human agency. Moreover, in their concern with the intimacies of race, gender, ethnicity and representation, recent critical historical studies of empire have continued to largely ignore the diversity of ethnic identity within the British emigration stream.

Modern historical geographies of colonialism pose similar problems. Despite their manifest concern with the ambiguous and contested meanings of colonial place, they, too, offer scant recognition of the varied engagement of the Scots and Irish as subaltern white settlers in constructing these. Their concern to destabilise the binarism evident in earlier postcolonial accounts of empire is admirable, but it has not yet extended to an adequate recognition of the ethnic diversity *within* the hegemonic British presence in nineteenth-century settler colonies in Australia and elsewhere. Nor have they considered the implications of this diversity for the ways in which differently ethnicised constructions of the white self may have destabilised hegemonic meanings of imperial or national identity within the colonial landscape. But to assert the role of ethnicity in colonial identity construction in this way is not to espouse some crude form of primordial ethnic essentialism.

[37]

Ethnicity – the constructive sense of shared cultural origins and memories, mediated through language, religion (perhaps) and other cultural signifiers – represented only one aspect of settler identity. Cross-cut by social and economic difference, amplified or diminished by the exigencies of colonial experience, its representation and mediation in the life-paths of individual settlers was inevitably elusive. Nevertheless, whether actively acknowledged or disregarded, ethnicity remained at some level a marker of difference, an element of selfhood which could connect or divide in equal measure. Our claim here is that, duly inflected by these other markers of identity, ethnic performances were integral to some at least of the settler place-narratives created by the Irish and Scots, giving meaning to these in ways which destabilised and fragmented hegemonic white colonial selfhood.

Notes

1 John Dunmore Lang, *Freedom and Independence for the Golden Lands of Australia; The Right of the Colonies, and the Interest of Britain and of the World* (Sydney, 2nd edn, 1857), p. 6.

2 A. Porter, 'Religion and Empire: British Expansion in the Long Nineteenth Century, 1780–1914', *Journal of Imperial and Commonwealth History*, Vol. 20, (1992) pp. 370–90; *Idem*, 'Religion, Missionary Enthusiasm and Empire', in A. Porter (ed.), *The Oxford History of the British Empire, Volume III, The Nineteenth Century* (Oxford, 1999), pp. 222–46.

3 S. Howe, 'The Slow Death and Strange Rebirths of Imperial History', Review Article, *The Journal of Imperial and Commonwealth History*, Vol. 29, No. 2 (May 2001), pp. 131–41.

4 C. Bridge and K. Fedorowich, 'Mapping the British World', in *Eidem* (eds), 'The British World: Diaspora, Culture and Identity', *The Journal of Imperial and Commonwealth History*, Special Issue, Vol. 31, No. 2 (May 2003), pp. 1–3; R. Robinson and J. Gallagher with A. Denny, *Africa and the Victorians: The Official Mind of Imperialism* (London, 1961). See also William Louis's comments on the influence of the 'Robinson Gallagher' thesis: W. R. Louis, 'Introduction', in R. Winks (ed.), *The Oxford History of the British Empire, Volume V, Historiography* (Oxford, 1999), esp. pp. 39–52.

5 Bridge and Fedorowich, 'Mapping the British World', pp. 1–15. The first 'British World' conference took place in London in 1998, followed by others in Calgary, Capetown, Melbourne (2004) and Auckland (2005).

6 R. W. Winks, 'The Future of Imperial History', in *Idem* (ed.), *Historiography*, p. 653.

7 D. R. Owram, 'Canada and the Empire', in Winks (ed.), *Historiography*, pp. 146–62.

8 S. Macintyre, 'Australia and the Empire', in Winks (ed.), *Historiography*, pp. 163–81; S. Macintyre, *Concise History*, p. 271. See also: N. Meaney, 'Britishness and Australia: Some Reflections', in Bridge and Fedorowich (eds), 'The British World', pp. 121–35.

9 Louis, 'Introduction', in Winks (ed.), *Historiography*, pp. 1–42; Winks, 'Future', in *ibid.*, pp. 653–68.

10 D. Kennedy, 'Imperial History and Post-Colonial Theory', *The Journal of Imperial and Commonwealth History*, Vol. 24, No. 3 (September 1996), pp. 345–6.

11 Howe, 'Slow Death', pp. 133–4.

12 Louis, 'Introduction', in Winks (ed.), *Historiography*, pp. 8–10; L. Proudfoot and

M. Roche, 'Introduction: Place, Network, and the Geographies of Empire', chapter 1 in *Eidem* (eds), *(Dis)Placing Empire. Renegotiating British Colonial Geographies* (London, 2005), pp. 1–3; Kennedy, 'Imperial History', *passim*.

13 S. Slemon, 'The Scramble for Post-Colonialism', in C. Tiffin and A. Lawson (eds), *De-Scribing Empire. Post-colonialism and Textuality* (London, 1994), pp. 16–17.

14 W. D. Ashcroft, G. Griffiths and H. Tiffin, *Key Concepts in Post-Colonial Studies* (London, 1998), p. 187.

15 E. Said, *Orientalism: Western Conceptions of the Orient* (London, 1978). Equally influential is his subsequent *Culture and Imperialism* (London, 1993). For a balanced though not uncritical assessment of Said's foundational importance to colonial discourse theory, see R. J. C. Young, *Postcolonialism. An Historical Introduction* (Oxford, 2001), pp. 383–94.

16 M. Foucault, *The Order of Things: An Archaeology of the Human Sciences* (English trans., London, 1970); *Idem, The Archaeology of Knowledge* (English trans., London, 1972); *Idem, The History of Sexuality. Volume One: An Introduction* (English trans., London, 1978). See also, R. J. C. Young, 'Foucault in Tunisia', in *Idem, Postcolonialism*, pp. 395–410.

17 Ashcroft *et al.*, *Key Concepts*, pp. 71–3; D. A. Washbrook, 'Orients and Occidents: Colonial Discourse Theory and the Historiography of the British Empire', in Winks (ed.), *Historiography*, esp. pp. 596–98.

18 R. J. Johnston, D. Gregory, G. Pratt and M. Watts (eds), *The Dictionary of Human Geography* (4th edn, Oxford, 2000), pp. 565–7.

19 Young, *Postcolonialism*, p. 384.

20 *Ibid.*, pp. 389–92; Washbrook, 'Orients and Occidents', pp. 604–7; J. McLeod, *Beginning Postcolonialism* (Manchester, 2000), pp. 37–50; F. Cooper, *Colonialism in Question. Theory, Knowledge, History* (Berkeley, 2005), pp. 3–22.

21 Kennedy, 'Imperial History', *passim*; J. M. MacKenzie, *Orientalism. History, Theory, and the Arts* (Manchester, 1995), pp. 1–19.

22 R. J. C. Young, *White Mythologies: Writing History and the West* (London, 1990), esp. chapters 1 and 2. For a trenchant critique of this position, see Kennedy, 'Imperial History', pp. 349–51.

23 See, for example, the papers brought together in K. Wilson (ed.), *A New Imperial History. Culture, Identity and Modernity in Britain and the Empire 1660–1840* (Cambridge, 2004). See also Mcleod, *Beginning*, pp. 46–8; Young, *Postcolonialism*, pp. 389–92.

24 Kennedy, 'Imperial History', p. 356; P. J. Marshall, 'British Imperial History "New" and "Old" ', Foreword, *History in Focus*, No. 6 (February 2004), Institute of Historical Research, www.history.ac.uk/ihr/Focus/.

25 C. Midgley, 'Introduction: Gender and Imperialism: Mapping the Connections', in *Idem* (ed.), *Gender and Imperialism* (Manchester, 1998), p. 5.

26 T. Ballantyne, 'Review Essay: Religion, Difference, and the Limits of British Imperial History', *Victorian Studies*, Spring 2005, pp. 429, 426–7.

27 K. Wilson, 'Introduction: Histories, Empires, Modernities', in *Idem* (ed.), *New Imperial History*, p. 19 ff.

28 *Ibid.*, p. 17, quoting C. A. Bayly, 'The British and Indigenous Peoples, 1760–1860: Power, Perception, Identity', in M. Daunton and R. Halpern (eds), *Empire and Others: British Encounters with Indigenous Peoples, 1600–1850* (London, 1999), p. 21.

29 F. Cooper and A. L. Stoler (eds), *Tensions of Empire. Colonial Cultures in a Bourgeois World* (Berkeley, 1997), p. 3.

30 Midgley, 'Gender and Imperialism: Mapping the Connections', pp. 5–6.

31 A. Coombes (ed.), *Rethinking Settler Colonialism. History and Memory in Australia, Canada, Aotearoa New Zealand and South Africa* (Manchester, 2006); L. Russell (ed.), *Colonial Frontiers. Indigenous-European Encounters in Settler Societies* (Manchester, 2001); D. Stasiulis and N. Yuval-Davis (eds), *Unsettling Settler Societies. Articulations of Gender, Race, Ethnicity and Class* (London, 1995).

32 Bridge and Fedorowich, 'Mapping the British World', p. 11.
33 S. Constantine, 'British Emigration to the Empire', in Bridge and Fedorowich (eds), 'British World', pp. 16–35.
34 See, for example, Meaney, 'Britishness and Australia', pp. 121–35; P. Buckner and D. R. Francis (eds), *Rediscovering the British World* (Calgary, 2005).
35 British World Conference IV, 'Broadening the British World', 13–16 July 2005, University of Auckland.
36 Midgley, 'Gender and Imperialism: Mapping the Connections', pp. 6–10.
37 The phrase is originally Salman Rushdie's. See: S. Rushdie, 'The Raj Revival', in J. Twitchin (ed.), *The Black and White Media Book. Handbook for the Study of Racism and Television* (rev. edn, Stoke on Trent, 1992).
38 A. Blunt, 'Imperial Geographies of Home: British Women in India, 1886–1925', *Transactions of the Institute of British Geographers*, New Series, 24 (1999), pp. 421–40.
39 C. Hall, *Civilising Subjects. Metropole and Colony in the English Imagination 1830–1867* (Cambridge, 2002), p. 13.
40 M. A. Procida, *Married to the Empire. Gender, Politics and Imperialism in India, 1883–1947* (Manchester, 2002), pp. 1–26.
41 T. P. Foley *et al.* (eds), *Gender and Colonialism* (Galway, 1995); J. A. Mangan, *The Games Ethic and Imperialism* (New York, 1986); M. Sinha, *Colonial Masculinity: The 'Manly' Englishman and the 'Effeminate Bengali' in the Late Nineteenth Century* (Manchester, 1995).
42 Procida, *Married to the Empire*, pp. 2–7.
43 H. Callaway, *Gender, Culture and Empire: European Women in Colonial Nigeria* (Urbana, 1987); N. Chaudhuri and M. Strobel, *Western Women and Imperialism: Complicity and Resistance* (Bloomington, 1992); K. Jayawardena, *The White Women's Other Burden: Western Women and South Asia during British Rule* (London, 1983).
44 M. Hunt, 'Women and the Fiscal-imperial State in the Late Seventeenth and Early Eighteenth Centuries', in Wilson (ed.), *New Imperial History*, pp. 29–47.
45 G. Russell, 'An "Entertainment of Oddities": Fashionable Sociability and the Pacific in the 1770s', in Wilson (ed.), *New Imperial History*, pp. 48–70.
46 J. T. Kenny, 'Colonial Geographies: Accommodation and Resistance – An Introduction', *Historical Geography*, Vol. 27 (1999), pp. 1–5; J. Nederveen Pieterse, 'Hybridity, So What? The Anti-hybridity Backlash and the Riddles of Recognition', *Theory, Culture & Society*, Vol. 18, Nos 2–3 (2001), pp. 219–45.
47 M. Bakhtin, *The Dialogic Imagination: Four Essays* (English trans., ed. M. Holquist, Austin, 1981); H. K. Bhabha, *The Location of Culture* (London, 1994). See also: R. J. C. Young, *Colonial Desire. Hybridity in Theory, Culture and Race* (London, 1995), pp. 1–28.
48 Bhabha, *Location*, esp. chapters 4 and 6; N. Papastergiardis, 'Hybridity and Ambivalence. Places and Flows in Contemporary Art and Culture', *Theory, Culture & Society*, Vol. 22, No. 4 (2005), pp. 39–64; G. Smith, 'The Politics of Hybridity: Some Problems with Crossing the Border', in A. Bery and P. Murray (eds), *Comparing Postcolonial Literatures: Dislocations* (London, 2000), pp. 43–55.
49 V. S. Kalra, R. Kaur and J. Hutnyk, *Diaspora and Hybridity* (London, 2005), pp. 70–85; Pieterse, 'Hybridity, So What?', esp. pp. 233–9.
50 L. Benton and J. Muth, 'On Cultural Hybridity: Interpreting Colonial Authority and performance', *Journal of Colonialism and Colonial History*, Vol. 1, No. 1 (2000), n.p.
51 F. Anthias, 'New Hybridities, Old Concepts: The Limits of "Culture"', *Ethnic and Racial Studies*, Vol. 24, No. 4 (July 2001), pp. 619–41; Papastergiadis, 'Hybridity and Ambivalence', pp. 39–64; A. Hughes, 'On Being in the Place of the Cultural Other. Marc Boulet's Travels in India and China', *Journal of European Studies*, Vol. 36, No. 1 (March 2006), pp. 43–60.
52 D. Denoon, *Settler Capitalism: the Dynamics of Dependent Development in the Southern Hemisphere* (Oxford, 1983).

53 Quoted by Lynette Russell in *Colonial Frontiers*, pp. 2–3.

54 Stasiulis and Yuval-Davis, *Unsettling*, pp. 2–3.

55 Coombes, 'Memory and History', in *Rethinking Settler Colonialism*, pp. 1–2.

56 S. Macintyre and A. Clark, *The History Wars* (2nd edn, Melbourne, 2004).

57 A. Curthoys, 'Mythologies', in R. Nile (ed.), *The Australian Legend and its Discontents* (St Lucia, 2000), pp. 11–41.

58 *Ibid.*, pp. 35–7. The intensity of the 'war' is illustrated by the controversy following Keith Windschuttle's re-evaluation of the evidential basis for the modern historical consensus that white settlers in Van Diemen's Land killed thousands of indigenous people there in the early nineteenth century. See K. Windschuttle, *The Fabrication of Aboriginal History, Vol. 1, Van Diemen's Land 1803–1847* (Sydney, rev. edn, 2003); J. Quiggin, 'The "fabrication" of Aboriginal history. Repudiating the past', The Evatt Foundation, University of New South Wales, Sydney, http://evatt.org.au/news/169.html, posted 26 January 2003; K. Windschuttle, 'The Return of Postmodernism in Aboriginal History', *Quadrant Magazine History*, April 2006, Vol. 50, No. 4, www.quadrant.org.au.

59 M. Dixson, *The Imaginary Australian. Anglo-Celts and Identity – 1788 to the present* (Sydney, 1999), pp. 6–11, 116–21, 162–65.

60 Russell, 'Introduction', in *Idem* (ed.), *Colonial Frontiers*, pp. 1–16.

61 N. Wolski, 'All's not Quiet on the Western Front – Rethinking Resistance and Frontiers in Aboriginal Historiography', in Russell (ed.), *Colonial Frontiers*, pp. 216–36.

62 Coombes, *Rethinking*, passim.

63 S. Howe, 'Historiography', in K. Kenny (ed.), *Oxford History of the British Empire, Companion Series, Ireland and the British Empire* (Oxford, 2004), pp. 241–46.

64 T. McDonough (ed.), *Was Ireland a Colony? Economics, Politics and Culture in Nineteenth-century Ireland* (Dublin, 2004).

65 D. O'Hearne, 'Ireland in the Atlantic Economy', in T. McDonough (ed.), *Was Ireland a Colony?* pp. 3–26; C. Kinealy, 'Was Ireland a Colony? The Evidence of the Great Famine', in *ibid.*, pp. 48–65; V. Crossman, 'Colonial Perspectives on Local Government in Nineteenth-century Ireland', in *ibid.*, pp. 102–16; T. Ballantyne, 'The Sinews of Empire: Ireland, India and the Construction of British Colonial Knowledge', in *ibid.*, pp. 145–64; P. Clayton, 'Two Kinds of Colony: "Rebel Ireland" and the "Imperial province"', in *ibid.*, pp. 235–48.

66 D. Fitzpatrick, 'Ireland and the British Empire', *The English Historical Review*, Vol. 121, No. 490 (2006), pp. 239–41; A. Jackson, 'Ireland, the Union, and the Empire, 1800–1960', in Kenny (ed.), *Ireland and the British Empire*, pp. 123–53; K. Jeffery, 'Introduction', in *Idem*, *'An Irish Empire?' Aspects of Ireland and the British Empire* (Manchester, 1996), pp. 1–24.

67 D. H. Akenson, *The Irish Diaspora. A Primer* (Belfast, 1996), pp. 141–52.

68 A. Bielenberg, 'Irish Migration to the British Empire, 1700–1914', in *Idem* (ed.), *The Irish Diaspora* (London, 2000), pp. 215–34.

69 K. Kenny, 'Ireland and the British Empire: An Introduction', in *Idem* (ed.), *Ireland and the British Empire*, pp. 1–25. For a critique, see Fitzpatrick, 'Ireland and the British Empire', pp. 239–41.

70 K. Kenny, 'The Irish in the Empire', in *Idem* (ed.), *Ireland and the British Empire*, pp. 92–3.

71 Fitzpatrick, 'Ireland and the British Empire', pp. 239–41.

72 S. Howe, 'Historiography', in Kenny (ed.), *Ireland and the British Empire*, pp. 229–30; Jeffery, 'Introduction', esp. pp. 5–10; Kenny, 'Ireland and the British Empire: An Introduction', pp. 1–25.

73 Jeffrey, 'Introduction', pp. 4–5; Kenny, 'Ireland and the British Empire: An Introduction', pp. 8–9, 12–17.

74 Kenny, 'The Irish in the Empire', pp. 96–7.

75 Clayton, 'Two Kinds of Colony', pp. 236–8.

76 Jackson, 'Ireland, the Union, and the Empire', pp. 142–5; Jeffrey, 'Introduction', pp. 11–17.

77 Jackson, 'Ireland, the Union, and the Empire', p. 123, citing A. Porter, 'Introduction', in *Idem* (ed.), *The Nineteenth Century*, p. 27.

78 A. Blunt and C. McEwan, 'Introduction', in C. McEwan and A. Blunt (eds), *Postcolonial Geographies* (London, 2002), pp. 1–6.

79 *Ibid.*, pp. 2–3; D. Clayton, 'Imperial Geographies', in J. S. Duncan, N. C. Johnson and R. H. Schein (eds), *A Companion to Cultural Geography* (Oxford, 2004), pp. 249–68.

80 J. Crush, 'Post-colonialism, De-colonisation, and Geography', in A. Godlewska and N. Smith (eds), *Geography and Empire* (Oxford, 1994), pp. 333–50. For a subsequent analysis which develops Crush's themes in a Southern African context, see: A. Lester, 'Introduction: Historical Geographies of Southern Africa', *Journal of Southern African Studies*, Vol. 29, No. 3 (September 2003), pp. 595–613.

81 N. Smith and A. Godlewska, 'Introduction: Critical Histories of Geography', in Godlewska and Smith (eds), *Geography and Empire*, pp. 1–8.

82 *Ibid.*, pp. 6–7.

83 McEwan and Blunt (eds), *Postcolonial Geographies*, esp. pp. 1–2; J. R. Ryan, 'Postcolonial Geographies', in Duncan, Johnson and Schein (eds), *Companion*, pp. 469–84.

84 A. Maddrell, 'Empire, Emigration and School Geography: Changing Discourses of Imperial Citizenship', *Journal of Historical Geography*, Vol. 22 (1996), pp. 373–87; T. Ploszajska, 'Historiographies of Geography and Empire', in B. Graham and C. Nash (eds), *Modern Historical Geographies* (Harlow, 2000), pp. 121–45.

85 N. Etherington, 'Genocide by Cartography. Secrets and Lies in Maps of the Southeastern African Interior, 1830–1850', in D. Trigger and G. Griffiths (eds), *Disputed Territories. Land, Culture and Identity in Settler Societies* (Hong Kong, 2003), pp. 207–32; S. Ryan, *The Cartographic Eye. How Explorers Saw Australia* (Cambridge, 1996).

86 J. M. R. Cameron, 'Agents and Agencies in Geography and Empire: The Case of George Grey', in M. Bell, R. Butlin and M. Heffernan (eds), *Geography and Imperialism 1820–1940* (Manchester, 1995), pp. 13–35; R. H. Grove, 'Imperialism and the Discourse of Desiccation: The Institutionalisation of Global Environmental Concerns and the Role of the Royal Geographical Society, 1860–1880', in *ibid.*, pp. 36–52; J. M. MacKenzie, 'The Provincial Geographical Societies in Britain, 1884–1914', in *ibid.*, pp. 93–124.

87 M. Bell, R. A. Butlin and M. Heffernan, 'Introduction: Geography and Imperialism, 1820–1940', in *ibid.*, pp. 1–12; D. N. Livingstone, *The Geographical Tradition* (Oxford, 1992), p. 160, cited in Ryan, 'Postcolonial Geographies', pp. 472–3.

88 J. D. Sidaway, 'Postcolonial Geographies. Survey–Explore–Review', in McEwan and Blunt (eds), *Postcolonial Geographies*, pp. 11–28.

89 J. S. Duncan, 'Complicity and Resistance in the Colonial Archive: Some Issues of Method and Theory in Historical Geography', *Historical Geography*, Vol. 27 (1999), pp. 119–27.

90 Clayton, 'Imperial Geographies', p. 460.

91 Kenny, 'Colonial Geographies', pp. 1–4.

92 R. Cole Harris, *Making Native Space. Colonialism, Resistance, and Reserves in British Columbia* (Vancouver, 2002), p. xvii.

93 N. Thomas, *Colonialism's Culture. Anthropology, Travel and Government* (Cambridge, 1994), pp. 15–16.

94 D. W. Clayton, *Islands of Truth. The Imperial Fashioning of Vancouver Island* (Vancouver, 2000), pp. xi–xix.

95 *Ibid.*, p. 71.

96 Cited in Clayton, 'Imperial Geographies', pp. 455–6.

97 A. Blunt, *Domicile and Diaspora: Anglo-Indian Women and the Spatial Politics of Home* (Oxford, 2005); *Idem, Travel, Gender and Imperialism: Mary Kingsley and West Africa* (London, 1994); A. Blunt and G. Rose, 'Introduction: Women's Colonial and Postcolonial Geographies', in *Eidem*, (eds), *Writing Women and*

Space: Colonial and Post Colonial Geographies (London, 1994), pp. 1–25; C. McEwan, *Gender, Geography and Empire: Victorian Women Travellers in West Africa* (London, 2000); S. Mills, 'Gender and Colonial space', *Gender, Place and Culture*, vol. 3 (1999), pp. 125–47.

98 P. Howell, 'Colonial Law and Legal Historical Geography: An Argument from Gibraltar', in A. R. H. Baker (ed.), *Home and Colonial. Essays on Landscape, Ireland, Environment and Empire in Celebration of Robin Butlin's Contribution to Historical Geography*, Historical Geography Research Series No. 39 (London, 2004); Idem., 'Prostitution and the Place of Empire: Regulation and Repeal in Hong Kong and the British Imperial Network', in Proudfoot and Roche (eds), *(Dis)Placing*, pp. 175–200; M. Satish Kumar, '"Oriental Sore" or "Public Nuisance"': The Regulation of Prostitution in Colonial India, 1805–1889', in *ibid.*, pp. 155–74; Idem., 'The Evolution of Spatial Ordering in Madras', in McEwan and Blunt (eds), *Postcolonial Geographies*, pp. 85–98; R. Phillips, 'Imperialism, Sexuality, and Space. Purity Movements in the British Empire', in *ibid.*, pp. 46–63.

99 Clayton, *Islands*, p. xiii.

100 M. Brayshay and J. Selwood, 'Dreams, Propaganda and Harsh Realities: Landscapes of Group Settlement in the Forest Districts of Western Australia in the 1920s', *Landscape Research*, Vol. 27, No. 1 (2002), pp. 81–101; M. Tonts, 'State Policy and the Yeoman Ideal: Agricultural Development in Western Australia, 1890–1914', *ibid.*, pp. 103–55.

101 K. D. Lilley, '"One Immense Gold Field!" British Imaginings of the Australian Gold Rushes, 1851–59', *Landscape Research*, Vol. 27, No. 1 (2002), pp. 67–82.

102 Lester, *Imperial Networks*; Idem., 'Colonial Settlers and the Metropole: Racial Discourse in the Early 19th-century Cape Colony, Australia and New Zealand', *Landscape Research*, Vol. 27, No. 1 (2002), pp. 39–49.

103 Lester, *Imperial Networks*, p. 4.

104 Idem., ' Trans-imperial Networks: Britain, South Africa, Australia and New Zealand during the First Half of the Nineteenth Century', in Baker (ed.), *Home and Colonial*, pp. 125–38.

105 Clayton, 'Imperial Geographies', pp. 459–61.

106 B. Yeoh, 'Historical geographies of the colonised world', in Graham and Nash (eds), *Modern Historical Geographies*, pp. 146–66.

107 J. McCann, 'The Unsettled Country: Landscape, History and Memory in Australia's Wheatlands', in Proudfoot and Roche (eds), *(Dis)Placing*, pp. 41–60.

108 Mitchell (ed.), *Landscape and Power*; Thomas, *Colonialism's Culture.*

109 *Ibid.*, pp. 2–15.

110 W. J. T. Mitchell, 'Imperial Landscape', in *Idem* (ed.), *Landscape and Power*, p. 9.

111 *Ibid.*, pp. 9–10.

112 J. Jacobs, *Edge of Empire. Postcolonialism and the City* (London, 1996), pp. 2–9.

113 *Ibid.*, p. 19.

114 K. Darian-Smith, L. Gunner and S. Nuttall, 'Introduction', in *Eidem* (eds), *Text, Theory, Space. Land, Literature and History in South Africa and Australia* (London, 1996), p. 3.

115 *Terra nullius*, or 'empty land', or 'land belonging to no-one', was the foundational concept of European settlement in Australia, and used to justify the appropriation of land already occupied by existing indigenous communities. The concept owed much to the thought of the English liberal philosopher John Locke (*fl.* 1632–1704). It represented (seemingly) unused land as being in a 'state of nature', and as available for acquisition as 'property' through the transforming agency of *labour* and improvement. See: J. Gascoigne, *The Enlightenment and the Origins of European Australia* (Cambridge, 2002), pp. 8–13.

116 D. S. Trigger, 'Introduction: Disputed Territories: Land, Culture and Identity', in Trigger and Griffiths (eds), *Disputed Territories*, pp. 1–4.

117 E. R. Hills. 'The Imaginary Life: Landscape and Culture in Australia', *Journal of Australian Studies*, Vol. 29 (1991), pp. 12–27.

118 A. Taylor, '"The Sun Always Shines in Perth": a Post-Colonial Geography of Identity, Memory and Place', *Australian Geographical Studies*, Vol. 38, No. 1 (March 2000), pp. 27–35.
119 Cole Harris, *Native Space*, p. xvii.
120 *Ibid.*, pp. 265–6.

CHAPTER 3

Place and diaspora

The exile shall return no more. In most instances he is dead and buried in the land of his adoption. But his children still live and remember his rehearsal of his boyhood days in the cradle land of his race. (Dr Nicholas O'Donnell, Melbourne, 1908[1])

The practice of empire provided one context for the local worlds imagined and inhabited by Irish and Scottish settlers and their descendants in nineteenth-century Australia. The wider issues of emigration, personal (dis)location and collective memory signalled in Dr O'Donnell's autobiographical memoir constituted another. The Irish and Scottish men, women and children who landed at Sydney, Port Phillip, Moreton Bay and elsewhere stood heirs to a long tradition of emigration that had taken their fellow countrymen to many parts of the world from the Middle Ages onwards. Plantation, rebellion and religious wars, as well as economic calculation, led to the displacement of significant numbers of migrants from both countries to continental Europe and beyond during the seventeenth and eighteenth centuries.[2] From 1800 the pace of emigration quickened, and was given an added fillip in each country by famine-induced agrarian social change and industrially led regional economic adjustment. But motives for emigration were complex. According to classical migration theory, emigration choices respond to perceived opportunities abroad as much as perceived constraints at home. They thus depend upon the nature, quality, volume and direction of information flows about possible destinations overseas, as well as the existence of intervening settlement opportunities and the presence (or absence) of supportive cultural networks in the chosen country.[3] The Irish and Scottish settlers who arrived in Australia are therefore likely to have only done so after a complex subjective process of opportunity and risk assessment.

Between 1815 and 1914 over 50 million people left Europe for various new worlds in North and South America, Africa, Australasia and elsewhere, including 23 million from the British Isles. Among the latter were the 7 million people who left Ireland, and the 2 million who emigrated from Scotland after 1830.[4] North America remained the most popular overseas destination for Irish and Scottish emigrants, though these flows, like those to other countries, were complicated by complex eddies of stepwise and return migration.[5] The precise number who emigrated to North America is impossible to determine. Akenson estimates that at least 5.5 million Irish men and women emigrated to the United States and Canada between 1825 and 1911. In comparison, approximately 1.25 million emigrants left Scotland for these countries during the same period.[6] Although always a less popular destination, Australia nevertheless also attracted significant numbers of Irish and Scottish emigrants during this period. Of the approximately 1.6 million emigrants from the British Isles who settled there during the nineteenth century, perhaps some 300,000 came from Ireland and between 250,000 and 300,000 from Scotland.[7]

These movements, together with their consequences in Ireland and Scotland, have long been the stuff of Irish and Scottish population history.[8] The empiricism and essentialism that characterised earlier accounts have come under increasing critical scrutiny as scholars in various disciplines have begun to consider the ways in which individuals and communities caught up in these transnational movements constructed their own sense of international selfhood. Central to this revisiting is the concept of *diaspora*. This has found considerable currency among cultural theorists, historians and others interested in emigration and its consequences, but has been used in ambiguous ways. Of ancient Greek origin, diaspora originally meant the scattering or dispersal of seed. In the Septuagint, the Greek translation of the Hebrew Scriptures made between the third and the first centuries BC, it is used to describe the deportation of Jews from Judah to Babylon *ca.* 586 BC, where it takes on the connotation of exile associated with the earlier Hebraic term, *galut*. This idea of diaspora as exile was reinforced by the banishment and enslavement of many Jews during the Roman occupation of Israel during the first and second centuries AD, and it was in this guise that diaspora eventually entered the modern lexicon.[9]

If twentieth-century scholarship initially acknowledged the paradigmatic nature of the Jewish experience of diaspora, the appropriation of the term by Africanist and Black Studies scholars in the 1960s significantly extended its meaning. The early emphasis on population movements that were coerced, involved exile from a traditional homeland with little or no possibility of return and were grounded in some form of religious or ethnic persecution gave way to a wider concern with 'almost any expatriate group . . . regardless of the conditions leading to the[ir] dispersion'.[10] Writing in 2005, Brubaker identified long-distance nationalist groups, labour migrants, trans-border linguistic communities, religious communities, ethno-cultural and nationally defined groups, as well as gays, whites, rednecks and fundamentalists as being among the diverse population segments recently assigned diasporic status. Following Akenson and Tölölyan, Brubaker also noted that this broader usage carries with it the danger that diaspora may lose whatever explanative purchase it once possessed. 'If everyone is diasporic, then no-one is distinctly so . . . The universalisation of diaspora, paradoxically, means the disappearance of diaspora.'[11]

Brubaker's concerns notwithstanding, the ideas of constructive selfhood that underpin both the original and later uses of diaspora remain central to our present concern with the place narratives of Irish and Scottish settler colonialism in Australia. Beyond this, difficulties ensue. A fundamental issue that distinguishes between earlier definitions of diaspora and its current critical rendition as transnational consciousness centres on the importance of locality as the *locus* of memory and identity within emigrant-descended communities. *Imperial Spaces* privileges ideas of place as an important referent in the construction of Irish and Scottish settler identities. Although these place narratives were framed by the practice of empire, they were also emigrant and arguably diasporic, some, possibly, in the original exilic sense of the word. In construing place in these terms, however, we ascribe an importance both to the locally grounded realities of the emigrant 'present' and to cultural invocations of a remembered or inherited national past which critical representations of diaspora currently downplay. Is accommodation possible?

We begin by considering the importance ascribed to locality and territory within earlier notions of diaspora as dislocation or exile, and contrast this with critical representations which represent diaspora as a state of transnational being. Our non-essentialist understanding of place as an imaginative construction allows us to combine a critical emphasis on diaspora as practice and experience with the insights offered by more conventional representations which emphasise the importance of located diasporic memory. The question remains, however, of the extent to which ideas of diaspora and place have informed existing accounts of nineteenth-century Irish and Scottish emigrant experience both within and beyond empire. In the second part of the chapter we examine recent representations of nineteenth-century Irish and Scottish emigration and consider the varying importance attached to different understandings of diaspora as a means of explaining this. In the final section, we focus our attention on Australia and New Zealand

and consider the relatively limited engagement with ideas of space and place in existing accounts of colonial Irish and Scottish settlement in these countries.

Rethinking diaspora

At the heart of the current debate concerning the importance of locality and territorial origin within diaspora lies the question of the extent to which diasporic identities are in any sense bounded, whether by the sedentary realities of the diasporic present or by the remembered places of the past. Alternatively, are people in diaspora so thoroughly de-territorialised, and their identities so hybridised, that they are always place-less, always occupying in-between space, neither here nor there? Initially, much late twentieth-century scholarship favoured the notion of territorially grounded identities and offered a geographically rooted understanding of diaspora which also emphasised the multi-generational nature of diasporic communities. Thus, in his 1996 survey of the Irish diaspora, Akenson drew a distinction between first-generation migrants, those who actually engaged upon an act of international movement and who generally left their country of origin for a foreign destination with the expectation of permanent or long-term residence there, and their own descendants born overseas. Akenson argues that it was the entire multi-generational global group who constituted the Irish diaspora. Later descendants of first-generation migrants may be expected to have had a more varied sense of their national origins than their migrant forebears, however. Consequently, Brubaker has concluded that Akenson's sort of demographically led definition is weak: in confusing evidence for numbers, and common ancestry with evidence of active diasporic consciousness, it denies the latter's constructive nature.[12]

Nevertheless, Akenson's demographically bounded and territorially rooted understanding of diaspora resonated with the work of other scholars in the 1990s, even as they sought to extend its meaning beyond the original Jewish paradigm. In *Global Diasporas. An Introduction*, for example, Robin Cohen offered a typology of five types of diaspora, classified according to their primary causation – victim/refugee, imperial/colonial, service/labour, trade/business/professional and cultural/hybrid/postmodern – but framed very much in ethno-cultural or national terms.[13] In this, Armenians and Jews are held to be paradigmatic of victim/refugee diasporas, the British, Spanish or Dutch to be representative of imperial/colonial diasporas, while indentured Turks and Indians personified labour/service diasporas. All, according to Cohen, share certain common characteristics (Table 3.1). Pre-eminent

Table 3.1 Diasporic characteristics (after Cohen, 1997)

Dispersal, frequently enforced, from an original homeland to foreign destinations.

Alternatively, the expansion from a homeland in search of work, trade or purposes of colonisation.

The maintenance of a collective memory, at least partially mythic, about the homeland, its location, characteristics and history.

The idealisation of this collective image of a 'homeland', and a commitment to its maintenance and prosperity, or creation or restoration.

An aspiration to return to the homeland.

A strong, distinctive, ethnic consciousness, based on a sense of common history and identity.

A troubled relationship with host societies in the countries of settlement.

A sense of empathy or shared identity and interest with co-ethnic members in other countries of settlement.

A potentially distinctive and creative life in those host societies with a tradition of tolerant multiculturalism.

among these are an idealised memory of the homeland, a distinctive sense of ethnic identity and an ongoing empathy with co-ethnic members in other host countries. Together, these capture the idea that, whether in the past or the present, diasporic consciousness is more than simply the individual's sense of being elsewhere, and also encompasses their feeling, however uncertain or conditional, of being, in at least part of their lives, defined by a wider, transcendant sense of (ethnic) belonging. Grounded in foundational beliefs and memory that are external to their present situation, this atavistic sense of a wider belonging – of being rooted elsewhere – positions these individuals in diasporic time and space. They live, therefore, in two worlds: their expatriate or expatriate-descended present and an imagined past that values this in terms that are at once broader, mutable and partial.

In a more recent but equally rooted approach to diaspora, William Safran has placed a similar emphasis on the maintenance of links with the homeland. Arguing that members of diasporas 'do not wish to cut themselves off completely from their homelands', he suggests that, habitually, they retain a memory of their homeland or some sort of general orientation towards it; create institutions which reflect something of its culture and religion; and continue to connect with it in other symbolic or practical ways. At the same time, while they remain committed to their survival as a distinct community, they doubt

[49]

whether they are fully accepted by their host country. Accordingly, many individuals preserve what Safran describes as 'a myth of return', the aspirational belief in the future possibility of their living in the homeland. The consequence of all this, Safran suggests, is a tension between being in one place physically – where the individual lives and works – and thinking regularly of another place far away. Thus, irrespective of whether members of a diaspora have adjusted to life in their host land, they still retain, and are characterised by, a spiritual, emotional and cultural attachment to their perceived – but physically distant – homeland. Framed in this way, diaspora provides a useful metaphorical designation that encompasses the disparate experiences of 'expatriates, expellees, political refugees, alien residents, immigrants and ethnic and racial minorities *tout court'*.[14]

Critical representations of diaspora as a transnational state of being and consciousness challenge the assumption underlying these sorts of approach that nations, regions or indeed any other form of bounded locality can provide a useful reference point for collective identities. The key issue is essentialism. In *Diaspora and Hybridity*, for example, Kalra, Kaur and Hutnyk dismiss Cohen's ethnographically framed diaspora typology as a form of 'essentialist primordialism' which accommodates neither the dynamicism of multiple diasporic moves nor, for some people, the absence of a homeland.[15] Borrowing from Vertovec's threefold conceptualisation of diaspora as social form, consciousness and cultural production, they emphasise its capacity to 'deterritorialise' the individual's sense of belonging.[16] Instead of being 'absolutist notions' based on 'prescriptive locations in territory and history' (i.e. a homeland), diasporic belonging and identity invoke shared experience, practices and loyalty, and the consciousness that derives from these.[17] In other words, diasporic consciousness, in their view, derives from routes rather than roots.

But the role of place and locality within diaspora is not as easily dismissed as this critique suggests. In a considered review that appeared a year earlier than *Diaspora and Hybridity*, Kokot, Tölölyan and Alfonso acknowledge the growing body of diasporic literature that criticises 'the general discourse of rootedness', but caution against too hasty a dismissal of the connection between diaspora and locality. Framing their analysis within a general critique of cultural essentialism, they argue that although diasporas 'cannot be usefully limited to any one type of community or historical situation', and transgress boundaries of culture, identity and locality which are themselves diffuse, the 'essences' of (diasporic) identity remain implicated within and reflected by the 'realities of sedentary diasporic life'.[18] In other words, no matter how inchoate, contingent and multiple the sense of selfhood constructed by people in diaspora, nor how liminal and in-between their sense of being, their lives still impart meaning to, and acquire meaning from, the material circumstances of their daily, local existence. Thus, historically, in Australia as elsewhere within the British Empire and beyond, localities acquired meaning as place through the constructive actions of communities of emigrants and their descendants whose lives, in diaspora, remained in a continual process of located becoming.

Our conception of place in *Imperial Spaces* as a subjectively constructed, imaginative site of memory, agency and identity accommodates this understanding and does not invoke the sort of territorialised essentialism that Kalra, Kaur and Hutnyk critique. Rather, we embrace their idea of diaspora as practice and experience but locate this within the material framework of the lived world that people in diaspora encounter. Place and practice were (and are) mutually formative. Because the meanings of place attached to different material locales are subjectively constructed, they will differ between individuals according to their social positionality and life experience and can never be primordial or essentialist. Rather, these meanings sustain precisely those sorts of ambiguous, fractured, transient, multiple and conditional senses of identity and belonging that have been argued to characterise the (diasporic) hybrid state. Lovell, for example, argues that the idea of hybridity, of mentally living in two places at once, reflects the transience of any sense of local belonging. The experience of emigration, for example, was not wholly encompassed by a global sense of being in between, but was also marked by the ever-changing materialities which derived from the actual processes of dislocation themselves.[19] According to Papastergiardis, these acts of displacement constitute the ambivalence at the heart of hybridity, simultaneously creating both an absence and a presence. This ambivalence produces new places or sites of identity, and these involve both an expansion of existing boundaries and attachments and progressively more complex nodes of attachment.[20] Diasporic hybridity, therefore, signals a desire for both separation and connection, which is expressed through the transient sites of memory and meaning (or places) created during the dislocating processes of emigration and its aftermath.

By locating diasporic identity in imaginative constructions of place in this way, we can accommodate both Brubaker's anti-essentialist notion of diaspora as 'a category of practice ... that makes claims, articulates projects, mobilises energies, and appeals to loyalties', and Kokot's warning that 'diaspora may transcend boundaries, but space, [place] and locality remain important points of reference on a symbolic as well as a physical level'.[21] Moreover, the subjective construction of place allows us to accommodate one self-evident fact. Not everyone sharing a common ethno-cultural or national ancestry but living trans-nationally sustained (or sustains) a similarly essentialised identity, either by making the same appeals to their putative homeland or by maintaining the same active sense of ethnic or other difference with their host society. In short, the changing narratives of place constructed by Irish and Scottish emigrants and their descendants reflected the strength – or absence – of each individual's continuing sense of origin as part of their evolving diasporic selfhood. How have existing representations of Irish and Scottish emigration within the Empire and beyond engaged with the possibility of such diasporic consciousness?

Irish and Scottish diasporas?

In her 2002 survey of diasporic literature relating to Ireland, Mary Hickman concluded that there were, in fact, remarkably few references to the country either by postmodern writers concerned with tran-snational identities and consciousness or by authors who privileged more conventional ideas of located diasporic identity and nationhood. Where claims for an Irish diaspora were made, they were invariably on the basis of victimhood, with the Famine migration cited as a typical example of coerced, exilic movement.[22] In Hickman's view, exist-ing Irish emigration literature hardly helped to remedy this lack of diasporic perspectives. Grounded in its by now traditional discourse of ethnic segment contribution history, it remained primarily concerned with post-arrival assimilationist narratives, or comparative empirical accounts of Irish migrants in different countries. Even work such as Akenson's *The Irish Diaspora* or O'Sullivan's series on *The Irish World Wide*, which adopted a global perspective, failed to engage with the issues of 'unsettling, recombination and hybridisation' that Hickman regarded as central to modern critical understandings of diaspora as a 'process of (transnational) becoming'.[23]

Hickman's own call, for an approach to the Irish world-wide which combined this critical sense of 'becoming' with the materiality of more conventional structural approaches, highlighted the continuing debate concerning the usefulness of diaspora as a mode of historical explana-tion for Irish emigration. Sociological studies of contemporary 'new Irish emigration' have tended to embrace critical readings of diaspora, and emphasise the hybrid and developing character of Irishness abroad.[24] Historians have been altogether more cautious in accepting the relevance of diaspora to the Irish case. Recognising the deficiency of much existing Irish emigration history as 'national history writ large', Kenny and Belchem have both argued for a cross-national as well as a transnational approach to historical studies of Irish emigration and its consequences.[25] That is, for an approach that explores both the migrant flows from Ireland to other countries and those which, independently, linked Irish-descended communities in different countries overseas, comparing each with other emigrant experience. Although subsequently criticised by McRaild for advocating an outmoded form of comparative history,[26] Kenny and Belchem argue that this perspective is necessary in order to assess the claims made for the uniqueness of Irish experience in diaspora.

Various scholars have adopted this approach, including David Doyle and Malcolm Campbell, who use it in their comparative analyses of Irish experience in Australia, the United States and the Pacific world, and its importance is gaining wider recognition generally.[27] But other concerns remain. Belchem has questioned whether critical ideas of diaspora as 'valorised, fluid, third space', would have had any particular meaning for Irish or other emigrants travelling steerage, say, to Boston or Grosse Île. He notes that Irish identities took on multiple and different forms globally as emigrants adapted to circumstance and chance. He argues that this diversity was not necessarily synonymous with postcolonial notions of hybridity as transcending essentialist ideas of nationhood and ethnicity. Expressions of Irishness were contingent on individual and community circumstance within the host society. The remembered or imagined 'Irelands' this consciousness invoked were no less real for the individual because of this. The major irony, according to Belchem, is that, despite the postmodern concern with diasporic hybridity, much diasporic writing on Ireland has remained thoroughly essentialist, privileging an exclusively Catholic ethnic Irish identity.[28] His critique carries some force. Although there is a growing body of historical literature on gender issues and socio-economic aspects of Irish emigration, the paucity of the treatment given to non-Catholic Irish emigrants has been notable. Whether for reasons of demography, the nature of the archives or because, as Hickman has argued, historically, host nations have perceived Catholics to enjoy hegemonic status within Irish emigration, conventionally, Irish Protestants have not figured largely in Irish emigration histories.[29]

Although this position is beginning to change, the continuing concern over the essentialist nature of much Irish emigration history mirrors the growing recognition of the heterogeneity of Irish experience both abroad and in Ireland, and the need to ground historical accounts of this in specific time-place moments.[30] For example, McRaild more or less dismisses critical understandings of diaspora when it is used in a 'relativist, presentist, [and] emotional way' to unify disparate communities of Irish people in terms of their shared but loose connection with 'a vague, stylised and romanticised patria'. Favouring its use as an analytical historical tool 'for something which actually happened', he argues that historians should concentrate on 'real events and processes' and test for the existence of social phenomena that together went to make up the existence of diaspora. In short, McRaild advocates historical questioning of the modern globalised connections that are embodied by diaspora. How is today's feeling of 'being Irish', whether in Santiago or Sydney, connected to the historical processes of emigration that created it?[31]

The point is exemplified by changing representations of Irishness in the United States, historically the single largest destination for Irish emigrants beyond Britain. Despite justifiable criticism that, in the past, scholars have too easily assumed that Irish migrant experience in the United States was representative of the Irish world-wide, our current understanding of Irish American ethnic solidarities reflects the increasingly nuanced – though by no means uncontested – ways in which Irish experience overseas is being represented.[32] Much twentieth-century Irish American historiography tended to characterise nineteenth-century Irish settlement in the United States as a whole in terms of the Famine emigration of the late 1840s and 1850s. Between 1846 and 1855, at least 1.8 million Irish men and women left Ireland for North America. Perhaps 80 per cent of this flow were Catholic; most were rural; many were impoverished. Their arrival at north-eastern American ports such as Boston or New York, and subsequent cultural impact there, acquired iconic status within this earlier discourse.

In this reading, Famine emigration was elided with Irish emigration in general; all were seen in essentialist terms to be rural, Catholic, impoverished and exilic, and thus, with the increasing fashionability of the term from the 1980s onwards, diasporic in the original sense of the word.[33] This image has proved to be tenacious, particularly in popular Irish American historical consciousness. It has given rise to a filopietistical contribution discourse that has celebrated victimhood at home in Ireland; triumph over initial adversity in America; and then, subsequently, success there. Bound up with this have been powerful undertones of exile, loss, suffering and injustice which have continued to resonate politically into the twenty-first century on both sides of the Atlantic.[34] This reading of Irish American origins is, however, at best partial. It ignores three things: first, the existence of significant Protestant Irish migration to North America during the eighteenth and early nineteenth centuries. Second, the existence of opportunistic economic Catholic migration to the United States from at least the late 1820s – and its effect in transforming the earlier Presbyterian-led Irish settlement pattern. And third, the growing evidence for the regional and socio-economic diversity displayed by Catholic Irish emigration to the United States both during and after the Famine.

The preponderance of Presbyterians among the quarter of a million migrants who left Ireland for North America during the eighteenth century has long been recognised,[35] but in fact, this early Protestant predominance continued into the first quarter of the nineteenth century. Irish emigration to North America increased steadily from *ca.* 1803 as rural conditions in Ireland deteriorated under the impact of accelerating population growth, and by 1845, a further 450,000 people had emigrated there from Ulster alone. On the assumption that the majority of these were Protestant, Doyle suggests that, as a proportion of the total number of Irish men and women arriving in Canada and the United States, Protestants fell to become only a minority (less than 40 per cent) in the United States after 1820, but continued to constitute at least 60 per cent of Irish arrivals in Canada.[36] The consequences of this early Protestant numerical dominance for the subsequent pattern of Irish denominational identities in the United States have been the subject of considerable debate. Akenson argues that despite the massively larger numbers of Catholics among successive generations of *arrivals* from the mid-nineteenth century onwards, the early preponderance of Protestants was sufficient to create a multiplier effect within the overall, *multi*-generational, Irish community. Because significant numbers of Irish Protestants settled in America far earlier than their Catholic counterparts, the longer passage of time over which more numerous generations of Protestant descendants emerged ensured the continued relative expansion of this part of the Irish diasporic community. Akenson argues that the consequences survive to the present day. He notes that despite the widespread assumption that the Irish-descended community in modern America is predominantly Catholic, in the 1970s and 1980s, over half the 44 million Americans claiming Irish descent identified themselves as Protestant.[37]

As Akenson demonstrates elsewhere, this sort of denominational head-counting is, in a sense, unimportant. It certainly does not account for variations in the emigrants' post-arrival economic performance.[38] It attains significance only in light of the religious essentialism that continues to characterise representations of the origins and character of Irish America as diagnostically Catholic. Unsurprisingly, Akenson's views have been challenged by those writing in this genre. First, on the grounds that acknowledging Irish descent does not necessarily imply possession of a constructive diasporic consciousness. Second, because of doubts over the relevance of the Canadian data that Akenson uses to infer historical patterns of social mobility within the Irish American community at large. The first subtly implies that (non-Catholic) denominational allegiance may affect your sense of being Irish. The second that, despite the numerous historical connectivities linking Canada and the United States, the differing historical construction of Irish Canada – with its far higher proportion of Protestants[39] – somehow vitiates meaningful extrapolation of Irish experience there: a curious conclusion for advocates of diaspora as transnational experience! Tellingly, some of this criticism simply reiterates that to be Irish in the United States was (and is) to be Catholic, because this – it is claimed – is how Irish Catholics have constructed their own experience and how they have periodically been perceived by nativist American society. In this view, 'further study of the Scotch-Irish [sic] or Irish Protestants in the United States, though important, will not necessarily deepen our knowledge about what is referred to as and was dynamically constructed as the Irish American ethnic experience in the United States'.[40]

Thus is essentialism perpetuated. Non-Catholic denominational groups arriving from Ireland are represented as having been somehow hybrid: possessors of a hyphenated identity that occluded their Irishness with some other – less authentic – marker of nationality. What is nevertheless clear, however, is that during the eighteenth century these 'other Irish' established themselves in a pattern of dispersed and largely rural communities that by ca. 1790 extended from Pennsylvania, Maryland and Virginia to the Carolinas, Kentucky and Tennessee. United by a shared experience of British colonial prejudice, and sustained by familiar Presbyterian leadership and the presence of entire congregations that had emigrated en masse, these communities exhibited – according to Doyle – a marked degree of social coherence that survived for several generations. But, ultimately, this particular Irish America did not last. Doyle also notes that the growing volume of (increasingly Catholic) Irish emigration between 1820 and 1845 was associated with a shift in migrant settlement towards the industrialising cities of America's north-east. With the growth of this urban-industrial nexus, the earlier rural pattern was obliterated or submerged. Within the cities, religious and other social organisations were established to cater for the needs of the numerous Irish Catholic migrants. Contrary to the stereotypical image of the impoverished Famine emigrant, however, the majority of these were young, opportunistic economic migrants, generally literate, and already equipped with the skills necessary to succeed in a capitalist economy.[41]

Consequently, although there is a strong case for arguing that the massive increase in Irish migration to the United States during and after the Famine, together with its increasingly urban and decidedly Catholic character, marked a highly significant phase in the development of Irish America, the framework for this transformation had been put in place twenty years earlier by migration flows which were far removed from the Famine stereotype. Moreover, it seems likely that, despite its emotive power, this stereotype, with its truly diasporic imagery of victimhood, destitution and despair,[42] really only applied to arrivals from the worst-hit and particularly impoverished counties of the south and west of Ireland, and to the unskilled generally. The marginalised post-arrival experience of the latter in the rookeries of New England's industrial city belt was equally untypical of Irish migrant life in general. Despite recent post-revisionist scholarship which has claimed to detect in the British government's response to the Famine if not malign geno-cidal intent, then at least coldly calculated social engineering, Doyle claims that most Famine emigrants were economic opportunists rather than driven exiles. Despite the undoubted suffering exhibited by some migrants at ports of embarkation like Liverpool, most arrived in the United States equipped with similar skills to their forebears twenty years earlier, and came from regions in Ireland where commercial agri-culture had long provided various means of petty capital accumulation. Through this, emigration, even in difficult years, became a considered economic strategy rather than a matter of headlong flight.[43] The spread of (English) literacy in the Irish countryside ensured that many more people were better able to take this decision in an informed way.[44]

Thus, as with other immigrant groups, Irish migrant experience in mid- and late nineteenth-century America depended on the individual's background in their country of origin and their ability to find a recep-tive niche in the new host society; in other words, on their 'first and second socialisation', to use Hoerder's phrase.[45] Hence the diversity of 'Irish Americas' that are currently being recovered. The individual migrant's gender, occupational status, educational attainment, linguis-tic and other skills, regional origins and cultural networks, as well as the economic opportunities, cultural receptivity and place identities of the communities they encountered in America, all determined the narrative of their emigrant life – and that of their descendants.[46] Broader patterns emerged, certainly. For example, the overwhelmingly urban profile of later nineteenth-century Irish America concealed fluctuat-ing regional preferences, as successive generations of Irish migrants and their descendants responded to the changing opportunities that they perceived to exist in their new world. The early concentration of Irish migrants in the largest Atlantic port cities, such as New York and Boston, prior to 1850 gave way to their more widespread disper-sal throughout the urban north-east over the ensuing decade; only for this pattern to slowly contract back to the north-eastern ports and their urban hinterlands after 1870. Only major inland centres, such as Chicago, Cleveland or Pittsburgh, retained significant Irish communities.[47] But whether in the urban America of the north-east or in far-flung western centres of Irish settlement such as San Francisco, for most Irish men and women, the rhythms and patterns of emigrant life reflected individual circumstance and opportunity, rather than a continuing narrative of exilic despair.

In short, if some Irish emigration to the United States was diasporic in the original exilic sense, that is, was unwanted and driven by circumstances that offered no alternative, by no means all of it was. Moreover, read in this historically precise way, the term would seem to be of equally limited utility in accounting for Irish movements to other destinations within and beyond empire. The numbers travelling to each destination varied greatly, but cannot be determined with any precision. They do not, in any case, tell us anything about the motives of those involved. As we have seen, Canada continues, perversely in Akenson's view, to be regarded as the other North American case, despite the fact that it formed an integral part of the complex emigration web that connected Ireland with the United States. Perhaps three-quarters of a million Irish men and women arrived in Canada between 1825 and 1900. By 1850, possibly one-third of that number had continued their journey south to the United States, a figure supplemented over the course of the nineteenth century by the movement of numerous Canadian-born descendants of Irish migrants. The continuing Protestant majority among those who remained in Canada has already been noted. Unlike the United States, Irish settlement in Canada also retained its early nineteenth-century rural and dispersed character, though with evidence of some (mainly Catholic) communities in the small towns of the Hudson valley and the industrialising suburbs of Hamilton and Toronto.[48]

Despite well-publicised cases of destitute Famine migrants from the west of Ireland being shovelled ashore at Shippigan, New Brunswick and St John's, Newfoundland in 1847, there is no *a priori* evidence to assume that a sense of exilic despair was any more or less prevalent among Canadian arrivals than among those travelling directly to the United States.[49] The evidence for such exilic consciousness among Irish migrants travelling to other destinations is no clearer – in some cases, less so. In nineteenth-century India, for example, Holmes concludes that the 'small minority' of Irish among the sub-continent's 'small white minority' were thoroughly embedded in the structures and practices of empire as soldiers, policemen, administrators, judges, missionaries and viceroys; a conclusion fully in accord with Akenson's judgement that the Irish were among the British Empire's 'most enthusiastic supporters'.[50] McCracken notes that while the Cape Colony and Natal's traditional reputation as the preferred destination for a socially elite Protestant settler class demands qualification, Ireland's 'huddled masses' still clearly went elsewhere. The 70,000 or so Irish men and women who did arrive before 1900 were characterised neither by poverty nor by gentry status. Rather, they possessed marketable skills which enabled many of them to flourish in the colonial economy.[51] In Argentina, the Irish Catholic Church established itself as a mediator between landowners and the state, on the one hand, and an Irish community that numbered perhaps 30,000 by 1860, on the other. Many of these emigrants had been encouraged to Argentina by the local Catholic hierarchy there, who were worried over the spiritual future of Irish emigrants in destinations such as the United States.[52] Paternalism, rather than coercion, would seem to have been the major driving force here.

In all of this, of course, we encounter the limitations of contribution history noted by Belchem and Kenny. Although these studies demonstrate the limited applicability to the Irish case of diaspora as enforced exile, they do not transcend the idea of the nation as the fundamental unit of analysis. Consequently, they fail to emphasise the extent to which Irish experience overseas may have been shared by other migrant national communities, or to explore the unsettling and recombination identified by Hickman as central to the diasporic condition. To an extent, therefore, the case for a diasporic approach to historic Irish emigration remains to be made – at least in critical transnational terms. If it is reasonable to argue that only some Irish emigrants (a minority?) were driven by an overwhelming sense of exile – in that they felt trapped in unwelcome circumstances in which emigration was the only option – then clearly, most historic Irish emigration cannot be considered diasporic in the original exilic sense. More recent, broader understandings of diaspora, as a condition in which the individual, though distantly located, still feels connected by memory and ethnic consciousness to an idealised homeland and to co-nationals living elsewhere, may offer greater intellectual purchase. Conceived of in this way, the term usefully accommodates the varied experience of a dispersed, multi-generational, ethno-national solidarity as it changes over space and time, while reminding us of the fluid nature of the sense of shared origins and identity that is central to this. But, as Hickman has already been quoted as arguing, these ideas have yet to be widely explored in a sustained, critical way by historians of Irish emigration.

Similar conclusions may be drawn concerning the ways in which diaspora has been applied to Scottish emigration. As in Ireland's case, representations of emigration from Scotland have been dominated by images of coercion and forced movement, but these really seem only to have applied to certain aspects of Highland emigration, particularly in the mid-nineteenth century. Despite the hegemonic power of this

'Highland myth of exile', as Eric Richards describes it, the only occasions where landlord evictions can clearly be shown to have resulted in intended *coerced* emigration, occurred on Barra, North Uist and Skye during the 1840s and 1850s.[53] Like earlier Clearances, such as those on the Countess of Sutherland's estates between 1811 and 1821, these evictions represented an attempt by landlords to rationalise the agriculture on their estates in the face of structural economic change. Between 1846 and 1856, they were also a response to the short-term ecological crisis induced by the Highland potato famine. The need for such change had become apparent in the later eighteenth century, but was given added impetus by the agricultural crisis that followed the end of the Napoleonic Wars in 1815. Faced with the collapse of cereal prices and the prospect of increasingly redundant crofting labour in what was becoming an inexorably pastoral economy, Highland landlords encouraged emigration as part of their plans for estate reconstruction and agrarian modernisation. Through their own subsidies and appeals for government aid, lairds increasingly represented emigration as a necessary step to prevent a Malthusian crisis developing in the Highlands, as well as an additional source of strategically important colonial manpower.[54]

The coercion that occurred on Barra and elsewhere appears to have been an extreme form of these policies, possibly prompted by the widespread destitution that had occurred as a result of the potato famine. After some reluctance, the government eventually conceded the landlords' case for regional assistance and extended the provisions of the New South Wales Bounty Emigration scheme to include the Highlands in 1837. Between 1852 and 1858 the scheme was complemented by the activities of the Highland and Island Emigration Society which, despite being philanthropically funded, was a government organisation in all but name. During these years, the Society paid for the kitting-out of over 5,000 Highland emigrants bound for Australia and the cost of their travel to their port of embarkation. Thereafter, the cost of their passage was subsidised by the Colonial Land and Emigration Commissioners in the normal way, and recovered from the emigrants after their arrival in the colonies.[55] But Australia was never the most popular destination for Highland emigrants, coerced or otherwise. Canada was. Harper estimates that, between 1815 and 1856, Highland landlords assisted some 14,000 of their tenants to emigrate there, of whom nearly 80 per cent left during the famine decade. Perhaps as many again left of their own volition between 1839 and 1849.[56]

The encouragement given by Highland landlords to their tenants to emigrate during the first half of the nineteenth century represented a considerable shift in attitude on the lairds' part. Rising rents and uncertain commodity prices at home, coupled with increasing awareness of betterment opportunities overseas, had created a tradition of Highland emigration to North America from at least the 1770s, but in the face of considerable opposition from landlords, who feared a shortage of labour and the loss of human capital generally.[57] Their *volte face* following the post-Napoleonic agricultural crisis demonstrates the truth of Richards' assertion that the Highland 'myth of exile' only ever captured part of what was a much more complex and spasmodic movement from the Highlands and Islands, and ignores altogether other forms of betterment migration from the Scottish Lowlands.[58] As Devine notes, this betterment emigration poses something of a paradox. Along with Norway and Ireland, Scotland was one of the three European countries which, proportionately, lost most of their population to emigration during the nineteenth century. But whereas Norway and Ireland were generally impoverished rural societies, in Lowland Scotland these losses occurred against a background of strengthening regional industrialisation, particularly from the mid-nineteenth century onwards, a development that should have enabled the economy to absorb whatever surplus agricultural labour became available.[59]

Devine explains this apparent paradox as the consequence of various factors. Although Scotland's industrialisation widened non-agricultural employment, it also encouraged further population growth and, in particular, attracted widespread Irish immigration to Glasgow and the surrounding region. Thus, as the industrial sector expanded, so too did the demand for these jobs, as a result of which Scottish industry paid notoriously low wages, paying perhaps 10 per cent below its English counterpart. In the countryside, on the other hand, industrialisation may have accelerated rural emigration by encouraging the substitution of capital for labour. Harper claims that in many parts of the Lowlands, the labouring class were particularly badly hit after *ca.* 1860 by the emergence of a new class of capitalist tenant farmer, intent on rationalising their farms in order to take advantage of new technology. Whereas labourers may once have aspired to rent their own smallholding, the imperatives of the capitalist farm economy now precluded this.[60] All of this, Devine argues, occurred in a society already characterised, as in Ireland, by a culture of emigration and had the twin effect of both equipping would-be Lowlands emigrants with highly marketable industrial and agricultural skills and enhancing their determination to go.[61]

Clearly, the *portmanteau* term 'betterment emigration' encompassed a wide variety of individual and regional circumstances, behaviours and motivations among nineteenth-century Scottish emigrants, just as it did in Ireland. Consequently, as Basu argues, it is probably misleading to insist on too clear a distinction between exilic and betterment emigration in every case.[62] Nevertheless, it seems reasonable to draw some distinction between instances such as those on North Uist, where crofters were compelled to leave, and the more numerous cases where individuals, whether they were textile workers in West Lothian or farm labourers in Perthshire, chose to emigrate on the basis of the rational calculation of relative advantage. But, as in the case of Irish emigration, so, too, these diverse motives and their consequences for identity formation among Scottish emigrants have yet to be systematically explored in terms of critical understandings of diaspora. Basu's own work on contemporary Highlands genealogical tourism, together with earlier explorations by Cowan and Bitterman of Scots Gaelic identities in Maritime Canada, represent a start.[63] But the case for an approach to historic patterns of Scottish emigration which combines the located materialities of emigrant experience with the subjectivities of diasporic consciousness has yet to be made. As we have argued above, our conception of place as a subjectively constructed, loosely bounded site of memory, agency and identity offers one means of accommodating this dualism. How far have such ideas been prefigured in existing representations of Irish and Scots settlement in colonial Australia and New Zealand?

Narrating the Irish and Scots in Australasia

Despite the conceptual sophistication of some recent analyses, which have begun to move the study of Irish and Scottish experience in Australasia away from its traditional, male-gendered contribution focus towards a more broadly gendered transnational understanding, few studies have offered explicitly geographical insights.[64] Most of the literature carries the implicit assumption – typical of much empiricist history – that the geographies of which individuals and communities formed a part were somehow inert, a passive backdrop against which human activity took place and on which it left its imprint. There are, of course, exceptions. David Fitzpatrick has used nineteenth-century census evidence to suggest that Irish settlement was evenly dispersed in cities and settled areas alike, reflecting the settlers' 'caution, prudence, and good economic sense', a model which Greiner and Jordan-Bychkov's flawed study of Anglo-Celtic material cultural geographies has done little to challenge.[65] Regional studies, too, have appeared, notably Malcolm Campbell's analysis of the cultural impacts of nineteenth-century Irish chain migration in the Boorowa district of southern New South Wales,[66] and Don Watson's account of the displacement of indigenous communities by Highland Scots settlement in Gippsland.[67] Lyndon Fraser has explored aspects of Catholic Irish settlement at Christchurch and on Aotearoa/New Zealand's west coast.[68] But the geographies inherent in these accounts remain, to a greater or lesser degree, empirical. Although all engage with identity, none explicitly grounds this in the imagined and material semiotic geographies of place in the way that we attempt here. The nearest approach to our position is found in Patrick O'Farrell's work on place and memory, although this remains framed within a more or less essentialist understanding of ethnicity.[69] We discuss the most important geographical perspectives offered by these contributions below. First, by way of context, we consider the broader changes that have characterised recent representations of Irish and Scottish settlement in colonial Australasia.

Studies of Irish Australian historiography by Bolton, Reece and Malcolm have stressed the filopietistical character of early contribution accounts, their grounding in a nineteenth-century discourse of supposed Irish marginalisation and the subsequent emergence of a more assertive narrative which transformed the Irish from 'passive victims' into figures of 'heroic political resistance'.[70] Personified by figures as diverse as Ned Kelly and the Catholic Archbishop of Melbourne, Daniel Mannix (1864–1964), the latter trope is most famously encapsulated in Patrick O'Farrell's seminal work, *The Irish in Australia*. Here, O'Farrell argues that the Irish formed an Anglophobic, radical catalyst for the emergence of Australia's modern national identity.[71] As Reece and Malcolm both note, O'Farrell's meta-narrative, with its emphasis on cultural difference and ideological conflict, was a deliberate riposte to what he saw as the sterile environmental materialism of Australian history during the 1970s and 1980s. It had the unfortunate effect, however, of underpinning the continued othering of the Irish as a troublingly separate group who, if they were noticed at all by Australia's historians, were assigned to the margins of the nation's history.[72]

O'Farrell's approach has fallen out of favour with younger generations of historians intent on the recovery of the complex, multi-layered and contingent meanings which attach to historical agency, practice and structure.[73] His view of the Irish was essentialist and pre-modern. He conceived of the Australian nation and its Irish-born citizens as definable entities: diverse in many respects, no doubt, but possessing sufficient commonalities and hegemonic qualities to allow each to be treated as a whole. Chief among the latter, as far as the Irish were concerned, was religion. Perhaps 80 per cent of all nineteenth-century Irish emigrants to Australia were Roman Catholic.[74] O'Farrell was alert to the existence of non-Catholic traditions in the Irish migrant stream, and to the significance of the emigrants' varied experience in Ireland before their departure, but he nevertheless emphasised the constructive importance of a peculiarly Irish brand of Catholicism in the reproduction of Irish migrant identities.[75] In doing so, he copper-fastened the popular historical belief that in nineteenth- and early twentieth-century Anglo-Celtic Australia, Irishness and Catholicism were synonymous: to be one was to be the other.[76]

This tacit assumption continues to colour much Irish Australian historiography, notwithstanding welcome signs of the broader perspectives mentioned above, particularly the work by Forth, McClelland and others in recovering the narratives of non-Catholic Irish settlement.[77] The conventional view carries with it the profound implication that nationality and ethnicity are synonymous and that religion was (and is) an important referent for both. Used in this way, Irish ethnicity has become a shorthand for one particular cultural group in Ireland (and Australia) which is Catholic, claims Gaelic (though in all probability genetically mixed) descent and which, in an echo of the North American debates described above, is presented as synonymous with the authentic Irish Nation. Moreover, such Irish-Gaelic-Catholic (national) ethnicity is frequently represented as an unchanging, primordial given which arrived fully fledged in Australia embodied in every (Catholic) migrant, and which was more important than factors such as class, occupation or gender in determining their post-arrival behaviour.[78] But how justifiable is this view? As we noted in chapter 1, modern representations of ethnicity suggest that it takes the form of performative cultural consciousness, which may invoke aspirations to national identity, and from which a sense of common selfhood derives. In this prescription, an ethnic group is a population segment set apart, either by itself or by others, on the basis of its perceived common ancestry, shared cultural traditions (including religion), language and social patterns; and sense of group belonging, the latter expressed in terms of experience, memory and loyalties.[79]

On this definition, the claims by advocates of the 'Gaelic Catholic Ireland abroad' model to authenticity and primordialism do not seem to stand up. When defined in these terms, other cultural groups in Ireland – the Anglo-Irish and Ulster-Scots, for example – can be argued to exhibit equally legitimate, though differently expressed, forms of Irish ethnicity. Each is set apart in its own and others' perception in terms of its origins in Irish history, and each shares in its own cultural traditions, social patterns and sense of group belonging, mediated, perhaps, in the case of the Anglo-Irish by their socially elite status.[80] Each also shares the material and imagined spaces of the island of Ireland with the Catholic majority. Like that majority, the Anglo-Irish and Ulster-Scots share, too, in a complex genetic pool that over time has mixed Celtic, Scandinavian, Flemish, Welsh, Norman,

[64]

Huguenot and Anglo-Saxon bloodlines to an extent that renders any claim to an authentically Gaelic Irish identity meaningless, except as a reflexive act of the imagination.[81] Moreover, experience and memory also change, and so, accordingly, does the individual or community's sense of ethnicity, which invokes both of these. Ethnic consciousness is thus performative, developmental and contingent on circumstance; which, of course, is also the claim made by critical understandings of diasporic consciousness. Lyndon Fraser goes further, and argues that ethnicity is also deliberately constructed, and invokes the support of a varied array of kinship and other connections to a create a solidarity which might vary from a loose sense of shared identity to a closely bounded and intricately linked community. In neither case is it unchanging.[82]

Fraser's analysis is one of a number of studies that have begun to challenge the (largely male-gendered) primordial ethno-national Irish model in both Australia and Aotearoa/New Zealand, though as yet not generally in critical diasporic terms. This revisiting has emphasised the instability and contingent character of Irish migrant identities.[83] Public spectacles such as St Patrick's Day parades have attracted particular attention. McIntyre's analysis of the politics inscribed in the Adelaide parades between 1900 and 1918, and Williams's account of the cultural memory and political symbolism that attached to the Melbourne parades prior to 1939, both stress the contingency and ambiguity of these meanings. In both cities, St Patrick's Day could variously – and often simultaneously – be an occasion for the expression of empire loyalism, of support for Irish independence, of a Catholic identity or of Australian nationalism: all depended on circumstance.[84] Similarly, in their analyses of Irish migrant women's experience in Victoria and Moreton Bay, Pauline Rule and Libby Connors emphasise the inadequacy of existing representations of this, grounded in ideas of victimhood and traditional female private sphere roles.[85] Both authors stress the capacity of individual women and girls to engage proactively in boundary-transgressing behaviour in order to improve their circumstances, a theme which Rule returns to in her analysis of Irish-Chinese marriages in Victoria in the 1850s. Here, the boundaries were those of endogamous marriage traditions within the Irish community. Rule argues that, in seeking Chinese partners, some Irish women attempted to redress in their own favour an Irish gender balance which encouraged footloose male behaviour.[86]

In doing so, these women exhibited much more flexible attitudes towards marriage outside the Catholic Irish community than commentators once believed to be probable. They provide further evidence of the inadequacy of the essentialist ethno-national model as a representation of Irish settlement in Australia. In Aotearoa/New Zealand, the higher proportion of non-Catholic Irish settlers – who accounted for somewhere between 25 and 40 per cent of all Irish immigration in the nineteenth century – and the disproportionate representation of Ulster Presbyterians among them (perhaps two-thirds), created a rather different Irish cultural mix.[87] Here, an elision in the literature between an allegedly marginalised and Anglophobic Catholic majority and Irish settlement *tout court* is less apparent. Indeed, recent scholarship has emphasised the limited sense of ethnic solidarity displayed by Irish communities. Fraser, for example, argues that conditions in the rapidly developing gold-field townships of Aotearoa/New Zealand's west coast in the 1860s precluded the development of 'a high order of ethnic incorporation' among the Irish who lived there. Rather, they relied on extraordinarily extensive kinship and neighbourhood networks, which might retain a truly transnational dimension, to provide material and other necessary forms of support.[88] In that place and at that time, not only was Irish ethnic consciousness contingent and unstable, it was also by no means necessarily always instrumental in defining the textures of Irish emigrant life – a conclusion Eric Richards also reached for the Adelaide Irish in the nineteenth century.[89]

Similar ambiguities have surrounded attempts to recover Protestant Irish identities in Aotearoa/New Zealand. As Malcolm Campbell warns in his contribution to a recent collection of essays devoted exclusively to migration and cultural transfers from Ulster, a too-easy acceptance of religion or regional origin as primary referents in framing migration studies carries with it the risk of reinforcing existing contribution perspectives. Rather, such contribution histories should be taken merely as a starting point. Analysis should focus instead on the silences, the unspoken, taken-for-granted spaces and meanings which imbued the migrants' colonial lives and which were created in the interactions between their national past and their colonial present.[90] Such silences would, by definition, be hard to disinter, but Campbell's intervention alerts us once again to the changing and conditional nature of Irish and Scottish migrant identities, whatever their religious affiliation. We should not be surprised, therefore, to find that even that most 'Ulster' of Aotearoa/New Zealand places, George Vesey Stewart's special settlement at Katikati, North Island, founded in 1875, had by the turn of the century lost most of its distinctively Protestant Irish cultural identity.[91] Nor that iconic Aotearoa/New Zealand Ulstermen, such as William Massey, the country's premier between 1912 and 1925, or politicians such as John Williamson and Crosbie Ward, or successful landowners and entrepreneurs like John Martin, constructed identities for themselves that were grounded as much in their (changing)

Aotearoa/New Zealand present as their Ulster past. Nor even that the most Protestant of Irish institutions, the Loyal Orange Order, did not survive for long unchanged in Aotearoa/New Zealand. Rather, like its Australian counterpart and despite Catholic opposition, it gradually shed its narrowly sectarian origins to become a vehicle for empire loyalism.[92]

Individuals such as Williamson and Crosbie Ward have been described as being 'among the most hidden' of pioneering Irishmen in Aotearoa/New Zealand.[93] Arguably, they embodied the Ulster-Scots' alleged potential for easy assimilation into the broader Scots Presbyterian emigrant community, which may have masked Ulster identities in both Australia and Aotearoa/New Zealand.[94] The truth of this has yet to be fully tested, but it seems reasonably clear that, as far as contemporaries were concerned, the benefits of such co-association would have been thought to be largely one way. Despite the arrival in Australia of impoverished Highland migrants from the 1830s onwards, lowland Scots in general remained the subject of a flattering stereotype which depicted them as entrepreneurial and successful. Moreover, despite (or perhaps, because of) their well-entrenched tradition of radical-liberal thought, most Scots did not share with the Irish in their long history of sometimes quite violent political dissent, particularly in Australia. Rather, the Scots' disproportionate involvement in colonial politics was entirely consonant with the structures of hegemonic civil authority.[95] For all these reasons, therefore, much may have been gained by individual Ulster Presbyterians from their gradual affiliation within an overall discourse of Scottishness which distanced them from the othered status of their fellow, Catholic Irishmen.

But we are in danger of caricature here. As Mackenzie notes, these (Australian) Scottish stereotypes were precisely that: collective imaginings which, although they were important in helping to construct Scottish identities *within* empire and, indeed, in establishing the importance of empire *to* those identities, fail to adequately account for their diversity. Collective myths of empire which invoked the 'Radical Scot', the 'Environmental Scot', the 'Enterprising Scot' or indeed the 'Military Scot', in Australia or Aotearoa/New Zealand or any other colony, might offer reassuringly 'heightened' narratives of imperial belonging – which could themselves become self-perpetuating – but they effaced the localism of migrant experience.[96] In short, the image of the enterprising, pioneering Scot may well have been a necessary myth of empire: crucial to the formation of collective historic Scottish settler identities, certainly, but altogether too broadly drawn to serve as the basis for the recovery of the emplaced narratives of individual migrant identity, memory and experience.

Earlier representations of Scottish settlement in Australia, such as A. D. Gibbs's *Scottish Empire*, G. Donaldson's *The Scots Overseas* and D. MacMillan's *Scotland and Australia 1788–1850* embraced these myths wholeheartedly, albeit with a varying degree of statistical rigour.[97] Some more recent accounts have continued in much the same vein, including, for example, national surveys such as Malcolm Prentis's *The Scottish in Australia*, the various entries on the Scots in James Jupp's *Encyclopedia* of the Australian people, and Tom Brooking and Jennie Coleman's collection of papers on the Scots in Aotearoa/New Zealand, *The Heather and the Fern*.[98] The 'great men' narrative looms large here, even though, as one contributor to the *Oxford Companion to Scottish History* suggests, the individuals concerned – be they colonial governors like Lachlan Macquarie, church leaders like John Dunmore Lang or graziers and investors like Sir Thomas Elder – were no more than a footnote in colonial history. In this view, the most significant Scottish contributions to Australasia remain under-researched: the widespread emigration of urban artisans to Australia in the late nineteenth and early twentieth century; the motivations and mechanisms involved in the three great pulses of Scottish migration to Otago and Canterbury between the 1850s and 1870s; and the cultural transformations that attended the rather earlier movement of Gaelic-speaking Highlanders to Australia between the 1830s and 1850s.[99]

Other recent contributions have begun address some of these issues in a way which begins to question the national contribution trope. For example, Angela McCarthy's edited collection of essays, *A Global Clan*, attempts to recover the individual voices of ordinary Scottish emigrants since the eighteenth century as they enacted the formal and informal transnational networks which (*pace* Malcolm Campbell) connected their colonial present to their national past.[100] These networks varied in intensity, expression and purpose over space and time, and were by no means necessarily endogamous; they frequently involved other colonial and indigenous ethnic groups. Despite Eric Richards's timely warning that the idea of formal migrant networks should not become a new orthodoxy and his evidence of mid-nineteenth-century un-networked 'colonial isolates' like Farquhar Mackenzie or John McKinlay in New South Wales, the book's general perspectives are welcome.[101] In its emphasis on the diversity of migrant identity and the capacity of this to change as migrant networks evolved, *A Global Clan* echoes Fraser's analysis of the unstable ethnic networks that characterised some Irish communities in Aotearoa/New Zealand. Like Fraser's work, it also points to the regionalism of Irish and Scots settler experience in Australasia and beyond.

Irish and Scottish geographies?

But, as we point out above, geographically informed representations of this settler experience have been relatively scarce in both countries. With the exception of Patrick O'Farrell's specifically place-related work, they are generally empirically framed and little concerned with the semiotic issues of place and landscape that underpin our approach. Moreover, in Australia, the conventional census-based model of widespread and relatively evenly dispersed Irish settlement is arguably misleading, at least as far as constructive narratives of place are concerned. While David Fitzpatrick is undoubtedly right to draw our attention to the relatively low proportion of the total population represented by the Irish-born and to the ubiquity of their presence, in very small numbers, in every census district, none of this tells us anything about the way the Irish-born were distributed *within* these districts.[102] We are, in short, faced with the ecological fallacy which attends all areal representations of census data: the assumption that the population characteristic which is being considered (in this case, the proportion of Irish-born) is uniformly distributed throughout the geographical space represented by the enumeration district in question.[103] This clearly is not necessarily so. The threshold statistic Fitzpatrick cites, that barely 25 per cent of the population in the most Irish of census districts, such as Kiama in New South Wales, or Shepparton in Victoria, were Irish born in 1871, tells us nothing about these settlers' local micro-geographies. Were they concentrated in particular parts of these districts, or more evenly spread across their entire area? Each outcome could be equally easily accommodated by Fitzpatrick's statistical measure, but each would have had very different implications for the contexts within which these settlers imagined, constructed and performed their own local worlds.

We may conclude, therefore, that the common assumption that Irish (and indeed Scottish) settlement was widely and evenly dispersed in colonial south-east Australia offers little intellectual purchase on the performative narratives of place and identity which are our present concern. Some regional analyses of Irish and Scottish settlement offer rather more insight, despite their underlying empiricism. For example, Malcolm Campbell's *The Kingdom of the Ryans*, his account of Irish settlement in and around Boorowa, New South Wales, is predicated on challenging what Akenson has described as 'ethnomorphicism'. This is the assumption, commonly made by historians, that 'national patterns, concerns and experiences [can be projected] onto local communities in the belief that these ought to have been shared by all communities'. Campbell emphasises instead the complex but intensely localised cultural practices and material outcomes that characterised Edward Ryan's successful attempt to establish himself as a major landowner in Boorowa. Originally transported as a convict following his participation in Whiteboy disturbances in County Tipperary in 1815, Ryan was emancipated in 1830. Thereafter, he took full advantage of existing kinship and ethnic networks, the economic opportunities offered by the prevailing system of land grants and the advent of assisted emigration to acquire – and settle – holdings which may have approached 1,000 square kilometres by the early 1850s. Campbell presents Ryan as something of a diasporic figure: a man whose values and sense of self were moulded in the (contested) moral economy of the Ireland of his youth but were also mediated by his experience in Australia. Campbell rejects the idea of an immutable, transportable Irish culture. He argues instead that the local worlds created and enacted by Edward Ryan and his Irish tenants and kinsmen were the result of continuous, though uneven, processes of individual and collective environmental and social negotiation. All sought accommodation between the changing circumstances of their new world and the remembered past of their old.[104]

Much the same emphasis on the importance of the intersections between cultural memory and colonial experience, and the unspoken, taken-for-granted spaces these created, pervades *Caledonia Australis*, Don Watson's account of Highland Scots settlement in Gippsland (south-east Victoria) between the 1830s and 1860s.[105] But other discourses also prevail here. In Australia, as in other parts of the 'Scottish empire', Gaelic-speaking Highlanders and Islanders have attracted particular attention for their alleged clannishness, their propensity to engage in group migration and the problems their supposedly pre-modern language and culture are thought to have posed for their attempts to engage with the narratives of colonial modernity. The conventional story, therefore, has been one of progressively more constrained and limited cultural survival following the peaks of Highlands and Islands immigration in the 1830s and 1850s. This was characterised by the gradual eclipse of Gaelic as a first language (save, ironically, among urban enthusiasts of the Highland Revival in Melbourne and Geelong in the 1860s and after).[106] Watson eschews these stereotypes and, like O'Farrell, explores the ideological conflicts enacted in the encounter in Gippsland between one set of displaced indigenes – the Highlanders – and another, the local Aborigine communities. The irony is inescapable. Displaced Scottish exiles, escaping the bewildering processes of economic and social modernisation in their homeland, but driven, too, by a conviction of Providential guidance, were instrumental in the displacement and attempted extermination of other marginalised

[70]

indigenes, the Kurnai people of Gippsland. *Their* gods proved altogether less capable in the encounter with Western modernity. Nevertheless, there are few villains in Watson's account: merely individual men and women of all races who, as morally charged beings, were caught up in externalities they could not control and who struggled to manage and understand the resulting impact on their lives.

The themes of memory and belonging which occur in both these studies are treated from a rather different perspective in Patrick O'Farrell's explorations of Irish migrant *mentalités* and their basis in imaginative reconstructions of remembered place.[107] These acts of the imagination recur throughout O'Farrell's work, and also figure in David Fitzpatrick's analyses of the representations of Ireland contained in Irish migrant correspondence from Australia.[108] O'Farrell's central thesis, that many Irish immigrants 'lived in a jumble of worlds, past and present, near and far, real and imagined'[109] or, quoting Seamus Heaney, had the capacity 'to live in two places at the one time, and in two times at the only place',[110] appears to prefigure later critical debates concerning transnational diasporic consciousness. But it is important to note two caveats. First, that O'Farrell was concerned primarily with Gaelic Ireland, whose authenticity he didn't question; and second, that he claimed that the 'jumbled worlds' of the Irish immigrant mind existed precisely because of their inability to escape the emotional and perceptual legacies of their place-bound identities in Ireland. O'Farrell, in short, prefigures the grounded approach of Safran and Cohen, rather than the liminal in-between spaces of Hickman.

Nevertheless, the places O'Farrell had in mind were both material and semiotic:

> [The Irish] were a people with a profound sense of locality, of Irish place, which was highly territorial, familial, and personal, rooted deeply in a pagan, pre-Christian past, and integral to the whole structure of Gaelic society. The individual's locality was a fundamental facet of his identity, his particular place was part of the person in a way that defined and positioned him in his own world and among his own people.[111]

O'Farrell emphasises the overwhelming localism of these place-bounded Irish identities, grounded in the minutely divided fieldscapes of rural Ireland and hedged about by the local parish and its world. All of this, he argues, provided a dislocating contrast with Australia. There, space, light and distance coloured an ancient, empty landscape seemingly devoid of both history and the intimate presence of God which was invoked so ubiquitously by religious sites in the Irish countryside. For Irish immigrants, or so O'Farrell claims, Australia provided a land of opportunity, but one which failed to engage their sense of selfhood at its most atavistic, spiritual level. It was a land, consequently, for sojourning. In contrast, Ireland grounded the self spiritually, in memory at least, and offered a sense of true belonging that the rawness of Australian society never could.

But there was also another factor: dispossession. In claiming for Gaelic Irish migrants this particular affinity with place in Ireland, and their deep sense of loss on leaving it, O'Farrell maintains that this resulted from the alienation these people felt in their own land. Sixteenth- and seventeenth-century plantation and land confiscation had created an *arriviste* class of colonial landowners who had displaced the traditional (authentic?) Gaelic owners of the soil. Accordingly, in leaving Ireland, Gaelic Irish emigrants felt a double loss: of their looked-for future among their own people, and of the possibility of future restitution of the land that was rightfully theirs. Framed in this light, Australia, the land of opportunity if not of emotional attachment, offered the prospect of creating a society which was everything colonised Ireland was not.[112] Hence the energy and importance of the Irish contribution to modern Australia; and the apparent paradox that Irish men and women who contested the structures of English colonial authority in Ireland might use these in a more constructive way to further their own ambitions in Australia.

As we noted above, O'Farrell's emphasis on the importance of place in the construction of human identity closely resembles our own, save in its overwhelming essentialism. Fundamentally, he is talking about *Irish* place as a bounded site of singular, authentic identity. Indeed, he goes as far as to suggest that place could not exist in Australia for Gaelic Irish migrants, because 'place only became itself when peopled, and only when those people were acting in their natural – which for the emigrant would have to be past – roles'.[113] According to O'Farrell, this element of naturalness was denied Irish migrants in Australia precisely because of the country's failure to engage them emotionally on a spiritual level. The absence of God and history from the empty Australian landscape prevented them from enacting their intensely localist, place-bound sense of Irish self. They did not belong. Opportunity might present itself to Irish migrants in Australia, but their response was always as outsiders: accepting the reality of their new circumstances, certainly, but never emotionally identifying with their new existence as home.

In contrast, we claim that a sense of place is ubiquitous: a mental construct that, although inflected by memory, is not constrained by particular territorialised, national narratives of belonging. Thus, as we argue in the following chapters, Irish and Scottish settlers inevitably enacted new, imaginative narratives of place in Australia simply *because* they were there in the present here and now, and no longer in the elsewhere of memory. These narratives may well have emphasised loss and disjuncture, but they will still have (re)constructed the migrants' sense of identity in terms of the meanings they inscribed in the material locales in which their lives were now performed. Complex, contingent and changing, and continuously reframed by the discursive ebbs and flows of memory and empire, this sense of place, we argue, grounded Irish and Scottish migrant identities in the New South Wales rangelands, or in the Victorian goldfields, or in Melbourne's suburbs, just as certainly as their earlier place narratives had constructed and sustained their previous sense of self in Antrim, Tipperary or Inverness.

Summary

Representations of Irish and Scottish settlement in Australia and New Zealand continue to engage with issues of identity construction from a variety of perspectives. The ethnic essentialism that characterised earlier approaches is showing signs of giving way to more diasporic understandings. Increasingly, these privilege ideas of transnationalism and emigrant networks as interpretive frames. The central debate within diasporic studies, between grounded and de-territorialised understandings of migrant consciousness, continues, however, and inflects these new approaches to Irish and Scottish experience in Australasia. Here, we claim that our non-essentialist understanding of place offers a means of resolving this debate. By emphasising the importance of the imagined meanings which attached to practices enacted as place, their materiality and capacity to evolve over time, we accommodate ideas of diasporic consciousness as both re-located identity and transnational becoming. In doing so, we also privilege ideas of regional and local diversity which have recently gained intellectual prominence in migration and diasporic studies, as scholars increasingly recognise the limitations of essentialist meta-narratives.

The place narratives we explore in the following chapters are, in essence, local stories, examples of local worlds imagined and constructed by individuals whose lives were enacted through them. But these colonial places did not exist in isolation. They acquired their meaning *as* place through their contingent relationship with other sites of identity, past and present. In short, the meaning of place for those individuals whose identities formed part of them was defined, in part, by the otherness of other places they had previously encountered. Hence the importance of memory and experience in the imaginative construction of these place identities. Narratives of place could only exist in the context of other imagined places; all were continuously redefined. The discursive networks of empire played a particularly important facilitating role in this process. The flows of ideas, information, people, goods and capital which articulated the Empire continuously transformed the geographical contexts within which places were imagined and enacted. A crucial and early stage in this was the transnational movement of the settlers themselves. What effect did the voyage to Australia have on migrant *mentalités* and their conceptions of place and home?

Notes

1 O'Donnell, Dr. Nicholas Michael, 'My Autobiography', Brennan Family Papers, NLA, Ms mfm G7703–7704.
2 Useful summaries in an extensive literature include: T. M. Devine, *Scotland's Empire 1600–1815* (London, 2003); D. N. Doyle, 'Scots Irish or Scotch-Irish', in J. J. Lee and M. R. Casey (eds), *Making the Irish American. History and Heritage of the Irish in the United States* (New York, 2006), pp. 151–70; *Idem*, 'The Irish in North America, 1776–1845', in *ibid.*, pp. 171–212; K. Kenny, *The American Irish. A History* (London, 2000); M. Harper, *Adventurers and Exiles. The Great Scottish Exodus* (London, 2003); J. J. Silk, 'The Irish Abroad in the Age of the Counter-Reformation, 1534–1691', in T. W. Moody, F. X. Martin and F. J. Byrne (eds), *A New History of Ireland III. Early Modern Ireland 1534–1691* (Oxford, 1976), pp. 587–633; J. G. Simms, 'The Irish on the Continent, 1691–1800', in T. W. Moody and W. E. Vaughan (eds), *A New History of Ireland IV. Eighteenth-century Ireland 1691–1800* (Oxford, 1986), pp. 629–56.
3 D. Hoerder, 'From Dreams to Possibilities: The Secularisation of Hope and the Quest for Independence', in D. Hoerder and H. Rössler (eds), *Distant Magnets. Expectations and Realities in the Immigrant Experience, 1840–1930* (New York, 1993), pp. 1–32; *Idem*, 'From Migrants to Ethnics: Acculturation in a Societal Framework', in D. Hoerder, and L. Page Moch (eds), *European Migrants. Global and Local Perspectives* (Boston, 1996), pp. 211–62; E. Richards, *Britannia's Children. Emigration from England, Scotland, Wales and Ireland since 1600* (London, 2004), pp. 91–232.
4 D. Fitzpatrick, *Irish Emigration 1801–1921* (Dundalk, 1984), p. 3; Harper, *Adventurers and Exiles*, p. 2; L. Proudfoot and D. Hall, 'Points of Departure. Remittance Emigration from South-West Ulster to New South Wales in the later Nineteenth Century', *International Review of Social History*, Vol. 50 (2005), pp. 241–77; Richards, *Britannia's Children*, p. 213.
5 See, for example, L. Fraser, *Castles of Gold. A History of New Zealand's West Coast Irish* (Dunedin, 2007); M. Harper (ed.), *Emigrant Homecomings. The Return Movement of Emigrants 1600–2000* (Manchester, 2005).
6 D. H. Akenson, *The Irish Diaspora. A Primer* (Toronto/Belfast, 1996), p. 258; Harper, *Adventurers and Exiles*, p. 3.
7 *Ibid.*, p. 2; M. D. Prentis, *The Scottish in Australia* (Melbourne, 1987), pp. 18–33.
8 See, for example; J. M. Brock, *The Mobile Scot. A Study of Emigration and Migration 1861–1911* (Edinburgh, 1999); T. M. Devine, *The Great Highland Famine: Hunger, Emigration, and the Scottish Highlands in the Nineteenth Century* (Edinburgh, 1988); *Idem* (ed.), *Scottish Emigration and Scottish Society* (Edinburgh, 1992); P. J. Duffy (ed.), *To and from Ireland: Planned Migration Schemes c. 1600–2000* (Dublin, 2004); D. Fitzpatrick, 'Emigration, 1801–70', in W. E. Vaughan (ed.), *A New History of Ireland Vol. V Ireland Under the Union I 1801–70* (Oxford, 1989), pp. 562–622; M. W. Flinn (ed.), *Scottish Population History from the 17th Century to the 1930s* (Cambridge, 1977); T. Guinane, *The Vanishing Irish. Households, Migration, and the Rural Economy in Ireland, 1850–1914* (Princeton, 1997); R.

A. Houston, 'The Demographic Regime', in T. M. Devine and R. Mitchison (eds), *People and Society in Scotland. Volume 1, 1760–1830* (Edinburgh, 1988), pp. 9–26; K. A. Miller, *Emigrants and Exiles. Ireland and the Irish Exodus to North America* (Oxford, 1985), pp. 9–130.

9   D. H. Akenson, 'A Midrash on "Galut", "Exile" and "Diaspora" Rhetoric', in E. M. Crawford (ed.), *The Hungry Stream. Essays on Emigration and Famine* (Belfast, 1997), pp. 5–16.

10 W. Safran, 'Deconstructing and Comparing Diasporas', in W. Kokot, K. Tölölyan and C. Alfonso (eds), *Diaspora, Identity, and Religion: New Directions in Theory and Research* (London, 2004), pp. 9–29.

11 R. Brubaker, 'The "Diaspora" Diaspora', *Ethnic and Racial Studies*, Vol. 28, No. 1 (January 2005), pp. 2–4. See also Akenson, *Irish Diaspora*, pp. 3–14; K. Tölölyan, 'Rethinking Diaspora(s): Stateless Power in the Transnational Moment', *Diaspora*, Vol. 5, No. 1 (1996), pp. 3–36.

12 Brubaker, 'The "Diaspora" Diaspora', pp. 12–13.

13 R. Cohen, *Global Diasporas. An Introduction* (London, 1997), pp. 177–96.

14 Safran, 'Deconstructing', pp. 9–14.

15 V. S. Kalra, R. Kaur and J. Hutnyk, *Diaspora and Hybridity* (London, 2005), pp. 11–12.

16 S. Vertovec, 'Three Meanings of "Diaspora", Exemplified by South Asian Religions', *Diaspora*, Vol. 6, No. 3 (1999), pp. 277–300.

17 Kalra *et al.*, *Diaspora*, pp. 29–34.

18 Kokot *et al.* (eds), *Diaspora, Identity, and Religion*, pp. 1–7.

19 N. Lovell, 'Introduction. Belonging in Need of Emplacement?', in N. Lovell (ed.), *Locality and Belonging* (London, 1998), pp. 1–24.

20 N. Papastergiardis, 'Hybridity and Ambivalence. Places and Flows in Contemporary Art and Culture', *Theory, Culture & Society*, Vol. 22, No. 4 (2005), pp. 53–9.

21 Brubaker, 'The "Diaspora" Diaspora', p. 12; Kokot *et al.* (eds), *Diaspora, Identity, and Religion*, p. 5.

22 M. J. Hickman, 'Locating the Irish Diaspora', *Irish Journal of Sociology*, Vol. 11, No. 2 (2002), pp. 8–26.

23 *Ibid.*, pp. 10–16; M. J. Hickman, 'Migration and Diaspora', in J. Cleary and C. Donnelly (eds), *The Cambridge Companion to Modern Irish Culture* (Cambridge, 2005), pp. 117–36.

24 Surveyed in L. Harte and Y. Whelan (eds), *Ireland Beyond Boundaries. Mapping Irish Studies in the Twenty-first Century* (London, 2007), *passim*.

25 J. Belchem, 'The Irish Diaspora: The Complexities of Mass Migration', *Przeglad Polonijny*, Vol. 31, No. 1 (2005), pp. 87–98; K. Kenny, 'Diaspora and Comparison: The Global Irish as a Case Study', *The Journal of American History*, Vol. 90, No. 1 (June 2003), pp. 134–62.

26 D. MacRaild, '"Diaspora" and "Transnationalism"'. Theory and Evidence in Explanation of the Irish World-wide.' Symposium: Perspectives on the Irish Diaspora, *Irish Economic and Social History*, Vol. 33 (2006), pp. 51–8.

27 M. Campbell, 'The Other Immigrants: Comparing the Irish in Australia and the United States', *Journal of American Ethnic History*, Vol. 14, No. 3 (Spring 1995), pp. 3–22; *Idem*, 'Ireland's Furthest Shores: Irish Immigrant Settlement in Nineteenth-century California and Eastern Australia', *Pacific Historical Review*, Vol. 71, No. 1 (2002), pp. 59–90; D. N. Doyle, 'The Irish in Australia and the United States: Some Comparisons 1800–1939', *Irish Economic and Social History*, Vol. 16 (1989), pp. 73–94.

28 Belchem, 'The Irish Diaspora', pp. 13–14.

29 D. N. Doyle, 'Review Article: Cohesion and Diversity in the Irish Diaspora', *Irish Historical Studies*, Vol. 31, No. 123 (May 1999), pp. 411–34; Hickman, 'Locating', p. 14; Kenny, 'Diaspora and Comparison', pp. 134–62; E. Malcolm, '10,000 Miles Away: Irish Studies Down Under', in Harte and Whelan (eds), *Ireland Beyond Boundaries*, pp. 39–47; P. O'Sullivan (ed.), *The Irish World Wide. History, Heritage, Identity. Volume 5. Religion and Identity* (Leicester, 1996), *passim*.

30 Akenson, *Irish Diaspora*, especially pp. 217–70; B. Patterson (ed.), *Ulster–New Zealand Migration and Cultural Transfers* (Dublin, 2006); A. Galbraith, 'The Invisible Irish? Rediscovering the Irish Protestant Tradition in Colonial New Zealand', in L. Fraser (ed.), *A Distant Shore. Irish Migration and New Zealand Settlement* (Dunedin, 2000), pp. 37–54; I. McClelland, 'Worlds Apart: The Anglo-Irish Gentry Migrant Experience in Australia', in O. Walsh (ed.) *Ireland Abroad. Politics and Professions in the Nineteenth Century* (Dublin, 2003), pp. 186–201; D. A. Wilson (ed.), *The Orange Order in Canada* (Dublin, 2007).

31 MacRaild, '"Diaspora" and "Transnationalism"', pp. 52–3.

32 M. Campbell, *The Kingdom of the Ryans. The Irish in South West New South Wales 1816–1890* (Sydney, 1997), pp. 13–14; Idem, *Ireland's New Worlds. Immigrants, Politics and Society in the United States and Australia, 1815–1922* (Madison, 2008), pp. vii–xii.

33 D. N. Doyle, 'The Remaking of Irish-America, 1845–1880', in Lee and Casey (eds), *Making the Irish American*, pp. 213–52; O. Handlin, *Boston's Immigrants: A Study in Acculturation* (rev. edn, Cambridge, MA, 1979); K. A. Miller, *Emigrants and Exiles. Ireland and the Irish Exodus to North America* (New York/Oxford, 1985).

34 J. J. Lee, 'Introduction: Interpreting Irish America', in Lee and Casey (eds), *Making the Irish American*, pp. 1–60.

35 The early literature is summarised in R. J. Dickson, *Ulster Emigration to Colonial America 1718–1775* (Belfast, 1966).

36 Doyle, 'Scots Irish or Scotch-Irish', pp. 151–4; Idem, 'The Irish in North America', pp. 184–7.

37 D. H. Akenson, 'The Irish in North America: Catholic or Protestant?' *The Irish Review*, No. 11 (Winter 1991/1992), pp. 17–22; Idem, *Irish Diaspora*, pp. 217–32. For an early and typically hostile response, see: L. J. McCaffrey, 'The Catholic and Urban Profile of Irish America', *The Irish Review*, No. 14 (Summer, 1993), pp. 1–9.

38 D. H. Akenson, *Small Differences. Irish Catholics and Irish Protestants 1815–1822* (Montreal/Dublin, 1988).

39 Akenson, *Irish Diaspora*, pp. 259–69; C. J. Houston and W. J. Smith, *Irish Emigration and Canadian Settlement. Patterns, Links and Letters* (Toronto/Belfast, 1990), pp. 43–78.

40 Hickman, 'Locating', p. 13.

41 Doyle, 'The Irish in North America', pp. 171–88.

42 Doyle, 'Remaking', pp. 218–24; Kenny, *The American Irish*, pp. 89–112; Miller, *Emigrants and Exiles, passim*.

43 Doyle, 'Remaking', pp. 219, 222–43.

44 J. R. R. Adams, *The Printed Word and the Common Man: Popular Culture in Ulster, 1700–1900* (Belfast, 1987); D. H. Akenson, 'Pre-University Education, 1782–1870', in Vaughan (ed.), *Ireland under the Union I*, pp. 523–37.

45 Hoerder, 'From Migrants to Ethnics', pp. 211–62.

46 Doyle, 'Remaking', pp. 213–52; Kenny, *The American Irish*, pp. 141–58.

47 D. N. Doyle, 'The Irish as Urban Pioneers in the United States, 1850–1870', *Journal of American Ethnic History*, Vol. 10 (1990), pp. 36–59; Idem, 'Remaking', pp. 227–34.

48 Akenson, *Irish Diaspora*, pp. 59–69, 258, 282 ff; Houston and Smyth, *Irish Emigration*, pp. 151–240.

49 T. Power, 'The Palmerston Estate in County Sligo: Improvement and Assisted Emigration before 1850', in Duffy (ed.), *To and from Ireland*, pp. 105–36.

50 Akenson, *Irish Diaspora*, pp. 142–8; M. Holmes, 'The Irish in India: Imperialism, Nationalism, and internationalism', in A. Bielenberg (ed.), *The Irish Diaspora* (London, 2000), pp. 235–50.

51 D. P. McCracken, 'Odd Man Out: The South African Experience', in Bielenberg (ed.), *The Irish Diaspora*, pp. 251–71.

52 P. McKenna, 'Irish Emigration to Argentina: A Different model', Bielenberg (ed.), *The Irish Diaspora*, pp. 195–212. For a detailed analysis which claims a unique

status for Irish experience in Argentina, see H. Kelly, *Irish 'Ingleses'. The Irish Immigrant Experience in Argentina 1840–1920* (Dublin, 2009).

53   E. Richards, 'Leaving the Highlands. Colonial Destinations in Canada and Australia', in M. Harper and M. E. Vance (eds), *Myth, Migration, and the Making of Memory: Scotia and Nova Scotia 1700–1900* (Halifax/Edinburgh, 1999), pp. 105–23.

54   Harper, *Adventurers and Exiles*, pp. 53–61.

55   Devine, *The Great Highland Famine*, pp. 245–72.

56   Harper, *Adventurers and Exiles*, pp. 50–3.

57   M. Gray, 'The Course of Scottish Emigration 1750–1914', in Devine (ed.), *Scottish Emigration*, pp. 16–36; Harper, *Adventurers and Exiles*, pp. 44–5.

58   Richards, 'Leaving the Highlands', pp. 121–2.

59   T. M. Devine, 'The Paradox of Scottish Emigration', in Devine (ed.), *Scottish Emigration*, pp. 1–15.

60   Harper, *Adventurers and Exiles*, pp. 61–5.

61   Devine, 'Paradox', pp. 1–15.

62   P. Basu, *Highland Homecomings. Genealogy and Heritage Tourism in the Scottish Diaspora* (London, 2007), pp. 10–17.

63   *Ibid., passim*; R. Bitterman, 'On Remembering and Forgetting: Highland Memories within the Maritime Diaspora', in Harper and Vance (eds), *Myth, Migration, and the Making of Memory*, pp. 253–65; E. J. Cowan, 'The Myth of Scotch Canada', in *ibid.*, pp. 49–72.

64   Malcolm, '10,000 Miles Away', pp. 39–47.

65   D. Fitzpatrick, *Oceans of Consolation. Personal Accounts of Irish Migration to Australia* (Cork, 1994), pp. 16–18; A. L. Greiner and T. G. Jordan-Bychkov, *Anglo-Celtic Australia. Colonial Immigration and Cultural Regionalism* (Santa Fe, NM, 2002).

66   Campbell, *The Kingdom of the Ryans*.

67   D. Watson, *Caledonia Australis. Scottish Highlanders on the Frontier of Australia* (Sydney, 1994).

68   L. Fraser, *To Tara via Holywood. Irish Catholic Immigrants in Nineteenth-century Christchurch* (Auckland, 1997); *Idem, Castles of Gold*.

69   P. O'Farrell, 'Landscapes of the Irish Immigrant Mind', in J. Hardy (ed.), *Stories of Australian Migration* (Sydney, 1988), pp. 33–46; *Idem, Vanished Kingdoms. Irish in Australia and New Zealand. A Personal Excursion* (Sydney, 1990); *Idem*, 'Defining Place and Home: Are the Irish Prisoners of Place?', in D. Fitzpatrick (ed.), *Home or Away? Immigrants in Colonial Australia* (Canberra, 1992), pp. 1–18; *Idem*, 'Varieties of New Zealand Irishness: A Meditation', in Fraser (ed.), *A Distant Shore*, pp. 25–35.

70   G. Bolton, 'The Irish in Australian Historiography', in C. Kiernan (ed.), *Australia and Ireland. Bicentenary Essays 1788–1988* (Dublin, 1986), pp. 5–19; Malcolm, '10, 000 Miles Away', pp. 39–47; B. Reece, 'Writing about the Irish in Australia', in J. O'Brien and P. Travers (eds), *The Irish Emigrant Experience in Australia* (Swords, 1991), pp. 226–42.

71   P. O'Farrell, *The Irish in Australia 1788 to the Present* (3rd edn, Sydney, 2000), *passim*.

72   Malcolm, '10,000 Miles Away', pp. 43–4; Reece, 'Writing about the Irish', pp. 230–2.

73   See W. Hudson and G. Bolton (eds), *Creating Australia. Changing Australian History* (Sydney, 1997); S. Macintyre, *A Concise History of Australia* (2nd edn, Cambridge, 2004), pp. 291–7.

74   Fitzpatrick, *Oceans*, p. 14.

75   O'Farrell, *The Irish in Australia*, pp. 5–21. O'Farrell explores the construction of non-Catholic Irish migrant *mentalités* in: *Letters from Irish Australia 1825–1925* (Sydney/Belfast, 1984).

76   Among numerous examples, see: P. S. Cleary, *Australia's Debt to the Irish Nation Builders* (Sydney, 1933); J. F. Hogan, *The Irish in Australia* (Melbourne, 1888);

C. McConville, *Croppies, Celts and Catholics. The Irish in Australia* (Melbourne, 1987); J. Waldersee, *Catholic Society in New South Wales 1788–1860* (Sydney, 1974).

77 Forth, '"No Petty People": The Anglo-Irish Identity in Colonial Australia', in P. O'Sullivan (ed.), *The Irish World Wide History, Heritage, Identity. Volume 2: The Irish in the New Communities* (Leicester, 1992), pp. 128–44; McClelland, 'Worlds Apart', pp. 186–201; L. J. Proudfoot, 'Landscape, Place, and Memory: Towards a Geography of Irish Identities in Colonial Australia', in Walsh (ed.), *Ireland Abroad*, pp. 172–85.

78 See, for example: P. Morgan, 'The Irish in Gippsland', in P. Bull, C. McConville and N. McLachlan (eds), *Irish Australian Studies. Papers Delivered at the Sixth Irish-Australian Conference, July 1990* (Melbourne, 1990), pp. 120–35; O'Farrell, *Vanished Kingdoms*, pp. 1–22.

79 B. Ashcroft, G. Griffiths and H. Tiffin, *Key Concepts in Post-colonial Studies* (London, 1998), pp. 80–4.

80 The literature on the place of the Anglo-Irish and Ulster-Scots in Irish history is voluminous. Useful accounts may be found in: T. Barnard, *A New Anatomy of Ireland. The Irish Protestants 1649–1770* (New Haven, 2003); J. C. Beckett, *The Anglo Irish Tradition* (London, 1976); S. J. Connolly, *Religion, Law and Power. The Making of Protestant Ireland 1660–1760* (Oxford, 1992); M. MacCarthy-Morrough, *The Munster Plantation. English Migration to Southern Ireland 1583–1641* (Oxford, 1986); P. Robinson, *The Plantation of Ulster. English Settlement in an Irish Landscape* (Oxford, 1986).

81 L. de Paor, *The Peoples of Ireland from Prehistory to Modern Times* (Boston, 1986); B. Sykes, *Blood of the Isles. Exploring the Roots of our Genetic History* (London, 2006).

82 L. Fraser, 'The Making of an Ethnic Collectivity: Irish Catholic Immigrants in Nineteenth-century Christchurch', *The Journal of Religious History*, Vol. 20, No. 2 (December 1996), pp. 210–27; *Idem, Castles of Gold*, pp. 1–22.

83 F. Molloy, 'An Irish Consciousness in some Australian Novels', in O. Macdonagh and W. J. Mandle (eds), *Irish Australian Studies. Papers Delivered at the Fifth Irish-Australian Conference* (Canberra, 1989), pp. 217–30; M. Strugnell, 'It's a Long Way From Home: Irish Exiles in Australian Drama', in R. Pelan, N. Quirke and M. Finnane (eds), *Papers Delivered at the Seventh Irish-Australian Conference, July 1993* (Sydney, 1994), pp. 111–19.

84 C. Macintyre, 'The Adelaide Irish and the Politics of St Patrick's Day 1900–1918', in Pelan et al (eds), *Papers Delivered at the Seventh Irish-Australian Conference*, pp. 182–96; C. M. Williams, 'Collective Identity and Memory in Melbourne's St Patrick's Day Celebrations, 1900–1939', in T. Foley and F. Bateman (eds), *Irish Australian Studies. Papers Delivered at the Ninth Irish-Australian Conference Galway, April 1997* (Sydney, 2000), pp. 273–85.

85 P. Rule, 'Honoria and Her Sisters: Success and Sorrow among Irish Immigrant Women in Colonial Victoria', in Pelan *et al.* (eds), *Seventh Irish-Australian Conference*, pp. 151–60; L. Connors, 'The Politics of Ethnicity: Irish Orphan Girls at Moreton Bay', in *ibid.*, pp. 167–81.

86 P. Rule, 'Challenging Conventions: Irish–Chinese Marriages in Colonial Victoria', in Foley and Bateman (eds), *Ninth Irish-Australian Conference*, pp. 205–16.

87 Galbraith, 'The Invisible Irish?', pp. 37–54.

88 Fraser, *Castles of Gold*, pp. 153–7.

89 E. Richards, 'Irish Life and Progress in Colonial South Australia', *Irish Historical Studies*, Vol. 27, No. 107 (1991), pp. 216–36.

90 M. Campbell, 'How Ulster was New Zealand?', in Patterson (ed.), *Ulster–New Zealand Migration*, pp. 17–30.

91 B. Patterson, 'New Zealand's "Ulster Plantation": Katikati revisited', in *Idem* (ed.), *Ulster–New Zealand Migration*, pp. 85–102.

92 R. Sweetman, 'Towards a History of Orangeism in New Zealand', in Patterson, (ed.), *Ulster–New Zealand Migration*, pp. 154–64; G. W. Rice, 'How

Irish was New Zealand's Ulster-born Prime Minister Bill Massey?', in *ibid.*, pp. 241–54.

93 E. Bohan, 'Carbuncle Jack and Mr Punch of Canterbury', in *ibid.*, pp. 229–40.
94 Galbraith, 'The Invisible Irish?', pp. 37–54; T. McLaughlin, 'Irish-Protestant Settlement', in J. Jupp (ed.), *The Australian People. An Encyclopedia of the Nation, Its People and Their Origins* (2nd edn, Cambridge, 2001), pp. 463–5.
95 I. L. Donnachie, 'The Making of "Scots on the make": Scottish Settlement and Enterprise in Australia, 1830–1900', in Devine (ed.), *Scottish Emigration*, pp. 135–53; Prentis, *The Scottish*, pp. 49–74; *Idem*, 'Scottish Recruitment to Australian Elites', in Jupp (ed.), *Encyclopedia*, pp. 659–65.
96 J. M. MacKenzie, 'A Scottish Empire? The Scottish Diaspora and Interactive Identities', in T. Brooking and J. Coleman (eds), *The Heather and the Fern. Scottish Migration and New Zealand Settlement* (Dunedin, 2003), pp. 17–32.
97 Cited in Donnachie, 'The Making', pp. 136–40.
98 Brooking and Coleman (eds), *The Heather and the Fern, passim*; Jupp, *Encyclopedia*, pp. 644–74.
99 M. Lynch (ed.), *Oxford Companion to Scottish History* (Oxford, 2007), pp. 32–5.
100 A. McCarthy (ed.), *A Global Clan. Scottish Migrant Networks and Identities since the Eighteenth Century* (London, 2006).
101 E. Richards, 'Scottish Networks and Voices in Colonial Australia', in McCarthy (ed.), *A Global Clan*, pp. 150–82.
102 Fitzpatrick, *Oceans*, pp. 16–18.
103 D. Martin, *Geographic Information Systems and Their Socio-Economic Applications* (London, 1991); Proudfoot, 'Landscape, Place, and Memory', pp. 176–8.
104 Campbell, *Kingdom of the Ryans*, p. 13–61.
105 Watson, *Caledonia Australis, passim*.
106 C. Cumming, '"In the Language of Ossian": Gaelic Survival in Australia and New Zealand – A Comparison', *Australian Studies*, Vol. 12, No. 2 (1997), pp. 104–22; E. Richards, 'Highland and Gaelic Immigrants', in Jupp (ed.), *Encyclopedia*, pp. 649–55.
107 O'Farrell, 'Landscapes of the Irish Immigrant Mind', pp. 33–46; *Idem, Vanished Kingdoms; Idem*, 'Defining Place and Home, pp. 1–18; *Idem*, 'Varieties of New Zealand Irishness', pp. 25–35.
108 Fitzpatrick, *Oceans, passim*.
109 O'Farrell, 'Landscapes of the Irish Immigrant Mind', pp. 35–6.
110 O'Farrell, 'Defining Place and Home', p. 8.
111 O'Farrell, 'Landscapes of the Irish Immigrant Mind', p. 37.
112 *Ibid., passim*.
113 O'Farrell, 'Defining Place and Home', pp. 14–15.

CHAPTER 4

Dislocations?

There are a good many Irish on board, from Ulster, Leinster and Munster and the 'Kingdom of Kerry' . . . all act as friends to each other, no matter what the respective creed may be, is it not strange that however parties contend at home in Ire[lan]d, so soon they meet 'foreigners' like Scotch or Eng[lis]h, the Irish become united – so it is in fact here. (Joseph Beale, on board *Sarah Sands*, 1852[1])

The day passed pleasantly, nothing occurring to break the harmony or disturb the monotony. At first we were continuously wishing for morning, for night, for day to come and go, but now it is different. Day may come and go without a wish or almost a thought, so listless have we become. We read without reflection and live without thinking and so the day passes. (William Lyall, on board *Kent*, 1854[2])

It is a strange life here . . . in this little world isolated on the sea, but when one can stay on deck, as today, till 8.30 in the fresh breeze, it is delightful, delicious, in fact wholesome idleness. I wish you were with me as I am now beginning to miss you all very sadly. (Alexander McNeill, on board *Macduff*, 1869[3])

These diary entries were written during the flood tide of emigration to Australia, when the lure of gold and the promise of prosperity had already fixed that continent as a possible destination in the minds of many would-be emigrants from the British Isles. Between 1832 and 1869 some 339,000 Britons were assisted to Australia, over 250,000 of them in the 1850s alone, when a further 373,000 unassisted emigrants also arrived.[4] The growth in this traffic, and the steady improvement in communications technology that facilitated it, significantly enhanced the amount of information available to would-be emigrants. Emigrant correspondence, the activities of colonial emigration agents, newspaper reports and numerous emigrant handbooks, like John Dunmore Lang's *Australian Emigrant's Manual*, all ensured that, as the century progressed, potential migrants were – in theory – better informed about prospects in the Australian colonies.[5] Yet, as these diaries demonstrate, the voyage under sail retained its capacity to disrupt even the most experienced and well-informed passengers' sense of self, time and space. Beale, an Irish Quaker, and McNeill, a Scotsman, were both first-time outbound emigrants; Lyall was a successful squatter, returning to Scotland for a visit after seventeen years in Victoria. For Beale, the voyage demonstrated the contingent nature of identity and the consequently uncertain basis of the primordial ethnic 'truths' governing life in Ireland. McNeill recognised the disconnected character of the shipboard life that revealed this. Lyall acknowledged a related paradox: that voyages to and from Australia by sailing ship were curiously timeless and aspatial experiences. The repetitive succession of night and day eventually lost real meaning, while the unending sea and sky remained a featureless constant, collapsing the imagined space between past and present, home and Australia.

The interplay between the performance of Scots and Irish passenger identities within these semiotic shipboard spaces and the temporal and spatial shifts identified by McNeill and Lyall provides the focus for this chapter. The outward voyage constituted an important formative phase in the construction of emigrant identities. It was an experience that all first-generation settlers shared. Despite changes in the size, technology and convenience of the ships themselves, in the routes and the time they took, and the increasing involvement of governmental bureaucracies in shaping the journey by arranging assisted passages, successive generations of emigrants shared in the same global maritime transition from a known past to an imagined future. Arguably, the geographical realities this involved were beyond most emigrants' imagination, while the alien character of the confined spaces on board ship only added to the newness of their experience. Brought face to face in daily contact with people and cultures they had not previously encountered, some migrants may have experienced a heightened sense of self-awareness. Equally, for some the necessity of intimate association with these others in the context of the voyage's shared dangers and uncertainties may have engendered a truly diasporic blurring of identity. In either case, the voyage mediated the emigrants' sense of belonging and selfhood and ensured that the passengers who stepped ashore at Port Phillip or Sydney could never be exactly the same people who had embarked at Glasgow, Londonderry, Plymouth or elsewhere.

We explore these issues using twenty-three voyage diaries that were written between 1836 and 1892 by Irish, Scottish and, for comparison, English passengers travelling between Australia and, in all but one case, the British Isles.[6] These represent a small sample of the 850 or so known nineteenth-century shipboard diaries and, like the remainder, pose questions concerning the representative status of the perspectives they offer. The vast majority of these diaries were written by first- and second-class cabin passengers; very few by emigrants travelling in steerage; and fewer still by women. Moreover, as Hassam observes, despite the commonalities of the global journey, there was no such thing as a single emigrant voice.[7] Individual positionality and the particular circumstances of each voyage combined to ensure that the texture of each emigrant's experience was subtly different. Accordingly, in line with our contention that settler colonialism was pre-eminently an experience of the local, we examine these diaries as evidence of individual encounters with the temporal and spatial shifts embodied in the voyage. We begin by outlining the improvements in shipping technology that framed this experience. These radically reshaped the length and character of the journey, and thus the contexts within which Scots, Irish and other emigrants performed place on board. In the following sections we turn to the testimony of the voyage diaries themselves. We consider Hassam's argument that they were a means of imbuing the voyage with meaning for their authors, and assess the evidence for Scottish and Irish ethnic consciousness within the on board places they narrated.

Routes

The diaries cited here were written within the shipboard spaces created by private and government-assisted free emigration to Australia. Convict transportation, which had begun with the First Fleet in 1788, finally ended in 1868, after decades of colonial protest over its social consequences and increasing metropolitan doubts as to its moral effectiveness. Altogether, over 162,000 British and Irish men, women and children were shipped to New South Wales (up to 1840), Van Diemen's Land and, later, Western Australia.[8] As Reece notes, Irish convict transportation to Australia had its own complex antecedents in various eighteenth-century North Atlantic projects, but formed an important part of this particular antipodean imperial discourse.[9] The transportation of the 'men of '98', for example, had an entirely disproportionate effect on the later production of nationalist Irish memory and identity in Australia. In the longer term, however, the assisted emigration of many Irish convicts' dependents from Ulster and elsewhere in the later 1820s had even more profound consequences. The passage of these dependents established regional links with New South Wales that were crucial in moulding the chain migration that subsequently characterised assisted Irish emigration.[10] In this way the narratives of convict transportation and early free emigration elided, as did the material technologies involved in each. In the 1830s convict transports and emigrant vessels were frequently one and the same. According to Bateson, 'a ship might carry prisoners one year and the next turn up in Australian waters with cargo and passengers or immigrants or simply as a freighter'. Little changed on board, other than in fitting the lower decks with the narrow, curtained bunks that were to become the hallmark of assisted emigration.[11]

But as the nineteenth century progressed, advances in shipping and navigation technology had a significant effect on the character of the voyage. Prior to the 1850s, journeys were characteristically slow. Charlwood suggests that none of the ninety-two convict transports that arrived in Sydney before 1820 completed the journey in less than three and a half months, while prior to 1840 a dozen took nearly seven months.[12] Various factors accounted for this. The design of the ships themselves, mostly broad-beamed vessels with deep drafts and modest rigging, was inimical to speed, but equally important was the route. Before the advent of 'great circle' sailing in the early 1850s, ships followed the 13,000-mile route the Admiralty had originally approved for the First Fleet. This led via the Azores and Cape Verde Islands across the South Atlantic to Cape Town (sometimes via Rio de Janeiro), to pick up the thirty-ninth parallel of latitude across the Indian Ocean to Australia. On the imagined spaces of the Mercator map projection this represented the shortest route, albeit with the double disadvantage of having to negotiate the Doldrums off the coast of equatorial Africa and the uncertain Westerlies in the Indian Ocean.

In reality, the shortest distance between any two points on the globe is represented by the arc of its circumference: the great circle. The implications of this for the Australia run were understood as early as 1847 by John Towson, scientific examiner of masters and mates at Liverpool, who in that year published *Tables to Facilitate the Practice of Great Circle Sailing*.[13] Realising, however, that a true great circle route would take ships into the Antarctic ice packs, Towson proposed a route that was divided into a series of straight segments that would take the vessel as far south as the ice would allow and which depended, crucially, upon accurate time-keeping and navigation. Once the ship had picked up the South-East Trades in the South Atlantic it would bear south to well below the fortieth parallel, where it would encounter much stronger prevailing Westerlies (the 'Roaring Forties') and begin its headlong dash to Sydney or Melbourne. The principle was well understood by some passengers at least. Writing on the *Macduff* in 1869, Alexander McNeill explained the ship's route:

Saturday 15th May. Our course will be shifted in a day, as we have to run due West to catch the trade winds and then come back in the direction of the Cape of Good Hope. This is round about but it must be done to get into these winds. You will understand this nicely by referring to an Atlas with all the currents shown. About the Cape we expect to run as far South as 44° after which we steer straight for Melbourne . . . Most ships do not go further south than 43° or 44° but the further that way the stronger the winds, which they like.[14]

Towson's modified great circle route eventually reduced the length of the average journey from around 120 days to 70 or 80 – the *Macduff* took 76 days on McNeill's voyage – but it required the demand for ever quicker passage times, fostered by the discovery of gold in Victoria in 1851, before great circle sailing was widely adopted. Even then, many masters adhered to the traditional route. The shorter passages were greatly aided by the appearance of a new and much faster type of ship, the clipper. Of American origin, clippers like the *Macduff*, *Lightning*, *James Baines*, or *White Star* were generally larger than anything previously seen on the Australia run and carried an enormous spread of sail: 12,000 square feet was not uncommon. With long, yacht-like hulls and steeply raked stems, some clippers were capable of 20 knots or more under ideal conditions. More important, however, was their ability to maintain good average speeds in any weather, as well as their capacity to catch the slightest breeze in the Doldrums. Sailing the great circle route, fast ships such as these transformed the passengers' onboard experience. On the *Kent* in 1854, William Lyall became increasingly aware of the advantages and disadvantages clippers offered:

The past night was one of the roughest we have had since we came on board. Our Captain, who at any time appears to carry a press of canvas, last night went the whole hog and frightened myself, and others into fits. [I] will never sail in a fast ship again . . .
. . . Several ships in sight but we pass them all as if they were at anchor. We pass everything.[15]

In the Southern Ocean, the clippers' speed, the wind and the high seas frequently disrupted the emigrants' shipboard lives. Donald McDonald's description of such disruption on the American clipper *Eagle* in 1853 could speak for many. A truly diasporic figure, McDonald was a Scot who had spent some time as a merchant in Natchez, Mississippi before deciding to join his brother William in business in Melbourne. En route there from New York, the *Eagle* encountered damaging seas south of the Cape of Good Hope:

Friday 6th May. We were roused from our midnight sleep by a very heavy sea having come off the cabin deck with a crash as if she was smashed against a wall. The cabin door being open it rushed down the steps like a cataract till the water was 12 inches deep in the lower end of the cabin. The first impression was that we were going down, and men in their shirt-tails were to be seen on the stairs and others in their state room doors anxiously enquiring what had happened. Having satisfied ourselves of its being nothing but a breaker we set to and bucketed the water out of our state rooms, and picking up the floating boxes, portmanteaux and the heavier books, boots, clothes that were to be found at the bottom only of the water . . . Pontius, one of my room mates who had the berth under mine, had all his books, ink, paper, pens, clothes, shoes etc all soaked with water. The sea smashed in the bulwarks opposite the deck house on the starboard side.[16]

In this instance, as in many others, the carefully specified routines and communal and private spaces that facilitated the shipboard community's shared existence were violently disrupted by uncontrollable elemental forces. The domestic space created by McDonald and his cabin mates was transgressed and thrown into confusion by the inrush of water, temporarily destabilising the materiality of their own sense of on board place. Sixteen years later, Alexander McNeill was witness to a similar experience during the *Macduff*'s voyage to Melbourne, but was phlegmatic about its cause and consequences:

Monday 21st June. We still have a westerly gale right with us and sea very heavy. I was on the poop at 1 o'clock when a 'crusher' came in washed right over us and broke down into the saloon through the skylights. The ladies being all sitting round the table got very much frightened. These seas strike the side of our ship sometimes with the force of a cannon ball, and make her whole frame shudder, still I don't count this as unpleas-ant as we are shortening our distance considerably. On the whole we are enjoying splendid sailing weather and a good voyage. We have all the comforts of life on board, and what more can we wish for?[17]

McNeill's comment reminds us that passengers made their own accommodation with the changing circumstances of the voyage, whether these were the disruptive effects of bad weather on the far southern segments of the great circle route, or the different time-spaces created during steamship journeys by the need for refuelling. Ancillary engines had become increasingly common on sailing ships working the Australia run since the launch of Isambard Kingdom Brunel's *Great Britain* in 1843. Until the introduction onto the route in the late 1870s of ships with more efficient compound steam engines and reliable screw propellers, however, they remained mere adjuncts to sail. These developments, together with the opening of the Suez Canal in 1869, signalled the end of the clipper's hey-day. Their ability to maintain high average speeds during the long eastwards dash across the Southern

Ocean became increasingly irrelevant as growing numbers of steamers took the shorter route to Australia via the Mediterranean, Red Sea and Indian Ocean. These steamers' prodigious demand for coal ensured that the long periods of shipboard isolation that had characterised the journey by sail became a thing of the past. Calls at coaling stations like Batavia, Colombo, Aden or Port Said segmented the journey and sustained the passengers' sense of the ship's progress. One English traveller encapsulated this difference, remarking that under sail 'passengers did not spend their time counting the days until the next port, as passengers on a steamer do'.[18]

In this way, steamship voyages offered emigrants and other passengers a very different spatial experience to those travelling by sailing ship. Some insight into the enhanced geographical awareness that could be engendered by these punctuated journeys is offered by the observations Bernard McIldowney made during his return trip to Ireland from Melbourne in 1892, after thirty-six years in Australia.[19] When his ship, the P & O steamer *Ormuz*, called at Colombo for two days to refuel, McIldowney was struck but also disconcerted by the other embodied in the city's inhabitants:

> But what strikes one at first so much is the swarming population. Men women & children all naked . . . the women just the same as the men in fact I could not tell the one from the other.[20]

Undeterred, McIldowney opted to tour the city and its environs, where his tourist gaze seems almost to have been overwhelmed by the verdant and decidedly alien Nature. His descriptive abilities and understanding were stretched accordingly:

> My first impression of Colombo from this drive was that if ever there was a Garden of Eden on this earth this was surely the place. The most lovely scenery I have ever set eyes on, groves of palms and coconut trees everywhere you went. Pineapple, Cinnamon trees which scented the air; Bread trees, Banana, Orange and most wonderful of all, the Banyan tree which would require a chapter to describe itself.
>
> Large trees I don't know their name covered with the most lovely blossoms in all the colours of the rainbow. Creepers, something like convolvulus, but far larger, flower and leaf hanging and creeping on fences and branches of trees, in fact I could compare it to nothing ever I seen [sic] except the gorgeous scenery in a well staged pantomime in one of the theatres.[21]

McIldowney's theatrical metaphor was apt. On his return to the *Ormuz*, the natural spectacle gave way to a different performance of the other: the process of ship refueling. His description of 'swarms of natives' transgressing the spaces of modernity on board the ship, yet in ways essential to it, suggests a sense of what Gelder and Jacobs term 'the uncanny': that troubling postmodern condition in which indigenous collaboration and authenticity combine to destabilise the Western self.[22]

> Strange sight coaling the ship, ten lighters on each side of the ship and all swarming with natives while the noise was a perfect babble, coaling all night and part of next day, natives do all the coaling, decks all swarming with natives selling fruit and nick nacks of every description. Ten large steamers coaling the same time, one being the Orient liner Austral bound for Australia . . . and several others for various ports in the east. All presenting the same busy scene as our own Ormuz.[23]

McIldowney's depiction of the other ships' refueling widens the spatiality inherent in his description of Colombo. His representation of his journey north on the *Ormuz* is now located within a wider network of steamship voyages connecting through Colombo to other parts of the Empire and the Far East. His voyage experience has thus become contextualised as part of a greater spatial encounter – made possible by the segmented nature of his own journey – stretching both backwards through time to the various countries and ports of origin where these other ships' journeys began, and forwards to their intended destinations. All of this stands in sharp contrast to the 'little world isolated on the sea' described by Alexander MacNeill on the *MacDuff* in 1869, or the listless monotony of time experienced by William Lyall on the *Kent* fifteen years earlier.

Writing the voyage

These descriptions of the different experience offered by sailing ships and steamers form part of what Hassam claims were attempts by diarists to shape and thus make sense of their journey.[24] Hassam's arguments apply to first-generation emigrants in particular. Stressing the liminal character of their voyages as transitional space between their past lives and new futures, he suggests that the act of writing a diary allowed them to try to control the uncertainty inherent in this transition by structuring it in narrative form, with a beginning, middle and end. In narrating and giving shape to the journey in this way, emigrants narrated and gave shape to their own lives at a time when the familiar values and practices of their old lives were being challenged by the unfolding, unfamiliar intimacies of shipboard life and the uncertain expectations for their future. Thus, Hassam argues, voyage diaries were much more than simply passive records of events. They were cultural performances which sustained the emigrants' sense of identity during the time-space shifts inherent in the voyage. Resolutely presentist in tone, they were written with their imagined readership in mind. Just as the voyage itself was an ongoing process of 'becoming' as the emigrants' past gave way to their future, so too these diaries represent this as a continuing experience of the immediate, depicting each day's events in relational rather than reflective terms.[25]

In narrating identity, these diaries also narrated space. Hassam explores this idea in relation to what he describes as the emigrants' 'non-temporal consciousness of space' on sailing ships, that is, their sense that time became meaningless while the external spaces beyond the ship – the unchanging sea and sky – remained unmarked by semiotic meaning. Once the Cape Verde Islands had been left behind, there was effectively nothing to be seen – save for an occasional passing ship – until the Australian coast was sighted. In order to narrate this timeless infinity of space and locate themselves within it, Hassam suggests, diarists needed to create a sense of on board domestic place by which this infinity might be humanised and comprehended.[26] This act of emplacement – the desire to create home on board – was normative and was engaged in irrespective of class or ethnicity. First- and second-class passengers might do so in the private spaces of their own cabins, where their more-or-less exclusive possession offered a greater chance of imbuing these places with their own – though still contestable – voices. Emigrants could only do so in more compromised fashion in the messes they shared in steerage, where the voice of each was only one among the subaltern many.

The contrast is exemplified by comments made on board two ships sailing to New South Wales from Scotland and Ulster in 1837. On the *North Britain*, which left Leith in May of that year, the ever socially conscious Reverend William Hamilton soon found that his 'closet and study assert their importance', despite his initial approval of his fellow cabin passengers.[27] Two months earlier, on the *Adam Lodge* riding at anchor off Londonderry, the surgeon Dr Alick Osborne noted the chaos and competition for space among the emigrants from Ulster that characterised preparations for the ship's departure:

> March 21st. Employed in berthing and messing the Emigrants, a good deal of confusion of course: everyone wanting all the accommodation to themselves.[28]

Hassam maintains that the confusion attending the ship's departure was as much social as spatial, and only added to the importance of the domestic sense of place created by diarists.[29] Establishing their home on board allowed them to cut through this initial uncertainty and establish the starting point that was so essential to the shaping effect of their narrative. On the *Macduff*, for example, Alexander McNeill devoted the second day's entry in his diary to a detailed, almost topographical, description of the private space he shared with his 'good friend Mr Sanderson from Edinburgh'. After locating the cabin within the ship's geography ('on the starboard side, entered from the saloon and half as large as an ordinary bedroom'), he continued:

> The lower [bunk] is occupied by . . . Mr Sanderson . . . and the top one is my property. The porthole is right above my knees in bed and this I take care to open in the mornings and shut in the evening, just as you would one of your bedroom windows at home. On the floor is a new carpet and at the door a crimson mat . . . On either side are our trunks, in the corner the wash stand and above it a long shelf for books etc. all around we have fixed brass knobs for our coats and hats . . . Everything we have got 'ship shape' and warranted perfect fitness.[30]

In this instance, it appears that the private spaces of this particular cabin were negotiated amiably enough between McNeill and Sanderson. Indeed, Sanderson only reappears in McNeill's narrative when he temporarily relocates to the captain's cabin to escape the below-decks heat in the tropics.[31] In other cases, however, creating an individual sense of domestic place out of the shared spaces of even first- or second-class cabins proved more problematic. In 1853, on board the *Indian Queen*, Thomas McKnight found his travelling companion's behaviour increasingly irksome and the spaces of their shared cabin charged with an underlying tension. McKnight had worked as a printer in New York but had returned to Scotland in the hope of persuading his mother to allow him to go to Australia. In the event, he went, but as the reluctant companion of a younger friend whose aunt had provided £500 capital for them to invest in the Victorian gold rush. Their voyage had not even begun before McKnight became angered by his companion's selfishness:

> [Dick's] egotistical feeling must be brought down during the voyage, or else it will be impossible to live with him. He has every intention of coming out the fine gentleman, so must be cooled down to a better level, but I fear we will quarrel, as neither of us have sweet tempers . . . Had I known he was such a sour tempered and selfish fellow I should never have agreed to go to Australia with him.[32]

Two months earlier, on the other side of the Atlantic, on the *Eagle*, Donald McDonald had encountered problems of a different order. Disconcerted at finding that half his cabin had been appropriated by the ship's carpenter and his wife, he was even more dismayed by the territorial behaviour of their dog, 'who considers the room as his rightful kennel', and by the intrusion into the already limited space of the fittings installed by the captain for the carpenter's use.[33] The matter was eventually resolved when, ten days later, McDonald was moved into the adjacent cabin, whereupon he immediately engaged in place making:

> Saturday 19th February. Our state-room is to be a medicine room and my berth changed into the next room. Spent half of the day in fixing shelves, nails etc about my berth for holding my books and hanging up my clothes ... My new berth is more comfortable than the one I left. I feel the motion of the ship less as my head is toward the stern. In my last, my head was toward the middle of the vessel.[34]

McDonald and McKnight's experiences demonstrate that place rarely sustains a single authentic meaning, even in the relatively private spaces of cabin accommodation aboard nineteenth-century sailing ships. It is always capable of contestation. Nevertheless, these domestic places still provided a reference point from which the wider social spaces on board ship might be negotiated, and this remained as true in the age of steam as it had been in the era of sail. Consequently, throughout the nineteenth century, ships constituted a 'landscape ... which was never fixed [but] was constantly made and remade physically and socially'.[35] Thus, Charlwood's claim that the social terrain on board ship simply replicated the mores and class relations of Victorian Britain is only partly true.[36] Social and spatial boundaries certainly existed between emigrants and cabin-class passengers, but were surprisingly ambiguous and permeable, at least as far as passengers were concerned. Thomas McKnight's description of what he encountered in the 'lower regions' of the *Eagle* in 1853 provides an instance of this boundary-crossing behaviour at its most extreme, but also a sense of the different social worlds that existed on either side of these divides. Following the loss of a man overboard, McKnight had been asked by the captain to ascertain who it was:

> Took a lamp in my hand, and made a thorough search through the whole of the ship but without success ... During my search I saw some queer scenes in the lower regions, as I forced my way into every berth. In some of them husband and wife were lying in a state of complete nudity, in others young men the same, while some of the young women were lying in sheets white as snow, and others in beds filthy with dirt. In berth 45 'the' celebrated berth, there were two women dead drunk, one lying in a fit on the floor, and one half sober endeavoring to bring her round.[37]

McKnight's delegated authority to force his way into every berth aptly symbolised the social differential that existed between cabin passengers and emigrants, as did his evident surprise at the scenes he encountered. On many ships, the raised poop or quarter-deck at the stern remained the preserve of first-class passengers and materialised one aspect of what Gothard calls the 'spatialised regime of authority' on board.[38] As Alexander McNeill found on the *Macduff*, this exclusive space provided an aptly elevated vantage point from which to observe the othered behaviour of more subaltern shipmates: 'We have been amused tonight looking down on the second class passengers' amusements from the poop, which place is my great favourite spot on board.'[39] Uninvited attempts to transgress this boundary from below were resisted, whether they came from second-class passengers attempting to renegotiate the fine differences of cabin-class status, or, more seriously and surprisingly often, from potentially mutinous emigrants or crew.[40]

But even socially nuanced transgressions were perceived as a threat. During Annie Henning's voyage to Melbourne as a first-class passenger on the *SS Great Britain* in 1853, the 'throng' of second-class passengers crowding onto the quarter-deck forced the captain to forbid their further access to this part of the ship, prompting informal retaliatory action on their part. Annie's indignation reflected the freedom habitually enjoyed by her class on board:

[The Fore Saloon passengers] retorted by another notice that none of the After Salooners should pass the line that separates the two parts of the deck: a piece of retaliation highly resented by our side, as first class passengers have a right to go into any part of the ship they like.[41]

This contested performance of the most exclusive social spaces on board the *Great Britain* provides a further reminder that the shipboard terrain consisted of more than a simple division between emigrant space and passenger space. Within and, as we have seen, between these spaces, passengers and emigrants performed and negotiated their own particular sense of place. By their nature, most voyage diarists offer their deepest insights into the nuanced production of place within the hegemonic spaces occupied by the first- and second-class passengers. These places were performed in a variety of ways beyond the confines of the passenger's own cabin: in the communal spaces of the shared saloon; at the dining table; and on deck, where entertainment, religious services and, on some voyages, frequent funeral services offered an opportunity for individuals to imprint these spaces with personal meaning. Consequently, as Goldsworthy notes, in the process of becoming that was the journey, new boundaries were formed and old ones disappeared as passengers continually enacted their unfolding identities – their changing sense of self and other – on board.[42]

In recording the changing semiotics of the journey, the diarists thus recorded their own changing sense of self and place. The Reverend

Hamilton's diary on board the *North Britain* in 1837 provides a notable early instance of this sense of the journey as a developing social experience which gave changing meaning to the shared spaces of the ship. We have already noted the short-lived nature of his early approval of his fellow passengers, and his gaze became increasingly critical as the journey progressed. His initial observations in early May were clinical and socially aware:

> Thursday 11th May. The company is agreeable though very mixed being composed of clergy men of different classes and adventurers of different ranks and characters. Hitherto conversation has not been very general or lively. Yet there are materials such as may be expected to render it both interesting and profitable once a good mutual understanding shall have been instituted.[43]

Three weeks later, Hamilton had become even more discriminating as he found opportunity to assess the passengers in terms of his own austere Presbyterian moral code. His analysis points to the transient but complex character of the places performed on board by his fellow passengers:

> Friday 2nd June. Our passengers may be divided into three classes. One who depend for their happiness on eating and drinking card playing and jesting and the examination and exhibition of their various goods and chattels. These seem sometimes to feel life irksome and are often distressed with the length of the interval from breakfast till dinner. They are however not destitute of good manners or wanting in civility.
>
> A second class have a more regular [approach] but want habits of reading and patient application to study. They turn from their books to their gun from their gun to their fishing tackle and from these to spie [sic] glasses and sextants. Then they betake themselves to light goodhearted conversation to trials of dexterity in climbing etc then return to their books and seem to find them agreeable for a short time.
>
> The third class is the most sedate and serious. They may be found for three or four hours daily walking the deck and enjoying conversation and as many hours engaged in reading in the open air or engaged in observing the wonders of the deep. The rest of their time they are engaged in study either with or without the pen but at any rate in private.[44]

Hamilton's tone was characteristically judgmental: self-improvement through sustained study was laudable; the dissipation of time in pointless activity was not, even though it was done in a civil manner. Yet all of these activities and pursuits gave personal meaning to the spaces of the ship for the individuals concerned.

By the middle of June the social terrain on board the *North Britain* had begun to change radically for Hamilton. In his view, 'the passengers of the lowest class have now lost all respect for one another and seek amusement in disgusting ribaldry', despite his periodic attempts to moderate their behaviour by sitting with them at meals.[45] The breakdown of the unspoken ties of civility evidently continued, with a consequent re-ordering of semiotic space on the ship. By late July the passengers had become 'almost entirely separated. Those of the coarsest class monopolising the lower cabin where they may enjoy all the liberty they wish . . . We who occupy the public cabin of the poop have no reason to regret that we are left to ourselves; we enjoy in consequence a more rational and agreeable conversation.'[46] But the performance of identity within even this more congenial space was dependent on circumstance and thus subject to change as the voyage continued. Towards the end of August, Hamilton concluded:

> Having been now so long together our conversation at table often halts or becomes frivolous. The more common subjects are nearly exhausted and Van Diemen's Land and New South Wales and South Australia have been so frequently before us that it is scarcely possible to suggest a new question or remark. Occasionally we have had a good natured discussion on some theological, literary or scientific subject.[47]

This failure of the collective imagination and consequent re-working of the passengers' shared discursive space found an echo in other diaries. In December 1838, towards the end of her five-month journey to Sydney from London on the *Earl of Durham*, Margaret Menzies was more emphatic: 'never was I so tired of any place as I am of this ship and never was I so tired of people as I am of some folks here, whose mean conduct is too despicable to take notice of and yet sufficiently annoying'.[48] A year later, on the *William Metcalfe*, Jonathan Binns Were felt similarly, but was conscious of a further discursive change as the ship neared its destination:

> Tuesday 25th October. We are all tired of each other's company (with but few exceptions) tired of the ship, and of the voyage, and very nearly tired of ourselves . . . Detraction in all its forms has been carried on to a great extent (which is usually the case on shipboard) and I regret to say those parties who should have shewn [sic] the better example in such cases, viz, the Captain, Parson and Dr have been the worst, to the annoyance of all on board at different times, but as we approach land the existing differences sink into oblivion.[49]

Seemingly, as the infinity of 'timeless space' under sail gave way to more material evidence of their destination, the passengers' self-absorbed negotiations of place and identity on board were replaced by an externalised sense of anticipation. As the ship moved back into 'real' space and 'real' time, so a perspectival shift occurred which reconnected – in Patrick McMahon Glynn's phrase – 'the little world' on board to the externalities of its collective future – evidence once again of the journey's transformative power.[50]

Ethnic encounters

McMahon Glynn's journey was made in 1880 on the SS Orient, and his observations on shipboard life survive in letters he posted from Cape St Vincent and Cape Town, where the ship refuelled. His descriptions make frequent and easy use of nationality as a readily understood marker of ethnic difference among his fellow passengers. Thus, he shared his cabin with 'a melancholic Scotchman' and 'a lay preacher who is nevertheless a perfect gentleman and an Irishman'.[51] At dinner, he sat at table with 'an ogre-like Scotch man and his wife, that seize everything on the table at once and pile them on their plates for fear of losing anything – with several skirmishes in the distance – principally Irish by birth, but all the right sort of fellows'.[52] McMahon Glynn's description of his encounters with more exotic others privileged race and ethnicity more explicitly. On the ship's arrival at Cape St Vincent, it was 'soon surrounded by young niggars [sic] who dived for any money we threw overboard and recovered it with remarkable quickness. They were perfectly naked ... Dancing at several "Public houses" [was] always possible to the music of the banjo and with black women – the latter being well built, but by no means prepossessing as regards facial structure.'[53]

The casual racism inherent in McMahon Glynn's remarks may offend modern sensibilities but formed part of his world-view, and in this ethnic and racial difference was a self-evident and unremarkable given. As such, McMahon Glynn incorporated it seamlessly into his narrative of the voyage, where it gave colour to his account of socially performed place. The question remains, however, of how widespread such ethnic sensibilities were among diarists as they sought to shape their voyage and locate themselves within its shifting time and space. Were ethnic representations particularly evident in Scottish and Irish diaries? Taking as his premise the idea that Irish peasant mentalité was intensely localist and place bound, O'Farrell claims that, consequently, Irish emigrants were often first confronted with the question of their Irishness – of what it meant to be Irish – in their chosen new world. Here, for the first time, they encountered other forms of Irish ethnicity – as well as people of other nationalities – in significant numbers.[54] But is it possible that this process had in fact already begun in the confined shipboard spaces and enforced intimacies of the outward voyage? Moreover, if this sensibility developed at sea, was it something that was contingent on social status? Was ethnicity equally important as a prop to identity among Irish cabin passengers as among emigrants? The latter, especially single women, may have felt less in control of their shipboard circumstances under the 'regime of surveillance' that was their lot. Having left the place of their home imagination, and with their own compensating sense of shipboard place constrained by the competing readings of authority and their fellow emigrants, is it possible that they had a particular recourse to their imagined past as a touchstone for their transitional present?

Similar questions might, of course, be equally well asked of Scottish emigrants, particularly the Gaelic-speaking Highlanders who arrived in Australia in significant numbers in the late 1840s. Prentis suggests that while Scottish cabin passengers and emigrants alike generally displayed less of a 'backward look' than their Irish counterparts, they nevertheless exhibited a 'taken for granted shared sense of Scottishness'. According to Prentis this was grounded in the uniquely non-political sense of civic nationalism that had developed in the country following the Treaty of Union in 1707. 'In other words, despite individualism and British affinities, Scots of all classes retained a subtle but deeply held and distinctive national consciousness.'[55] Hassam goes further, and argues for an important general distinction between the spatial semiotics of cabin and steerage accommodation. Whereas the former were negotiated informally between passengers on the basis of fine differences in their social status, Hassam claims that the semiotic spaces in steerage reflected deliberate attempts by the ships' authorities to maintain existing religious, ethnic and national differences among the emigrants. On most ships, emigrants represented a culturally disparate but numerically dominant body, who nevertheless shared a common background of relative social disadvantage – and the potential for collective protest. Communal protests of this sort occurred, for example, on the *Adam Lodge* in 1837 and the *Asia* in 1850. In each case the cause was an assumed infringement of the emigrants' moral rights – usually concerning food or supplies – by the captain or crew.[56] By housing different nationalities in separate messes, the captain might hope to lessen the possibility of such class-based resistance to his authority. The end result, according to Hassam, was that emigrants thought of themselves primarily as Scots or Irish or English, and not as emigrants – much as Joseph Beale's quotation at the beginning of this chapter suggests.[57]

While suggestive, this interpretation remains speculative. The limited survival of steerage diaries and the marginal literacy of many emigrants means that we simply do not know whether the majority saw themselves primarily in ethnic or in social terms, whatever the fears and intentions of the ships' authorities may have been. Much would have depended on circumstance and neither ethnicity nor social identity is likely to have been expressed in a primordial or unchanging way. The evidence that does survive is ambiguous. Among the steerage diaries analysed here, there are certainly references to ethnic messing and difference, but also references to the social effects of the surveillance regime under which all assisted emigrants lived.[58] This regime, and the opportunities it provided for ethnic performance, was gendered: single female emigrants experienced particularly rigorous controls on their daily lives. For example, while Mary Maclean's account of her voyage to Sydney on the *Africana* in 1865 carefully distinguishes between the various English, Scottish and Irish girls' messes in her part of the ship, it also complains about the onerous restrictions she and they were placed under as single women. Commenting that her diary in fact contravened the ban on single girls taking notes ('on account of so many writing to the men'), she continued: '[it] seems as if they tried to Deprive us of Every Liberty. We are to be allowed to Come on Deck this Evening if We behave Well during the Day.'[59]

Seven years earlier, on the emigrant ship *Conway*, Fanny Davis had been subjected to a similar regime. During the ship's voyage to Melbourne, the surgeon regulated the single girls' daily regime in minute detail. In bad weather they were forced to stay below; insolence towards the matron was instantly punished; and hygiene was maintained by a competitive cleaning regime in which messes were set against each other.[60] Both Fanny Davis and Mary Maclean appear to have inhabited shipboard spaces that were imbued with presentist ethnic and social meanings that could invoke memory in various ways. Sometimes this memory was painful. Mary found Old Year's Night (31 December) particularly trying:

> Last night I dreamt of my Father and the rest of our house hold as plain as Ever I Seen them. But I Was thinking of them in the Evening as it Was So neare the Close of the year. I Was thinking of the past and its Events Mary Wilkinson how I Wished my Self With you that We might talk of our Dear parents as We have often Done But now I have no one to Speak to. All here are Strangers and I Can onley relieve my hart By Crying When No Eyes Sees me But one and ask him to keep and guide me through my pilgrimage.[61]

As an Englishwoman, Fanny Davis observed the same elision between Scots (and Irish) ethnicity, memory and social meaning on the *Conway* from an external perspective. Describing a typical evening scene on deck, she delineated the complex ways in which the social spaces of the shipboard present intertwined with the ethnic past:

It would amuse anyone to be suddenly introduced onto our poop on a moonlight night – in one of the corners will be about two dozen singing, in another a lot talking scandal about everybody . . . In another place will be a lot of Scotch girls dancing with one of them imitating the bagpipes and not one of them with either shoes or stockings on; then the Irish will be squatting down under the boats talking over everybody's business but their own and vowing eternal hatred to the English, and even the children must have a game to themselves . . .[62]

But these were essentially *female* spaces, and subject to a particularly rigorous surveillance regime. Single male emigrants, like Fitzwilliam Turner, who travelled to Sydney on the *Camperdown* in 1880, were subject to less onerous restrictions, though they still came under the general authority of the ship's doctor.[63] Turner's diary is written in a literary and observant style and suggests that he was a man of far greater educational accomplishment than many of his fellow Irish emigrants. Of prosperous Protestant stock, he offers an unusually articulate perspective on the performance of ethnicity in the less overtly gendered – and constrained – emigrant spaces of the *Camperdown*. From the start, Turner positions himself as a non-participant observer. Acknowledging that the Irish men and women around him were his fellow countrymen, he carefully distinguishes himself from them in social and ethnic terms. The emigrants embarked on St Patrick's Day:

All the Irish boys and girls sported green ribbons (in honour of the day). Got up a dance in a large empty store and marched round in procession to air St Patrick's Day played on fifes, fiddles, concertinas etc. Quite a treat to see the animals feeding (especially at dinner time) and the washing up of utensils after.[64]

The social division between Turner and these 'animals' is almost palpable. Thereafter, the tone of amused superiority continues as Turner locates his fellow countrymen's behaviour within the broader array of ethnic performance around him. After a week, a pattern had been established that Fanny Davis would have recognised:

Wednesday 24th March. Well, after tea it is quite amusing – groups of Irish boys all playing fifes and concertinas and dancing jigs or singing Irish ditties, 'real come all yus!!' Groups of Scotch ladies singing 'Auld Lang Syne' or other Scotch airs – other groups playing cards, drafts or dominoes – some promenading the deck – others, more serious, talking of future prospects in a strange land or speaking of home or dear ones left behind whom they may never see again in this world.[65]

As the voyage proceeded, Turner continued to represent Irishmen as variously comic or uncivilised, but invariably as other. His initial assessment was far from flattering: 'Of all the passengers on board, my own countrymen are the roughest, the dirtiest and the most rowdy!'[66] Subsequently, the messing system provided a further opportunity for comedic othering, and this was given an added note of veracity by Turner's own remembered Irish past. Describing the system of appointing captains for each mess, Turner continued:

> Friday 26th March. Well it is amusing to hear these fellows (most of them clods) called by the members of their mess, 'Captain', 'I say Captain' . . . One gentleman they call 'Captain Taypot' from the fact of his trying to steal a teapot from another mess, this circumstance has immortalised him on board the Camperdown. He seems quite proud of the title and struts and swaggers about the deck in regular 'buc-caneer' style (an Irishman of course), he reminds me of one of those 'swells' I have often seen my mother fighting about the price of a load of turf . . .[67]

There was, in reality, no 'of course' about the fact that the figure in question was an Irishman, and thus Turner's aside is particularly telling. From his vantage point as an educated, detached insider, someone who occupied a liminal position on the *Camperdown*, he provides us with compelling evidence for the continuing low-level performance of ethnicity on that ship at that time.

There were other spaces and occasions that privileged ethnicity even more consistently. Religious services, for example, were performative events that pointed up differences between ethnic traditions but could also blur the social divisions within them. In the context of Australian emigration, the main ethnic division lay between Roman Catholic and Protestant services of various denominations, as the vast majority of Catholic emigrants were Irish men and women from a variety of pre-modern rural backgrounds. Catholic services were held separately from the Anglican services conducted by the captain or a clergyman in the privileged spaces of the saloon or quarter-deck.[68] Attendance at these Anglican services by the crew, emigrants and passengers alike was encouraged, and ensured that they were socially hybrid affairs which transgressed the otherwise exclusive material space they occupied. These complex, socially layered religious sites were thus shared by all on board except the resolutely othered Catholics: their rituals were performed in less privileged spaces elsewhere.

Unsurprisingly, the semiotics of religious observance were a source of frequent comment by emigrants and passengers alike. On the *North Britain*, the redoubtable Reverend Hamilton saw the fine weather on successive Sundays and the consequent lack of crew activity as provi-dential: 'Yesterday like all our previous sabbaths was so fine a day that little or nothing was requisite to be done working the ship and not the least disturbance was given to our public worship.'[69] Less sabbatarian passengers also noted the change in demeanour among passengers and crew on Sundays. Fitzwilliam Turner noted that 'everything on board today had more the appearance of what a Sunday should be – all looked cleaner and neater. The sailors looked very nice in clean white trousers and jackets, and the passengers in their Sunday best attire, no work done except what was really necessary . . .'[70] During Andrew McDonnell's voyage on the *Falcon*, the general quietness was facilitated by Sunday's provisions being handed out the night before, but also on one occasion by the influential effect of a preacher: '[Mr Ray] preached . . . a most impressive sermon . . . which was listened to with the greatest attention by all, the Captain among the rest . . . His very impressive address appeared to have a good effect on all as might be seen from the quietude and order that prevailed during the afternoon.'[71] Similarly, at a service on the *Eagle* in 1853, 'almost all the passengers gathered round on the Quarter Deck to hear the sermon, some climbing up ladders some crowding on the Deck House and some standing on the Spanker Beam'.[72]

But the social meaning of these religious services could be contested by those taking part. If the sermon on the *Eagle* commanded the attention of crowds of passengers, another on the *Lightning* a year later attracted less support from the cabin elite. Conceivably, nuances of social difference may have played their part in this. A second-class passenger, John Fenwick, observed: 'A stranger officiated (from the Intermediate); he showed his ignorance & bored us tremendously. Some of these chaps have far more vanity & impudence than Religion, or they could never stick themselves up & talk the nonsense they do.'[73] On the *Macduff* Alexander McNeill was more trenchant: 'No one seems interested in the Service on board as our Baptist parson is but a poor "fish".'[74]

Other comments reinforce the sense that religious services were thought of by some primarily in ethnic terms. Presbyterians wrote warily of services held 'in the Church of England fashion', but it was the othered spaces of Catholicism that drew particular comment.[75] On the *Africana* only forty of the emigrant girls were Protestant, but Mary Maclean, a Presbyterian, noted that the Catholic majority still needed to have their services conducted by one of their own girls. For her part, the formal parade for prayers 'in the English fashion' prompted memories of her minister, Mr McDougall: 'Well Did my Dear father Call him our moses. I hope he has not forgot an absent member in the Body but present in Spirit.'[76] For Andrew McDonnell on the *Falcon*, the Catholic services were a complete unknown: 'The Roman Catholics also mustered on the forecastle of the ship at the same time (11 o.c.)

and had some sort of service but as I did not hear it I am unable to say of what it consisted.'[77]

Subsequently, McDonnell reflected more widely on the social and denominational divisions that inflected religious space on the *Falcon*:

Today (Sunday) was spent as the previous ones. The Roman Catholics and the Church people each having services in the forenoon and Mr Ray, the Dissenting Minister, preached in the afternoon.

There is just as much religious party feeling exhibited on board the FALCON as there is in Liverpool or any other town in England and many discussions and debates has [sic] taken place between the advocates of the different classes. Some of the most enthusiastic of the adherents of the Church of England showed their zeal for their own Church – or their rigidity – I will not say whether, by objecting to Mr Ray preaching in the morning as they could not think of dispensing with the reading of the Church prayers. Consequently the Doctor performed that service – although there is a Minister on board who can preach a better sermon than you will hear in two thirds of the Churches in England – but as they were chiefly First Cabin passengers [they] must be attended to.[78]

Clearly, this party feeling extended beyond the primary (and presumably ethnicised) division between Catholics and Protestants. Not only were Catholics othered, Dissenters, too, were unacceptable to some at least of the hegemonic Anglican elite. Members of other Protestant denominations might be tolerated in the spaces of Anglican observance, but only on Anglican terms. On this occasion at least, there were obviously limits to the blurring of social and denominational boundaries that would be tolerated within the spaces of non-Catholic religious observance.

All of which points to the complexity of the semiotic places performed on board ship. If emigrant accommodation was deliberately ethnicised in order to maintain shipboard authority, the social spaces created by that authority loomed equally large in the emigrants' lives and intertwined with ethnicity to create complex, ever-changing places on board. Moreover, as we have seen, neither can we totally separate these emigrant spaces from those of the cabin passengers. As far as first-class (and other) cabin passengers were concerned, the boundaries between them and emigrant space were surprisingly permeable, as Annie Henning was quick to point out. Yet the cabin diaries examined here suggest that there was one sense in which ethnic performance differed between cabin passengers and emigrants. For whatever reason, possibly because, as Hassam suggests, cabin passengers were primarily concerned with negotiating their own social position, references to ethnicity, whether of their fellow passengers or the emigrants, were muted. In the saloon and on the poop-deck, gentlemanly and ladylike behaviour were of far greater importance than Scottish or Irish origins. Cabin passengers might perform their ethnicity by reading Scott's *Waverley* novels, or listening to Scottish or Irish airs, or musing on the increasing distance between themselves and their remembered home in Scotland or Ireland, but these were essentially private matters, internalised through the lens of memory.

Alexander McNeill's diary on the *Macduff* exemplifies this tendency. At the start of his voyage, McNeill carefully positioned himself within the social geography of the cabin accommodation by cultivating social networks with other Scottish cabin passengers: 'Mrs Cameron has been to Australia before and was a fellow passenger with Mr and Mrs McNeill, ... [she] is a relation of the McKellars, Glenrisdale, Kintyre.' As the voyage proceeded, he read extensively on Scottish literature (Burns) and history, and took part in the predominantly Scottish concerts put on by his fellow passengers. At one, Mr McKellar read 'Mary Queen of Scots', the ship's captain (a Scotsman) read 'Burns' address to the deil', and McNeill sang 'Anchors away'.[79] More tellingly, as time passed, McNeill's diary entries became increasingly reflective. Two weeks into the voyage he described his growing feeling of separation from home and family:

> I stood before dinner today behind the man at the wheel and looking back thinking of *Dear friends!!* I was conscious every passing hour was taking me miles and miles further away from you all and then I could not help thinking to myself 'How is this?' and 'Will I ever again see them all?'[80]

The mood continued. The following day, McNeill's memories of place and home, were again framed by his sense of changing time and space:

> Saturday 1st May. I now enter a new month, and this is the first day of summer with you all at home! I can well picture you all going out and speaking of the May dew. I am only sorry that I cannot join you. Do you remember, dear Johnnie, the long walk you and I took before breakfast this day one year, and of the two pence worth of milk we bought from the dairywoman in or near Partick? These recollections are pleasant to me now and come up quite vividly to my mind.[81]

The next day, Sunday, McNeill acted as precentor at the morning service, and this provided a further prompt for memory, based this time on shared religious experience:

> Today I led off first with 'Hursley' (the tune you use for Rock of Ages in your church at Sandyford and which I was so much attached to) ... Occasionally I take up my album and see all your dear faces there before me – your very images and I wish you only knew the comfort I derive from that Book.[82]

For a time, McNeill's attention became distracted by the weather and the routine of shipboard life, but six weeks later, an anniversary of a different sort prompted further memories which disrupted his presentist narrative once again:

> Wednesday 9th June. It is six years this date since I first saw Glasgow – it was then that I first left my native Isle to enter the business of our Commercial World and here I am today – within 3 weeks sailing from Melbourne.[83]

The note of surprise in this last comment is plain enough, and adds to the sense that, for McNeill as for every other migrant, the voyage to Australia was a transitional experience. In his case, memory played an ongoing part in shaping his adjustment to the changing circumstances in which he found himself. Although sometimes painful, these memories reinforced his sense of place and belonging on board by connecting him to his past, underpinning his present and contextualising his future. Hymns learnt in his youth allowed him to lead the singing in the ship's religious services; memories of his home on Gigha and his early business career in Glasgow sharpened his anticipation of Melbourne. In every sense, McNeill was a prime example of Prentis' 'taken-for granted Scottishness'. In the polite spaces on board the *Macduff*, this occasionally coloured otherwise normative social behaviour, but could also give rise to deep-seated private reflection.

Summary

Arguably, it was inner transformations of self and identity such as these that constituted the emigrant voyages' most lasting effect. Death, particularly infant mortality, might reduce the number on board by the time a ship reached Sydney or Melbourne, but the most significant changes occurred in emigrant and passenger attitudes and understanding. Although progressive improvements in shipping technology and changes in the preferred route significantly shortened the journey time to Australia as the nineteenth century progressed, the emigrant voyage remained what it had always been: an uncertain transitional space between a remembered past and an imagined future. The unsettling shifts in time and space were compounded by the enforced intimacies of life on board for emigrants and cabin passengers alike. While these differed in both degree and kind for different status groups, the close proximity of previously unfamiliar national, cultural and ethnic others remained an abiding hallmark of the emigrant voyage. Moreover, each ship developed its own social landscape which itself evolved as the journey progressed, and individuals negotiated their own place on board.

Some, mainly cabin passengers, may have tried to control the uncertainty and newness of their shipboard lives by shaping these through acts of narration. Most did not, or at any rate have left no record that they did. Nevertheless, the diaries and journals that do survive suggest that social status and ethnicity elided in complex ways to form ambiguous and nuanced spaces that were performed as place on board. Despite possible attempts by shipboard authorities to use nationality and ethnicity as a means of control among emigrants, and the ethnicity inherent in religious practice, there is little evidence among the diaries examined here for consistently primordial expressions of Scots or Irish ethnicity. Instead, these represent ethnic consciousness as thoroughly unremarkable, a matter of private introspection rather than public assertion. But there was an exception. Catholic emigrants, most of whom would have been Irish, had their otherness periodically asserted for them by the marginalisation of their shipboard religious practices. But every traveller who landed in Australia for the first time, whether Scots or Irish, English or some other nationality, only did so after prolonged personal exposure to newness and change. Their imagined futures had already begun at sea. What place did Australia offer to the Scots and Irish among them?

Notes

1 Joseph Beale to Margaret Beale, 'First Letter', entry for 4 October 1852, cited in Edgar Beale, *The Earth between Them. Joseph Beale's Letters Home to Ireland from Victoria 1852–53* (Sydney, 1975), p. 35.

2 William Lyall, Diary, entry for 28 February 1854, 'Extracts Collected from the Diaries of William Lyall, Esquire, of "Harewood", Westernport, Victoria, by his granddaughter, Bertha Irene Ricardo', RHSV, Box 60/1.

3 Alexander McNeill, 'My Diary', entry for 4 May 1869, SLV, Ms 8887, MSB 440.

4 B. Fraser, *People of Australia. Key Events in Population, Society, the Environment*, Macquarie Reference Series (Sydney, 1998), pp. 64–6.

5 J. D. Lang, *Australian Emigrants' Manual or A Guide to the Gold Colonies of New South Wales and Port Phillip* (London, 1852). For a general survey of the information fields within which assisted emigration took place from the British Isles, see R. F. Haines, *Emigration and the Labouring Poor. Australian Recruitment in Britain and Ireland, 1831–60* (London, 1997).

6 Manuscript diaries: W. J. Douglas, Diary 1891–94, NLA, Ms 1629/1; Daniel Halfpenny, Journal 1840–47, SLV, Ms 13300; Hugh Hamilton, Diary and Reminiscences, 1841–1882, NLA, Ms 956; William Hamilton, Diary 1837, NLA, William Hamilton Mss, Ms 2117; John S. Henry, Travel Diary 1851, SLV, Ms 8359, Box 1868/5; William Lyall, Diary; Donald McDonald, Diary 1852–53, SLV, Ms 8484, Box 818/2; Andrew McDonnell, 'Diary of a Voyage from England to Australia' (n.d.), SLV, Ms12436, Box 3220/a; Bernard McIldowney, Diary 1892, RHSV, Ms 001016, Box 235/15; Robert McKean, 'Voyage to Australia in 1868', SLV, Ms 9580; Thomas B. McKnight, Diary 1852, SLV, Ms 9271, Box 1127; Alexander McNeill, 'My Diary'; George Main, Diary 1887–8, NLA, Ms 8749; Margaret Menzies, Diary 1838–39, NLA, Ms 3261; Dr Alick Osborne, 'Journal of occurrences connected with Emigration, 1836–37', hereafter ML, Ms 248, CY Reel 2294; Fitzwilliam Turner,

Diary 1880, ML, Ms 6652. Published diaries: Beale, *The Earth between Them*; J. Binns Were, *A Voyage from Plymouth to Melbourne in 1838* (Melbourne, 1964); 'Fanny Davis, 1858', in D. Charlwood, *The Long Farewell* (Warrandyte, 2000 edn), pp. 251–64; G. Glynn O'Collins, S. J. (ed.), *Patrick McMahon Glynn: Letters to His Family (1874–1927)* (Melbourne, 1974); 'Mary Maclean', in A. Hassam, *No Privacy for Writing. Shipboard Diaries 1852–1879* (Melbourne, 1995), pp. 93–126; J. Thomas (ed.), *The Sea Journals of Annie and Amy Henning* (Sydney, 1984); 'William Shennan, 1870', in Hassam, *No Privacy*, pp. 127–58.

7   A. Hassam, *Sailing to Australia. Shipboard Diaries by Nineteenth-century British Emigrants* (Manchester, 1994), pp. 10–11; *Idem, No Privacy*, pp. 1–17.

8   A. Brooke and D. Brandon, *Bound for Botany Bay. British Convict Voyages to Australia* (Kew, 2005), p. 13.

9   B. Reece, *The Origins of Irish Convict Transportation to New South Wales* (Basingstoke, 2001), *passim*.

10 T. Parkill, '"That Infant Colony": Aspects of Ulster Emigration to Australia, 1790–1860', *Familia*, Vol. 3 (1987), pp. 57–72.

11 C. Bateson, *The Convict Ship 1787–1868* (Sydney, 1974), p. 83, cited in Charlwood, *Long Farewell*, p. 25.

12 Charlwood, *ibid.*, p. 25. This paragraph draws on Charlwood's admirable study of the material technologies of emigration.

13 John T. Towson, *Tables to Facilitate the Practice of Great Circle Sailing and Determination of Azimuths* (15th edn, London, 1854). Cited in Charlwood, *Long Farewell*, p. 17.

14 McNeill, 'My Diary', entries for 15 May and 3 June 1869.

15 Lyall, Diary, entries for 22 March and 16 May 1854.

16 McDonald, Diary, entry for 6 May 1853.

17 McNeill, 'My Diary', entry for 21 June 1869.

18 Cited in H. R. Woolcock, *Rights of Passage. Emigration to Australia in the Nineteenth Century* (London, 1986), p. 88.

19 McIldowney, Diary, 1892.

20 *Ibid.*, entry for 5 and 6 May 1892.

21 *Ibid.*

22 K. Gelder and J. M. Jacobs, *Uncanny Australia. Sacredness and Identity in a Postcolonial Nation* (Melbourne, 1998), pp. 23–42.

23 McIldowney, Diary, entry for 5 and 6 May 1892.

24 Hassam, *Sailing*, pp. 20–45.

25 *Ibid.*, pp. 53–7.

26 *Ibid.*, p. 58. See also the diary of John Fenwick, reproduced in Charlwood, *Long Farewell*, p. 232.

27 William Hamilton, Diary, entry for 12 May 1837.

28 Osborne, 'Journal of occurrences', entry for 21 March 1837.

29 Hassam, *Sailing*, pp. 46–73.

30 McNeill, 'My Diary', entry for 19 April 1869.

31 *Ibid.*, entry for 7 May 1869.

32 McKnight, Diary, pp. 64–5, *ca.* 10 April 1853.

33 McDonald, Diary, entry for 7 February 1853.

34 *Ibid.*, entry for 19 February 1853.

35 J. Gothard, 'Space, Authority and the Female Emigrant Afloat', *Australian Historical Studies*, Vol. 111 (1999), pp. 96–115.

36 Charlwood, *Long Farewell*, p. 91.

37 McKnight, Diary, entry for 20 June 1853.

38 Gothard, 'Space', p. 97 ff.

39 McNeill, 'My Diary', entry for 30 April 1869.

40 Charlwood, *Long Farewell*, p. 120 ff. See also McKnight, Diary, entry for 14 June 1853.

41 Thomas (ed.), *Sea Journals*, pp. 18–19.

42 K. Goldsworthy, 'The Voyage South: Writing Immigration', in K. Darian-Smith *et*

al. (eds), *Text, Theory, Space. Land, Literature and History in South Africa and Australia* (London, 1996), pp. 53–64.

43 William Hamilton, Diary, entry for 11 May 1837.

44 *Ibid.*, entry for 2 June 1837.

45 *Ibid.*, entry for 13 June 1837.

46 *Ibid.*, entry for 21 July 1837.

47 *Ibid.*, entry for 21 August 1837.

48 Menzies, Diary, entry for 14 December 1838.

49 Binns Were, *Voyage*, pp. 232–3.

50 O'Collins (ed.), *Patrick McMahon Glynn*, p. 16. See also Hassam, *Sailing*, pp. 161–91.

51 *Ibid.*, pp. 10–11.

52 *Ibid.*, p. 17.

53 *Ibid.*, pp. 12–13.

54 P. O'Farrell, 'Defining Place and Home: Are the Irish Prisoners of Place?', in D. Fitzpatrick (ed.), *Home or Away? Immigrants in Colonial Australia* (Canberra, 1992), pp. 7–8.

55 M. Prentis, 'Haggis on the High Seas. Shipboard Experiences of Scottish Emigrants to Australia 1821–1897', *Australian Historical Studies*, Vol. 124 (2004), pp. 296–7.

56 Henry, Travel Diary, entry for 17 July 1851; Osborne, 'Journal of occurrences', entry for 14 April 1837.

57 Charlwood, *Long Farewell*, p. 252; Hassam, *Sailing*, pp. 107–34.

58 Charlwood, *Long Farewell*, pp. 240, 263; Hassam, *No Privacy*, p. 71.

59 Hassam, *ibid.*, pp. 108–10.

60 Charlwood, *Long Farewell*, pp. 257, 259, 261; Hassam, *No Privacy*, pp. 47, 194.

61 Hassam, *ibid.*, p. 107.

62 Charlwood, *Long Farewell*, p. 258.

63 Fitzwilliam Turner, Diary, 1880.

64 *Ibid.*, entry for 17 March 1880.

65 *Ibid.*, entry for 24 March 1880.

66 *Ibid.*

67 *Ibid.*

68 Henry, Travel Diary, entry for 18 May 1851.

69 William Hamilton, Diary, entry for 10 June 1837.

70 Turner, Diary, entry for 28 March 1880.

71 McDonnell, 'Diary of a Voyage', entry for 28 May (no year).

72 McDonald, Diary, entry for 13 February 1853.

73 Charlwood, *Long Farewell*, p. 240.

74 McNeill, 'My Diary', entry for 13 June 1869.

75 McKean, 'Voyage to Australia', entry for 31 May 1868.

76 Hassam, *No Privacy*, p. 102.

77 McDonnell, 'Diary of a Voyage', entry for 5 June (no year).

78 *Ibid.*, entry for 21–26 June (no year).

79 McNeill, 'My Diary', entries for 21 and 28 April 1869.

80 *Ibid.*, entry for 30 April 1869.

81 *Ibid.*, entry for 1 May 1869.

82 *Ibid.*, entry for 2 May 1869.

83 *Ibid.*, entry for 9 June 1869.

CHAPTER 5

Relocations: land, legislation and memory

At Port Phillip . . . the squatting class had from the first been respectable, and attained in this particular, both as to the means and the social status of its members, a position equal or even superior to that of any other colonial vocation. (William Westgarth, Edinburgh, 1853[1])

Now we in Belfast, unfortunately find ourselves . . . manacled as it were on every side by landlordism. Every thing pines beneath its accursed yoke. Like the upas tree, it withers everything beneath its fatal shade. (*The Banner of Belfast*, Port Fairy, 1857[2])

Despite the seductive romanticism of representations of Australia as a 'timeless' land, the colonial cultural landscapes encountered by settlers like William Westgarth on their arrival in the country were anything but stable. Regionally varied and subject to complex processes of social, economic, political and environmental change, these landscapes were the discursive outcome of the continuing interaction between the demands of settler capitalism on the one hand and environmental learning, the encounter with indigeneity and the uneasy interplay between imperial and colonial interests on the other. One result, in urban centres, the settled districts, the bush and the outback alike, was the creation of meanings of place that were subtle, elusive and changing. In this and the following chapter, we focus on Scottish and Irish participation in the pastoral geographies that, until the 1850s gold rushes, sustained the colonial economy in Australia and remained of major importance to it thereafter. Of particular importance in framing these landscapes was the colonial legislation that attempted to regulate social access to land ownership. This provided the basis on which squatters and pastoralists might consolidate their existing claims to land, or alternatively, find them drastically curtailed.[3] Thus the history of this legislation offers an insight into the changing opportunities for property acquisition that determined the Irish and Scottish squatters' ability to engage with the landscape through place. Here, we explore this legislative framework, its consequences for Scottish and Irish pastoral investment, and one interpretation placed on it from within the Irish emigrant community. In the following chapter we consider various narratives of environmental learning, indigenous relations and property ownership that were embodied in the pastoral places imagined and enacted by Scottish and Irish squatters within this legislative framework.

Imperial contexts: legislating for land

If, as Said suggests, in the final analysis empire was all about the 'actual geographical possession of land', then the legislative alienation of land for constitutionally desirable purposes was one of the Second British Empire's great discursive themes, albeit one which led to very different outcomes in the colonies of white settlement and the British Isles.[4] The place identities imagined and inscribed by Irish and Scottish settlers in Australia represented one outcome of the varied processes of territorial acquisition that characterised this particular discourse. The nature of this territorial aggrandisement depended on the colonial relationship in each area, but was invariably characterised by a racial or ethnic subtext. In the Australian colonies the prior claims of the indigenous inhabitants were simply ignored, and the political debate over property rights and social access to land was an internal one within the white settler community. In Ireland, the land debate invoked different claims to ethnic identity and political legitimacy; in Scotland, it embodied an encounter between indigenous cultural authenticity and modernity. In India, both under the East India Company Raj (to 1858) and in the modern colonial state that followed, the frequent employment of indirect rule, coupled with the absence of widespread land alienation, ensured that European settlement remained a matter of cantonments, civil lines and coastal enclaves.[5] In tropical Africa, too, the extensive territories incorporated within the British Empire by the end of the nineteenth century were generally administered rather than widely settled. Only in environmentally favourable areas such as Kenya's 'White Highlands' did widespread European settlement occur.[6] By contrast, in both hemispheres, the neo-Europes of the temperate zone offered forest and grassland environments which were regarded as ecologically less hostile to white settlement than the tropics, and more conducive to culturally familiar forms of agrarian production.[7] Accordingly, in these zones, settler colonies such as Victoria, New South Wales, New Zealand or Upper and Lower Canada developed extensive pastoral and agricultural systems that encouraged progressively wider European settlement.

These transformations were facilitated by imperial and colonial land policies which invoked the power of the state, individual economic self-interest and a discourse of civilising improvement to re-inscribe the landscape with colonial meaning.[8]

In Australia, the sequence of land legislation as an instrument of sometimes conflicting imperial and colonial policies is well attested. Earlier representations of the initial British penal settlement in New South Wales as a mere dumping ground for convicts no longer transportable to the lost American colonies have given way to a more nuanced appreciation of the economic expectations which surrounded the First Fleet, and the competing discourses of individualism and collectivism it embodied.[9] As Gascoigne has argued, the whole enterprise was grounded from the start in a deeply engrained enlightened utilitarianism that promoted rational enquiry as the basis for social progress.[10] However fictive it may have been, *terra nullius* constituted part of this ideology. It offered a belief in an 'empty land' – claimed by the Crown – whose very emptiness sanctioned the morally redemptive improvement required to bring order out of chaos and rescue both the land and its indigenous inhabitants from 'a state of nature'.[11] The ultimate goal of this redemptive act was the creation of an ordered, agricultural society. Farmers, in tilling the land, would bring it within the orbit of European knowledge and experience, and bestow upon it the mark of civilisation.[12]

Successive land policies and legislative instruments in New South Wales and Victoria (after the latter's separation as a colony in 1851) reflect the tenacious survival of this sedentary yeoman ideal in the face of environmental reality. Until the Ripon Regulations put an end to the system in 1831, land was normally allocated on the basis of free grants.[13] Initially the emphasis, officially at least, was on the creation of numerous small farms but, following Commissioner Bigge's report in 1823 into Macquarie's governorship (1810–21), this switched to the promotion of pastoralism on larger estates. These were confined within Limits of Location set in 1826 (and extended in 1829), beyond which the governor would neither sell, grant nor lease land, but within which settlers might continue to select land before survey (Figure 5.1).[14] These provisions had little effect on pastoral expansion. The illegal occupation of land without title (squatting) continued to spread beyond the proclaimed limits of settlement, driven by what Weaver describes as a 'robust cultural trait: the desire to possess territory, nurtured in a densely settled European society where land was power'.[15] The Ripon Regulations accelerated this process by requiring all remaining public land within the Limits of Location to be disposed of by auction. By 1839, most of the 1.5 million acres bought under the regulations had

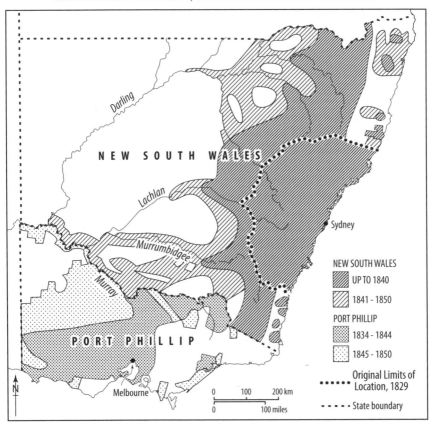

5.1 The Limits of Location to Settlement in New South Wales, 1826–29

been acquired by wealthy settlers, keen either to invest in land or consolidate existing holdings. Much of the remaining land was of inferior
quality. Faced with the prospect of having to pay substantial sums for
this, many pastoralists continued to opt to pasture their flocks illegally
beyond the limits of settlement. Following Thomas Mitchell's pioneering journey along the River Murray into Australia Felix (Western
Victoria) in 1836, increasing numbers sought out the better grasslands
of this area in which to do so, overlanding their flocks and herds south-
west along the Murrumbidgee and Murray valleys before heading south
into the Port Phillip District proper.[16]

By the 1840s, the triumph of pastoralism in south-east Australia
appeared complete. Despite the best efforts of the Colonial Office, the
Wakefieldian principle of setting a minimum price for land to encourage adequately capitalised agricultural settlement had been adopted

only in South Australia.[17] In New South Wales, governors such as Sir George Gipps (1838–46) realised the importance of pastoralism to the economy and strove – often in the face of the squatters' opposition and the imperial government's misunderstanding – to regularise the illegal squatting districts in ways that would benefit the colony at large. Annual licences were introduced for runs in these areas in 1836 and adjusted to reflect stock densities in 1839. Thereafter, successive Acts sought to redefine the balance between the imperial interest and the individual's rights in these lands. In 1842 the Imperial Waste Lands Act extended the principle of sale by auction to include them. Two years later, Gipps' Land Sales Act provided occupiers with a pre-emptive right. By purchasing 320 acres of their run at the minimum (upset) price of £1 an acre, an occupier could secure their possession of the remainder for the next eight years.[18]

The 1846 Imperial Waste Lands Act and Orders in Council of 1847 extended this right to allow the purchase of the entire run at the upset price, and introduced leases to the squatting districts alongside the principle of purchase at auction. These leases varied according to the presumed agricultural potential of the land. In the settled districts, mainly along the coast and around the larger towns and on land intended primarily for agriculture, only annual pastoral leases were available. In intermediate districts, eight-year leases were available for 1,600 acre blocks, while in unsettled districts further inland twice that area could be leased for fourteen years.[19] This legislation represented the last metropolitan attempt to solve the squatting issue. Following the grant of Responsible Government to Victoria and New South Wales in 1855, the direction of future land policy lay in colonial hands. The consequences of the 1846–47 legislation were considerable, however. By retaining the high minimum purchase price for land of £1 an acre, it enhanced both the security of tenure offered by the new pastoral leases and the viability of the leasehold system. No leaseholder would pay the upset price for land he already rented more cheaply, unless for very good reason, nor would any potential rival when the lease came up for renewal. Leases might be forfeited (often with remarkable frequency) through non-payment of rent or environmental exigency, but they were unlikely to be lost through direct commercial competition. Rather, by using their pre-emptive right to purchase those parts of their runs which contained essential water resources, for example, occupiers could reduce the likelihood of others bidding for the remainder at the end of the lease, and secure their own continued occupation.

But the pastoralists' world was changing. Among the radical social changes that were either instigated or accelerated by the discovery of

gold in New South Wales and Victoria in 1851 was a growth in democratic sentiment, allied with demands for increased self-government
and an end to transportation.[20] However well licensed, the leasehold
pastoral system, with its presumption of the rights of a small propertied elite and overtones of aristocratic privilege, formed a particular
target for goldfields egalitarianism. For many diggers, the search for
gold was simply a means to an end – the purchase of land, and in
Victoria their concerns were given increasingly effective voice from
1853 by the Melbourne press campaign to 'unlock the lands'.[21] Despite
the pastoralists' strenuous and continuing opposition, the New South
Wales and Victorian legislatures proved responsive, and policy in both
colonies shifted decisively in favour of widening social access to land.
As Waterhouse has argued, however, this was for significantly different
motives: radical agrarianism in Victoria, and more overtly anti-squatter
egalitarianism in New South Wales.[22] Over the next twenty-five years,
beginning in 1860 in Victoria and in 1861 in New South Wales, a series
of Selection Acts were passed which were designed to make available
for small-scale farming Crown Lands that had previously been leased
by pastoralists.[23]

Complex in legislative detail, widely evaded in practice and limited
and regionally uneven in effect, these Acts quickly came to be regarded
as failing in their primary purpose. Whatever gains they provided for
farmers were more than offset by the success of pastoralists in manipu-
lating them to consolidate their existing possessions.[24] In New South
Wales, for example, approximately 29 million acres were bought as
freehold during the life of the Robertson Land Acts between 1861
and 1884, but of this barely half a million acres were cultivated by
1879.[25] By 1891, the amount of alienated land in the colony had risen
to over 49 million acres, but only 21,000 new farms had been created
and fewer than 200,000 new selectors placed on the land. As Williams
notes, in areas such as the Riverina, the pastoralists' monopoly was
extreme: there, ninety-six people owned over 8 million acres.[26] In
Victoria, the Nicholson (1860) and Duffy (1862) Acts met with equally
little success, and for similar reasons. Deficiencies in the legislation
allowed pastoralists to circumvent regulations designed to restrict
their capacity to amass land. The small size of the holdings available
for selection (no more than 640 acres under the Nicholson Act), and the
onerous financial and residence obligations imposed on the generally
under-capitalised selectors acted as a further serious obstacle to their
success.[27] Five-sixths of the 900,000 acres sold under the Nicholson Act
in the Western District of Victoria were bought by pastoralists. Three-
quarters of the 1 million acres sold in the same part of the colony under
the Duffy Act were bought by fewer than 100 men.[28]

Thereafter, the pace of land alienation in Victoria quickened. The 1869 Grant Act eased the processes involved by offering free selection before survey, and by 1872 some 2 million acres had been sold.[29] Powell estimates that by 1881 approximately 20 million of Victoria's 56 million acres had been sold under successive Land Acts, at least half of them since the 1869 Act.[30] But the pastoralists' manipulation continued and the condition of many selectors did not improve. In 1879 the Royal Commission on Crown Lands in Victoria reported that, of selectors who had acquired lands under the 1869 Act, one-third had subsequently lost these; one-fifth of the remainder were heavily mortgaged, and arrears were running at nearly £200,000, or roughly one-quarter of Victoria's annual income from land.[31] In both colonies, selection as a means of promoting the radical transformation of the agrarian landscape from extensive leasehold pastoralism to intensive freehold yeoman agriculture had proved illusory. The pastoralists' hegemony had – through manipulation or purchase – either survived or, in some areas, been reinforced. In many areas this was inevitable, given the mineral-deficient nature of the soils, the seasonal variations in hydrology and the semi-arid and uncertain climate. All of this bore witness to the limited applicability to Australian conditions of a model of dense agricultural settlement based on Atlantic European experience.[32]

Nevertheless, closer – though not necessarily freehold – settlement remained the political goal in both colonies. Driven by economic pragmatism and the need to encourage population growth, closer settlement also reflected the ideas of social reformers like the American Henry George, who advocated heavy taxation on the unimproved value of all land (the 'single tax') as a means of encouraging public rather than private land ownership and ensuring that maximum social benefit accrued from it.[33] Subsequent land legislation in New South Wales and Victoria, as in Queensland and South Australia, reflected these changed priorities. In Victoria, the 1884 Land Act more or less extinguished squatting – in its earlier sense as the temporary (by now usually leasehold) occupation of Crown Land – in many districts, not least because of the growing pressure from selectors as land became scarcer. This provided the background for extensive debates in the late 1880s over the desirability of substituting leasehold tenure for selectors in place of freehold alienation, as a means of retaining public ownership of the remaining Crown Lands and controlling their future use. The continuing gross inequality in the social distribution of landownership remained a further concern. Closer Settlement Acts in Victoria from 1893 and in New South Wales from 1901 attempted to resolve both issues. Land confiscation was considered but rejected. Instead, land taxation (effective more as a threat than a reality) and land repurchase schemes were used, first to encourage and latterly to coerce pastoralists to sell freehold runs in accessible agricultural areas to government for sub-division and leasing to smallholders.[34]

Scottish and Irish parallels

As elsewhere in colonial Australia, the New South Wales and Victorian legislation represented an attempt to manage the disposal of public lands in accordance with what government perceived to be socially and politically desirable goals. Whether different sections of the public accepted the legitimacy of these depended on what they stood to gain – or lose. The pastoralists' opposition to the Selection Acts was as predictable as was their ruthless exploitation of the legislation's deficiencies – and the public outcry that ensued. This was particularly so in Victoria, where the absence of pre-1831 freeholds meant that squatters did not have the same protection against selection that some of their counterparts in New South Wales enjoyed.[35] At heart, the issue in both colonies remained one of the allocation of land within the white settler community; questions of indigenous rights and prior claims to land were soon lost sight of.[36] In Highland Scotland and – more particularly – in Ireland, the contemporaneous Land Question took on a subtly different form. In this north-western and supposedly Celtic region of the British Isles, indigenous dispossession was as much a subtext of nineteenth-century land debates as in Australia and was, arguably, equally potent. In Ireland, contemporary agitation for land reform encompassed a wide variety of social groups and regional agendas. After the Potato Famine of 1845–50, it became increasingly politicised in the cause of national autonomy, culminating in the Land War of 1879–82.[37] Despite Gladstone's Pauline conversion to Home Rule in 1886, the Irish Land Acts of 1870–1909 represented a continuing attempt by government to defuse the structural causes of this violence. In particular, they strove to decouple demands for Home Rule from wider dissatisfaction with the landlord system inherited from the Plantations.[38] As inequitable as the white pastoral hegemony established in New South Wales and Victoria, Irish landlordism was characterised by the concentration of landownership in the hands of an aristocratic and gentry elite of Scottish and English extraction. These were perceived to be separated from the mass of Ireland's (Gaelic and Catholic) population by their disproportionate wealth, their Anglicanism, ethnic origins and leisured, Anglophile *mentalité*. Although Ireland's landlord class was far from uniform or unchanging in size and composition, there was nevertheless sufficient truth in these claims to sustain an irredentist nationalist rhetoric that portrayed it as an oppressive foreign class of culturally alien, socially predatory economic parasites.[39]

Through a combination of rent control, judicial recognition of customary tenant rights and government loans to assist tenant land purchase, the major Irish Land Acts of 1870, 1881, 1885 and 1903, undermined the economic basis of the landlord class. They transformed Ireland's farming community from tenants into owner-occupiers, providing a model for land reform elsewhere in the Empire.[40] The 1881 Land Law (Ireland) Act, which offered a combination of judicial rent reviews, security of tenure and limited tenant purchase, was used as a basis for the Bengal Tenancy Act of 1885 and, closer to home, the 1886 Crofters' Holdings (Scotland) Act.[41] This was passed in an attempt to defuse the worsening violence of the Crofters' War. This had broken out in 1882 in Skye, Lewis, Tiree and elsewhere in Caithness, Ross and Cromarty, and Sutherland as crofters attempted to defend their customary rights and prevent renewed attempts at eviction by modernising landlords.[42] Contemporary events in the Irish Land War seemingly helped to radicalise the crofters' movement, but the government's attempted 'Irish' solution failed. In offering the sort of rent controls and security of tenure embodied in the 1881 Irish Land Act to the crofting counties of Orkney, Shetland and the north-west Highlands, the Scottish Act failed to address the crofters' major grievance – their lack of land. Accordingly, protest and disaffection continued into the 1890s and after.[43] As in Ireland, the crofters' protests embodied a sense of ethnic difference and indigenous authenticity encroached upon by external modernity.[44] None of this was apparent in the contemporary discourse of agrarian improvement in England, where the same sense of ethnic dispossession simply did not exist. Rural social divisions existed, certainly, and were exacerbated by periodic downturns in the agricultural economy, such as the depression of the 1890s, but these were normally expressed in economic, not ethno-cultural or religious terms.[45]

Patterns of pastoral engagement

In Australia, the opportunities offered by the colonial land legislation attracted men of varying condition. Like their landed counterparts in Britain and Ireland, Scottish and Irish pastoralists were diverse and changing in their acreable wealth and economic interests, social and cultural values and, perhaps to a lesser extent, their politics. At one end of the spectrum were people like Hugh Glass or Samuel Gordon, both from County Down, who built up extensive property portfolios in New South Wales and Victoria by the mid-nineteenth century, or Scotsman Andrew Chirnside, who by the 1860s held or owned 170,000 acres in Victoria's Western District. In 1862 Glass's mining, suburban and pastoral interests in Victoria were reputedly worth £800,000, while on his death in 1882 Gordon left pastoral property in New South Wales valued at £250,000.[46] More numerous were less wealthy pastoralists like Robert Atkinson, who owned 3,800 acres at Belfast, Western Victoria, or Peter Clement, who bought 5,000 acres at Coady Vale in Gippsland, following the death in 1872 of its original Irish owner, Patrick Coady Buckley.[47] Unlike their counterparts in Ireland and Scotland, none of these men could claim that their material presence in the colonial landscape was the embodiment of an ancient, naturalising moral order.[48] Rather, as part of a raw and recent colonial society whose claims to legitimacy rested on the morally redemptive quality of an imposed Western modernity, they and other squatters like them were complicit in an alien discourse of property ownership which transfigured Australia's ancient landscape and people. Grounded in environmental optimism and ignorance, pastoral settlement was characterised by a steep and often painful learning curve. Only gradually did squatters acquire the environmental knowledge and competencies necessary to sustain production in the face of drought, unfamiliar and infertile soils, uncertain water supplies, periodic bushfires and outbreaks of pests and disease.[49] Moreover, these environmental uncertainties were compounded by the ongoing legislative attempts described above to regulate and transform squatting districts into areas of closer settlement. The upshot was that, despite the pre-eminence accorded to settler property rights under colonial capitalism, the leasehold pastoral cartographies created by the industry were anything but stable.[50]

The point is well made by the evidence from Victoria. Between 1851 – which marked the end, more or less, of the initial pioneering phase of squatting – and 1884, when leasehold squatting was about to be extinguished by the Land Act of that year, the total number of pastoral runs in the colony rose by over three-quarters, from 933 to 1,638.[51] This increase reflected the secondary expansion of pastoralism, northwards into the Wimmera region of the River Murray basin and into the forests of eastern Gippsland and the Great Dividing Range (Figure 5.2). It also reflected the effects of government adjudication between the competing and often heroically ambitious land claims made by neighbouring pioneer squatters.[52] But within these expanding and intensifying pastoral cartographies other, countervailing processes were at work. The ongoing pursuit of the yeoman ideal through selection led to the forfeiture of over 800 run leases between 1860 and 1884, most of them in the Portland Bay and Wimmera and Murray districts. Although squatter

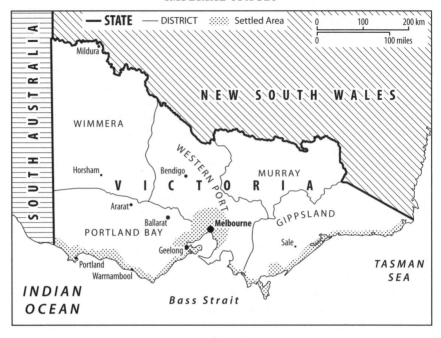

5.2 Squatting districts in Victoria

evasion and manipulation ensured that much of this land remained in the same hands, and a small minority of runs were subsequently re-let on annual grazing licences, these forfeitures still represented a net loss of pastoral leaseholds. Moreover, financial exigency and continuing environmental problems ensured that, between 1848 and 1884, the average length of individual pastoral leases was no more than five and a half years.[53]

The overall extent of Scottish and Irish involvement in these changing pastoral landscapes is reasonably well known. The conventional view is that the Scots were disproportionately involved in the industry, particularly in South Australia, Victoria and Queensland. Here, from the late 1830s onwards, the activities of Scottish joint stock and investment companies like the Clyde Company, the Aberdeen-based Scots Australian Company and the Australian Mercantile Land and Finance Company, encouraged chain-migration of Scots emigrants and capital into pastoralism. In New South Wales, particular concentrations of Scottish squatters were established by 1848 in the Hunter Valley and New England (originally New Scotland) in the north; along the Illawarra valley to the south of Sydney and in the Riverina region to the south-west, where they constituted around one-third of the squatting popu-

[116]

lation.[54] The major concentration of Catholic (and, the conventional presumption is, Irish) settlement also lay to the south and south-west of Sydney. Waldersee explains this as a consequence of the early settlement of Irish political convicts ('the men of '98') immediately south of Sydney. Their emancipation and subsequent success in obtaining land on the expanding settlement frontier, and their descendants' clannish behaviour in selectively encouraging the migration of fellow Irish men and women are all processes to which Campbell's account of Edward Ryan's pastoral empire around Boorowa amply testifies.[55]

In Victoria, Margaret Kiddle's classic account of pastoral society, *Men of Yesterday*, uses various secondary sources to suggest that three-quarters of the pioneer squatters in the Portland Bay District were Scottish.[56] Reliable data to test this estimate are hard to come by, as colonial land registries did not record the nationality of licence applicants. Surrogate surname analyses are suggestive but rely on necessarily heroic assumptions in assigning ethnicity. One such analysis of the 1851 *Return of Crown Land Licences* in Victoria suggests that Scots pastoral involvement was everywhere significantly greater than that of the Irish. Scottish occupation varied from a minimum of just under a quarter of the runs in the Murray district in the north-east, to over 40 per cent of those in the Portland Bay and Wimmera districts in the west (see Figure 5.2). The Irish figures varied from around 3 per cent of the runs in Gippsland and the Murray to 8 per cent of those in Portland Bay and the Wimmera.[57] While we clearly cannot assume that the people concerned were in every case of immediate Scottish or Irish descent, it is nevertheless noteworthy that these results are very much in line with Paul de Serville's analysis of the national origins of Victoria's squatters in 1879. Among the 360 pastoralists listed in the Government *Register of Landowners* who owned over 5,000 acres in the colony in that year, 45 per cent were Scottish and 11 per cent Irish. Between them, the Scots owned over 3 million acres, as compared to the Irish total of 640,000 acres. Individually, the Scottish runs were also marginally larger, averaging 19,500 rather than 16,400 acres.[58] De Serville's analysis provides us with only part of the picture, since he excluded 500 or so squatters listed in the *Register* who owned much smaller amounts of land and we do not know how the undoubted presence of Scots and Irish among them would have affected the overall pattern of Irish and Scottish land ownership.[59] Nevertheless, it seems clear that the difference between Scottish and Irish involvement was a real one, and may have reflected both more extensive capitalisation among the Scots and the possibility that Scottish sheep farming provided better experience for would-be emigrants than the labour-intensive potato and dairying economy of pre-Famine Ireland.[60]

Local representations: remembering the land in Belfast (Port Fairy)

But whatever the size of their holdings and the opportunities offered by their tenure and wealth, all squatters performed their identities as place in ways informed by the social behaviours, gender roles, cultural values and economic activities they encountered around them, as well as by their own memory and past experience. Or, to put it another way, in light of their diasporic roots and routes. While some emigrants may have viewed emigration as a conscious break with a past that, having offered them little, retained scant purchase on their allegiance, for others, colonial events and circumstances were invested with additional ethnic meanings precisely because they were viewed through the frame of diasporic memory.[61] Accordingly, it is plausible to argue that some at least among the Irish and Scottish Highland migrants may have viewed the conflicts and opportunities created by colonial land legislation through a lens of remembered agrarian grievance. Local newspaper representations in Belfast (Port Fairy) of the activities of landowners and of the probable effects of Haines's intended Land Bill of 1857, and the evident results of the Nicholson and Duffy Land Acts of 1860 and 1862, suggest that this was so. Given an appropriate opportunity, colonial land legislation had the capacity, seemingly, to evoke both rooted and routed forms of cultural memory among Irish settlers.

How widespread this was is hard to determine. All was contingent on place and circumstance. Belfast (so named between 1843 and 1887) served as the outport for one of a number of districts in Victoria and New South Wales, where unusually fertile soils supported relatively dense agricultural settlement, including significant numbers of Irish tenant farmers. The district around Kilmore (north of Melbourne) was similarly endowed. O'Farrell argues that these and other areas, including Bungaree near Ballarat (Victoria) and Boorowa and Kiama in New South Wales, attracted this Irish presence because of their perceived environmental similarity with Ireland and capacity to support a potato and dairying economy that was familiar to Irish emigrants.[62] These Irish communities provided a ready-made and potentially receptive audience for calls to interpret the colonial land legislation in terms of a visceral cultural memory which privileged ideas of Irish landlord predation and oppression. But this memory expressed itself differently – though not necessarily inauthentically – in the changed contexts of the colonial present.[63] These forms of representation were epitomised by *The Banner of Belfast* (1855–72), which was edited by an ex-Young Irelander, Michael O'Reilly. Like its local rival, *The Belfast Gazette* (1849–90), *The Banner* adopted a consistently anti-squatter stance.

Unlike *The Gazette*, which professed no particular ethnic affiliation, *The Banner* was also one of a number of local and regional Irish-Australian newspapers which sought, in O'Farrell's phrase, to convey an Irish rather than an Irish-Australian perspective on events in Ireland and Australia. They included, notably, the *Australasian* (later *Sydney*, then *Morning*) *Chronicle* (1839), the *Sydney Freeman's Journal* (1850), the Melbourne *Catholic Tribune* (1853) and *Advocate* (1868), and O'Reilly's own subsequent short-lived venture in the same city, *The Irishman* (1872–73).[64]

How far individual papers in this self-consciously 'Irish' press in Australia succeeded in influencing their readership with a particular Irish imaginary is uncertain. Authorial intent and readership positionality are rarely perfectly aligned. In the case of *The Banner*, O'Reilly's criticism of the squatters' landed hegemony was given local colour by the highly personal editorial attacks he made on the activities of three other Irishmen: James Atkinson, William Rutledge and R. H. Woodward. Born in County Armagh to a professional family, Atkinson arrived in Sydney aged 24 in 1830. A year previously, the similarly aged Rutledge had been persuaded by his uncle, a retired military surgeon, to leave the family farm in County Cavan and join him in Parramatta. Atkinson, too, took advantage of existing family networks to join his brother-in-law, Colonel William Ward, in the same town.[65] Both Atkinson and Rutledge proved financially astute, and by 1844 each had taken advantage of legislation introduced by the New South Wales government in 1841 to form syndicates to invest in Special Surveys.

By purchasing a Land Receipt for at least 5,120 acres (at the upset price of £1 an acre) from either the colonial government in Sydney or the Colonial Land and Emigration Commissioners in London, investors could have that amount of land surveyed in a locality of their choice, provided that this was at least five miles distant from existing major towns.[66] Altogether, some ten Special Surveys are known to have been gazetted in New South Wales, each with the intention of encouraging well-capitalised agricultural settlement. Initially Atkinson attempted to obtain a Survey at Two Fold Bay, on the southern New South Wales coast, while Rutledge was involved in protracted negotiations for Surveys in Gippsland and near Geelong, both of which he eventually abandoned. In naming his final purchase Belfast, Atkinson indulged in just one of a series of Irish toponymic inscriptions in the district. Rutledge's Farnham Survey lay adjacent to the east, and this, too, was conceivably a toponymic reference to the landed estate of that name in County Cavan. It included eight square miles of the best agricultural land in the colony. Rutledge's other Special Survey, at Kilmore, was similarly well endowed.[67]

In effect, the Special Survey legislation provided investors with the opportunity to act as fee-simple landlords to what the government hoped would become closely settled agricultural communities of tenant farmers (the yeoman ideal in yet another guise). The presence of significant numbers of Irish-born tenants on the Belfast and Farnham Surveys gave particular colour to this relationship, and provided the context for O'Reilly's attacks on Atkinson and Rutledge. By 1857, perhaps 40 per cent of the local population were Irish-born, some, according to local memory, brought out directly from Ireland by Rutledge.[68] The narratives of place performed in Belfast (Port Fairy) by these groups were framed and inflected by a disbursement of landlord authority that was similar in many ways to that customarily exercised in Ireland. As fee-simple landowner and patron, Atkinson laid out his town and endowed it with sites for churches and other public buildings in a manner typical of improving urban landlords in Ireland. Like Rutledge on the Farnham Survey, he also offered tenures that would have been instantly familiar to Irish emigrants: twenty-one-year building leases in Belfast and con-acre for agricultural smallholders. Additionally, after a brief period during which Rutledge acted as his middleman and chief merchant tenant in the town, in 1848 Atkinson appointed his nephew, R. H. Woodward, to act as his resident agent in Belfast. Woodward held this position until 1869, exercising day to day managerial control and occupying various positions of local governmental authority very much in the manner of Irish land agents.[69]

The Banner's critique of these practices located them within its broader criticism of squatting in general. Both critiques were morally charged and grounded in an explicit invitation to the paper's readership to interpret colonial events through the lens of memory. For O'Reilly the danger was clear enough: the erection of a landlord class in Australia whose monopoly of land ownership would allow it precisely the same latitude for unilateral and – in his view – predatory action that had characterised its counterpart in Ireland and the Scottish Highlands. Local events on the Belfast and Farnham Surveys merely demonstrated the probability of this happening. In February 1857, for example, O'Reilly invoked the different ethnic background of local tenants to highlight their present shared experience of the 'evils' of colonial landlordism:

> 'Homesteads for working classes'. Such is the alluring title of an advertisement of an auction by R. H. Woodward at Yangery! . . . If we mistake not, there are some of the honest 'working classes' at the present moment about to surrender their 'homesteads' to this grasping agent . . . These hardy but unfortunate sons of toil, many of whom left their cosy English cottages, where at least they did not fear the frown of the landlord or

the 'monstrous visage' of his hungry agent, who perhaps heard only such things (sceptically as they would listen to ghost stories) existing in Ireland or the highlands of Scotland, came to this land of plenty and after stepping from the immigrant ship, and toiling some two or three years from morn to night under summer sun and winter rain, now find the little homestead they raised by their savings clutched in the merciless grip of landlordism. This is the man who will now provide 'homesteads for the working classes'! But there is a Road Board election at hand and this is bait. Every man who has erected a homestead on land on which he has the slightest hold has but riveted his chains![70]

Several authorial subtexts are evident here: O'Reilly's apprehension of re-created Old World social barriers; his emphasis on class as much as ethnicity; his recognition of politically motivated tenurial relations in the Irish mode; but above all, his representation of Irish landlordism as preying promiscuously upon English tenants. In this way the traditional stereotype of predatory English landlordism in Ireland is neatly inverted, while retaining its oppressive authority in the colonial context. We may detect here a diasporic consciousness on O'Reilly's part: an awareness that the landlordism which played such an antagonistic role in his own remembered past in Ireland mutated to take on a different colonial form that was still, nevertheless, recognisably familiar. In short, the translation of landlordism from Ireland to Australia was, as so often the case, culturally transformative.

But for O'Reilly and *The Banner*, landlordism, whether in the Old World or the New, remained an essentially malign social force and was represented as such during the early life of the paper. In April 1857, following the defeat in the Legislative Assembly of Sir John O'Shanassy's ministry (which *The Banner* had supported) by adherents of the previous Haines administration (which it had not), *The Banner* alleged that an unholy combination of squatting and political interests had sought to foment sectarian discord in order to protect the pastoralists' land monopoly. This was a period of considerable political turmoil in Victoria, with six short-lived ministries between 1856 and 1861.[71] By alleging that the short-lived O'Shanassy government in the spring of 1857 had been intent on establishing a Catholic Irish hegemony in Victorian politics, the squatting interest and its adherents in the pro-Haines press (notably *The Melbourne Argus*) had, *The Banner* claimed, tried to distract the electorate from the real issue of land ownership.[72] The paper continued:

Hear this, ye toiling slaves who tolerate every scheming land jobber who tells you that when you want land you must go to an auction and submit to competition with them, while they are to plunder you and your posterity of ten millions of acres – not purchased at auction – but

[121]

smuggled by act of parliament from the people. Can you now see why these fellows would set you all fighting about straws? They would set Irish at English and English at Scotch, because if they can induce you to fight about what particular degree of latitude or longitude you were born in; whether your ancestors were Saxons or Celts – whether you believe in seven sacraments or two; whether you adopt the Thirty-Nine Articles or the Westminster Confession; or believe in latter day saints – if we say the squatters and land jobbers and place hunting schemers who have been rushing the public treasury for the last seven years can get you to fight about these things they will have time (while you are squabbling) to make away with the lands, to tax your industry – to leave you landless and penniless – to create an odious tyrant aristocracy, risen from the scum of society, who will rule you and plunder you (as in England and Ireland and without the resources of these countries to sustain you), one half of you will be condemned to poor houses and the other half to support them . . . We boldly assert that this is the real issue of the present struggle . . . It is utterly false to say an attempt has not been made to excite religious and national feuds to divide the people and distract their attention from the real designs of their enemies to possess themselves of the lands of the colony . . . If some people really desire to hate each other 'for the love of God', to fight about their religious tenets . . . If they will fight about their respective countries, which they loved so well that they fled them as they would a pestilence, if as we say some will persevere in this course, let them agree to a truce until the land question is settled and not play the game of the squatters.[73]

Once again, this representation of colonial landlordism employs rhetoric that does not always sit easily with contemporary nationalist images of landlordism in Ireland that O'Reilly himself subsequently used. For example, in contrast to the binary essentialism of much of the language of nineteenth-century land reform in Ireland, there is no assumption here of a simple denominational equivalence between Protestantism and landlordism, on the one hand, and Catholicism and tenant status, on the other.[74] Rather, the squatters and their allies are represented as a predatory economic class, capable of attempting to repress anyone with aspirations to land ownership, irrespective of their religious affiliation or ethnicity. English and Irish, Protestants, Presbyterians and Catholics, all are held to be equally vulnerable to the squatters' manipulation simply by virtue of their non-elite economic status. Yet the references to ethnic memory, religious denomination and national origin also defined these other forms of difference among the groups in a quite explicit way. The text acknowledges not only that these ethno-religious differences existed as a discordant element within colonial society, but that they were also primordial, connecting these settlers' past with their present. O'Reilly, it would appear, employed a colonial imaginary of landlordism that was truly diasporic. While it framed his own (and others') current encounter with the social consequences of colonial land policy in light of the 'there and then' of memory, it also acknowledged that these encounters took on a different form to those in the remembered past.

Nevertheless, the 'backward look' was still evident in *The Banner*'s subsequent representations of Duffy's Land Act in 1862, but much more so in its analyses of land-related events in Ireland generally. Initially, *The Banner* welcomed Charles Gavan Duffy's arrival in Melbourne in 1856 and his early entry into Victorian politics, not only on the grounds of his Young Ireland pedigree, but also because of his non-sectarian approach to Catholic rights in the colony and his opposition to the 1857 Haines Land Act.[75] As Duffy's political career developed, however, *The Banner*'s early high expectations of him as an acclaimed land reformer – which were framed with reference to his (assumed) experience of Irish landlordism – gave way to reproach as the deficiencies in his own 1862 Land Act became apparent. Commenting in May 1858 on reports of the Derryveagh evictions in County Donegal, the paper made explicit the insights it thought Duffy (who was by then Minister for Lands in the second O'Shanassy administration) might have on these, and the lessons he should learn:

> We copy the following excellent article from the Melbourne Age in reference to the late evictions in the County Donegal, and other miseries from the same prolific source of national misery – landlordism. Taken in conjunction with the signs of the times in our own district, we think the time has come for our legislators to ameliorate by some tenant protection enactment, the evils which are distinctly traceable to legislative blundering and jobbery in dealing with public lands. Mr Duffy justly regarded landlordism as the main cause of the miseries of his countrymen at home, and we presume his sagacity as a statesman will point out to him that the same effects may result from the same causes in Australia.[76]

The Derryveagh evictions, like the regional harvest failures and distress in Ireland in 1862, offered an opportunity for *The Banner* to reassert its convictions concerning the malign intent of Irish landlordism. In August 1858, the paper appealed to its readership's own experience of this to validate the continuing reports of distress in Donegal: 'No one who knows anything of the workings of Irish landlordism and the wretched condition to which it has reduced the Irish peasantry can doubt the truth of the statements respecting the sufferings of the Donegal victims.'[77]

Four years later, the paper went further, and gave this sort of authenticating memory a moral charge while locating it within a specific ethno-religious frame. Describing the effects of the 1862 harvest failure in parts of Ireland, it asserted:

> To the humane efforts of every country but especially their countrymen in Australia do these starving people appeal for food. How lightly do hundreds of them squander more than would suffice to relieve the sufferings of one of these families who pine in hunger. The aged parents sent to die by the ditch side by the landlord or his agent, the grown up sons and daughters emigrated, and none but the helpless little ones left, who writhe in hunger by their sides . . . Collections will be made in all the catholic churches in the colony . . . To give liberally – to give promptly – is the duty of all, but more especially it is the duty of the countrymen and co-religionists of the starving poor, whose piercing wails come across the ocean from the south and west of Ireland.[78]

Here, explicitly, is an elision between religious affiliation, social oppression and economic vulnerability. In this representation, the suffering in Ireland is located within one particular denominational community, and so too is the intended colonial relief. Colonial prosperity, unimagined in Ireland, carried – according to *The Banner* – a moral obligation to the remembered familial past. By implication, therefore, the agents of this oppression, the landlord and his agent, are othered in religious, kinship and cultural terms, just as the adult siblings of the most innocent young victims of this injustice are portrayed in terms of an immediately understood exilic family victimhood. All of this is far removed from the more inclusive victim imagery that O'Reilly employed in 1857 in his representations of the dangers of colonial landlordism. In re-engaging with Irish landlordism, O'Reilly reverts to the more essentialist tone he had employed in his capacity as chairman of the local Donegal Relief Committee in 1858.[79] On each occasion, the Ireland O'Reilly remembered was a subjective construction of his own imagination, simply one among many possible Irelands carried in the memories of Irish emigrants to Australia. They are a reminder, nevertheless, of the rootedness of O'Reilly's own colonial imaginary of land and landlordism, and of the sense, issuing from this, of dispossession and of opportunity grasped in exile, which he invited his readership to share.

One irony, however, is inescapable. At much the same time as O'Reilly was inviting *The Banner*'s readership to share in his remembered Ireland, the limitations of Charles Gavan Duffy's Irish past in equipping him to deal with the land question in Victoria were becoming increasingly apparent. As O'Farrell notes, the magnitude of the Duffy Land Act's failure to provide cheap land for selectors was heightened by the expectations raised by Duffy's own rhetoric, not least in Ireland, where his Act was widely represented as a land charter for the

Irish poor.[80] Duffy subsequently laid the blame for his Act's failure on the errors and omissions made by the lawyers drafting it, and the strict legal interpretation of these subsequently insisted upon by government law officers and other legal advisers, which had the effect of negating the Act's intended purpose. On the other hand, Duffy still thought its fundamental principle, the orderly transfer of land from the squatting to the agricultural interest while making fair provision for the squatters' existing investment, to be justified. He acknowledged, too, his original intention 'to see a multitude of my own countrymen, who had been driven from the land in Ireland, find a safer and more prosperous home on the genial soil of Victoria'.[81]

The Banner's assessment was more ambivalent. Initially, the paper was surprisingly conciliatory towards the squatting interest, particularly given its continuing strictures against Irish landlordism in general and the failure of the earlier 1860 Nicholson Land Act to promote a significant expansion in agricultural selection.[82] Welcoming the Duffy Act's intention to widen social access to land ownership, the paper claimed that it had no objection to pastoralism *per se*, but simply to the exclusive land rights pastoralists claimed:

> Any attempt to open the pastoral lands of the colony is denounced as an infringement of the 'property' of squatters and an innovation of their rights; we must repudiate any desire to do them an injustice or drive them from their holdings merely for the purpose of letting others take their place. We regard the squatting interest as one which should be carefully conserved at this stage in our progress, as essential to the present well being of the colony. But we also repudiate any exclusive rights which the present occupants of the pastoral lands may claim thereto. They have no more right to exclude others from possession than others have to drive them out from possession . . . [83]

Thereafter, *The Banner* remained cautious, and certainly did not acclaim the Act as being self-evidently favourable to Irish selectors in the way that Duffy implied. Although the paper eventually reluctantly accepted that ten-year leases were necessary to ensure continued squatter investment on runs not opened for selection, it remained critical of the large amount of land to be thrown open and the short time scale for this, warning that both could lead to a glut of land and consequent speculation.[84] It also remained convinced that however judicious the provision for pastoral interests might be, this completely contravened the spirit of Duffy's unequivocal opposition to the 1857 Haines Land Act, from which he had gained much early political support. On that occasion Duffy had made it clear that 'nothing deserved the name of a settlement . . . which did not terminate, on whatever basis appeared equitable, but terminate at once and for ever the claims of a handful of graziers to the whole territory of the colony'.[85] Nevertheless, by September 1862, shortly after the Act became law, and despite the growing evidence for the squatters' widespread 'dummying' and other forms of evasion, *The Banner*'s assessment of its initial effect remained sympathetic. Although the Act was 'not the masterpiece of legislation it was represented to be', and had manifestly failed in its professed aim of 'providing homes for the people' and 'excluding capitalists', it might still benefit the colony by securing the pastoral interest, providing funds for roads and other improvements and for immigration. The paper continued, 'we feel . . . certain that in opening up the country and bringing population to our shore, [the Act's] disadvantages will be fully counterbalanced.'[86]

The Banner maintained its qualified support for Duffy's Land Act in the face of mounting press criticism of the Act's failure to prevent squatters from consolidating their existing runs in the areas opened for selection, or speculators from amassing lands there. In this we may detect a significant shift in the paper's position. In dealing with this latest manifestation of colonial land policy, *The Banner* employed rhetoric that was inclusive not merely of would-be selectors of all origins, but also, increasingly, of the pastoralists or squatters themselves. Their attempts at engrossment were now represented as a legitimate defence of their runs against predation by land-jobbers.[87] All of this was a long way from the paper's strident anti-squatter language of the late 1850s, embodied in its critique of Atkinson and Rutledge. But it was this local embodiment of landlordism within a recognisably translated Irish context that may provide the explanation for *The Banner*'s altered perspective. By September 1862, these local contexts with their resonances of a remembered Irish past had altered radically. Earlier that year, William Rutledge's merchant firm had collapsed, a victim of the current agricultural depression, while two years previously both he and James Atkinson had begun the sale of tenancies on their respective Farnham and Belfast Surveys under the provisions of the Nicholson Land Act.[88] Consequently, the local narratives of place which supported O'Reilly's claims of a hostile colonial landlordism in the late 1850s no longer did so as clearly by the early 1860s. Local manifestations of allegedly malign landlordism were no longer so apparent, nor provided so immediate a target. Arguably, this allowed *The Banner* to qualify its representation of the squatting class. In contrast, the discursive networks linking O'Reilly, his paper, its readership and their locality with Ireland could still be enacted in the same essentialist way as before. The continuing narrative of Victoria's land question might well provide an opportunity for O'Reilly's paper to demonstrate the contingent nature of his colonial consciousness, but the rooted part of this remained locked in memory, and ensured that his remembered Ireland changed but little.

Summary

The land legislation described in this chapter constituted one of the discursive networks of empire that, we argue, were important in framing the place narratives created by Irish and Scottish settlers in Australia. Nineteenth-century Land Acts in Victoria and New South Wales, like their counterparts in Ireland and Scotland, were designed by government to achieve politically desirable social and economic change. In Ireland, the great flurry of land legislation introduced by Gladstone at the close of the century was intended to defuse a growing political and constitutional crisis, as well as stem the tide of nationalist-inspired agrarian violence. In Highland Scotland, too, the government's immediate concern during the Crofters' War was the widespread and often violent expression of peasant discontent at the progressive inroads made by agrarian capitalism into their traditional way of life. In New South Wales and Victoria, on the other hand, the land legislation evolved over a longer period and was designed to bring about a progressive and orderly adjustment to the balance between early established and exclusive rights of private property and the public interest in the land.

In all three countries there was an implicit ethnic – and in the case of the colonies, racial – subtext. In New South Wales and Victoria, these legislative attempts at property adjustment were the exclusive preserve of the white settler community, and were made on an economic and social basis. They created pastoral cartographies that were fundamentally unstable, but in which the Scots in particular figured to a disproportionate extent. In Ireland and Scotland, similar legislation invoked differing claims to ethnic authenticity and political legitimacy. The presence of significant numbers of Irish settlers in the colonies ensured a potentially receptive audience for these contested metropolitan readings, but all depended on individual circumstance. At Belfast (Port Fairy), the creation of the Belfast and Farnham Special Surveys permitted the erection of tenurial structures and practices which closely replicated experience in Ireland, and perhaps for this reason the issue of remembered landlordism was especially potent. How widespread this particular form of contested memory was is not certain, but its clear articulation at Belfast (Port Fairy) suggests its potential wherever local circumstance permitted. And here lies the nub of our argument. White settler experience of empire was essentially an experience of the local, however much framed by discursive networks and impulses of the sort described in this chapter. The material places through which Irish and Scottish and other settlers enacted and inscribed their lives were essentially loosely bounded local worlds which, as this chapter has shown, sustained a variety of sometimes conflicting and certainly changing meanings for those whose lives connected through them. For Scottish and Irish squatters these 'loosely bounded local worlds' centred on the pastoral properties they acquired under the changing provisions of the land legislation. What narratives of identity did these embody?

Notes

1   William Westgarth, *Victoria; late Australia Felix or Port Phillip District of New South Wales Being an Historical and Descriptive account of the Colony and its Gold Mines* (Edinburgh, 1853), p. 89.
2   *The Banner of Belfast*, Editorial, 27 November 1857.
3   Originally, 'squatters' were graziers who illegally occupied (without licence) Crown Lands beyond the Limits of Location in New South Wales. As their presence became accepted as a *fait accompli* by colonial governors and their holdings regulated, so the term entered more general currency as a synonym for pastoralists holding land on all forms of tenure.
4   E. Said, *Culture and Imperialism* (New York, 1994), p. 78. See also D. Cannadine, *The Decline and Fall of the British Aristocracy* (New Haven and London, 1990), pp. 54–71; R. Douglas, *Land, People and Politics. A History of the Land Question in the United Kingdom, 1878–1952* (London, 1976).
5   B. D. Metcalf and T. R. Metcalf, *A Concise History of India* (Cambridge, 2002), pp. 91–122.
6   P. Burroughs, 'Imperial Institutions and the Government of Empire', in A. Porter (ed.), *The Oxford History of the British Empire. Volume III The Nineteenth Century* (Oxford, 1999), pp. 191–4; T. C. McCaskie, 'Cultural Encounters: Britain and Africa in the Nineteenth Century', in *ibid.*, pp. 644–89.
7   B. R. Tomlinson, 'Economics and Empire: The Periphery and the Imperial Economy', in Porter (ed.), *The Oxford History of the British Empire. Volume III*, pp. 55–6.
8   R. Cole Harris, 'How Did Colonialism Dispossess? Comments from an Edge of Empire', *Annals of the Association of American Geographer*, Vol. 94, No. 1 (2004), pp. 165–82.
9   A. Atkinson, *The Europeans in Australia, A History. Volume One. The Beginning* (Oxford, 1997), pp. 3–18; *Idem*, 'Conquest', in D. M. Schreuder and S. Ward (eds), *The Oxford History of the British Empire Companion Series. Australia's Empire* (Oxford, 2008), pp. 49–53; R. Waterhouse, 'Settling the land', in *ibid.*, pp. 54–5; *Idem*, *The Vision Splendid. A Social and Cultural History of Rural Australia* (Fremantle, 2005), pp. 18–19.
10 J. Gascoigne, *The Enlightenment and the Origins of European Australia* (Cambridge, 2002), *passim*.
11 M. Williams, 'More and Smaller is Better: Australian Rural Settlement 1788–1914', in J. Powell and M. Williams (eds), *Australian Space. Australian Time. Geographical Perspectives* (Melbourne, 1975), pp. 61–103, citing J. F. Bennett, *An Historical and Descriptive Account of South Australia founded on the Experience of Three Years' Residence in that Colony* (London, 1843), p. 43.
12 Gascoigne, *The Enlightenment*, pp. 69–102; J. M. Powell, *An Historical Geography of Modern Australia. The restive fringe* (Cambridge, 1988), pp. 30–66; Williams, 'More and Smaller', pp. 61–103.

13   P. Burroughs, *Britain and Australia 1831–1855. A Study in Imperial Relations and Crown Lands Administration* (Oxford, 1967), pp. 35–58.

14   *Ibid.*, pp. 120–30; D. N. Jeans, 'The Impress of Central Authority', in Powell and Williams, *Australian Space*, pp. 5–9; Waterhouse, *The Vision Splendid*, pp. 20–1. For a study of the extent to which British agrarian social practices were adopted at this time in these areas, see A. Atkinson, *Camden. Farm and Village Life in Early New South Wales* (Melbourne, 1988), *passim*.

15   J. C. Weaver, 'Beyond the Fatal Shore: Pastoral Squatting and the Occupation of Australia 1826–1852', *The American Historical Review*, Vol. 101, No. 4 (October 1996), pp. 981–1007. This effectively amounted to New South Wales's first land boom, driven by the inflow of speculative capital. See D. N. Jeans, *An Historical Geography of New South Wales to 1901* (Sydney, 1972), pp. 135–56.

16   Burroughs, *Britain and Australia*, pp. 35–58; J. M. Powell, *The Public Lands of Australia Felix* (Melbourne, 1970), pp. 12–20; Stephen N. Roberts, *The Squatting Age in Australia 1835–1847* (Melbourne, 2nd edn, 1970), pp. 168–70.

17   Burroughs, *Britain and Australia*, pp. 169–251.

18   *Ibid.*, pp. 296–330.

19   Powell, *Public Lands*, pp. 26–30; Williams, 'More and Smaller', pp. 68–9.

20   The literature on the discovery of gold in Australia and its consequences is extensive. Standard accounts include G. Blainey, *The Rush that Never Ended: A History of Australian Mining* (3rd edn, Melbourne, 1978); and N. Keeting, *History of the Australian Gold Rushes* (Hawthorn, 1967). For more recent surveys see G. Blainey, *A History of Victoria* (Cambridge, 2006), pp. 39–58; and D. Day, *Claiming a Continent. A New History of Australia* (4th edn, Sydney, 2005), pp. 115–31. For a collection of revisionist essays, see I. McCalman, A. Cook and A. Reeves (eds), *Gold. Forgotten Histories and Lost Objects of Australia* (Cambridge, 2001).

21   T. Dingle, *The Victorians. Settling* (Sydney, 1984), pp. 60, 89; Powell, *Public Lands*, pp. 66–7.

22   Dingle, *Settling*, pp. 58–76; Waterhouse, 'Settling the Land', pp. 65–7.

23   Powell, *Public Lands, passim*; Waterhouse, *The Vision Splendid*, pp. 25–31, 86–9.

24   B. Gamage, 'Who Gained, and Who Was Meant to Gain, from Land Selection in New South Wales?' *Australian Historical Studies*, Vol. 24, No. 94 (April 1990), pp. 104–22.

25   M. E. Robinson, 'The Robertson Land Acts in New South Wales, 1861–84', *Transactions of the Institute of British Geographers*, No. 61 (March 1970), pp. 17–33.

26   Williams, 'More and Smaller', pp. 80–1.

27   Powell, *Public Lands*, pp. 76–7, 84–8, 96, 105–9, 117–18, 123–5, 138, 128–41.

28   Dingle, *Settling*, pp. 58–63.

29   'Free selection before survey' was first introduced (in New South Wales) by the 1861 Robertson Land Act. It allowed selectors to stake claims up to a stipulated amount of any Crown Land in any area that was not already reserved, part of an existing or intended township, or in close proximity to a goldfield. See Robinson, 'The Robertson Land Acts', *passim*.

30   Powell, *Public Lands*, pp. 145–72, 180, 188.

31   *Ibid.*, pp. 191–223.

32   J. M. Powell, *Mirrors of the New World. Images and Image-makers in the Settlement Process* (Folkestone, 1977), *passim*; *Idem*, 'Enterprise and Dependency: Water Management in Australia', in T. Griffiths and L. Robin (eds), *Ecology and Empire. Environmental History of Settler Societies* (Keele, 1997), pp. 102–24; A. Young, *Environmental Change in Australia Since 1788* (2nd edn, Oxford, 2000), pp. 1–93.

33   Powell, *Public Lands*, pp. 192–200.

34   *Ibid.*, pp. 191–223.

35   B. Kingston, *A History of New South Wales* (Cambridge, 2006), pp. 64–6.

36   R. Foster, 'Coexistence and Colonisation on Pastoral Leaseholds in South Australia, 1851–1899', in J. McLaren, A. R. Buck and N. E. Wright (eds), *Despotic Dominion.*

Property Rights in British Settler Societies (Vancouver, 2005), pp. 248–65; A. McGrath (ed.), *Contested Ground. Australian Aborigines under the British Crown* (Sydney, 1995).

37 P. Bew, *Land and the National Question in Ireland 1858–1882* (Atlantic Highlands, 1979), *passim*; Philip Bull, *Land, Politics and Nationalism. A Study of the Irish Land Question* (Dublin, 1996); K. Theodore Hoppen, *Ireland since 1800: Conflict and Conformity* (London, 1989), pp. 83–109; T. Garvin, *The Evolution of Irish Nationalist Politics* (Dublin, 1981), pp. 53–88.

38 In a voluminous literature on Irish landlordism, useful general summaries include T. Barnard, *Making the Grand Figure. Lives and Possessions in Ireland, 1641–1770* (New Haven and London, 2004); L. J. Proudfoot, 'Spatial Transformation and Social Agency: Property, Society and Improvement, c. 1700 to 1900', in B. J. Graham and L. J. Proudfoot (eds), *An Historical Geography of Ireland* (London, 1993), pp. 219–57; W. E. Vaughan, *Landlords and Tenants in Ireland 1848–1904* (Dundalk, 1984); *Idem, Landlords and Tenants in Mid-Victorian Ireland* (Oxford, 1994).

39 For contrasting perspectives on these readings, see: T. J. Hughes, 'The Estate System of Landholding in Nineteenth-century Ireland', in W. Nolan (ed.), *The Shaping of Ireland. The Geographical Perspective* (Cork, 1986), pp. 137–50; L. Proudfoot, 'Hybrid Space? Self and Other in Narratives of Landownership in Nineteenth Century Ireland', *Journal of Historical Geography*, Vol. 26, No. 2 (2000), pp. 203–21.

40 The classic survey of the Irish Land Legislation remains B. Solow's *The Land Question and the Irish Economy, 1870–1903* (Cambridge, MA, 1971). See also Vaughan, *Landlords and Tenants*, pp. 177–216.

41 Cannadine, *Decline and Fall*, pp. 60–1; D. Fitzpatrick, 'Ireland and the Empire', in Porter (ed.), *The Nineteenth Century*, pp. 517–20; M. Lynch (ed.), *Oxford Companion to Scottish History* (Oxford, 2007), pp. 373–6.

42 J. G. Kellas, 'The Crofters' War, 1882–1888', *History Today*, Vol. 12 (1962), pp. 281–8.

43 Lynch (ed.), *Scottish History*, pp. 373–6; A. G. Newby, *Ireland, Radicalism and the Scottish Highlands, circa 1870–1912* (Edinburgh, 2007), *passim*.

44 T. M. Devine, *The Great Highland Famine: Hunger, Emigration, and the Scottish Highlands in the Nineteenth Century* (Edinburgh, 1988), pp. 245–72; E. Richards, 'Leaving the Highlands. Colonial Destinations in Canada and Australia', in M. Harper and M. E. Vance (eds), *Myth, Migration, and the Making of Memory: Scotia and Nova Scotia 1700–1900* (Halifax/Edinburgh, 1999), pp. 105–23.

45 F. Crouzet, *The Victorian Economy* (London, 1982), pp. 147–84; C. Ó Gráda, 'Agricultural Decline, 1860–1914', in R. Floud and D. McCloskey (eds), *The Economic History of Britain Since 1700. Vol. 2. 1860 to the 1970s* (Cambridge, 1981), pp. 175–97; J. R. Walton, 'Agriculture and Rural Society 1730–1914', in R. A. Dodgshon and R. A. Butlin (eds), *An Historical Geography of England and Wales* (2nd edn, London, 1990), pp. 323–50.

46 J. Ann Hone, 'Chirnside, Andrew Spenser (1818–1890)', *Australian Dictionary of Biography*, Vol. 3 (Melbourne, 1969), pp. 391–2; J. E. Senyard, 'Glass, Hugh (1817–1871)', in *ibid.*, Vol. 4 (Melbourne, 1972), pp. 254–5; G. J. Abbott and M. Rutledge, 'Gordon, Samuel Deane (1811–1882)', in *ibid.*, Vol. 4 (Melbourne, 1972), p. 271.

47 P. de Serville, *Pounds and Pedigrees. The Upper Class in Victoria 1850–80* (Oxford, 1991), p. 465; *The Gippsland Times*, 'Obituary: Patrick Coady Buckley', 18 July 1872.

48 For a summary of the debate over Irish landlords' claims to authenticity in place, see L. Proudfoot, 'Hybrid Space?', pp. 203–21. For general considerations of improvement in Ireland and Scotland, see: T. Barnard, *Improving Ireland? Projectors, Prophets and Profiteers 1641–1786* (Dublin, 2008); D. Turnock, *The Historical Geography of Scotland since 1707* (Cambridge, 1982), pp. 37–96; T. C. Smout, 'The Context of the Scottish Enlightenment', in A. Broadie (ed.), *The Cambridge Companion to the Scottish Enlightenment* (Cambridge, 2003), pp. 9–30.

49 J. M. Powell, *Environmental Management in Australia, 1788–1914* (Melbourne, 1976), *passim*; L. Proudfoot and D. Hall, 'Imagining the Frontier. Environment,

Memory, and Settlement: Narratives from Victoria (Australia), 1850–1890', *Journal of Irish and Scottish Studies*, vol. 3, No. 1 (2010), pp. 27–48.

50 McLaren *et al.* (eds), *Despotic Dominion*, *passim*. These essays make the point on a comparative basis across the 'white' spaces of Empire.

51 Calculated from: Votes and Proceedings of the Legislative Council (Victoria), 'Crown Land Leases Victoria 1856', Return to Address, 8 June 1855. Tabled, 18 March 1856; R. Spreadborough and H. Anderson, *Victorian Squatters* (Melbourne, 1983).

52 Exemplified in the career of Foster Fyans. See S. Sayers, 'Captain Foster Fyans of Portland Bay District', *Victorian Historical Magazine*, Vol. 40 (1969), pp. 45–66.

53 Calculated on the basis of a 20 per cent sample of the runs gazetteered in Spreadborough and Anderson, *Victorian Squatters*.

54 M. D. Prentis, *The Scottish in Australia* (Melbourne, 1987), pp. 34–48; *Idem*, 'Lowland Scottish Immigration until 1860', in P. J. Jupp (ed.), *The Australian People. An Encyclopedia of the Nation, its People and Their Origins* (2nd edn, Cambridge, 2001), pp. 646–9.

55 M. Campbell, *The Kingdom of the Ryans. The Irish in Southwest New South Wales 1816–1890* (Sydney, 1997); J. Waldersee, *Catholic Society in New South Wales 1788–1860* (Sydney, 1974), pp. 105–59.

56 M. Kiddle, *Men of Yesterday. A Social History of the Western District of Victoria 1834–1890* (Melbourne, 1961), p. 14, n.

57 Votes and Proceedings, 'Crown Land leases'. These estimates are conservative. Surnames of probable Scottish or Irish origin were identified on the basis of D. Dorward, *Scottish Surnames* (Edinburgh, 2003), and E. MacLysaght, *The Surnames of Ireland* (6th edn, Dublin, 1985). Surnames of English origin but of widespread provenance in Ireland and/or Scotland were excluded from these totals.

58 Calculated from de Serville, *Pounds and Pedigrees*, Appendix 3, 'Landowners of Victoria in 1879', pp. 456–94.

59 *Ibid.*, Appendix 3a, 'Colonists owning less than 5,000 acres', pp. 494–502.

60 D. S. MacMillan, *Scotland and Australia 1788–1850* (Oxford, 1967), pp. 83–4; Prentis, *The Scottish*, pp. 39–41. L. Proudfoot and D. Hall, 'Points of Departure. Remittance Emigration from South-West Ulster to New South Wales in the later Nineteenth Century', *International Review of Social History*, Vol. 50 (2005), pp. 241–77.

61 P. O'Farrell, *Stories of Australian Migration* (Kensington, 1988), pp. 33–46; *Idem*, 'Landscapes of the Irish Immigrant Mind', in J. Hardy (ed.), *Stories of Australian Migration* (Sydney, 1988), pp. 33–46; *Idem*, 'Defining Place and Home. Are the Irish Prisoners of Place?', in D. Fitzpatrick (ed.), *Home or Away? Immigrants in Colonial Australia* (Canberra, 1992), pp. 1–18.

62 P. O'Farrell, *The Irish in Australia 1788 to the Present* (3rd edn, Sydney, 2000), pp. 124–8, 136–7.

63 N. C. Johnson, 'Historical Geographies of the Present', in B. Graham and C. Nash (eds), *Modern Historical Geographies* (Harlow, 2000), pp. 251–72.

64 O'Farrell, *The Irish in Australia*, pp. 108, 143, 191–2; R. B. Walker, *The Newspaper Press in New South Wales, 1803–1920* (Sydney, 1976), pp. 145–60.

65 J. W. Powling, *Port Fairy. The First Fifty Years 1837–1887. A Social History* (Melbourne, 1980), pp. 48–76; L. Proudfoot and D. Hall, 'Memory and Performance in Irish Australia: Belfast (Port Fairy), 1850–1890', in M. McCarthy (ed.), *Ireland's Heritages: Critical Perspectives on Memory and Identity* (Aldershot, 2005), pp. 69–84.

66 Proudfoot and Hall, 'Memory and Performance', pp. 91–2; Maya V. Tucker, *Kilmore on the Sydney Road* (Kilmore, 1988), pp. 32–3.

67 Tucker, *Kilmore on the Sydney Road*, pp. 36–9, 93–4; Powling, *Port Fairy*, p. 31.

68 Powling, *Port Fairy*, pp. 62–3; Proudfoot and Hall, 'Memory and Performance', pp. 69–84.

69 For a detailed case study of the urban role of Irish land agents that illustrates this comparison, see: L. J. Proudfoot, *Urban Patronage and Social Authority.*

The Management of the Duke of Devonshire's Towns in Ireland, 1764–1891 (Washington, DC, 1995).

70   *The Banner of Belfast*, Editorial, 10 February 1857.

71   S. M. Ingham, 'O'Shanassy, Sir John (1818–1883)', *Australian Dictionary of Biography*, Vol. 5 (Melbourne, 1974), pp. 378–82; D. McCaughey, N. Perkins and A. Trimble, *Victoria's Colonial Governors 1839–1900* (Melbourne, 1993), pp. 65–98.

72   *The Banner of Belfast*, Editorial, 17 and 27 March 1857.

73   *Ibid.*, Editorial, 21 April 1857.

74   For two regional studies that acknowledge these rhetorical assumptions, see D. E. Jordan Jr., *Land and Popular Politics in Ireland. County Mayo from the Plantation to the Land War* (Cambridge, 1994), and J. O'Shea, *Priest, Politics and Society in Post-famine Ireland. A Study of County Tipperary 1850–1891* (Dublin, 1983), pp. 52–118.

75   *The Banner of Belfast*, Editorial, 27 March 1857; *Ibid.*, 'Domestic Intelligence', 16 June 1857.

76   *Ibid.*, 'Landlordism in the Old Country', 13 May 1858.

77   *Ibid.*, 'Town Talk', 5 August 1858. For an analysis of the emigration of some of the Donegal victims to Australia, see B. Barrett, 'The Mystery of a Long Lost Irish Village', in C. Kiernan (ed.), *Australia and Ireland. Bicentenary Essays 1788–1988* (Dublin, 1986), pp. 207–14.

78   *The Banner of Belfast*, 'Distress in Ireland', 9 September 1862.

79   *Ibid.*, Editorial, 17 June and 5 August 1858.

80   O'Farrell, *The Irish in Australia*, pp. 134–8.

81   Charles Gavan Duffy, *My Life in Two Hemispheres*, Vol. II (London, 1898), pp. 226–35. For a relatively hostile analysis of Duffy's Land Act, see Eugene Doyle, 'Sir Charles Gavan Duffy's Land Act, 1862: Victoria through Irish Eyes', in Kiernan (ed.), *Australia and Ireland*, pp. 145–55.

82   *The Banner of Belfast*, Editorial, 7 April, 29 September and 6 October 1860.

83   *Ibid.*, Editorial, 14 January 1862.

84   *Ibid.*, Editorial, 11 February and 15 April 1862.

85   *Ibid.*, Editorial, 28 January and 25 February 1862.

86   *Ibid.*, Editorial, 16 September 1862.

87   *Ibid.*, Editorial, 23 September 1862: 'The government now needs to amend the loop-holes which squatters perforce have to exploit for their own protection of their own runs against Speculators.'

88   *Ibid.*, Editorial, 7 January 1860; 'Town Talk' 10 November 1860 and 29 April, 3 June and 24 June 1862.

CHAPTER 6

Pastoral places

At Hamilton I made the acquaintance of Acheson Ffrench of Monivae, and his large family . . . Ffrench was the type of the well-bred Irish gentleman – a most delightful man, and clever, and none more hospitable. At Monivae you got a real Irish welcome . . . [it] was run on the old generous Irish lines . . . (Cuthbert Fetherstonhaugh, Melbourne, 1917[1])

We had some of the black cricketers with us one shearing season, before they became travelling gentlemen . . . Blacks don't need to be too civilised to make good workers. I always paid any blackfellows who worked for me, putting as much of it in clothes as possible. (William Moodie, Melbourne, 1913[2])

By imposing European concepts of bounded, alienable property on an as yet barely comprehended Australian landscape, nineteenth-century land legislation in New South Wales and Victoria provided an opportunity for Irish and Scottish settlers like Fetherstonhaugh and Moodie to inscribe their identity on that landscape in an act of possession. In embodying a high level of environmental ignorance, the legislation also militated against the likelihood of the settlers' doing so in anything other than functional terms – initially at least. In displaying near-total indifference to the competing claims of existing indigenous communities, the legislation also ensured that the pioneers' environmental difficulties were likely to be compounded by potentially hostile Aborigine encounters. Thus the pastoral places created within this legislative framework by Irish and Scottish settlers formed complex and continuously changing sites of identity as the settlers' environmental experience grew, their encounters with indigenous communities widened, their colonial property relations formalised and their social networks deepened.

The Irish and Scottish squatter identities we explore here were characteristically ambiguous. They were emplaced in the landscape via the social and cultural practices that the squatters and others enacted through the material spaces of the pastoral runs, and the symbolism that was ascribed to them. Some aspects of these place narratives were common to all squatters; others were unique to, or uniquely performed by, individual Scots and Irish pastoralists. Consequently, while ethnic consciousness played its part in creating these unstable cartographies of meaning, it was never primordial or essentialist but depended, rather, on individual performance, experience and circumstance. Here we examine the narratives of meaning produced on Scottish- and Irish-owned runs in Victoria and eastern New South Wales and use this evidence to sustain our argument for the discursively framed localism of settler experience in general, and for the conditional and hybridised nature of the imagined places that embodied it.

Four narratives of place

Environmental learning

Some of the clearest evidence for the contingent nature of the narratives of pastoral place created by Scottish, Irish and other squatters in Australia derives from the environmental encounters that formed part of these. Early official and other public environmental appraisals of the colony were decidedly optimistic. They were grounded in the assumption that European knowledge and agricultural practice would be immediately transferable to this as yet unknown land. This vision was of a decidedly enlightened modernity, endowing civilisation and progress upon a land and people still in a state of Nature.[3] Thus, during his exploratory journey along the Darling and Murray Rivers into Australia Felix in 1836, the New South Wales Surveyor General, Major Thomas Mitchell, repeatedly imagined the country's future in terms of an untrammelled colonial prosperity. Detecting a Creatorial hand at work, his used a biblical imagery which constructed the future in terms of human endeavour guided by the Almighty:

> We have at length discovered a country ready for the immediate reception of civilised man and fit to become eventually one of the great nations of the earth . . . this highly interesting region lay before me, with all its features new and untouched as they fell from the hand of the Creator! Of this Eden it seemed to me that I was the only Adam, and it was indeed a sort of Paradise to me, permitted thus to be the first to explore its mountains and streams – to behold its scenery – to investigate its geological character – and finally, by my survey, to develop those natural advantages, all still unknown to the civilised world, but yet certain to become, at no distant date, of vast importance to a new people.[4]

[134]

Despite mounting evidence for climatic and other environmental variability that might render these 'Edens' less salubrious, subsequent published accounts of the colony frequently continued in this vein. Favourable comparisons were made with England and rival destinations in Australia. According to the editor of the *Port Phillip Gazette* in 1840, the pastoral potential of much of Australia Felix rivalled 'the sward of Old England . . . [while] the general characteristics of fertility, including richness of soil and abundance of pasture, place it far above the older districts [in New South Wales] in those advantages which immigrants naturally seek for'.[5] Clearly, Mitchell's imagined Eden still existed for this writer, as it did for William Westgarth when he published *Victoria: Late Australia Felix or Port Phillip District of New South Wales*, in 1853:

> The park-like open forest with its grassy carpet beneath forms a striking and unique aspect of the country, which affords pastoral facilities, ready-made, as it were, at the hand of Nature . . . [These] explain the rapid progress of these colonies . . . and more particularly of Victoria, which abounds in these pastoral lands.[6]

But, as surviving station diaries and journals make clear, this early optimism gave way to altogether more cautious assessments as squatters sought to establish viable runs and cope with a seemingly fickle and perverse environment that rendered European knowledge and experience irrelevant. The presence of adequate water supplies and good forage was of crucial importance in initial run selection, as the journals of the Henty brothers near Portland Bay in the late 1830s make clear, but offered no guarantee of future sustainability.[7] Consequently, concerns over water management and related issues of drought, bush-fires and excessive rainfall occur as a *leitmotif* in station archives throughout the nineteenth century and constitute a continuing thread of environmental anxiety within these narratives of place.[8] For example, at Dunmore, the 47,000-acre property near Port Fairy acquired by three Scottish partners, Charles MacKnight, James Irvine and William Campbell in 1842 (Figure 6.1), the early station records frame the mundane rhythms of pastoral life (fencing, clearing paddocks, mustering stock) within an acute environmental consciousness. Routine variations in the weather were recorded, as on many other stations, as a matter of course. This created a local settler environmental memory, but one couched in terms of an external objective knowledge of temperature, rainfall and wind direction, rather than subjective indigenous understanding.[9] Consequently, extreme events such as floods and bush-fires retained their capacity to surprise and threaten the European narrative of place at Dunmore, as elsewhere. For example, in September 1843 several days' 'torrential' rain breached a newly completed dam in which six months' labour had been invested, prompting Charles MacKnight to conclude that:

> This ill-fated occurrence is calculated to teach many valuable truths, touching the vanity of human wishes and endeavours in general. But in particular it should check that tendency (so incident to frail humanity) to an over-weening confidence in the success of scheme and operation ... We may read another inference ... from the circumstance of labour of weeks and months having been dissipated in a short hour, viz, that the first wicked action – the first plunge into the downward stream, may burst the barriers which it has taken a long course of good action to erect. Lastly, however zealously you may labour to effect a particular object, your labour will be unavailing unless you employ the true and legitimate means.[10]

MacKnight's reaction mirrors Rolf Boldrewood's assessment of him as a man of high moral principle and stern – though fair – integrity.[11] Both these qualities were subsequently put to the test by the bush-fires which threatened to destroy Dunmore station in 1851 and 1863. If the failure of his initial attempt at water management prompted MacKnight to reflect on the hubris and futility of human endeavour, his escape from the capricious but still mortal threat posed by bush-fires elicited an overtly religious sense of gratitude. The diary entry for 6 February 1851 is relatively laconic, but records 'Black Thursday', when numerous settlements in Victoria were destroyed by fire. 'The station nearly burnt down but was preserved with great exertion. Memorable day! The station within an ace of being burnt, much cause for thankfulness for the Providential escape ... A slight shower during the night, a perfect god-send as it will afford a chance of stopping the fires ... Some part of the run unburnt.'[12] Twelve years later, in January 1863, the threat to Dunmore was even more immediate. Earlier in the month, fires had broken out widely on adjacent runs and had moved progressively nearer the station. By Monday the 12th, all hands were fighting a fire that posed a direct threat to the buildings. This culminated the following day:

> Tuesday 13th. A very momentous day. Had the wind remained in the south-east no human exertion could have saved the station from total destruction. It pleased God to send a light breeze in the morning from the east and north. It came on very hot in the middle of the day. A heavy dew fell last night which prevented the grass from burning early. First thing in the morning marked out a line for burning a trail and cleared all the timber off it ... and afterwards began to burn a trail backwards from the creek. But then a strong south-west gale sprang up which prevented the trail being burned that way ... Before the trail was finished

a tremendous thunder storm broke, rendering the ground quite wet and effectually saving the station, which no exertion could have done without a favourable wind and rain. It is a great cause of thankfulness and gratitude to Almighty God. This the second time within a few days that the destruction of the station seemed inevitable, and yet was averted by God's mercy alone.[13]

The consistency with which MacKnight ascribed religious meaning to the environmental problems he encountered at Dunmore provides an apt reminder of the subjectivity of these environmental narratives. For MacKnight, Dunmore was a site both of environmental learning and of environmental deliverance, a reading that reflected his deeply held religious beliefs. How widespread this sort of religious construction of Nature was among Scots and Irish squatters in general is a matter for conjecture. For some, at least, the 'continuing thread of environmental anxiety', although real enough, was constructed in different ways. Thirty years later, Margaret McCann's diary offers the perspectives of a rather out-of-place young Irish woman on the environmental issues confronting the still male-gendered world of pastoralists and selectors in the 1890s. Born in Ireland ca. 1867 as Margaret Ashwood, she emigrated with her family to Australia, where her schoolmaster father settled at Archdale, a small settlement on the central Victoria goldfields. In a typical display of post-arrival Irish mobility, various members of the family also lived for a time in Sydney, where Margaret's brother established a successful general store and where she taught at a girls' school. Eventually, she married John McCann, whose father had selected land in Archdale but who, with his brother Arthur, had taken up land near Stradbroke in south Gippsland, in 1884.[14]

Margaret's diary begins in 1894 and portrays her struggling to cope with the multiple demands of young children, domestic life and a gendered division of labour that left her responsible for various ancillary agricultural activities. These were reminiscent of traditional female roles in the Irish rural economy and included butter making, poultry keeping, horticulture and milking.[15] The tensions engendered by these competing prior claims were exacerbated by her husband's frequent absences buying sheep, and also by Margaret's own constant anxious awareness of the weather. Local drought and high temperatures were carefully recorded and set against a contrapuntal theme of low water supplies. Rain, when it came, was either 'badly wanted' – and only occasionally filled their water tanks – or else disruptively heavy.[16] Other threats were more immediate. Bush-fires in 1895, 1898, 1899 and 1907 destroyed fencing, burnt paddocks and on one occasion threatened the farm buildings themselves.[17] Dingoes and feral dogs were a constant menace to the sheep that constituted the McCanns' livelihood.

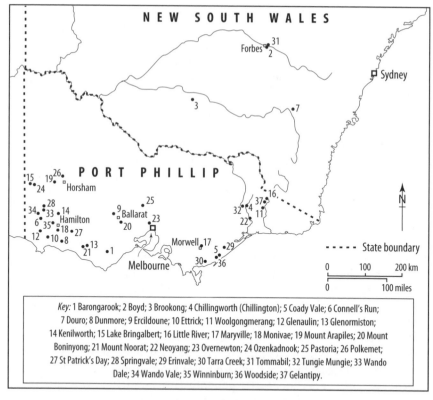

6.1 Major pastoral runs mentioned in the text

Their attacks, the consequent stock losses and the counter-measures that were taken (poisoning and shooting) were carefully detailed and constituted another subtext of continuing hardship.[18]

Despite the gradual improvement in the family's circumstances as it acquired more land, and the consistent if modest profits the property made each year, Margaret's diary suggests that Stradbroke remained for her a place of unending, wearisome toil.[19] In March 1901, seven years after her diary started, she summed up her feelings thus:

My arms ached cutting so much maize. It is hard work here, is there no end to it? I am a veritable house drudge. I love the children so that nothing I can do for them is too much, but the cows, the churning, the slopping about is too much, I am sick of it. I wish I had £200 I would buy a house in Sale and give this sort of life up.[20]

While droughts, fires and dingo predation formed a major part of her struggle, Margaret's representation of these hazards betrays no sense of the elemental that characterised Charles MacKnight's reaction to similar problems, nor yet of his sense of Divine purpose in them. Rather, she presents the continuing round of bad weather and stock losses as a pragmatic narrative of disheartening but unavoidable set-backs that hindered and circumscribed the family's attempts at improvement. The McCann's continuing involvement in the local Methodist church provided no point of reference for these encounters. For Margaret, the environmental narrative at Stradbroke was subjectively constructed in terms of its economic consequences rather than its religious content – Mammon rather than God.

Diaries such as these inevitably depict place as a narrative of the present, as they record the unfolding environmental problems and management practices on a run or farm. However unpredictable and damaging these events may have appeared to be when viewed in this way, other squatter narratives indicate that, in the longer term, hazardous environmental encounters might form a part of more positive constructions of identity. These were grounded in remembered place as part of an imaginary heroic epoch in white settlement. Charles Fetherstonhaugh, James Hamilton, and William Moodie were among a number of Irish and Scottish pastoralists with Western District connections who wrote autobiographies in the early twentieth century celebrating Australia's pioneering era and their role in it.[21] In all three accounts bush-fires are remembered as events when the extraordinary collective efforts necessary to contain the threat acted to reinforce the squatters' sense of belonging in place. At Ozenkadnook, Hamilton's station close to the South Australian border, neighbouring squatters mustered in the 1850s to fight fires approaching out of the dry Mallee scrubland to the north.[22] Twenty years later, similar co-operation was required to prevent the destruction of the station at Brookong, the 315,000-acre run in the Riverina, New South Wales, managed by Cuthbert Fetherstonhaugh:

> There was no possibility of beating the fire out, a frontal attack was impossible – no man could get near it . . . the only hope of saving the station was to burn alongside the southern track, and let the new fire work back into the big blaze . . . All hands worked like Trojans. This went on for nine days and nights, and on the ninth day we had run the fire into the main beaten Wagga road to the south . . . I can honestly say that I did as much work at the fire as any man who was at it, and beside that I had all the bossing of the show and the responsibility, and every night after the men turned in, I had to go and reconnoitre and lay schemes how to circumvent the enemy.[23]

Fetherstonhaugh's sense of involvement is palpable, and was clearly sufficient to sustain his memory of that particular enactment of place until the publication of his autobiography, *After Many Days*, in 1917. But in 1871, when the fire occurred, Brookong was for him a site of heroic collective endeavour, and one in which his own role was crucial. A squatter's agency encountering bush-fires might construct place in other ways, however. For example, William Moodie, the Scots owner of the 19,000-acre Wando Dale run in Victoria's Western District, remembered the effects of bush-fires in more hybrid terms. In his 'Reminiscences', compiled in 1914, he recalled his childhood experience of the events of 'Black Thursday' in 1851 as both exhilarating and terrifying.[24] His mature recollection of fire, on the other hand, was that it was beneficial as well as destructive. After describing a particularly extensive bush-fire in the 1850s which destroyed buildings, paddocks, fencing and livestock at Xongbool, Springvale and other runs near Wando Dale, Moodie concluded:

> [Fires] had their good side in keeping the country free from plagues . . . There is no doubt that the country is much sweetened by a good heavy fire and I saw the proof of that very plainly in the effect of the fire above mentioned . . . On the 2,000 acres that were saved, Mr Willis put the best of his wethers expecting to sell them fat. They had grass enough for double that number but in spite of that they fell away, while those in the burnt country put on condition. The lambs were the finest I have ever seen before or since.[25]

Moodie makes it clear that he and his fellow pastoralists were so taken by the beneficial effects of controlled burning that its use became widespread in the Western District, copying an indigenous practice that had modified the Australian landscape for thousands of years.[26] But neither Moodie's environmental learning nor that of the other Scottish and Irish squatters considered here was ethnically framed. Drought, fire, floods and plagues were the common lot of all European settlers. The personal constructions placed on such events by the Scots and Irish might be replicated in any ethno-cultural group. MacKnight's devout sense of Providential deliverance was hardly unique to Scottish Presbyterianism. Margaret McCann's troubled appraisal of the quality of her rural life was driven by economic hardship and personal disappointment, not by her origins in Ireland. Nor was Fetherstonhaugh's memory of his own efforts in defence of Brookong framed by his Anglo-Irish background. Rather, these and other encounters with the all-too-real physical hazards of the colonial landscape added meaning and a sense of located identity to the lives of squatters who were, in a real sense, living in the colonial present. Other narratives of place might invoke ethnic memory more strongly. The challenges of a new environment, with its need for new learning and skills, did not. What of the Irish and Scots squatters' encounters with Aborigine communities?

Indigenous engagements

Recent claims that some Irish emigrants developed a particular rapport with Australia's indigenous inhabitants because of their supposed cultural affinities and 'shared experience of English colonialism' find little support among the squatters' lives narrated here.[27] Rather, these men and women shared attitudes towards aboriginal people that were widespread among settlers. Moulded by personal experience, most indulged in a nuanced racialist discourse which distanced itself from earlier white violence towards indigenous communities, but still accepted the eventual extinction of Australia's aboriginal peoples as the inevitable outcome of their encounter with more advanced (white) races. This view was tenacious, and gave local colour to the racialism that constituted one of the Empire's discursive themes.[28] Westgarth's influential *Victoria: Late Australia Felix* spoke for many in the early 1850s. Acknowledging that 'in their natural state . . . aborigines stand out with a species of rude dignity', Westgarth nevertheless concluded that these 'barbaric excellencies' stood them in little stead in the face of the 'cold, quiet [and] merciless encroachment . . . of civilised habitation', which would soon 'drive off and exterminate their feeble and scanty race'.[29] 'Other and more favoured races' would develop the country's 'boundless resources'.[30]

Westgarth's tone throughout is one of regretful, patronising disinterest. Aboriginal people were, for him, objects of scientific curiosity whose predilection for the 'vices of civilisation', cultural dependence on 'barbaric' social practices that ran foul of civilised values and incapacity in the face of Western progress would ensure their eventual demise. 'Absurd, useless or mischievous as these superstitions or barbarities may appear to us, they are everything to the aborigines and deprived of their time-honoured practices and vocations, they live without object or motive beyond that of mere brute creation.'[31] For Westgarth, the best policy was separation. Where possible, Aborigine communities should be left to follow their traditional way of life; but in thickly colonised districts where this could not be done, 'the hand of religious zeal should minister to the scattered remnants that still linger among the resistless invaders of their soil, and that hand should at least smooth the path that is so directly leading to their extinction'.[32] In this Scotsman's colonial imaginary, at least, indigenous people had no future place.

Occasionally, other voices disagreed. As early as 1836, Joseph

Gellibrand, one-time Attorney General for New South Wales and founder member of the Port Phillip Association, professed 'not the slightest doubt but that they [the aboriginal people] may all be brought to habits of Industry and Civilisation' through agriculture, and that this would inculcate a respect for property in both Aborigines and settlers alike.[33] But Westgarth's was the hegemonic voice, and one which continued to find trenchant expression into the early twentieth century. In 1917, Cuthbert Fetherstonhaugh – who had found the fellow Irishness of other pioneer squatters so engaging – concluded that 'the whites had a perfect right to take possession of this great Continent, sparsely peopled as it was with a decadent race of savages, but little removed now from mere animals . . . Had the whites never discovered and taken possession of Australia, the blacks would never have risen any higher, and they would in time most surely have died out.'[34] Little sign here of alleged Irish-Aboriginal *rapprochement*. Rather, Fetherstonhaugh employed the same rhetoric of racial superiority and moral authority as Westgarth, but used this to draw a patronising distinction between the behaviour of 'whites' and 'blacks' in the initial racial encounter. While acknowledging the violence committed by both groups, Fetherstonhaugh held the settlers to higher account: 'I do not call the killing of whites by the blacks murder; the blacks did not know any better, poor things, and in many instances they had great provocation.'[35] For Fetherstonhaugh, Australia's indigenous people were capable neither of exploiting the land to its full potential nor of realising the extent of their own shortcomings. But these were the marks of an externally imposed modernity in which aboriginal people were, variously, both participants and victims.

It is evident, however, that Aborigine victimhood was neither quiescent nor uncontested, and this is reflected in the place narratives enacted by pioneer Scottish and Irish squatters in Victoria and elsewhere.[36] Individual attitudes and circumstance counted for much in determining the nature of the squatter–Aborigine encounter. For some early squatters, indigenous hostility marked their runs, initially, as spaces of loss and fear, sites of stock depredation and violent assault on shepherds and stations alike. For others, pastoral stations became places of cautious, mutual accommodation with local Aborigine tribes. Arguably, however, narratives of suspicion and hostility predominated, at least at first, in Victoria; or so the descriptions of pioneering squatter life collected in 1853 by Charles La Trobe, Victoria's first Lieutenant Governor, suggest. Thus, Hugh Murray, a Scotsman who had arrived from Van Diemen's Land in 1837 and established the Barongarook run on the future site of Colac, in the Portland Bay District, described the Aborigines he encountered as 'always treacherous and dishonest

... They never lost an opportunity of stealing our sheep.'[37] For John Robertson, another Scot who arrived from Van Diemen's Land in 1840 and took up the 11,000-acre Wando Vale run in the Glenelg valley, the initial encounter with indigeneity involved the murder of his shepherd, the 'wanton destruction' of a flock of 600 sheep and threats to his neighbour's wife.[38]

Other Scots and Irish sources extend these early negative narratives. James Hamilton's account of his pioneering days in Western Victoria includes a description of a punitive raid in 1845 against Aborigines who had murdered a squatter at Hynam, near Bringalbert. Writing in 1914, he represented the ensuing massacre as justifiable in its day, but less so subsequently. 'It was a bad day for the ill-fated darkies . . . [The horsemen] opened fire and many of the blacks went under. They made no show of resistance but scattered and ran for their lives . . . What happened that day is a scene from the past and a curtain is drawn over it . . . The lesson given to the blacks that day made them understand they must respect the lives of white men.'[39] Some more contemporary accounts lack Hamilton's belated scruples. In the same year as the Hynam raid, Patrick Coady Buckley recorded his attempts to stop Aborigines preying on cattle on his run at Coadyvale in Gippsland, and the casual violence this involved.

20th January 1845. Took Betty the mare and went down to the beach. I saw two blacks coming along from near the creek. I waited behind the sand hummock until they came opposite me. I then rode towards them and they took to the sea. I had pistols with me and I fired blank shots to keep them in the sea, which I did for about four hours, and drove them along the water to near the mouth of the Merriman creek which is about a mile. The blackfellow got very weak. The gin seemed quite strong. I pointed to her several times to leave but she stuck to the blackfellow faithfully. At last she thought there was no chance for him consequently she left him. At this time he seemed nearly drowned in the breakers. I rode into the surf after him, got a rein round his neck and pulled him out onto the sand and nearly hanged him in doing so. On the sand he pretended to be dead, but when I pulled out his hands to look at them he used to jerk them in again. I planted back of the hummocks for some time but he would not move so I came away and left him. Only my mare was too frightened I would have brought him home to the hut. The blackfellow must have been very weak from being so long knocked about among the surf.

21st January. Black George and I went down to the beach to see if the blackfellow had died but he was gone.[40]

Buckley had a penchant for personal violence, but even so there is a matter-of-factness to his account which is chilling.[41] For this Irishman, whose own origins as the illegitimate son of a transported convict mother should surely have equipped him with exactly the sensibilities towards Aborigines that the *rapprochement* model predicts, indigenous people remained an objectified other, a troubling source of economic loss and disturbance in the rhythms of pastoral life.[42] In fact Buckley's attitude points to a greater truth. His and other similar accounts highlight the inevitable clash in values and understanding that occurred when property-based settler capitalism came into contact and competed for space with territorial hunter-gatherers.[43] The rhetoric of capitalism had no vocabulary to accommodate the ancient indigenous meanings that attached to the land – or the settlers' livestock, still less the flexibility to absorb these into its own practices.[44] Yet there were those among La Trobe's correspondents – and others later – who showed some awareness that, even in terms of the values of Western capitalism, settler behaviour towards Aborigines had frequently been morally reprehensible.[45] By the 1850s, retaliatory white violence and sexual predation towards Aborigine communities were acknowledged as major causes of their hostility, but were consigned to history as aberrant forms of behaviour typical of an earlier age.[46] Thus, Thomas Learmonth, who held Boninyong as part of a larger Scottish pastoral enterprise, claimed 'never to have come into personal collision with the blacks', despite their killing of a shepherd. He continued:

> Nor have we been instrumental in taking the life of a single individual, and more over, I am free to confess that, considering the wrong that has been done to the aboriginals in depriving them of their country, they have shown less ferocity and less desire to retaliate than might have been expected.[47]

As Victoria's settlement frontiers closed, so the indigenous encounters which inflected the pioneering place narratives of Irish and Scottish squatters with sometimes hostile meaning gave way to a truly ambivalent colonial embrace.[48] Aboriginal people began to find accommodation within settler capitalism, in employment on runs, for example, or as Native Police, but always in a manner which reinforced their otherness, and hence their distance from the white colonial self.[49] Signs of this repulsion/attraction were evident from mid-century, and were tellingly expressed by objectifications of indigenous labour. Various of La Trobe's pastoral correspondents set clear limits to the working relationship they had with Aborigines. John Mcleod, for example, who held the Borhoneyghurk run before buying Tahara and Winninburn in 1849, initially refused to allow his Aborigine workers near his hut, and instead sent their provisions to them.[50] Thomas Chirnside, founder of one of the greatest Scottish pastoral dynasties in Victoria, thought similarly. Describing his early relations with Aborigines on his first station in the Wimmera, he explained:

> I went to meet them and gave them to understand that I wished to be friendly with them; that if they did not steal they would be at liberty to wander about as usual. They seemed quite delighted and pleased. I, at times, gave them a little flour and mutton. But it was some time before I would allow them to come closer than two hundred or three hundred yards to the huts.[51]

Chirnside's behaviour personified white ambivalence. Setting limits to indigenous behaviour which were based entirely on his own colonial values and ignored the Aborigines' own prior claims to the now colonised land, he was prepared to accommodate them within this newly imposed order, but only insofar as it was necessary to secure his own position.

Other squatters recognised the particular (but still other) skills that the Aborigines possessed, and their usefulness to pastoralists. William Taylor, who in 1844 occupied 206,000 acres in the Wimmera with his partner and fellow Scotsman, Duncan McPherson, claimed that many stations in the region found their services 'of great value in looking for strayed horses and especially sheep. Some of them shepherded for eight or ten months at a time and were the best shepherds in the district. Not being afraid of losing the sheep, they allowed them to spread over a large tract of country.'[52] But their utility was a function of difference, and it is this same sense of difference – of an anonymised collective black other which the occasional references to named individuals only served to heighten – that continued to inflect many later descriptions of indigenous engagements with settler capitalism. For example, in discussing 'The Blacks at Wando Dale' (sic) in his autobiography in 1913, William Moodie described the indigenous workers on his run almost as a form of animate labour:

> We could not work our blacks if the bullocks were near. The bullocks, more especially the old ones brought from Tasmania, went perfectly mad, something of the same aversion a horse shows to a camel . . . if the blacks had remained with us long enough, no doubt the bullocks would have become reconciled, but they were as wild as ever up to the time the blacks left.[53]

There is a disturbing equivalence evident in Moodie's imagination between bullocks and 'blacks'. Given the racialism inherent in comments like this one, it is unsurprising that when Aborigine people transgressed the imagined boundaries set for them by people like Chirnside and Moodie, the results could be troubling for the narratives of place and identity these settlers had so carefully constructed for themselves. Hence, perhaps, Moodie's comment, quoted at the beginning of this chapter, concerning the Aborigine cricket team that played in Western Victoria before touring England in 1868.[54] The tour resonated with Moodie, writing over forty years after the event, not because of its sporting significance – the team was the first of any kind to represent Australia abroad – but because it elevated the Aborigines involved from their accustomed, marginalised place in his personal narrative of identity.

It is important to remember that the subjective construction of place in Moodie's colonial imagination was precisely that: a personal narrative which reflected his own circumstances and understanding vis-à-vis those around him. Other squatters read the events that underpinned Moodie's narrative in different ways. For example, Adam Turnbull, who managed the nearby Winninburn run on behalf of his Presbyterian minister father, was able to accept the boundary-crossing activities of the Aborigine cricket team more easily, albeit in terms of their sporting achievements rather than of their race.[55] Nevertheless it is apparent that for some, perhaps many, squatters the indigenous presence formed a disquieting element within their colonial present. Memory played its part in coming to terms with this indigeneity, as it did in the environmental narratives that helped to shape the squatters' sense of pastoral place. But this was not ethnic memory. Rather, among the squatters discussed here, it was a distancing acknowledgement of earlier events in the colony's history that no longer had a place in the imagined narrative of these squatters' colonial selves. Increasingly, these narratives were enacted in terms of the property-based values of settler capitalism and the complex pastoral cartographies they created. We have already remarked that the material inscriptions of place that formed part of these exhibited varied social and ethnic meanings. What is the evidence for this?

Property's progress

The pastoral cartographies created by settler capitalism represented the progressive re-imagining of the Australian landscape in terms of ideas of bounded, allocated and valued property which were entirely alien to indigenous people. These cartographies were also semiotic. They provided white settlers with the opportunity to inscribe meanings in the landscape that memorialised and reinforced the discursive links between their colonial lives and their remembered homelands. The upshot was the creation of complex colonial geographies of place which embodied not only the environmental learning and indigenous encounters described above, but also the need of some squatters to

Table 6.1 Pastoral run names, New South Wales and Victoria, 1884–90

	New South Wales 1890		Victoria 1884	
	Number	Percentage	Number	Percentage
Aboriginal	1,181	71.6	584	42.5
Irish	33	2.0	43	3.1
Scottish	47	2.9	115	8.4
Colonial topography	246	14.9	316	23.0
Colonial other	143	8.6	316	23.0
Total	1,650	100.0	1,374	100.0

Source: W. Hanson, *Pastoral Possessions of New South Wales* (Sydney, 1889);
R. Spreadborough and H. Anderson, *Pastoral Possessions of New South Wales*
(Melbourne. 1983).

signal both their diasporic routes – their colonial experience, especially if successful – and roots – their ethnic origins. One early means of signalling all of these was place naming, which, as Arthur notes, embodied claims both to particular forms of knowledge and to ownership.[56] But in making these claims, and invoking memory and belonging in this way, these place names used a vocabulary that, arguably, was exclusionary. By signalling particular forms of memory and particular claims to status, place naming might distance the squatters' emplaced selves not only from the indigenous people whose claims to place their runs supplanted, but also from other white settlers of different ethnicities – or different social standing. By the same token, of course, Irish or Scottish semiotics of place might also encourage a broader discourse of shared ethnic identity and association with other settlers.

Table 6.1 addresses aspects of these colonial vocabularies of place and memory. It classifies the pastoral run names in Victoria and New South Wales *ca.* 1884–90 according to their likely provenance.[57] The majority of the names in the Irish and Scottish categories commemorate not only localities (Ben Lomond, Cavan) but also people, usually but not always associating them with a particular topographical feature: thus Campbell's Island or Paddy's Land. The category 'Colonial topography' includes all other European names which identify landscape features without a Scottish or Irish connotation (Fiery Creek, Mount Misery), while 'Colonial other' includes the remaining commemorative and other non-indigenous names (Salisbury, Tiara, Zig-Zag). The aboriginal names are identified on the basis of their English redaction. Clearly, given the propensity for run names to change, and the ubiquity of some of the British place and personal names that are commemorated, such a classification can be only approximate.[58] Nevertheless, two things are apparent: first, the widespread appropriation of aboriginal names by squatters, particularly in New South Wales. Second, the relative scarcity of run names of specifically Scottish or Irish origin. By comparison, in both colonies the physical features of the newly encountered landscape seem to have provided much more fertile ground for the colonists' lexical imaginings of place.

On first inspection, the extensive number of aboriginal run names appears to invite the conclusion that, contrary to the claim made here, the vocabulary of pastoral places did not particularly exclude indigeneity. Thus, we might argue that their extensive use reflected a willingness on the part of many squatters to incorporate indigenous land relations into their own ascriptions of place. In this way, so the argument might run, these aboriginal names could be seen as evidence of the imbricated nature of the place identities constructed by colonialism in Australia, and their capacity to support multiple readings by different authorial groups. In a broad sense, this may well be true, but caution is needed. As Blake and Arthur have argued, these aboriginal run names were still, in fact, acts of the colonial imagination. At best, they represented a European phonetic rendering of local indigenous names that were ephemeral, and which were as likely to reflect the colonist's own dialect as the original, transient, aboriginal meaning. There is evidence, moreover, that some squatters adopted aboriginal names from other parts of Australia for their runs, completely severing the intimate link between locality and community that underlay indigenous relations to the land. Blake suggests that this localism was incapable of sustaining a generic conceptual framework for indigenous place names and that, for this reason alone, many of them were inappropriately used by Europeans.[59]

But more than this, these aboriginal run names were also deliberate acts of colonial selection and, therefore, erasure. By choosing one redacted form of an intensely local indigenous name to signify a broader, white colonial space (the run), squatters inevitably obscured the other. aboriginal meanings that had been embedded within this landscape. Through this process of selective imposition, the vocabulary of colonial place stripped the indigenous landscape of its rich diversity of meaning and fixed in its stead a simplified European indigenous sensibility.[60] Like the squatters' encounters with individual Aborigines, this representational lexicon was truly ambivalent. Appropriated indigenous meanings were incorporated within the language of colonial place but, lacking real context, they served only to locate the Aborigine presence in the landscape as a now marginalised other in the hegemonic discourse of colonialism. In effect, the widespread use of indigenous run names simply served to secure the privileged position of the white presence in the pastoral landscape.

The limited invocation of Scottish and Irish run names as part of this white presence points to the individualism and diasporic character of colonial identity construction. Although the semiotic content of these names might be interpreted differently by various social or cultural groups, they remained, above everything else, a mirror of individual authorial experience. Whether the names privileged or ignored the squatters' roots depended on the importance of these in continuing to define each person's sense of self in the colonies. Not all Scottish and Irish settlers felt an equal and ongoing affinity with a homeland that they might, variously, have left with very little, or great regret. Accordingly, we might expect the realities of colonial life to have been embraced more readily by some settlers than others, and to have figured more prominently in their developing sense of colonial selfhood as a result. The Portland Bay District in Victoria illustrates the point. By 1851, 360 runs had been established in the district, but of these only thirty-one (8.6 per cent) bore indisputably Scottish names, such as the 39,000-acre Ettrick run, licensed to W. Learmonth in 1849, and Glenlivet, licensed in 1845 to Duncan McRae.[61] If, as suggested earlier, in 1851 at least 40 per cent of the region's squatters were Scottish (and, if Kiddle is correct, considerably more), then clearly few among them felt it either necessary or appropriate to commemorate their ethnic or national origins in this way. Nor were the minority of Irish squatters in the district any more prone to 'authentically' Irish toponymic commemoration. In 1851, the thirty or so Irish-owned runs mustered barely eight Irish names between them, including Connell's Run and St Patrick's Day. Evidently, in this part of Australia at least, the majority of squatters in both groups found it more meaningful to signal their new-found place in the landscape in terms of a toponymy of their current experience rather than in echoes of their remembered past.

Whether commemorative or resolutely presentist, naming land as a run was an act of possession: a redefinition of the land as property that could be identified, defined, valued, owned and represented. In the acts of demarcation that inevitably followed these claims to ownership, squatters created bounded local worlds, material sites of agency and practice which helped to define their sense of place and self. References to bounding and demarcation occur throughout the pastoral archive and provide a sensitive measure of the competing claims to land that characterised the progressive closure of the pastoral frontier as the process of settlement intensified. Earlier accounts provide a sense of the openness of the land on the pastoral frontier and of its seemingly infinite capacity for white settlement, but also of the evolving capitalist cartographies that framed this. Thomas Lennox Gibson's description of his move from Kilmore to Lake Bringalbert in the Wimmera in 1845 provides an example. Gibson was born in Perthshire in 1810, and in 1828 emigrated to Van Diemen's Land to join his uncle, David Gibson, an emancipist and pastoralist. In 1835 he moved to Port Phillip, where he established the Long Hills run near Kilmore, north of Melbourne. Six years later he sponsored his sister, Janet, and brother-in-law, Francis Hamilton, as bounty migrants to Australia, where they joined him at Kilmore. In 1845 Gibson sold the Long Hills run, leaving other property in trust to his sister and her family, and overlanded sheep to the Wimmera, where he squatted at Lake Bringalbert.[62]

Writing to his parents in Scotland in August of that year, Gibson portrayed something of the as yet unbounded frontier life of the squatter. After explaining that he had sold his Kilmore run because it was no longer large enough to sustain his flocks, he continued:

> I started into the woods, steering a north-westwards course. I travelled about 300 miles, I was better than three months on the way before I reached this. I have got a large country to myself at present, but I expect I shall have some neighbours soon. There are [sic] no one within 30 miles of me . . . I do not know whether I am in the District of Adelaide or Port Phillip, it is to be decided this summer. I am about 300 miles from Melbourne, 200 miles from Adelaide. If I am in the District of Adelaide I shall have to go there for a license. There are no houses on the road for 150 miles.
>
> We are something like the Children of Israel roaming from place to place. We think nothing of riding a 100 miles. We take some bread and meat, some tea and sugar and [a] tin pot. We make a fire and boil some water, get supper, tether the horse lay down by the fire and go to sleep.[63]

Gibson's portrayal was of a world that was already on the cusp of change as successive Land Acts began to take effect and property rights became both more formal and disputed. In Gibson's own case, the opportunity to formalise his claim came two years later, in 1847, in the wake of boundary survey between what were to become the colonies of South Australia and Victoria. Despite Gibson's assertion that his was a poor country of stringy bark forest and extensive swamps, his initial claim for 204 square miles to run 10,000 sheep was rejected. His proposed stocking density was too low, in view of the large number of licence applications for the area. Instead, the Wimmera Lands Commissioner, W. R. Wright, granted him 120,000 acres on which to run 12,000 sheep, although this was subsequently increased to 150,000 acres when his application was formally approved a year later.[64]

Figure 6.2 is based on the sketch map that accompanied the 1848 modification of Gibson's successful licence application. Like the language of Gibson's application, the map is notable for its imagined geometry, even as it appropriated a misunderstood Aborigine place

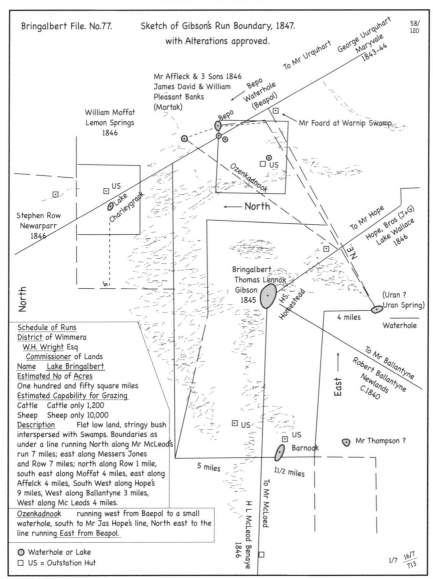

6.2 Lake Bringalbert run, *ca.* 1847–48

name to denote the white spaces of this newly imposed capitalist cartography. For Gibson, Bringalbert was defined in terms of its relationship to other white places ('situated about 35 to 40 miles W.S.W. of Mount Aripiles') and its rigid demarcation: 'I claim four miles to the

East, half the distance betwixt R. and G. Hope's Esa station and mine, that station is about ten miles S.E. of this. Half the distance betwixt R. Ballantyne Esq.'s station, it is about nine miles S.S.W. of this. Eight miles to the Nor'ard and eight miles to the Westward or half the distance betwixt K. Mcleod's station and an outstation of mine known as Barnork.'[65] In similar vein, the map depicts an imagined geography of settler names and spaces. European artefacts – out stations and homesteads – as well as economically important resources – water holes – are carefully delineated, and provide reference points for blocks of land that are marked with geometric precision and identified in terms of white possession. Spaces are given meaning because of this ownership. Messers Ballantyne, Ford, Hope, McLeod, Moffat, Thompson and Row are named and located, and all brought singular identities to this pastoral landscape which helped to define and distinguish between its constituent, Europeanised parts. This was now a capitalist landscape of property and commodification, and in it indigenous understandings played little part.

But, as the narrative of the successful Catholic Irish squatter Patrick Coady Buckley shows, the symbolism inherent in cartographic lines such as those which demarcated the Bringalbert map was conditional on time and circumstance. Buckley has already been represented as a man of humble origins and violent temperament, but he was also a significant figure in the early European colonisation of Gippsland.[66] Together with his stepfather, Edmund Buckley, he joined the southwestwards push of Irish Catholic settlers from Sydney into the Monaro and beyond in the early nineteenth century. From his arrival in Gippsland in 1842 until his death in 1872 Patrick Buckley held nine stations at various times (Figure 6.3) and helped to finance another three for his stepfather.[67] The extensive station diary he kept from 1844 bears witness to the importance he placed on demarcating and knowing his land. But this was a discourse that changed over time as Gippsland became progressively more heavily imprinted with the marks of European settlement and as the issues that Buckley faced as a squatter changed. Initially, Buckley's primary concern was to establish his legal claim to the lands he had applied for and to prevent his neighbours from encroaching on their boundaries. In March 1844, having given up the first run he had held, TungieMungie, on the Tambo river in north-west Gippsland, Buckley agreed with the Crown Lands Commissioner the extent of what was to be his main property, Coady Vale, on the coast:

March 7th. Rowley and I went to Mason's on this south side of [Merrimans] creek. Heard there that the Commissioner of Crown Lands, Mr Tyers, had gone down to my place. I turned for home and met Mr Tyers, William

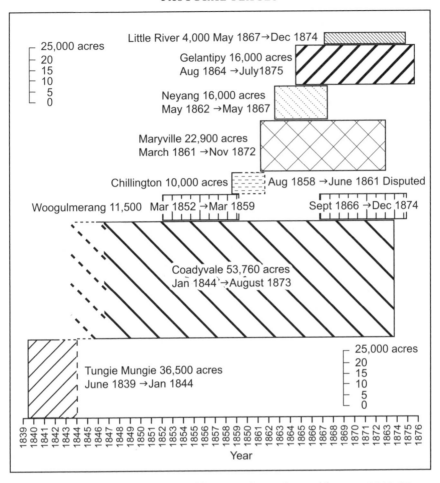

6.3 Gippsland stations owned by Patrick Coady Buckley, *ca.* 1842–90

Scott and H. B. Marley and four policemen within about 3 miles of my place. I returned with them to the Big Flat and Scot and I agreed upon a boundary about where the dogleg fence now stands, running one point to east of north from Merriman's creek. Tyers gave me up to the road on the south side of the creek – the old crossing at Erin Vale . . .[68]

Further licence applications quickly followed. Despite, or perhaps because of, the apparent ease with which they were made, Buckley's possession did not remain uncontested. In August 1846 he evicted Neil McDonald, a neighbouring Scottish squatter, from occupation of part of Coady Vale and later in the same year he began the first in a series

[153]

of court cases against his neighbours to defend his property interests. These culminated in 1859 when Buckley and his then partner, Leonard Mason, were sued by Archibald McLeod in the Melbourne Supreme Court for their alleged illegal occupation of the Chillingworth run. Mason and Buckley eventually lost the case in 1861, but not before Mason was imprisoned for twelve years for attempting to shoot McLeod's overseer.[69]

Buckley sought compensation for his losses at Chillingworth from Victoria's Legislative Assembly, but with what degree of success is not known.[70] What is clear is that his energetic legal defence of his various properties represented only one aspect of his discourse of run owner-ship. If the lines on station maps represented boundaries which had to be defended against fellow squatters, they also enclosed spaces which, by the 1860s, had to be protected against enforced subdivision under the Selection Acts. Buckley had already bought the Pre-emptive Right to 640 acres at Coady Vale in 1854, and under successive Land Acts in the 1860s he engaged a wide variety of friends and employees to select on his behalf as 'dummies'. In August 1865, for example, at a 'monster land sale with 1,300 selectors present' in Sale, his long-time compan-ion, Miss Ricketts, together with her father and one Frank Taylor, acted for him, but eventually withdrew as drawing the lots continued into the early hours of the following day.[71] Four years later, in May 1869, Buckley bought four lots on the Woodside run, but failed in his attempt to buy others under Clause 42 of the Grant Act, which encouraged the subdivision of runs near goldfields to support the mining population. Buckley attempted to prove the admissibility of his intended pur-chases under this clause, but his case was referred for appeal before the Land Commissioners. His appeal failed, leading him to complain that 'there is no justice for the squatter. Hearsay evidence against me was recorded. The other applicants . . . all recommended. I failed.'[72]

But if Buckley was only partly successful in exploiting the changing land legislation to secure or extend his existing runs, those he did hold were increasingly closely inscribed with the material signatures of pastoralism. As the pastoral industry developed and tenures improved, so shepherding, with its characteristically ephemeral landscape imprint, gave way to more manageable – and permanent – systems of paddock grazing wherever environmental conditions allowed.[73] New boundaries appeared in the landscape as squatters divided their runs into smaller units, and the rhythms of pastoral life now routinely included fencing, which station records indicate might absorb a high proportion of the available labour.[74] In the longer term, the economic advantages were considerable: labour costs were reduced and both livestock and grazing resources could be managed more efficiently. In Buckley's case much of

the work of fencing was done by him with his own men, and this subsequently took on a performative quality in local memory. Writing in
1872, his obituarist commented that he 'was a man of gigantic stature
and nearly everything around partook of this particular feature of his
personal appearance. The fencing of his paddocks and around his homestead was larger and more substantial than anyone else's, and it was his
habit to put the corner posts in with a block and tackle.'[75]

Acts of enclosure such as those by Buckley created a new and,
for settlers, arguably universal vocabulary of landscape. Terms like
paddock, yard, homestead or run formed part of a lexical currency that
connected squatters in a shared system of functional understanding
that transcended ethnic consciousness or national origins. Thus the
neatly geometric boundaries of the Bringalbert and other station maps
took on additional meanings as the cartographic frame for a capitalist
system that assigned value to the land in terms of its productivity and
net worth. On many runs, the value ascribed to the land within this
capitalist imaginary constituted by far the largest proportion of the
enterprise's capital. Thus, at Dunmore, where Charles MacKnight had
seen Providential purpose in the station's preservation from bush-fires
in 1863, the annual account for 1869 was balanced at £49,720, but
nearly three-quarters of this (£35,600) was made up of the land valua-
tion. By 1873 the balanced account stood at over £79,000 and returned a
net profit of £11,000.[76] Australian historians have long recognised that
this sort of capital accrual, driven by the expanding imperial market
for Australia's pastoral produce and copper-bottomed by the increasing
security of many pastoral tenures, was an important enabling factor
from the mid century onwards in promoting the widespread rebuilding
of squatters' homesteads.[77] By indulging the squatters' own aesthetic
sensibilities and incorporating the 'polite' architecture of their choice,
these buildings constituted the most obvious, yet also ambiguous,
material statements of identity and belonging in the pastoral landscape.

Irish and Scottish squatters were as wholeheartedly engaged in
this activity as any other group, but very few can be shown to have
built houses that were intentionally Scottish or Irish in appearance.
Care is needed here, however. In Ireland, 'polite' architecture of the
sort that might be expected to have influenced an Irish squatter's
choice of design was heavily influenced by European fashions for
Enlightenment Classicism and nineteenth-century Romanticism, both
of which were also widely adopted in Australia.[78] Thus, homesteads
built in these styles in Australia by Irish squatters may simply have
signalled their owners' wider sense of architectural fashion rather
than any particular ethnic consciousness. A case in point is Cooma
Cottage, on the Southern Tablelands near Yass in New South Wales

6.4   Cooma Cottage, Yass, New South Wales

(Figure 6.4). The original wooden homestead was built in 1835 by a pioneer Irish squatter, Cornelius O'Brien, who, with his brother Henry, established several runs (including Douro) on the Yass Plains and the Murrumbidgee and Lachlan rivers.[79] In 1839 Cornelius sold the cottage and 100 acres to Hamilton Hume, the Parramatta-born explorer and eldest son of Captain Andrew Hamilton Hume, who was originally from Hillsborough, County Down. Hume was responsible for constructing the present house in a debased Palladian style, with colonnaded Grecian portico and projecting wings.[80] The design offers a fair imitation, in a simplified colonial idiom, of the architectural sensibilities of many of the 'big houses' that existed in County Down and other parts of Ireland during his father's upbringing there. But without further evidence, its provenance either as a deliberate diasporic echo of the family's Irish origins or as an aspirational statement of status and aesthetic sensibility within the colonial present remains unknown.

Scottish architecture offers firmer grounds on which to establish deliberate invocations of ethnic memory, though these still appear to have been relatively rare. Architecturally, nineteenth-century Scottish Romanticism found expression in the Scottish Baronial style, which was based on the country's seventeenth-century buildings.[81] Consequently, pastoral homesteads built in this style may be fairly thought to invoke a specific Scottish ethnic consciousness. In Victoria, examples include Ercildoune near Ballarat and Overnewton Castle at Keilor, both of which were built in 1859. Architecturally, Overnewton Castle is more correctly detailed and offers a convincing repertoire of gabled dormer windows, bartizans, crow-stepped gables and spired turrets. These were regarded locally at the time of the homestead's construction as good examples of 'the oldest Scottish architecture'.[82] However, the juxtaposition of this against a simpler, verandahed extension lacking any Scottish stylistic reference points to the owner, William Taylor's, reflexive choice of the Baronial for the main house. The Scottish part of the homestead stands as a conscious act of imagination, actively asserting – in its design and name – a claim to a particular ethnic origin and identity. Taylor had this part of the house constructed after returning from a visit to Scotland and his birthplace, Overnewton, allegedly using Scottish craftsmen.[83] The verandahed block was an altogether more appropriate response to the local environment.

Ercildoune's design is more eclectic. Built in bluestone by the Scottish Learmonth family, it is a rambling affair of massive compositional forms and occasional Baronial detail, including battlements, drip moulds above some windows, and stepped gables. In a particular act of memory, however, it also incorporates a copy of the pele tower that formed part of the Learmonth's ancestral home on the Scottish borders. If Overnewton Castle was deemed by contemporaries to be an authentic representation of a shared remembered past, Ercildoune was altogether more imaginative: a *pot pourri* of borrowed stylistic detail applied with no great understanding. Whether this is to be explained in terms of personal idiosyncracy or of the lack of an immediate exemplar is unclear. Either way, the contrast between Ercildoune's eclecticism and Overnewton's authenticity highlights the subjective and selective nature of ethnic consciousness and memory. Even when a sense of ethnic origins and belonging actively shaped the settler's identity, their existence in the colonial here and now militated against total recall of both their roots and routes. The passage of time and the tyranny of distance distorted memory. The past they brought to mind was an act of imagination – in varying degree, perhaps – but it was never complete or fully authentic.

But however distorted by the lens of memory, such deliberate architectural invocations of ethnic consciousness were the exception rather than the rule. In common with other squatters who engaged in the great rebuilding of the later nineteenth century, most Irish and Scottish pastoralists for whom records survive commissioned houses which were, above all, statements of their current wealth and standing. Ethnically valorised homesteads like Ercildoune were also this, of course, but

6.5   Monivae, Hamilton, Western Victoria

the majority of the houses constructed by Scottish and Irish squatters appear to have simply reflected colonial fashion – and the rigours of the local climate. A case in point is Monivae, near Hamilton in the Western District of Victoria (Figure 6.5). The present house was built by James Thompson, a Scotsman who bought the run for £34,000 following the death of its previous Anglo-Irish owner, Acheson Ffrench, in 1870. Ffrench's original house – where Cuthbert Fetherstonhaugh had found such a friendly Irish welcome – was a sixteen-room prefabricated corrugated iron structure which had been imported from Britain. Neither this house nor Thompson's replacement embodied any statement of its owner's origins. The broad verandahs of the later house were an entirely pragmatic response to the heat of the summer climate, while the imported Oregon pine, Welsh slate and Italian marble used in its construction signalled taste – and the wealth to materialise this.[84]

The same point could be reiterated for any one of a number of Irish-and Scottish-owned pastoral stations in the later nineteenth century. For example, the romantic Italianate and Gothic architecture of Niel Black's homesteads at Glenormiston and, following the dissolution of his partnership with Alexander Finlay and Thomas Gladstone in 1868, Mount Noorat in Victoria's Western District, signalled his wealth and status as a pastoralist and colonial politician, not his origins as the Gaelic-speaking son of a Scottish tenant farmer.[85] In sum, it seems likely that the polite architectural spaces created by Irish and Scottish pastoralists at their homesteads were more commonly mirrors of their present, not embodiments of their past. Only occasionally did circumstance and personal preference dictate otherwise. But however mute their architecture might be in terms of essentialist ethnic symbolism, these homesteads were also performative sites imbued with continuously changing meanings by the behaviour of those whose lives flowed through them. The steep environmental learning curve and unsettling indigenous encounters exemplified by the experience of the Irish and Scottish squatters discussed here formed an essential part of this. But additionally, these homesteads' meanings as place were also constructed out of the intimacies of domestic life and the discursive social and cultural links that connected these to the immediate region and beyond. And here, different degrees of ethnic consciousness, expressed in the quotidian details of everyday life, might more commonly be found.

Social enactments

The place meanings which attached to pastoral stations depended on the attitudes, values and experience of those who invoked them. As the frontier closed and property relations formalised, larger stations supported increasingly complex communities. The squatter, his family and their dependents; governesses, domestic servants, gardeners and station hands; itinerant visitors – swagmen, and sheep shearers employed for the annual clip – all brought their own perspectives and understanding to the white colonial spaces they shared. These perspectives were variously hegemonic or subaltern. The ethnic or social symbols inscribed in the architecture of the homestead buildings normally represented the squatter's own gaze of ownership and, like his environmental and indigenous encounters, were grounded in the hegemonic propertied perspectives of settler capitalism. By contrast, the sometimes differently gendered voices of other family members and station employees offer perspectives that were variously positioned from below in what remained – despite the rapid pace of regional transformation – a resolutely patriarchal world.

Daniel Halfpenny's diary provides an early example of one such subaltern voice. Originally from Belfast, he and his wife arrived in 1840 in Melbourne, where they were employed on various runs in the Port Philip District until 1847.[86] His diary provides a relatively rare insight from the labourer's perspective into the moral economy of labour on a pioneer pastoral station. His daily routine of caring for stock, shifting hurdles, carrying water and so forth was framed by his strong sense of the mutual contractual obligation he and his employer shared. Halfpenny was prepared to carry out those tasks he 'had agreed for', not those he hadn't. His first employer, William Piper, who held the Pastoria run near Kineton, thought otherwise. Between 1840, when Halfpenny began work there, and 1843, when he and his wife left, his diary records a litany of confrontation and complaint as the abusive Piper tried to insist that he carry out additional tasks.[87] Despite the difference in their status – to Halfpenny, Piper was always 'Master' and the tasks he was required to do were always 'ordered' – their relationship was one of mutual dependence. The depression of the early 1840s caused economic difficulties for squatters and labourers alike, and this may have accounted for Piper's repeated refusal to allow the Halfpennys to terminate their employment early – and for their otherwise surprising willingness to re-engage as his employees.[88] But whatever the proximate cause of their decision, it signalled the hybrid nature of the meanings of place that the Pastoria run held both for the Halfpennys and their employer. On the one hand, the homestead was a site of oppressive authoritarian behaviour and abuse; on the other, as Halfpenny defended his moral claims, it became a site of resistance.

A different subaltern understanding of place is provided by Margaret Youngman's description of domestic life at Polkemmet station in the Wimmera in the 1860s.[89] A well-educated and genteel young lady, Margaret was driven by reduced circumstances to accept the post of governess to the unruly daughters of the wealthy but (to her) uncouth Scottish owner of Polkemmet, Robert Calder, 'a rough and unrefined man ... ready to guffaw at his children's most rude and vulgar sayings'.[90] A profound clash of cultural values is evident throughout her memoir. Her sense of belonging was unsettled by the limited horizons of Mrs Calder, 'the daughter of an Edinburgh farmer', who had never once left the station in fifteen years and whose capacity for gossip with the servants offended Margaret's sense of social propriety. Her authority over the children was undermined by their parents' tolerance of their ridicule of her; while visits to a limited network of neighbouring Scottish and Irish squatters provided only partial relief. Her admiration for the elegance and style of some was matched by her disgust at the wild and drunken behaviour of others and at their willingness to break the conventions of polite society.[91] The arrival of shearers for the annual wool clip confirmed her social misgivings and reinforced her sense of isolation. Disgusted by the brutality of the shearing process, and astounded at the liberties Calder's daughters were allowed in mixing with the shearing gangs, she withdrew from her expected role as observer of the spectacle.

Thus, for Margaret Youngman, Polkemmet became, at least in part, a site of 'misery' and alienation.[92] Yet there were compensations. The gardens surrounding the homestead elicited unalloyed pleasure, while Margaret found true companionship in the company of the carpenter's wife, whose (well-behaved) children she also taught and whose 'bush hut was ... clean and tidy beyond belief. Many an afternoon I have spent with pleasure and profit sitting with this poor woman in her hut.'[93] The comment is telling, and suggests that many of Margaret's problems at Polkemmet stemmed from her liminal social position there. Attached to, yet not part of, the Calders' inner domestic circle, and ever conscious of her own superior upbringing, she appears to have felt comfortable only in circumstances which confirmed her sense of social order. Hence her liking for the company of tradesmen's wives who knew their place. But the upshot was that, like Daniel Halfpenny at Pastoria, for her the meanings of place at Polkemmet were hybrid and conditional. If the performative spaces she created in her role as governess were unavoidably negative, those she encountered elsewhere at the station reaffirmed her sense of self-worth in more positive ways. All, however, contributed to her understanding of Polkemmet as place.

The subaltern positionality of Halfpenny and Calder was socially led, yet in each case there was also an ethnic dimension. Halfpenny's Ulster *mores* were counterpoised against Piper's Englishness; Youngman's English gentility contrasted with the Calders' Lowland Scots culture as 'rough and ready' Berwickshire farmers. How far these ethnic differences contributed to the divisions between the squatters and their employees is hard to determine. What is clear is that, like other Scottish squatters, the Calders indulged in patterns of behaviour that resonated directly with their Scottish origins. Chief among these was their continuing Presbyterian affiliation, which connected them not only to local and regional ethnic networks within Victoria but also to the wider discursive Presbyterian network within the Empire at large.[94] As Hoerder notes, religious practice provided emigrants with a comfortingly familiar set of values with which to order their lives in the new country, as well as a social arena in which connections with 'home' and like-minded émigrés could be maintained.[95] Local Presbyterian churches performed all of these functions for Scottish (and Irish) squatters, including Niel Black at Glenormiston and Robert Scott at Mount Boninyong, just as the Episcopalian church at Port Fairy did for others like Charles MacKnight and Andrew Suter.[96]

By virtue of their standing in the local community, squatters such as these tended to assume a leadership role in the creation of local religious networks. For example, in 1847 Niel Black was one of a number of wealthy Scottish squatters who initially funded and then, as members of the elders' committee, ran the first Presbyterian church in the Western District, at Kilnoorat. Their call to the Reverend William Hamilton, from Goulburn in New South Wales, as their first minister connected them with a major figure in the early development of the Presbyterian Church in Australia. While he had never felt truly in place at Goulburn, Hamilton found the 'liberal stipend and convenient dwelling', and the forbearance, kindness and social deference of his new congregation much more amenable to his (considerable) sense of self-worth.[97] Elsewhere in the Western District, John Mackersey, a 'son of the manse' who had bought the Kenilworth run in 1857, was instrumental in constructing the new Presbyterian church at Cavendish in 1862, two years after Robert Scott had been similarly involved at Boninyong. Mackersey's role was particularly extensive and involved laying out the church site with the architect and contractors, managing the building costs and allocating the pews to the congregation.[98]

But, as the records of these and other runs make clear, this Presbyterian ethos could inflect the whole tenor of station life. Alex Turnbull's frequent preaching on the Balmoral–Cavendish–Coleraine Presbyterian circuit in the 1870s was one instance of this and formed part of a religious imaginary which gave additional meaning to the Winninburn run for the Turnbulls. Not only was this a site of pastoral endeavour, it was also a place where they actively performed their faith, holding religious services and Sunday School picnics, and entertained visiting preachers.[99] For Hugh Hamilton, another Scottish pastoralist, the religious sensibilities enacted at his station were no less profound but were more troubling. The son of a Scottish gentry empire family with property in Jamaica and military connections in India, Hamilton arrived in Sydney in 1840 with £3,000 capital.[100] After two years acquiring experience on runs near Bathurst owned by Arthur Rankin, a family friend under whose protection he had come out to Australia, Hamilton bought two runs, Tommabil and Boyd, on the Lachlan River in south-east New South Wales. For the next eight years he raised cattle there, but was thwarted by periodic floods, drought and low livestock prices. Only between 1844 and 1848 'was there good grass in all the country; my cattle prospered and I had great pleasure in all my work'.[101] The disastrous drought of 1849–50 proved a near-final straw, and for the next eleven months he worked as Gold Commissioner on the Bathurst goldfield before returning to his stations and developing the overland droving trade in beef cattle from the Lachlan to the thriving gold-enriched Melbourne market.[102]

As Hamilton's economic circumstances worsened after 1848, so his diary began to record periods of intense, self-absorbed and entirely self-critical religious introspection. These continued intermittently until 1852, which suggests that the onerous demands of station (and goldfields) life frequently effaced Hamilton's daily sense of religious duty, only for this to re-assert itself in outbursts of guilt-ridden self-reflection. Thus, his main residence, Tommabil, became for him a site of spiritual conflict. In August 1848, for example, Hamilton confessed not only to a profound feeling of 'sinfulness' but also to a general luke-warmness in his faith and a willingness to allow others to distract him from his religious duty. 'I am conscious of having done wrong in several ways every day ... My prayers are not attended to with all my heart. My mind wanders from the subject of meditation on my bed. I do not give God thanks for all I have received at his merciful hands ... During the past week what has been the progress if any or my declension if any in religion? The question is of great importance but very hard to answer.'[103] By January of the following year Hamilton was confessing to 'swearing and using intemperate language', and by May to 'neglecting his religious duties', all the while counterpoising these bouts of self-excoriation with routine accounts of station life and practice.[104]

The dawn of the New Year of 1851 found Hamilton in even more reflective mood than usual. Concluding that his time in Australia had left him 'in the same position in life as I was ten years ago, with a smaller sum of money to my credit and a seventh part of the term of man's life passed without improvement', he nevertheless acknowl-edged the importance of the Christian precepts his mother had taught him as a means of setting these disappointments in proper perspective. 'Suppose I gain a fortune ... will the houses, the land, the family ties which at the end of my life I have possession of give me any advantage in the endless ages of eternity?'[105] Ultimately, Hamilton's fortune did improve, and, on the strength of this, in 1853 he married Margaret, second daughter of George Innes of Thrumster in Caithness. In 1852 his first sale of bullocks in Melbourne had realised £10 a head, and by the mid-1850s purchasers were coming from Victoria to the Lachlan to buy his stock. A speculative purchase of the Waroo run (also on the Lachlan) in 1856 proved successful, and four years later he was able to sell the station and its stock at a net profit of £7,000, having sold Boyd and 2,000 of its cattle two years previously for £16,000.[106] Intriguingly, as Hamilton's material situation improved, so his religious introspec-tion faded. Seemingly, as a spiritual battleground, Hamilton's stations exhibited their most profound meanings of place during times of economic hardship.

Hamilton's success in developing the specialised beef trade with Melbourne reflected the modernisation that characterised the pastoral industry. For some Scottish and Irish squatters, this modernising urge took on a moral quality of improvement which involved many of them in the evolving structures of local government and the active promotion of their districts, much as landlords had conventionally done in Scotland and Ireland. Adam Turnbull typified this sort of paternalistic, patronal community authority and service. A member of the Dundas Road Board, in 1872 he was elected president of its replacement, Wannon Shire, a role he retained for twenty-two years. Vice-president of the Coleraine Caledonian Society between 1864 and 1870, he was also secretary and treasurer of the town's Presbyterian church and joint president of the local Pastoral and Agricultural Society.[107] Other local squatters performed similar roles. William Moodie, owner of Wando Dale, was first elected to the Glenelg Shire Council in 1864, before joining Adam Turnbull on the Wannon Council in 1873, a post he held almost uninterruptedly until his retirement in 1913.[108] At Hamilton, Acheson Ffrench, owner of the Monivae run and a not uncritical observer of the colonial government, accepted roles as a stipendiary magistrate and member of the local National Schools Board. By the late 1850s he had established a reputation not only as one of the Grange district's leading landowners but also as one of its foremost advocates, keen to promote its case for improvement in Victoria's Legislative Assembly.[109] Ffrench was descended from a leading family of Galway landowners with a long history of involvement in agricultural and social improvement in that county.[110] McClelland suggests that his enthusiasm for educational and infrastructural development in the Grange reflected a sense of *communitaire* responsibility that had been inculcated in him by these family values; another form, in short, of ethnic memory.[111]

Public roles like these enhanced the squatters' local standing and arguably reinforced the otherness of their pastoral stations as sites of authority in the eyes of subaltern groups in the community. These public offices thus added another layered meaning of place to these stations, as well as constituting a different form of discursive network connecting them to the immediate locality and beyond. Participation in council meetings in local towns like Casterton, Coleraine or Hamilton, a judicial role as a magistrate, or a role as an office bearer in local improving clubs or societies ensured that, for much of the nineteenth century, the Ffrenches, Moodies and Turnbulls of pastoral Australia not only personified their locality to its community but also represented it to the wider world. Politically, of course, this representation did not remain uncontested, as *The Banner of Belfast*'s representation of squatting interests in the Western District demonstrates.

Other squatter networks were altogether more private affairs, and might extend far further than the local Shire Council or a seat in the colony's Legislative Assembly. Family networks, assiduously maintained by correspondence or by occasional personal visits, might connect with other colonies or 'home' to Scotland or Ireland, reinforcing in either case a continuing sense of ethnic connection and identity.[112] At Mount Boninyong, Robert and Sarah Scott maintained a lengthy correspondence in the late 1850s and early 1860s with Sarah's mother in Glasgow, which they used to acquaint her with family news from Victoria and to reassure her of their continued adherence to their shared Presbyterian values. Each letter included a journal or diary which detailed the daily routine of station life as well as the Scotts' social networks in the locality and beyond. The Presbyterian church at Boninyong was one focus of this, and its completion ('the new church is universally admired and a great ornament to the township'), the quality of services there, and visits by various preachers, formed a recurring theme.[113] Counterpoised against this were frequent allusions to the acute social consciousness which framed the Scotts' own constructions of place. Not all of their neighbours were socially acceptable: 'Mr Norsey gave a pic nic . . . I wonder they asked us for we have only called once, we do not care to be intimate'; and both the Scotts and their employees knew their place.[114] Robert's attendance at the opening of the Victoria Legislative Assembly in April 1860 was carefully recorded, and when his newly married younger brother, Thomas, arrived at Mount Boninyong a month later the gratifyingly enthusiastic welcome by the station hands was noted. 'All the men and servants on the place met them as they entered the gate and gave them a right good hearty cheer, after which they came into the kitchen and drank their health . . . '.[115]

For the Scotts, as for other Scottish and Irish squatters, ethnic consciousness and identity was not a matter of primordial inscription, but rather a matter of performance, of maintaining active links and associations with family and with acquaintances of the same ethnic background, whether in Australia or in the home country. Later generations of the Scott family maintained these connections. In the 1880s Robert's son trained in medicine at Glasgow University, before returning to take up the management of Mount Boninyong on the death of his father in 1896.[116] At Mount Boninyong, as elsewhere, this ethnic performance was socially constructed, and consequently gave rise to ambiguous meanings of place in which ethnicity and social symbolism elided. All were conditional on time and circumstance, and susceptible to different interpretation.

Summary

The Scottish and Irish squatters discussed here performed their identities in and as place in ways that defy essentialist description. Their runs formed part of an unstable pastoral cartography that imposed the property values of settler capitalism on a landscape that was neither known nor understood, and on an ancient indigenous people whose knowledge and culture Western enlightenment deemed barbaric. Individual squatters made their accommodation with these circumstances in different ways, but environmental learning and encounters with indigeneity were common to all. Whether these indigenous encounters invoked cautious co-operation or outright hostility depended upon the individual's circumstance and experience and their subjective construction of the other. Similarly, each squatter's engagement with the physical landscape depended upon cognitive behaviour and environmental learning that were equally subjective. For some, runs and homesteads periodically became places of heroic resistance to environmental threats like bush-fires, deliverance from which might invoke a religious sensibility. For others, particularly in the pioneering phase of settlement, stations were sometimes places of fear and loss as squatters enacted with local indigenous communities the initial, mutually uncomprehending, encounter between Aborigine culture and the values of settler capitalism.

Although these meanings invoked – and subsequently formed part of – memory, this was of colonial life and experience, not of a distant past in some remembered homeland. Other aspects of the squatters' performance of place did invoke ethnic memory and consciousness, but in ways which emphasised the individualism of the white colonial experience. Some Scottish and Irish squatters used a toponymic vocabulary to imprint the imagined spaces of their runs with the remembered associations of place and locality in Scotland or Ireland. On the evidence presented here, most did not, and preferred instead to signify their act of possession of the landscape in terms of a presentist understanding of the colony's topography and people. As economic conditions improved and tenures became more secure, some few also chose to symbolise their claims to ethnicity in the architecture of their homesteads. Again, most of the squatters represented here did not, and were content to commission buildings that conformed to colonial architectural fashion and environmental imperatives. Presentism again.

But an adherence to colonial architectural norms represented only part of the squatter's inscription of his or her identity in place. Whatever the semiotics of their architecture, homesteads were also performative spaces in which the different meanings that the run held for those whose lives connected with it could be enacted. The squatters' own gaze of ownership and construction of self were undoubtedly hegemonic within these, but there were other gazes enacted in the same homestead spaces: views from below which inflected the runs with multiple meanings. It was here, in the mundane details of everyday station life, that ethnic memory and consciousness was most commonly to be found, but as performative practice, not primordial inscription. Presbyterian affiliation connected Scottish and Irish squatters to local religious networks and, through these, to the wider Empire beyond. Active church membership provided them with an opportunity to perform their faith locally in ways which reinforced its ethno-cultural content. Scottish ministers preaching to Scottish squatters reinforced the ethnicity of both. Family networks were equally effective in maintaining similar discursive ethnic links across the spaces of empire.

But the evidence recited here demonstrates that the place meanings enacted in the pastoral landscapes of Victoria and New South Wales by Irish and Scottish squatters were characteristically ambiguous. Few can be made to sustain a single, authentic, ethnic reading. Most were testaments to the squatters' truly diasporic condition, in which past and present came together to produce a third space of identity that relied fully on neither. How else to explain the performative Irishness at Monivae or Scottish Presbyterianism at Glenormiston within material spaces that were resolutely presentist in their semiotics? But one question remains. Was this liminality a function of privilege? The squatters whose lives we have depicted here were, by definition, relatively wealthy men and women, despite the exigencies of the colonial economy and environment. Possessed of far more material wealth than most Irish and Scottish settlers, they were also afforded the opportunity – potentially – to move more easily than most between the worlds of the remembered past and the colonial present. Did this encourage them to perform their ethnicity more – or less – assiduously than those whose material circumstances kept them in Australia?

Notes

1   Cuthbert Fetherstonhaugh, *After Many Days. Being the Reminiscences of Cuthbert Fetherstonhaugh* (Melbourne, 1917), p. 62.
2   William Moodie, 'Reminiscences of Wando Dale (Nareen)', p. 52, RHSV, Box 160/6.
3   J. Gascoigne, *The Enlightenment and the Origins of European Australia* (Cambridge, 2002); A. M. Whitaker (ed.), *Distracted Settlement. New South Wales after Bligh. From the Journal of Lieutenant James Finucane 1808–1810* (Melbourne, 1998).
4   Sir Thomas Mitchell, *Three Expeditions into the Interior of Eastern Australia* (2 volumes, London, 1839), vol. 2, p. 171.
5   George Arden, *Latest Information with Regard to Australia Felix, the Finest Province of the Great Territory of New South Wales* (Melbourne, 1840), p. 315.
6   William Westgarth, *Victoria: Late Australia Felix or Port Phillip District of New South Wales* (Edinburgh, 1853), pp. 31–2, 41.
7   L. Peel (ed.), *The Henty Journals. A Record of Farming, Whaling and Shipping in Portland Bay, 1834–1839* (Melbourne, 1996), *passim*.

8   See, for example, Patrick Coady Buckley, Journal 1844–1872, RHSV, Box 37/4;
    Hugh Hamilton, Diary and Reminiscences, 1841–1882, NLA, Ms 956, Folders 1–2;
    Miscellaneous correspondence to Andrew Vernon Suter and others, 1844–1888,
    RHSV, Suter Mss, Box 160/4; M. A. Bunn (ed.), *The Lonely Pioneer. William Bunn,
    Diarist, 1830–1901* (Braidwood, 2002), *passim*.
9   Dunmore Station Journal, Vols 1–3, MacKnight Papers, SLV, Ms 8999, Box F
    1839.
10 *Ibid.*, Vol. 1, 16 September 1843.
11 *The Australasian*, 'Obituary: Charles Hamilton MacKnight', 10 May 1873.
12 Dunmore Station Journal, Vol. 1, 6 February 1851, MacKnight Papers, SLV, Ms
    8999, Box F 1839.
13 *Ibid.*, Vol. 2, 13 January 1863.
14 Margaret McCann, Diary Stradbroke Station, SLV, Ms 9632, Call No: MSB 480.
15 *Ibid.*, 2 and 12 January, 23 September 1895; 3, 11 and 12 August, 2 and 31 October
    1896; 19 April 1897; 8 February 1898.
16 *Ibid.*, 30 October 1895; 24 February, 15 March 1896; 9 November, 6 December
    1897; 4 May, 20 October 1898.
17 *Ibid.*, 4, 20 and 21 February, 7 March 1895; 12, 20 and 22 January, 8 February 1898;
    23 February, 13–16 March 1899.
18 *Ibid.*, 14 May, 4 June 1896; 12 and 18 July 1897; 1–5 March, 12 May 1898; 7 June
    1899.
19 *Ibid.*, 4 April 1896; 3 December 1897; 7 April 1898; 11 September 1900.
20 *Ibid.*, 22 March 1901.
21 Fetherstonhaugh, *After Many Days*; J. C. Hamilton, *Pioneering Days in
    Western Victoria. A Narrative of Early Station Life* (Melbourne, 1914); Moodie,
    'Reminiscences'.
22 Hamilton, *Pioneering Days*, p. 37.
23 Fetherstonhaugh, *After Many Days*, pp. 407.
24 Moodie, 'Reminiscences', pp. 14–15.
25 *Ibid.*, 25–6.
26 *Ibid.*, pp. 37–8; D. Day, *Claiming a Continent. A New History of Australia* (4th
    edn, Sydney, 2005), pp. 5–6; P. J. Hughes and M. E. Sullivan, 'Aboriginal Burning
    and Late Holocene Geomorphic Events', *Search*, Vol. 12 (1981), pp. 277–8.
27 Cited in B. Reece, 'The Irish and the Aborigines', in T. Foley and F. Bateman
    (eds), *Irish-Australian Studies. Papers Delivered at the Ninth Irish-Australian
    Conference Galway, April 1997* (Sydney, 2000), pp. 192–204.
28 T. Ballantyne, *Orientalism and Race. Aryanism in the British Empire* (London,
    2002); J. M. MacKenzie, 'Empire and Metropolitan Cultures', in A. Porter (ed.), *The
    Oxford History of the British Empire. Volume III The Nineteenth Century* (Oxford,
    1999), pp. 270–93.
29 Westgarth, *Victoria*, pp. 46, 50.
30 *Ibid.*, p. 47.
31 *Ibid.*, p. 53. See also, S. Ryan, *The Cartographic Eye. How Explorers Saw Australia*
    (Cambridge, 1996), pp. 128–52.
32 Westgarth, *Victoria*, p. 54.
33 H. Vellacott and C. E. Sayers (eds), Thomas Francis Bride, *Letters from Victorian
    Pioneers* (3rd edn, Melbourne, 1983), p. 31.
34 Fetherstonhaugh, *After Many Days*, pp. 293–4.
35 *Ibid.*, p. 294.
36 Day, *Claiming*, pp. 43–114; A. McGrath (ed.), *Contested Ground. Australian
    Aborigines under the British Crown* (Sydney, 1995), *passim*.
37 Vellacott and Sayers, *Letters*, pp. 103–4.
38 *Ibid.*, pp. 161–6.
39 Hamilton, *Pioneering Days*, pp. 32–3.
40 Patrick Coady Buckley, Journal 1844–1872, Vol. 1, 20 and 21 January 1845, RHSV,
    Box 37/4.
41 Buckley's Journal also records his physical assaults on Chinese and other labourers

who worked for him. *Ibid.*, Vol. 1, 26, 27 September 1855; 23 September 1856; Vol. 2, 5 April 1863.

42 The last entry in Buckley's Journal recording stock losses as a result of Aborigine depredation is in August 1847.

43 Exemplified by the various contemporary accounts in Vellacott and Sayers, *Letters*.

44 J. M. Arthur, *The Default Country. A Lexical Cartography of Twentieth-century Australia* (Sydney, 2003), pp. 72–83.

45 Vellacott and Sayers, *Letters*, p. 165.

46 *Ibid.*, pp. 28–9, 109, 165–7, 293, 368.

47 *Ibid.*, pp. 98–9.

48 For a perceptive critique of the concept of frontier 'closure' see: R. Howitt, 'Frontiers, Borders, Edges: Liminal Challenges to the Hegemony of Exclusion', *Australian Geographical Studies*, Vol. 31, No. 2 (July 2001), pp. 233–45. Howitt claims that this constitutes an unhelpful exclusionary epistemology that denies the possibility of hybrid interaction across borders.

49 This debate is summarised in F. Devlin-Glass, 'The Irish in Grass Castles: Re-reading Victim Tropes in an Iconic Pioneering Text', in L. M. Geary and A. J. McCarthy (eds), *Ireland, Australia and New Zealand. History, Politics and Culture* (Dublin, 2008), pp. 104–18.

50 Vellacott and Sayers, *Letters*, pp. 147–9.

51 *Ibid.*, pp. 334–5.

52 *Ibid.*, p. 312.

53 Moodie, 'Reminiscences', pp. 51–2.

54 D. J. Mulvany, *Cricket Walkabout. The Australian Aboriginal Cricketers on Tour 1867–1868* (Melbourne, 1967).

55 Adam Turnbull, Diary 1865–6, entry for 27 March 1866, Turnbull Family Papers, RHSV, Ms 000681, Box 231/2.

56 Arthur, *Default Country*, pp. 72–3.

57 Data derived from William Hanson, *The Pastoral Possessions of New South Wales* (Sydney, 1889); R. Spreadborough and H. Anderson, *Victorian Squatters* (Melbourne, 1983).

58 Arthur, *Default Country*, *passim*. For an example of the instability of run names even as recalled in pioneer memory, see Moodie, 'Reminiscences', pp. 23–30.

59 L. Blake, *Place Names of Victoria* (Melbourne, 1977), pp. 9–14.

60 Arthur, *Default Country*, pp. 72–83.

61 Calculated from Spreadborough and Anderson, *Victorian Squatters*, pp. 82–146.

62 Thomas Lennox Gibson Papers, RHSV, Ms 000786, Box 58/20.

63 Thomas Lennox Gibson to J. Gibson, 16 August 1845, *ibid.*

64 Thomas Lennox Gibson to W. R. Wright, 5 January and 24 April 1847, Letters from Crown Lands Department Files, *ibid.*

65 Thomas Lennox Gibson to W. R. Wright, 24 April 1847, *ibid.*

66 Buckley's violence was something his local obituarist ignored, choosing rather to represent him as 'widely respected . . . a man of giant stature, prompt, energetic and truthful, guileless as a child and most conscientiously industrious. For integrity and honour he bore the highest character . . .', *The Gippsland Times*, 18 July 1872.

67 Letter M. Hancock to A. J. Hopton, 16 May 1860, Patrick Coady Buckley, Journal 1844–1872, RHSV, Box 37/4.

68 Patrick Coady Buckley, Journal 1844–1872, RHSV, Box 37/4, Vol. 1, 7 March 1844.

69 *Ibid.*, Vol. 2, 25 November 1859; 5 October 1860; 11 March, 17 April, 6 and 23 May 1861.

70 *Ibid.*, Vol. 3, 2, 4 and 6 February 1862.

71 *Ibid.*, Vol. 3, 23 July 1865.

72 *Ibid.*, Vol. 3, 27 May and 25 June 1869.

73 T. Henzell, *Australian Agriculture. Its History and Challenges* (Melbourne, 2007); J. Pickard, 'The Transition from Shepherding to Fencing in Colonial Australia', *Rural History*, Vol. 18, No. 2 (2007), pp. 143–62; Idem, 'Shepherding in Colonial Australia', *Rural History*, Vol. 19, No. 1 (2008), pp. 55–80; G. Raby, *Making Rural*

Australia. An Economic History of Technical and Institutional Creativity (Oxford, 1996).

74 See, for example, Patrick Coady Buckley, Journal 1844–1872, RHSV, Box 37/4; Scott Family papers, SLV, Mss 13178 and 8853, Box 915/1–4, call no: MSB 438; Turnbull Family Papers, RHSV, Ms 000681, Box 230/1–4, Box 231/1–2, Box 233/11–12.

75 *The Gippsland Times*, 'Obituary: Patrick Coady Buckley', 18 July 1872.

76 Dunmore Account Book 1865, Dunmore Station Records 1847–1873, MacKnight Papers, SLV, Ms 13180, Box 3826/4.

77 M. Kiddle, *Men of Yesterday. A Social History of the Western District of Victoria, 1834–1890* (Melbourne, 1961), pp. 307–18; S. Priestly, *The Victorians. Making Their Mark* (Sydney, 1984), pp. 92–5; R. Waterhouse, *The Vision Splendid. A Social and Cultural History of Rural Australia* (Fremantle, 2005), pp. 94–8.

78 B. Andrews, 'Revival or Reminder: the Gothic in Australia', in Peter Reynolds (ed.), *Conference of Architectural Historians in Australia* (Adelaide, 1984); M. Dupain *et al.*, *Georgian Architecture in Australia* (Sydney, 1963); J. M. Freeland, *Architecture in Australia: A History* (Melbourne, 1974).

79 P. Scott, 'O'Brien, Cornelius 91796–1869)', *Australian Dictionary of Biography*, Vol. 2 (Melbourne, 1967), pp. 292–3.

80 Stuart H. Hume, 'Hume, Hamilton (1797–1873)', *Australian Dictionary of Biography*, Vol. 1 (Melbourne, 1966), pp. 564–5.

81 J. Summerson, *Architecture in Britain 1530–1830* (New Haven and London, 1993), pp. 502–7.

82 Sarah Scott, Mount Boninyong, to Sarah Mitchell, Glasgow, 14 April 1860, Letters from Robert Scott and Sarah Scott (née Mitchell) to Sarah Mitchell, Glasgow 1859–1862, Scott family papers, SLV, Ms 13178, Box 3840/12.

83 C. Laskowski, *'Overnewton': The Castle on the Hill* (Essendon, 2005).

84 I. McClelland, 'Landscape and Memory: Irish Cultural Transmissions in Australia, c.1840–1914' (unpublished PhD thesis, Queen's University, Belfast, 2002), p. 88 ff.

85 Kiddle, *Men of Yesterday*, pp. 307–9; Russell Ward, 'Black, Neil (1804–1880)', *Australian Dictionary of Biography*, Vol. 3 (Melbourne, 1969), pp. 171–2.

86 Daniel Halfpenny, Journal August 1840–June 1847, SLV, Ms 13300, call no: SAFE 3.

87 *Ibid.*, 3, 10, 13, 15 November and 1 December 1841; 24 January 1842; 2, 20 October 1842.

88 *Ibid.*, 13 November 1841; 2, 21 October 1842.

89 Memoirs of Margaret Emily Brown (née Youngman), SLV, Ms 11619.

90 *Ibid.*, p. 51.

91 *Ibid.*, pp. 47–9.

92 *Ibid.*, pp. 51, 53–4.

93 *Ibid.*, pp. 55–6.

94 L. Proudfoot, 'Place and Presbyterian Discourse in Colonial Australia', in L. J. Proudfoot and M. M. Roche (eds) *(Dis)Placing Empire. Renegotiating British Colonial Geographies* (Aldershot, 2005), pp. 61–80.

95 D. Hoerder, 'From Migrants to Ethnics: Acculturation in a Societal Framework', in D. Hoerder and L. Page Moch (eds), *European Migrants. Global and Local Perspectives* (Boston, 1996), pp. 211–62.

96 Memoirs of Margaret Emily Brown (née Youngman), SLV, Ms 11619, p. 27; Proudfoot, 'Place and Presbyterian Discourse', pp. 75–6; Robert Scott at Mount Boninyong to Sarah Mitchell, Glasgow, n.d. but September 1860, Scott Family papers, SLV, Ms 13178, Box 3840/12; Churches and Yambuck Cemetery, Suter Family Papers, RHSV, Ms 000656, Boxes 155–164, Box 160/3.

97 Proudfoot, 'Place and Presbyterian Discourse', pp. 67–80.

98 John Mackersey, Diary 1857–1870, Turnbull Family Papers, RHSV, Ms 000681, Box 230/2; Robert Scott at Mount Boninyong to Sarah Mitchell, Glasgow, 16 April 1860, Scott Family papers, SLV, Ms 13178, Box 3840/12.

99   Alex G. Turnbull, Diary 1873–1885, Turnbull Family Papers, RHSV, Ms 000681, Box 230/3 (5).

100 Hugh Hamilton, Reminiscences pp. 1–2, Diary and Reminiscences 1841–1882, NLA, Ms 956.

101 *Ibid.*, p. 14.

102 *Ibid.*, pp. 31–5.

103 Hugh Hamilton, Diary, 6, 13, 20 and 27 August 1848, Diary and Reminiscences 1841–1882, NLA, Ms 956.

104 *Ibid.*, 8 and 9 January 1849; 27 May 1849.

105 *Ibid.*, 1 January 1851.

106 Hugh Hamilton, Reminiscences pp. 32–51, Diary and Reminiscences 1841–1882, NLA, Ms 956.

107 A. G. Turnbull, Draft notes: 'Streets of Coleraine', Turnbull Family Papers, RHSV, Ms 000681, Box 230/4; *Idem*, Draft notes: 'Coleraine settlement, Wannon Valley History', *ibid.*, Box 231/7.

108 Moodie, 'Reminiscences', pp. 55–62.

109 McClelland, 'Landscape and Memory', pp. 88–108.

110 T. Barnard, *Improving Ireland? Projectors, Prophets and Profiteers 1641–1786* (Dublin, 2008), pp. 143–66.

111 McClelland, 'Landscape and Memory', pp. 97–8.

112 Exemplified by the Suter family, whose lives in Victoria were informed by their relatives' previous service in the Indian Army and who maintained close contacts with, and periodically visited, relatives in Aberdeen and Queensland. Suter Family Papers, RHSV, Ms 000656, Boxes 155–164.

113 Robert Scott at Mount Boninyong to Sarah Mitchell, Glasgow, 16 April and (-) September 1860, Scott Family papers, SLV, Ms 13178, Box 3840/12.

114 Sarah Scott at Mount Boninyong to Sarah Mitchell, Glasgow, 14 April 1860, *ibid.*

115 Sarah Scott at Mount Boninyong to Sarah Mitchell, Glasgow, 15 May 1860, *ibid.*

116 'Mount Boninyong 1839–1989', Scott Family papers, SLV, Ms 13178, Box 3840/11(e).

CHAPTER 7

Urban enactments

It is surely then not only a harmless but a pleasing thing that Irishmen should still continue to show that love of country which ennobles them and serves to make them better citizens of their adopted home. In nearly every town of any importance whatever in this colony Irishmen assemble on the 17th March to do honour to St Patrick's day. (*Kilmore Free Press*, 1873[1])

He was always a Scotchman, which did not deprive him of his real love for this adopted country – Ilawarra . . . Of course we have always to make allowances for Scotsmen, who stand up at all times and on all occasions for noted Scotchmen. (Thomas Brown, Obituary, 1925[2])

As a townsman, his interests are identical with my own, I will therefore vote for him. What do I care what his religion is or where accident placed his birth? Signed A BURGESS. (*Kilmore Free Press*, 1865[3])

Just as pastoral runs formed part of the colonial re-imagining of Australia's landscape, so too, towns and villages were central to the re-materialisation of this landscape and its inscription with new place meanings. As Anthony Trollope noted in 1873, even the smallest towns might possess a surprisingly wide range of functions and were thus, as Jeans observes, truly urban in character.[4] Accordingly, as Thomas Brown's obituary and the excerpts from the *Kilmore Free Press* suggest, it is likely that they had the capacity to sustain a wider variety of 'voices' and provided more complex opportunities to contest hegemonic narratives of place than even the largest pastoral stations. The assemblies of Irishmen 'in nearly every town of any importance' in Victoria on 17 March were defined by the assertion of a particular and often subordinate form of ethnic Irish selfhood. In much the same way, Thomas Brown's declarations of his Scottishness necessarily also defined himself in terms of what he was not – not English, not Irish; nothing, apparently, that was not Scottish. That these ethno-national self-designations could sometimes prove troubling is amply testified by the anonymous burgess's letter, but so too is the diasporic realisation that these primordial affinities offered progressively less purchase on the realities of the colonial urban present.

In this chapter we examine aspects of the ways in which the four towns that form part of this study, Belfast (Port Fairy), Kiama, Kilmore and Stawell were performed as place by the Irish and Scottish settlers and their descendants who formed a significant part of their nineteenth-century populations. The populations of all four towns fluctuated as the colonial economy developed, but never exceeded 2,000 or 3,000, save Stawell's, which rose to over 7,500 during its' mining hey-day of the 1870s. In common with the other towns, however, Stawell's population declined (to *ca.* 5,000) during the depression of the 1890s. Both Kilmore and Port Fairy were regarded by contemporaries as Irish Catholic enclaves, though this denomination (regardless of nationality) never exceeded 45 per cent of the population in either settlement.[5] Kiama, by contrast, acquired a reputation from the start as a centre of Protestant Irish settlement, largely in consequence of the chain migration of Anglicans from West Ulster that was actively encouraged by local Ulster-born leaseholders from the 1830s onwards.[6] At Stawell, the cosmopolitan and footloose workforce attracted by the diggings ensured that the proportion of Scots- or Irish-born never exceeded 15 per cent of the town's population during the nineteenth century.[7]

As noted in chapter 1, these towns were variously ports, agricultural markets or, in the case of Stawell, a mining settlement, and this functional diversity ensured that they embodied a particularly wide array of the social, cultural and economic discourses that formed part of the urban signature of settler capitalism. They therefore held a multi-faceted mirror to Irish and Scottish experience of colonial urbanism in Australia. As in the case of pastoral runs or on board emigrant ships, a reflexive self-identifying sense of ethnicity appears to have played a part, but only a part, in this experience. Just as in these other 'imperial spaces', so too in towns, ethnic performance bore upon and was borne upon by other imperatives, such as economic survival, gender and social status. Memory played a significant part in these elisions by helping to sustain the continual re-imagining and re-staging of the performative spaces they created. In this way, further layers of meaning were continually added to already inchoate diasporic place identities which, crucially, were given further local shape by the performances themselves.

We begin by outlining various discursive aspects of colonial urbanism in Victoria and New South Wales that provided the imperial context for the narratives of urbanism in our chosen towns. Both

colonies quickly established primate urban hierarchies that were characterised by the rapid growth and disproportionate size of their capitals,
Melbourne and Sydney, as the major ports of entry. In this, they bore
a remarkable functional resemblance to the mercantilist urban hierarchy which existed in Ireland prior to the industrialisation of Belfast
and its hinterland from the 1820s onwards, and which was dominated
by Dublin.[8] We then explore three narratives which highlight different aspects of the ways in which Scottish and Irish settlers performed
urban place in Australia. In the first, 'Constructing the civic', we
examine the ways in which the materiality of urban place might be
imbued with ethnic signifiers, and the varied interpretations different
socio-economic readership groups placed on these. The second, 'The
spectacle of memory', considers the ways in which different ethnic
solidarities periodically performed their collective identities in the
shared spaces of these towns. The most prominent of these were the St
Patrick's Day celebrations on 17 March, but there were others: the
Scottish St Andrew's Day celebration on 30 November, for example,
as well as celebrations of Queen Victoria's birthday and local cultural
events. All trod a fine line between ethno-cultural essentialism and
social inclusivity as the primordial ethnic imperatives of the Old World
gave way to the diasporic sensitivities of the New. The final narrative,
'Gendered spaces', explores particular instances of ethnicised gendered
and sexual behaviour which reinforced the authority of existing urban
patriarchies. All three narratives bear witness to the discursively
bounded localism of Scottish and Irish colonial urban experience.

A cartography of settler urbanism

If the perceived 'timelessness' of Australia's landscapes masked the
reality of rapidly changing colonial geographies, it also helped to frame
a particularly enduring national foundation myth which invoked the
rural rather than the urban. In this, diggers, drovers, swagmen and
selectors, rather than counter-clerks and urban artisans, were held to
embody the qualities of mateship, endurance and fortitude that were
said to have created 'white' Australia. Yet the myth itself was urban
and arguably, mirrored the growing disassociation from 'the timeless
land' that was felt by the increasing majority of Australia's population who were, in fact, town or city dwellers.[9] In the 1850s perhaps 40
per cent of Australia's population lived in towns of over 2,500 people;
by 1881 over half the population were urban dwellers.[10] Not that the
colonies' overall population growth rate fell; simply, the towns and
cities grew faster.[11] Moreover, a significant component in this urban
growth was due to the increasing attraction of the colonial capitals. For

example, in 1861 a quarter of Victoria's population of just over 538,000 lived in Melbourne; by 1911 that proportion had risen to half the state's total of over 1.3 million.[12] In New South Wales a similar story ensued as Sydney increased its primacy throughout the nineteenth century. In 1851, with a population of 54,000, the city was thirteen times larger than Maitland, the second-largest town. By 1911 Sydney's population had grown to over 488,000, or 38 per cent of the state total, and was over nineteen times larger than the next largest town, the mining settlement of Broken Hill.[13]

Carter argues that such primate urbanism was typical of pre-industrial economies characterised by extensive rather than nodal modes of production and the highly centralised exercise of state authority, and this was true of both Ireland (up to the mid-nineteenth century) and settler colonies in general.[14] Consequently, many of the reasons Jeans adduces for Sydney's disproportionate growth during the nineteenth century could also stand for Melbourne from the 1850s and for Dublin prior to the Act of Union of 1801.[15] These cities' monopoly of central political, governmental and administrative functions attracted the wealthy and ambitious – speculators and pastoralists to the Melbourne clubs, no less than Anglo-Irish aristocrats to Dublin Castle. This created a thriving internal market for an ever-expanding array of goods and services that fuelled the cities' further growth.[16] Moreover, all three cities developed one further advantage. As road, rail and, in the earlier case of Dublin, canal networks developed, linking them to their hinterlands, so they became increasingly well placed to dominate inland markets by offering goods and services advantaged by economies of scale in production and decreasing real transport costs. By the mid-nineteenth century Melbourne and Sydney had become *entrêpots* where the products of British industrial capitalism could be circulated in exchange for primary exports; import substitution was to develop later.

Dublin's position in the nineteenth century was more complex. The loss of its capital status under the Act of Union deprived it of precisely those high-status consumerist functions which had driven its primate population growth to 180,000 by 1800. Thereafter its growth was comparatively modest and geared to an increasingly redistributive role as its own agrarian-based industries struggled to cope with growing competition from British imports. By 1901 the city's population stood at *ca.* 290,000, considerably less than Belfast's 350,000, and an apt reflection of Ireland's shift from a colonial urban pattern to one dominated by the regional industrialisation of Ulster.[17] By contrast, in New South Wales and Victoria the discoveries of gold in the 1850s and the continued exploitation of the Hunter Valley, Illawarra and Western coalfields led to comparatively limited urbanisation that did not challenge Melbourne and Sydney's primacy. Although used to fuel the two capitals' growing industries, New South Wales' coal was largely exported – to Valparaiso, San Francisco, South Africa and beyond. Consequently, the main coalfield centres, Newcastle and Wollongong, remained primarily coal-exporting ports.[18] Similarly, even the largest and functionally most complex gold-mining towns, such as Ballarat or Sandhurst (Bendigo) in Victoria, survived as little more than regional service centres once their alluvial and quartz reef gold reserves ran out.[19]

But, whatever their future success in developing a wider service role, goldfield towns such as Bendigo, Castlemaine or, indeed, Stawell, remained in the end a particular form of colonial urbanism. Driven, certainly, by the same logic of settler capitalism as other settlements, they nevertheless represented an opportunistic response to the adventitious economic opportunities presented by unexpected goldfield discoveries. The majority of country towns and villages had a different origin, either as official planned components in the government's initial land surveys or as private initiatives – retrospectively sanctioned by government – as settlement spread into the intermediate and pastoral districts. By 1842, fifty-three town sites had been surveyed in the settled districts of New South Wales as part of the 1825 Parish Survey instigated under Governor Brisbane, and their orthogonal plans provided a model for future inland urban initiatives in the colony.[20] Each parish or township comprised twenty-five square miles and included designated sites for four villages where land was reserved for churches, schools and other public use. Paralleling historical English practice, the Survey established a hierarchy of administrative units that ultimately proved to be unsuitable for the sparsely populated Australian landscape. Four parishes were amalgamated into a 'hundred', while sixteen hundreds formed a county of approximately 1,600 square miles. Each county was, in theory, to be served by its own county town, again after the English fashion.[21] In the Port Phillip District the Parish Survey was begun in 1837 under Robert Hoddle, though with less detailed attention to the provision of village sites. In 1851, the new Victorian legislature, under the first lieutenant governor, Charles La Trobe, proclaimed ninety-one existing settlements as towns or villages and set aside a further 681,000 acres for future township reserves. In 1853, 250 townships were officially gazetted.[22] Not all of the village sites they contained eventually achieved urban status or were proclaimed as municipalities or boroughs, but nevertheless, as Powell suggests, nearly 90 per cent of Victoria's inland towns originated in this way.[23]

It is hard, accordingly, to over-estimate the extent to which the cartographies of settler urbanism in New South Wales and Victoria were imprinted with the discursive stamp of imperialism and mirrored the colonial imagination. As Heathcote has noted, the European colonisation of Australia was, in a sense, an urban project that channelled flows of people, goods, capital and ideas from towns and cities on the coastal periphery into the rural interior.[24] Accordingly, towns of every size were, above all, sites of the colonial self. In them, imperially sanctioned but sometimes informal discourses of cultural, social and economic authority were enacted, and various 'white' hegemonies were established and contested. Many were also sites of the political, judicial and legislative authority that sustained these. Thus, the grand narratives of land allocation and redistribution were administered by urban elites and attracted urban capital, while the assisted-passage schemes which brought a large proportion of Australia's first-generation migrants to its shores were orchestrated through Sydney and Melbourne. Moreover, in these as in other matters, colonial politicians increasingly responded to the demands of the growing urban electorate. At a local level, once police districts had superseded counties as the basic unit of administration in the 1840s, many towns in the intermediate and pastoral districts were founded as a simple collection of judicial and other government buildings. Perhaps comprising no more than a police station and a lock-up located at a some river crossing or other strategic point, they nevertheless exhibited and disbursed colonial authority – and the imperial power which it manifested – to the surrounding area.[25]

Urban plans and morphology gave physical shape to these acts of colonial discourse. Most of the colonial authorities' planned towns existed on paper before they were laid out on the ground, and their rigidly bounded and regimented orthogonal spaces frequently ignored the local physical reality of steep slopes, gullies and flood-prone land. For example, Port Pirie and Pinnaroo in South Australia remained subject to devastating floods because their ill-chosen, low-lying sites were surveyed during the 'dry'.[26] Robert Dixon's original 1828 survey of Goulburn at the junction of the Wollondilly and Mullwaree Rivers in New South Wales suffered from a similar deficiency. Following his visit to the town in 1832, Governor Richard Bourke ordered that a new site be laid out on higher ground to the east.[27] In much the same way, according to Jeans, Thomas Mitchell's 1829 plan for East Maitland combined aesthetic sensibility, environmental awareness and topographic maladaptation in equal measure. The town was sited on a ridge overlooking the flood plain of the Hunter River, and Mitchell paid careful attention to the juxtaposition of the public spaces along its major axes and to their visual potential. He thought it 'important to supply by art the natural defects of the country even with the respect to the ornamental'. His concern did not extend to the town's suburbs. These were laid out in rectilinear fashion across the broken terrain which fell away on either side of the ridge. In the event, Mitchell's plan suffered further disruption as traders vied for plots along the Newcastle Road. Originally peripheral to Mitchell's intended town centre, this subsequently emerged as East Maitland's major commercial axis.[28]

If the regimented character and topographical insensitivity of urban planning such as this bore witness to the limits of the colonial imagination, the toponyms attached to these sites embodied a greater diversity of personal meaning. Just as the pastoral cartographies created by settler capitalism offered opportunities to memorialise the settlers' diasporic past through place naming (chapter 6), so too, towns offered the possibility of complex and contested semiotics of place. Naming settler towns and villages was as important in shaping meaning and building identity as bounding and naming the colonists' pastoral properties. In town and countryside alike, demotic language was used to incorporate the alien and unknown into the settled and familiar.[29] Near Stawell, for example, Sisters Rocks, a significant granite rock formation, was given its English name to describe the spot where the three Levy sisters camped with their family en route to the goldfields, thus fixing the location as a white place in the contemporary colonial imagination.[30] Similarly, William Rutledge named Kilmore after the ancient cathedral in Cavan, his home county in Ireland, thus imprinting Irish meaning in the Australian landscape. As with James Atkinson's foundation at Belfast (Port Fairy), Kilmore proclaimed both Rutledge's ethno-national origins and the commonly understood Irishness of the town and its people.[31] Where settlers adopted Aborigine names for towns or villages, as at Kiama, Gerringong and Jamberoo in the Illawarra, indigenous meaning was largely eradicated. As on the pastoral runs, in appropriating these names settlers demonstrated their limited understanding of indigeneity, even as they tried to locate this particular other within the landscapes of their colonial imagination.

Urban, village and mining toponyms also reflected subaltern as well as hegemonic 'white' performances of place. On the Pleasant Creek (later Stawell) goldfield, claims and mines were named and renamed by hopeful licence holders in imaginative acts that, as on the runs, located these individuals' diasporic past in their colonial present. Philips' Flat was named after Wexford-born Philip Scallan and colloquially known by local diggers as 'Philips'.[32] Similarly, the scrubby surrounds of Pleasant Creek were transformed into evocative sites of memory by names such as Scotchman's, Hibernia Reef, Perthshire and Emerald.[33] Martin Doyle, Wexford-born town clerk of Stawell and a prominent member of local Irish organisations, was the business manager of the

Emerald Isle and Hibernia mines as well as of the Starlight mining company. His friend, fellow Wexford-born David Scallan, was manager of the Prince Alfred Mining company and the Victoria Reef company.[34] Scallan, a lawyer and former Stawell Shire President, was both a fervent supporter of Irish Catholic causes and an Empire Loyalist. His impassioned speeches supporting the British Crown after the attempted assassination of Prince Alfred in Sydney in 1868 are a reminder of the layered and contingent nature of the cultural and political identities embodied in these naming practices.[35]

Street and building names too were of varied authorship, and signified diverse and sometimes controversial meanings to different readership groups.[36] In 1868, shortly after the attempted assassination of Prince Alfred, the Stawell correspondent of the *Ararat and Pleasant Creek Advertiser* reported that 'A new street named by one class of the community "Patrick" and by the other "Alfred" had been settled'.[37] As the street was known as Patrick Street in all the official documents, 'Alfred Street' clearly embodied a pointed ethnic, and presumably politically inspired, objection by some residents to the use of a name with connotations of Irish Catholicism and – in their view – disloyalty. Naming appears in this instance to have been a deliberate act of ethnic politics. In other places, ethnically inspired naming practices operated at different levels to indicate not only a generalised Irishness but also specific remembered places in Ireland. For example, at Kiama, James Barton, from Kesh, opened the Fermanagh Hotel sometime in the late 1840s. The hotel retained this name for more than twenty-five years, during which time large numbers of Ulster Scots Protestants settled in the area.[38] To name or run a hotel called the Fermanagh signalled more than just the owner's personal memory. It established the hotel and its proprietors' political and cultural identity in the eyes of outsiders – those from elsewhere in Ulster, Ireland, England and the new colony of New South Wales – as a place where compatriots from Ulster would find a familiar welcome. In this case, it also signalled a political and religiously defined space. Catholics were not welcome in the Fermanagh Hotel, and seemingly preferred to seek comfort in the neighbouring Beehive Hotel, run by the Irish Catholic O'Toole family.

Like all ethnicised toponyms, the Fermanagh Hotel evoked both memory and belonging as well as self and other for its customers. Although forming only a fractionally small part of the complex and ever-changing cartography of settler urbanism, the hotel, the people it served (or excluded) and the town they lived in all played a role in the continuing discourse of British colonialism in Australia. However indifferent to the geographical realities of the Australian landscape some planned towns may have been, and whatever the source of their toponymic identity, they remained resolutely part of the projection of a particular form of European imperialism. Beyond this they had no meaning; within this their meaning as place was contested along every conceivable axis of identity. What part did Irish and Scottish settlers play in this, in the towns that concern us here?

Three urban narratives

Constructing the civic

Throughout the colonies of white settlement, urbanisation facilitated the growth of local government, but in Australia the trajectory of this relationship varied. In New South Wales, local government incorporation was not mandatory until the 1905 Local Government (Shires) Act divided the whole state (save the Western Division and existing municipalities) into shires. The municipalities were accommodated under a second Act in the same year, and both Acts were combined as The Local Government Act a year later. An earlier attempt under the 1842 Constitution Act to replace the elected Parish Road Trusts of 1840 with District Councils failed because of inadequate resources, while the elevation of settlements to municipal status remained a matter of local initiative. The 1858 Municipalities Act allowed groups of at least fifty ratepayers to petition for this status, leading to the proclamation of some thirty-five new municipalities, including Kiama. The second Municipalities Act of 1867 extended municipal powers and allowed settlements with a population of at least 1,000 within existing municipal districts to be designated as boroughs in their own right.[39]

Prior to the separation of Victoria in 1851, the earliest local government bodies in the Port Phillip District followed the New South Wales pattern. Parish Road Trusts were set up under the 1840 Act; two counties, Bourke and Grant, centred on Melbourne and Geelong, were proclaimed by the governor in 1843, and the two towns were incorporated in 1842 and 1849 respectively. Following separation, Victoria's provision for local government varied between urban and rural areas. The 1853 Roads Act established Road Boards as rate-collecting bodies charged with maintaining roads and bridges in their local rural Road Districts. Belfast (Port Fairy) was among the first boards to be proclaimed in 1854, and by the time that the 1863 Local Government Act amended the system, ninety-eight boards had been established.[40] Under the 1863 Act, any Road District larger than 100 square miles and with a minimum annual rateable income of £1,000 could apply for shire status. As the number of shires increased so the number of Road Districts gradually declined, until they were finally abolished under the Shire Statute of 1869.[41] In urban areas, corporate local government was initially provided for by the 1854 Municipal Institutions Act, which offered existing towns and suburbs the opportunity to apply for municipal status. Among the first to do so, in 1855, were Brighton, Richmond and Collingwood on the outskirts of Melbourne, and Sandhurst (Bendigo) on the central goldfields. Nine years later, the 1863 Local Government Act devolved yet more authority to the towns. Existing municipal districts were reconstituted as boroughs and charged with responsibility for all public infrastructural improvements, including roads, streets, cemeteries, water supply, drainage, public health, pounds and markets. Eventually the 1874 Local Government Act brought together rural and urban government under a single statute, ratified existing city, borough and shire boundaries, set electoral property qualifications and confirmed local rating powers.[42]

This seemingly straightforward narrative of administrative expansion and adjustment embodied complex meanings of place. At one level, the buildings that materialised these systems of governance – the court houses, shire halls, hospitals, bridges and other infrastructural improvements – stood as symbols of local civic achievement, albeit ones aligned with the broader discourse of colonial authority. As a visitor to Stawell Shire Council in 1886 observed, these places embodied the self-confident values of middle-class British imperialism. Describing the men attending a meeting in the council chamber, he concluded that they possessed

> that indefinable something – which tells the observer that it is of that stuff the colonies are made; men who know their own mind; fathers of the coming rulers of this great country.[43]

It was not just the individual men that this visitor saw, it was their collective demeanour and performance within the empowering hegemonic setting of the council chamber that attracted his attention. Their deliberations formed part of the place meanings embodied within this particular colonial space and both gave and received authoritarian substance from it.

These meanings, however, varied for each individual, and in this ethnic consciousness and performance evidently played their part. Irish and Scottish settlers were conspicuous in the governance and growth of all four towns in this study, but in different capacities. At Stawell, where the shire and municipality were proclaimed under the 1863 Local Government Act and the borough was declared in 1869, Scots, Ulster-Scots and Southern Irish men figured prominently among the list of urban officers, even though collectively these groups constituted less than a fifth of the borough's population of 5,166 in 1871.[44] For example, the four Wexford-born Scallan brothers were, variously, miners and storekeepers, but in David Scallan produced the first Shire President. Martin Doyle, also from Wexford, was the first Town Clerk, while fellow Irishman Thomas Kinsella was Mayor in 1881–82. John McLaren, the first Shire Engineer, and John D'Alton, the first Borough Engineer, were both Ulster-Scots Presbyterians from County Down. Various Scotsmen, including Ronald Campbell, Thomas Smith and John Sinclair, occupied the offices of Mayor and Town Clerk between the 1860s and 1880s.[45]

At Belfast (Port Fairy) and Kilmore, Irish involvement was of a rather different order. The circumstances surrounding the foundation of these towns under the Special Survey regulations by their Irish land-lords, James Atkinson and William Rutledge, have already been noted (chapter 5). By the time each community acquired the trappings of more formal local government, its landlord's patronal role had either been surrendered (at Kilmore) or was beginning to wane (in Belfast). Both towns were proclaimed Municipalities in 1856 and achieved Borough status in 1863–64, by which time Rutledge had long since sold his Kilmore property to his sitting tenants and a Sydney-based (and partly Irish) syndicate.[46] The decline of landlord influence in Belfast was more gradual. Despite selling some land to sitting tenants under the 1860 Nicholson Land Act, the Atkinson family retained ownership of most of the town and surrounding lands after James Atkinson's death in 1864, before selling out to a local property syndicate in 1883.[47] It is debatable whether the Atkinson family could have maintained its patronal authority for very much longer in Belfast, in any case. There, as elsewhere, the advent of increasingly democratic local government created opportunities for representatives of previously othered groups to contest existing forms of authority, be they those of an Irish landlord or anyone else.[48]

The question remains, however, of how ethnic consciousness may have inflected these negotiations of urban governance. Some insight into this can be gleaned from the diary of William Wall, one-time schoolmaster and, latterly, local government official and councillor at Belfast. The son of Catholic Irish immigrants, Wall was born in Belfast in 1859 and died there in 1899. After a brief career teaching in the local Catholic school, he was elected first as Shire Secretary in 1881 and then as Shire Auditor in 1885, a post he held until 1889. Various appoint-ments, including Rabbit and, later, Road Inspector, followed, and in 1894 he qualified as Municipal Auditor. He was appointed as a Justice of the Peace in 1895 and elected as a Borough Councillor a year later.[49] As secretary and auditor he was responsible for the minutes of council meetings and for overseeing local elections and rate collections, and he was thus privy to the inner workings of local government. His diary contains frequent references to the often acrimonious exchanges between councillors on a variety of improvement and other issues. These confrontations usually had a decidedly *ad hominem* flavour, as when the Town Clerk, John Davidson Burnie, was dismissed from his post in September 1884. An undiplomatic figure who had habitually antagonised a significant number of borough councillors through his part-time journalism, Burnie had relied on the patronage of a clique of local businessmen for support in the Council. Having survived an earlier attempt at dismissal in September 1883, he finally lost his post when his supporters were defeated – over the issue of his employment – in the Borough Council election of August 1884.[50]

Like Burnie, who went on to become a full-time journalist in New South Wales, Wall's career in local government represented only one aspect of his identity; his growing business interests represented a second, and his actively cultivated sense of Irishness, a third. There were others. In addition to the increasingly prominent role he played in Irish associational networks such as the Hibernian Association and the Hibernian Australian Catholic Benefit Society, he was also a member of various local self-improvement organisations such as the Mechanics' Institute, as well as the militia and the Australian Natives Association.[51] Yet it is clear that, as time went on, Wall's claims to a particular form of Irish Catholic ethnicity (which in his case can only have been learnt behaviour) increasingly coloured the other parts of his life, including his local government responsibilities. Initially, his Irishness was a matter of social and cultural performance: attendance at Hibernian dinners and involvement in organising the St Patrick's Day races at the nearby village of Koroit, for example. As the 1880s unfolded, however, Wall's claims to ethnicity became increasingly politicised in the cause of Irish nationalism and he grew more ambivalent about the displays of imperial loyalty expected of him as a militia sergeant and local government official.[52]

Throughout the decade, Wall continued his active political support for Irish-born candidates for the local seat in Victoria's Legislative Assembly: Sir John O'Shanassy in 1880 and 1883, and Sir Bryan O'Loghlen in 1889 and 1897. He was also prominent in organising visits to Belfast by the Redmond brothers and Sir John Esmonde during their tours of Australia in 1883 and 1889.[53] All of this marked him out as a man of particular ethno-cultural sensibilities in the shared spaces of the town. As Wall's political activism increased, so his willingness to participate in public expressions of loyalty to the British Crown waned, culminating in his refusal, as Shire Auditor, to attend the ball and banquet held in the town to celebrate Queen Victoria's Fiftieth Jubilee in 1887. As a leading member of the local branch of the

Hibernian Catholic Benefit Society, he had already been party to that organisation's decision to boycott Belfast's Jubilee parade, when it was the only local association to do so. Both these decisions stood in sharp contrast to his earlier willingness in 1881 to take part in royal celebrations as a member of the militia.[54] In a town as deeply riven by competing ethnicities as was Belfast, Wall's increasing political activism was unlikely to pass unnoticed. Nor did it. In August 1889 he was defeated in the annual election for Shire Auditor, partly, he alleged, because of his 'Home Rule sympathies'.[55]

Wall's performance as Shire Secretary and Auditor demonstrates the complex and subjective character of governance in Belfast, and the role ethnic consciousness might play in this. Elsewhere, the process of governance produced other material signatures in the landscape, and these too can be read for ethnic meaning. In such cases, the commonly understood imperial and colonial symbolism that imbued these places was overlain with cultural performances that shifted and complicated their seemingly neutral meaning. For example, one of the earliest civic acts of the Stawell Shire Council was the construction of a much-needed bridge over the Wimmera River on the road to the farming district of Callawadda. This was opened on 23 November 1863 to

> a blast from the bagpipes played by the prize piper, Mr Donald Rowan who by his frequent displays of a variety of Highland music throughout the day, added materially to the enjoyment of the many Celtic settlers with which the surrounding areas are peopled.[56]

The bridge was named after Ronald Campbell, the Shire Councillor (later Shire President) who had overseen its construction. Thus, at the time of its opening, the bridge was inscribed with particular ethnic meanings by the pipe music, the local settlers' accents and, of course, its name. In representing this event, the *Pleasant Creek News* appears to have subsumed both Irish and Scottish identities under the same 'Celtic' ethnic category. Whether intentional or not, this had the effect of investing the performative spaces of the bridge's opening with hybridised meanings as a temporarily non-English 'othered' place. This hybridity was further marked when the Shire President, Galway-born George Jennings, spoke at the opening ceremony in an Australianised Irish accent. There was no irony in this performance. Seemingly, the local community fully approved of its varied ethnic inflection and consequent elision of different remembered pasts within the collective colonial present.[57]

Not all civic inscriptions of place were marked with such diasporic harmony. At Stawell, the community decided early on in its history that a benevolent hospital was required to care for sick and injured miners.[58] Local fund raising began in 1858 and, with the addition of a government grant, quickly raised enough money to open a fifteen-bed temporary hospital. A permanent building designed by Thomas Turnbull and George Lorimer was completed in 1861 and subsequently extended in 1869, and again in 1876–77. The hospital's construction embodied a great deal of Stawell's civic pride. The opening of the 1869 extension was the occasion for a civic ball, and this reflected the iconic status the building had achieved in the locally imagined landscape.[59] Predictably, the hospital's management committee meetings were fully reported in the local press, while the institution itself received widespread charitable support throughout the area.

From the outset, however, the management committee's meetings were confrontational. Different interest groups attempted to appropriate the hospital project and stamp it with their own ethno-cultural values, and in this Irish Catholics were heavily embroiled. Irish-born miners and businessmen had been involved in the hospital's planning from the start. The committee's first president was Richard Codd; Patrick D'Arcy and Thomas Hodges were among its members and David Scallan was one of its four trustees.[60] Matters came to a head over arrangements for the foundation ceremony. In an inevitably controversial move, Masonic members of the committee asked the Grand Master of the local Masonic lodge to lay the foundation stone, despite the stated objections of the Catholic committee members. As the *Ararat and Pleasant Creek Advertiser* put it:

> The objection is, briefly, that several influential supporters of the institute are Roman Catholics and it is a matter of notoriety that persons of this denomination object to Masonic and all other secret societies.[61]

A vigorous correspondence to the editor of the *Advertiser* ensued, most writers declaring that the dispute would do irreparable damage to the harmony of the town and the management of its hospital. One correspondent summed up the general mood:

> I regret and most sincerely that it will be very very long ere the bitter words expressed and the party feeling displayed will be forgotten by a good many public men of Pleasant Creek.[62]

The 'party feeling' demonstrated the primordialism of local Irish diasporic politics and their continuing division along religious and ethnic lines. All the Catholic members of the management committee were Irish and, in an orchestrated and well-understood protest, they boycotted the opening ceremony, whereupon Richard Codd immediately resigned as president.[63] Evidently, at this particular moment of empire, the mutual accommodations of the colonial present, as demonstrated by the shared civic pride in the new hospital, were insufficient to overcome the atavistic cultural certainties imported into Australia by some Irish immigrants.

Similar cultural memories found physical inscription in the urban spaces of Victoria in more quotidian ways as well. The desire for the comfort of the known and familiar was common to immigrants of all nationalities. For example, in September 1863, *The Ararat and Pleasant Creek Advertiser* invoked almost Arcadian imagery to place Stawell's cemetery as a visible reminder of civilisation and England's ordered landscapes amid the chaos of colonial life:

> It is quite a satisfactory feature to see so many graves substantially fenced in and evidently taken care of by relatives or friends. The cemetery looks more like a little village church-yard than the last resting place of a diggings town.[64]

By comparison, Kilmore's appearance evoked specifically Irish connotations in the minds of some observers, and presumably this, too, reflected the successful recreation of the familiar by its numerous Irish inhabitants. Writing in 1854, the Irish author, writer and traveller William Kelly was struck by the authenticity of its apparent Irishness:

> I was much astonished at the appearance of Kilmore in more than one respect, for it appeared to me like a place at least half a century old. And again, it gave the idea that Tubbercurry or Ballerodare, was rafted over holus-bolus from the Emerald Isle, so completely and intensely Irish was the entire population in appearance, in accent, and in the peculiarly Milesian style of huckstering arrangement in which the shops were set out.[65]

Yet beneath this apparent ethno-cultural hegemony lay divisions which only became apparent on longer acquaintance, as Caleb Collyer, an English school-teacher appointed to the town in the mid-1860s, found out. Collyer's observations on the social performance of place in Kilmore suggest that its semiotics were complex and layered, rather than singular and primordial. The people were 'either very kind or very hard to get along with. I found the Irish element most sympathetic. The English folk bitter, the Scotch loving and the native growth careless . . . There was too little moral fibre in the mental constitution and considering the number of religious institutions in Kilmore this would strike one at once . . . I found an absence of those honourable opennesses to which I had been accustomed and in its place a peculiar reticence and continuous suspicion.'[66] This suspicion may well have been due to local perception of Collyer as a recently arrived English government employee whose status and nationality placed him firmly outside the community's existing informal ethnic and social networks.

[186]

Some indication of this is given by Collyer's own account of the local Irish community's behaviour at the height of the 'Kelly scare':

> Many relatives and friends of the Kellys were residents in the neighbourhood, and Miss Kelly was a well known figure to all. It was expected that the banks in Kilmore would be raided. It was not far from the school where Ned Kelly was known to shelter, and every turn nearly of that adventurous gang was understood and though words were few that passed, signs followed signs that were unmistakeable.[67]

The 'signs [that] followed signs' suggest the existence of circuits of knowledge within the Irish Catholic community at Kilmore to which outsiders like Caleb Collyer – and perhaps members of other ethnic communities in the town as well – were not privy. Yet, at Kilmore as in the other study towns and beyond, civic endeavour resulted in the creation of buildings whose symbolism transcended, in however contested a fashion, such ethnically bounded understandings of place. Both these discourses – of inclusive colonial presentism and exclusive ethnic memory – played their part in the civic performance of these and other places. How else were they performed by Irish and Scottish settlers?

The spectacle of memory

Like many towns in colonial Australia, Belfast, Kiama, Kilmore and Stawell all witnessed periodic cultural performances of a more structured kind. In these, ethnic memory elided with presentist colonial experience to inscribe frequently hybrid social, political, cultural and religious meanings in the shared spaces of each town. Associational groups and energetic committees of community-minded men and women organised and attended a wide array of entertainments and commemorations. These events – parades, balls, games and picnics – inscribed their meaning in the townscape in ways which invited varied interpretation by different readership groups. The inevitable contestations that followed added to the semiotic complexity of these towns as place.

Foremost among these events in urban Victoria – and among the most ethnically inflected – were the celebrations of St Patrick's Day on 17 March, the Battle of the Boyne on 12 July and St Andrew's Day on 30 November, as well as various Caledonian Games on other dates. Each of these performances temporarily imprinted the public spaces of Melbourne and other towns with particular inscriptions of cultural memory and identity. In doing so, they reinforced the participants' sense of membership of a wider diasporic community that extended beyond their immediate colonial circumstances to connect them not only in memory to Ireland or Scotland, but also to a 'Greater' Scotland or Ireland overseas.[68] This sense of diasporic connection was embodied in annual toasts such as those of the Melbourne St Patrick's and Caledonian Societies to 'Our Native Land' and 'The Land We Live In', but it was also occasionally articulated by individual settlers with surprising clarity.[69] On St Patrick's Day in 1863, beneath a Harp of Erin and other 'authentic' symbols of Irishness which decorated the Shamrock Hotel at Ararat, William O'Callaghan gave a speech that acknowledged the diasporic contexts and consequent complexities of identity formation among Irish men and women living in Australia:

> Sir, this night and at this hour, how many social gatherings there are throughout the world to commemorate that old land . . . That this love of Father land is supereminently the characteristic of the Irish race is exemplified even in Australia, for whilst the children of the members of other nationalities content themselves with being called natives, the children of Irish parents invariably contend they are Irish. Nor does this love for one moment affect our allegiance for our adopted country, for by the same rule that an obedient son makes a good husband, does a man who loves the land of his birth make a good citizen in the country of his adoption.[70]

O'Callaghan's speech included frequent warmly received references to heroes of the struggle against the English in Ireland as well as to Irishmen who held high civic office in the Australian colonies, but also asserted Irish loyalty to the imperial crown that these men served. This dualism – between a growing concern for Ireland's position within the Empire and loyalty to that Empire – became increasingly characteristic of St Patrick Day speeches as constitutional nationalism, agrarian reform and Home Rule began to dominate the political agenda in Ireland and 'Greater' Ireland alike. By its nature, this particular trope of Irish diasporic consciousness was susceptible to the march of political events. Thus, in 1885, speeches at the St Patrick's Society ball and supper in Melbourne were framed by a desire, and perhaps the need, to distance Irish Australians from allegations of support for recent Fenian attacks in British and American cities. Responding to the toast 'Our Native Land', Martin Hood was reported by *The Argus* as expressing

> his great satisfaction at the patriotism evinced by the rising race of Irish Australiana. Amidst general applause he denied that Irishmen of Australia had a particular sympathy with dynamiters and assassins . . . Irishmen had no sympathy with the miserable wretches who promoted assassination and outrage [Applause]. Irishmen regretted such men's existence and looked upon them as the vilest enemies they had [Renewed applause].[71]

Further assurances of Irish imperial loyalty were given by the Catholic Archbishop of Melbourne, Thomas Carr, to the Governor of

[188]

Victoria, the Earl of Hopetoun, at the St Patrick's Day celebrations in 1890 and 1895, along with references to 'the cause of Ireland' and the welcome support of 'those who deeply sympathised with it'.[72] By 1900, the elision between Nationalism and Empire Loyalism was (temporarily) complete. In that year the organising committee of the St Patrick's Day celebrations in Melbourne sent a telegram on behalf of the Festival to the Secretary of State for the Colonies, to be forwarded to the Queen. The message combined loyal gratitude with political aspiration in equal measure:

> The Irish people of Victoria, enjoying the blessings of self government, desire most respectfully to thank Her Most Gracious Majesty The Queen for the kind friendliness displayed by her proposed visit to Ireland, and cherish the hope that it may be the prelude to Home Rule. Signed: N. M. O'Donnell and J. F. Cody, Chairmen of the Celebration Committee.[73]

Cody and O'Donnell's hopes were, of course, not realised and, as Williams's analysis has demonstrated, in early twentieth-century Melbourne, St Patrick's Day parades became increasingly politicised and dominated by the Church and its ever more essentialist – and divisive – reading of Irish ethnicity.[74]

Celebrations of St Andrew's Day by Caledonian Societies, Highland Games and celebrations of the Battle of the Boyne by the Protestant Irish Loyal Orange Lodge were equally discursive and contingent affairs, but for different reasons. Scottish celebrations were always less politicised than their Irish counterparts: questions of contested constitutional status within the United Kingdom did not arise. Consequently, St Andrew's Day celebrations in Melbourne and elsewhere tended to be less public events, marked by cultural nostalgia and charitable purpose, rather than an anxious renegotiation of claims to loyalty and nationalist aspiration. In 1868, *The Argus* noted that 'the holiday of St Andrew's Day, as celebrated yesterday, caused very little change to the appearance of the city', while in 1884 the Caledonian Society's first annual dinner in the city was a high-status affair, marked by the presence of the Governor, Sir Henry Loch. His speech, praising the national pride of Scotsmen and the success they attained in every walk of life, also enumerated the Society's charitable objectives and resulted in a subscription of £300. Thus, although the speeches celebrated an inclusive myth of Scottishness, the perspectives were patrician and those of the leadership of the self-identifying Scottish community in Victoria.[75]

The elite performative spaces of this dinner echoed events at an earlier and less august Scottish gathering, the New Year Caledonian Games held at Pleasant Creek (as Stawell was then known) in 1862.

Like the Melbourne dinner, the ball which followed these games demonstrated the nuanced ways in which social status interacted with ethnic consciousness to produce complex place meanings. The ball was held in West Stawell, an area then inhabited by professionals and government officials, who had previously complained that all local entertainment was held up the hill at the Quartz Reefs, where the miners lived and worked.[76] However, no one from West Stawell attended the ball because, as the *Ararat and Pleasant Creek Advertiser* reported, it was not considered 'respectable'.[77] The event was unquestionably signified as Scottish by the inclusion of activities such as putting the stone, hammer throwing, Highland dancing, bagpipe competitions, performances of 'Rob Roy' and, of course, its name.[78] Whether these cultural markers had by now also become signifiers of a working class *mentalité* increasingly distanced from the middle-class and elite entertainments favoured in metropolitan centres is unclear. The inclusion of many local civic office bearers, prominent business men and professionals on the organising committee would suggest not. Arguably, it may have been the participation of miners from the Quartz Reefs district at this particular event that limited local middle-class participation. Either way, the social meanings read into this particular event provide a reminder that ethnicity was not an untrammelled driver of place in colonial Australia.

The Loyal Orange Order's celebrations of the Battle of the Boyne stood somewhere between the Irish celebrations of St Patrick's Day and the Scottish commemoration of St Andrew. While undeniably more politicised than the latter – as the associational embodiment of one outcome of Ireland's turbulent history they could hardly be otherwise – the 'Twelfth Day' celebrations lacked the radical political subtext of later St Patrick's Day celebrations. Insofar as the Order made political claims in Australia, these were for the maintenance of the constitutional and religious *status quo* in Ireland and, latterly, for Empire loyalty. For, as O'Farrell notes, the character of the Orange Order changed substantially in Australia during the course of the nineteenth century. True to its narrowly sectarian and ethno-national origins until the late 1860s, it remained a numerically small organisation in the demotic cultural spaces of the colonies. The attempted assassination of Prince Alfred in 1868 by Henry James O'Farrell, a Catholic Irishman and alleged Fenian sympathiser, transformed the organisation's appeal. In the highly politicised and culturally divisive aftermath of O'Farrell's assault, the Order was rehabilitated in the popular imagination as an instrument of imperial loyalism in which its anti-Catholicism caught the popular mood. It grew rapidly, attracting much wider and more numerous social and ethno-national support, which very quickly eclipsed its northern Irish and working-class origins. As O'Farrell notes, at its peak in 1882 the Order had 25,000 members and over 130 lodges in New South Wales alone.[79]

The Orange Order's early narrowly conceived sectarianism elicited a hostile response from Catholic Irish immigrants, and this had significant repercussions for the public performance of both cultural traditions in the urban spaces of Australia. Like St Patrick's Day, the Battle of the Boyne had been commemorated in the Australian colonies from an early period.[80] The advent of Irish mass immigration in the late 1840s shifted the tenor of both celebrations and introduced tensions that had not previously been apparent.[81] In Melbourne, the first Orange Lodge was established in 1843, a year after the St Patrick's Society was founded. By 1846 the Order had a sufficient presence in the city to plan a formal – and, for Irish Catholics, unwelcome – celebration on the Twelfth of July. The chosen venue for the Boyne celebration, the Pastoral Hotel, was besieged by a large group of Irish Catholics who at one point attempted to storm the building.[82] The fracas became a *cause célèbre* in the colonial press, *The Argus* describing it as being caused by 'an armed rabble of the lowest description of the Irish papists'.[83] Its most lasting consequence, however, was the adoption of the 1847 Party Processions Act, which banned contentious parades in an attempt to avoid similar confrontations in future.[84]

The ban on parading in Melbourne was officially lifted in 1879, when processions were allowed at the discretion of the mayor, but parading had in fact resumed from at least the mid-1870s in the city, and earlier still in inland towns.[85] At Kilmore, the relatively large Irish Catholic population recommended St Patrick's Day parades in 1870, when the 'rather hastily got up' procession marched from the church after mass to the paddock where sports were held.[86] Matters were more orderly the following year, when the town's St Patrick's Society paraded in their new green and gold silk regalia to the sound of Irish music and before a crowd estimated at 2,000.[87] Elsewhere, after the ubiquitous performance of mass, horse racing and sports days featuring suitably 'Irish' events continued to be the preferred method of celebration, usually under the auspices of one or other of the Irish associational groups, such as the St Patrick's Society or the Hibernian Association. In 1875 at Geelong, the St Patrick's Society first attended high mass at St Mary's before parading to the cricket ground for its annual sports, led by bands 'playing national airs'. In the same year, *The Argus* reported that the St Patrick's Day races at Kyneton proved to be their usual formidable attraction, with many of the crowd of 6,000 coming by train from Melbourne. This was apparently very much at the expense of the Hibernian Australian Catholic Benefit Society's celebration at nearby Sandhurst (Bendigo), where the morning parade 'attracted little attention' and the afternoon sports were poorly supported.[88]

The competition between the events at Sandhurst and Kyneton is a reminder that these celebrations created their own performative geographies of place within the colonial urban landscape at different times of the year. Contemporary press reports make it clear that, until the end of the nineteenth century at least, these performances were far from essentialist. Rather, they attracted different ethno-cultural groups whose attendance effectively hybridised these events' semiotic meaning as place. So much is apparent from Stawell, where a meeting to re-constitute the local Caledonian Society was held in 1868 and was attended by locally prominent Irishmen as well as Scots.[89] One, David Scallan, was also a member of various committees organising the St Patrick's Day celebrations and the construction of St Patrick's Catholic school and church during the 1860s.[90] Such dual member-ship suggests the shared cultural appeal of an organisation that, in the diasporic spaces of this part of Victoria, was defined by its non-Englishness. Similar pan-Celticism – however subjectively imagined – is suggested by the participation of Irishmen in subsequent Caledonian games. In 1863, Irish-born John Kinsella won the putting the shot and Wexford man Michael Cowman won the tilting the ring contest.[91] The St Patrick's Day sports events in Kilmore in 1870 were similarly hybrid and featured Caledonian events such as throwing the hammer as well as ostensibly more authentic 'Irish' competitions such as Irish dancing.[92]

Newspaper reports of the resumed Melbourne St Patrick's Day parades from the 1880s provide the most detailed *vignettes* of how this hybridity was performed, and of the ways in which the proces-sions imprinted their own temporary meanings on the cityscape. *The Melbourne Age*'s description of the city's parade in 1900 is worth quoting in extenso for its nuanced if slightly patronising description of these ambiguities:

A member of the St Patrick's Day committee declared – in his own words – that there were 'more Irishmen by profession' in Melbourne on Saturday than on any St Patrick's Day in the past. 'Hello, Llewelyn', said an acquaintance to a green-bedecked Welshman in Bourke Street, 'I didn't know you were an Irishman before'. 'Well I've got a strain in me' was the reply. 'My mother's cousin was in the Dublin Fusiliers and my father's uncle was a non-commissioned officer in the Inniskillen Dragoons!' But many more who could not claim so close a relationship sported the shamrock and the green on Saturday ... Young men claim-ing descent from sturdy old Scottish Covenanters discovered for once that Scots and Irish had always taken common cause, and the weird skirl of their bagpipes completely smothered the excellent music that might otherwise have been produced by the Milesian who laboured unceasingly on the Irish harp.

The procession was to parade through Bourke Street to the Exhibition Grounds, and in that thoroughfare tram and vehicular traffic was for some time suspended. The real patriots, about whose nationality there could be no question, assembled on the hill near St Patrick's Hall. Elderly gentlemen from the country, with shaven upper lips and chins, and whiskers on their necks, proudly strode to the gathering ground, clamping ferruled bludgeons upon the pavement with every stride. One in national pride and sentiment, but 227 in their disparity of size, costume and methods of marching, that number of lodge members flaunted their green banners and sashes as they marched up the hill to Queen Street . . . Beautiful silk banners with representations of saints and patriots were drawn up on lorries by powerful horses whose saddle cloths in one or two cases proclaimed the virtues of a particular brewery . . . Matronly ladies, somewhat to the discomforture of their prim and pretty but less enthusiastic daughters, waved their parasols and overcome by the raptures of the moment, shouted 'God bless you' to a newly arrived section of the procession more Irish in appearance than the rest . . . A few yards away, a different type of the big hearted Irishwoman, 'with laughter holding her sides' plied badinage with one of the elderly gentlemen of the whiskers and ferruled stick. 'Faith' the man was saying, 'you're one of the good old sort'. 'Indade I am, Irish to the backbawne'.

Above the merry buzz of the throng rose the blare of brass instruments, one declaring the joys of 'St Patrick's day in the morning', another proclaiming the intention of the musician to 'wear the green' in spite of everything and everybody, and a third reminding all present that the minstrel boy had gone to war and intended to stick fast to his harp, no matter who might envy him possession of it. A dozen youths and men vended 'Songs of Ireland' for a penny; numberless street boys traded in a variety of St Patrick's Day emblems . . .

To the indescribable tones of the Scottish pipes, the procession moved off along Bourke Street. The line of march was perhaps the longest ever seen in Melbourne on a similar occasion, and its progress through the streets was heralded with evidence of delirious enthusiasm . . .[93]

In this particular performative space, the over-arching discourse of 'authentic' Irishness was evidently read in a variety of ways by those who participated in it. For the elderly gentlemen whose rustic appearance immediately identified them as non-urban others, its appeal appears to have been that of national pride, a statement of essentialist identity that their years in Australia had done nothing to diminish. For the hucksters and street vendors, the parade was an economic opportunity when money could be made from others' need to belong. But, as the careful delineation of the various female responses suggests, the semiotics created by the parade as it shaped and moulded the shared spaces of the city streets were also gendered and socially constructed. The 'big-hearted' Irishwoman was clearly of a different caste to her matronly sisters, whose temporary loss of decorum so embarrassed their daughters. However stereotyped her representation by *The Age*, that anonymous Irishwoman still speaks across the years with a raw authenticity which the urbane but enraptured Melbourne ladies could only mimic.

But the parade's claims to cultural authenticity were also subverted by its very success. The presence of Scottish pipe bands, descendants of 'sturdy Covenanters', and numerous people claiming apparently spurious Irish connections in an attempt to appropriate the parade's ethno-cultural meaning all added to its hybridity. Evidently, at this particular moment, before the imposition of the sectarian essentialism that was to colour future Melbourne parades, the city's St Patrick's Day parade had taken on a wider cultural significance that transcended its ethnic origins. It was truly hybrid space, in which its hegemonic 'Irish' meaning was rewritten in translation by the numerous groups who ascribed to it.

Not every town whose population included Irish Catholics celebrated St Patrick's Day or had organised Irish Catholic committees. By the 1860s, the largely Protestant Irish farming district of Kiama did not have any Catholic associational groups, and local Catholics depended on the church for expressions of their religious identity.[94] Given the history of sectarian animosity in the town, this is unsurprising. In the early 1840s, local Catholics invited a delegation of their co-religionists from Sydney to visit Kiama. As they paraded past the hotel owned by James Marks (an Orangeman from Dromore, Co. Tyrone), a shot was fired through the flag carried by the procession.[95] This violent opposition to the ethno-religious symbolism embodied by the flag was understood by local Irish Catholics for the hostile act it was, and there were no more Catholic performances in the public spaces of the town.

Although the Orange Order had been well established in Kiama since the 1840s, it too, felt constrained by the threat of local violence, and until the 1860s its commemorations were normally held in private houses.[96] The narrative of these threats points to the contested and subjective nature of the meanings of place in Kiama, as in the other study towns. At the height of the Fenian scare following the attempted assassination of Prince Alfred in 1868, relations between members of the Orange Lodges and their Catholic neighbours in the Kiama region were tense.[97] That year, on the evening of 28 April, the calm of Kiama's streets was shattered by shouts of 'murder'. John Grey, a Fermanagh-born dairy farmer, had been riding home to his farm, Loyal Valley, when he was allegedly shot at by someone lurking in the bushes. Grey and his horse avoided injury, though the ball lodged itself in the horse's saddle.[98] Grey, a prominent member of a local Orange Lodge, had received threatening letters, purportedly from Irish Catholics, in previous years.[99] He immediately reported that Fenians had attempted to kill him. Arguably, the sense of dread and anxiety generated by this sort of event would have transformed Kiama into a space of fear and insecurity for Catholics and Protestants alike. Such an outcome was unlikely to have been alleviated by the subsequent dismissal of murder charges against the three Catholic labourers who had been accused of the attack on Grey, nor by the widespread belief among Irish Catholics that he had orchestrated the attack himself in order to increase sectarian tension.[100] Whatever the truth of this, it seems reasonably evident that, by the 1860s, Orangeism in Kiama constituted a dominating cultural presence against which locally culturally subaltern Irish Catholics were occasionally prompted to react in a traditional manner. Thus, in performing their allotted roles, Grey and his alleged assailants were acting out sectarian narratives of identity which had been prescribed for them by their respective Irish pasts. As at Stawell, for these men at least, the shared experiences of the colonial present had still to ameliorate the certainties engendered by their remembered origins in Ireland.

But, as we have already noted, the character of Orangeism in Australia altered radically in response to the attempted assassination of Prince Alfred. By the 1880s, Orange performances in Kiama had changed. Significant dates in the Order's calendar were now commemorated by public teas and picnics rather than by tense private gatherings, symbolising, perhaps, the Order's new inclusiveness and acceptability.[101] At Broughton Creek over 2,000 attended the annual November picnic in 1883.[102] At Stawell, where the Orange Order was established in 1880, the Twelfth of July and the Fifth of November were marked by soirees, musical evenings, prayer meetings and lectures which generally attracted a large and enthusiastic attendance.[103] Although the Irish origins of the Order were stressed in the speeches and songs, the leaders and probably most of the membership and audience for these events were not Irish. They were overwhelmingly either English or native born, and had been moved to join the Order through their shared Protestantism and Imperial Loyalism.

The narratives of place and identity offered by the Orange Order in Stawell were publicly contested on at least one occasion. In 1882 an advertisement for one of its gatherings was rejected by the editor of the *Pleasant Creek News* on the grounds that it might provoke disharmony:

> We have received an advertisement which reflects in terms the reverse of agreeable on a meeting which is to be held this evening. We do not publish it because it is calculated to stir up ill feeling and our community is too sensible to foster within it feelings which lead to disunion and bitterness. The author of the advertisement can have his money returned by calling at the place where he left it for insertion.[104]

Walter Swan, the Presbyterian, Monaghan-born editor of the newspaper had interpreted the advertisement as a provocative challenge to peaceful relations in the town. His own cultural background may provide the key to his reaction. Although a Monaghan-born Presbyterian, he had married a Tipperary-born Catholic, Mary O'Brien, but also maintained close relations with his sister Jane and brother-in-law, Samuel Kelso, a Presbyterian minister who also came from Monaghan. After his death, Swan was buried with his wife's family in the Catholic section of the nearby Ararat cemetery. He had embraced his Australian identity in his writing and rarely publicly mentioned his Irish birth.[105] Viewed in this light, Swan's refusal to publish material that may have re-ignited past sectarian rivalries offers some insight into the depth of his commitment to colonial life. His actions also highlight, yet again, the varied importance that Scottish and Irish settlers placed on cultural memory in performing urban place in Australia. If the implacable certainties of sectarian dissent remained a present reality for John Grey in Kiama in 1868, for Walter Swan in Stawell in 1882 they held no further purchase on who he thought himself to be.

Gendered spaces

When William O'Callaghan made his speech on Irish history and nationalism at the Ararat St Patrick's Day ball in 1863, he ended with several toasts, the last being 'To the Ladies'. Everyone then began to dance.[106] Although the presence of both men and women was considered necessary for the success of the occasion, the Irish identities being performed in the hotel's dining room were overwhelmingly masculine. The subaltern status accorded to those women who were present was entirely typical of most Scottish and Irish performative spaces of the period. Although women were generally present at St Patrick's Day speeches, Orange Order meetings and Caledonian Games, their attendance rarely attracted specific attention other than to the ornamental value they brought to the occasion. Studies of gendered behaviour at Irish diasporic events in the United States have argued that, while St Patrick Day parades were largely masculine affairs involving overt expressions of ethno-nationalism and stereotypically rowdy and drunken behaviour, other events, such as church fairs or bazaars, were gendered feminine. These were associated with respectability and the affirmation of middle-class values.[107] Here, women's activities invariably involved a public translation of their private domestic roles as they provided catering and large tables of food for teas. Nevertheless, this gendered elision of the public and private spheres constituted a form of boundary crossing, and this may have helped in the long term to destabilise the normative female colonial role as respectable spouse and home maker.

Such gendering of public religious and cultural events was not limited to Irish Catholics. Jane Grey, in whose home near Kiama Orange Lodge meetings were held for many years, was awarded a special trophy for her services in providing food for lodge members.[108] Plentiful food was a key marker of the success of colonial associational functions and was usually commented upon in newspaper reports of these events. Thus, in 1868 the largely Scottish Presbyterian community at Stawell celebrated in style when 'about 150 children belonging to the Presbyterian Sabbath school were regaled with tea, cakes, buns, lollies and other good things, bountifully provided by liberal members of the congregation'.[109]

The entertainment offered at Irish and Scottish soirees and balls was also frequently gendered feminine, adding particular piquancy to the performance of songs, poems and plays in small and remote colonial halls. In 1884, for example, 'Miss Baily recited Shamus O'Brien and Miss O'Callaghan and Miss Dowling played purely Irish airs on the piano' at an Irish function in Kilmore.[110] As well as participating in these public renditions of cultural memory, women were also often the repositories of family songs, words and language from home. Their role was evoked in poems such as 'The little Irish mother' by 'John O'Brien', which celebrated the cultural fortitude of Irish mothers in alerting their Australian-born children to their Irish heritage through words, stories and domestic customs.[111] There were also examples in family stories where Irish words and stories were told and re-told, often by mothers. Frank McCaffery, historian of the Kiama region, recorded how his mother, Mary, who migrated from Kesh in Fermanagh in 1846, always referred to the township of Fairy Meadow, north of Kiama, in Irish as 'Cluain Sithe'.[112]

These representations alert us to the fact that, in many instances, narratives of women's place in colonial Australia were primarily performed within the intimacy of homes or the kitchens of church halls. Two of the most common spatial markers of identity for women were their marital status or status as servants. European women running homes in the demanding conditions of colonial Australia frequently called on other women for help. Sometimes this was paid for, but at other times neighbours merely helped out when needed. Domestic servants were most widely employed in urban areas, although they were present in rural settings as well. Many single Irish and Scots women migrated as domestic servants and worked, for a time at least, in the households of other women. In the Australian colonies, as in other diasporic contexts, domestic service was culturally marked as Irish in the popular press.[113] Domestic servants who subsequently married frequently acquired an elevated status as the mistress of, often, Irish servants. The roles of servant and mistress were thus usually differentiated by age and marital status, rather than by class backgrounds.

Servants and mistresses shared the domestic spaces in which they lived and worked, and this demanded continuous delicate negotiation so that the social difference between them was maintained. The servant's identity was often spatially constrained by her relegation to the working areas of the house – the kitchen, laundry and nursery – while the mistress was identified by her occupation of the 'polite' and leisured spaces of the house – the dining room (if there was one), parlour and bedroom. Although the boundaries between these domestic spaces were necessarily fluid, especially in small households, it was in the mistress's interest to ensure that her identity continued to be spatialised in this way. As Margaret Youngman observed of Mrs Calder at Polkemmet station in the 1860s, any collusion between a mistress and her servants in crossing these boundaries had the potential to dislocate the structures of authority in the entire household.

The importance of these spatial boundaries was highlighted in a very public brawl between an Irish mistress and her Irish servant in the small village of Glenorchy, just outside Stawell, in 1863. The mistress, Limerick-born Honora Jenkins (who until very recently had been a servant herself), and her servant, Belfast-born Martha O'Kane, came to blows in an argument over the use of household space. Martha had usurped her mistress's keys and was sitting sewing in the parlour – a room and activity usually marked out for the mistress. Martha told Honora that the parlour was 'her place that night' and that Honora was not her mistress but a 'thing'.[114] In this instance the delicate balance between mistress and servant had been irrevocably upset and the dispute was pursued through the contested occupation of personal and private feminine spaces. While it is unusual to get such insight into the fine nuances of spatial meaning within households, the situation of an Irish woman moving from the position of servant to that of mistress was very common.

It was not only in private spaces that gendered meanings might be contested. In public spaces of all sorts, various factors, including behaviour, the time of day or night, class, age and ethnicity were crucial in imparting meaning to gendered activities. For example, in July 1863, the people of Stawell were enthralled by a scandal that illuminated the complex and layered meanings that might attach to ethnicised sexual behaviour. An Irish woman, Mary Honan, alleged that she had been raped by three Welshmen as she walked home from Miss Nihill's hotel one Saturday night around midnight. One of her assailants yelled at her 'You're Irish', during her ordeal.[115] In common with other diggings towns, in Stawell there was a great deal of movement and socialising late at night, centred around the many hotels in the town. The nocturnal meanings which attached to these material places were very different from their daytime reading for both men and women. Moreover, women were likely to interpret the noises and darkness of the untidy streets differently to men, perhaps seeing danger lurking outside the boundaries of their tent or house. Thus, although a certain Brigit Hall heard the noise the group made as Mary Honan struggled with her assailants, and tried to stop the assault by throwing a bucket of water over them from her tent, she was 'too frightened to follow the men'.

Mary Honan alleged that her recognisable identity as an Irish woman was one reason why the men had attacked her. Their obviously derogatory claim, 'You're Irish', may have reflected a cultural antipathy on their part to the Irish in general. Alternatively, it may also have signalled their assumption that, because Honan was Irish, drunk and alone without her husband on the cold streets late at night, her behaviour placed her beyond the boundaries of respectability and thus made her sexually available. Honan's use of alcohol affected the authorities' reaction to her account of the event. Just before the criminal trial took place in February 1864, she was involved in another court case where she (somewhat incoherently) alleged that she had been defrauded of money by the butcher. The case was dismissed because she was found to have been drunk at the time and her actions were deemed to be inappropriate. Her social position was thought to be undeserving because of her class, Irishness and history of public alcohol use, and this is likely to have been a factor in her alleged assailants' acquittal.[116] Seemingly, for Mary Honan the semiotic spaces of Stawell were relentlessly negative and threatening.

Summary

Like its pastoral counterpart, the urban performance of place by Scots and Irish settlers in south-east Australia was characteristically ambiguous and layered in meaning. The places which these men and women enacted formed part of a discourse of urbanism that was as fundamental to the success of the colonial enterprise as the pastoral cartographies it served. The towns and villages that were laid out in New South Wales and Victoria formed part of the signature of colonial capitalism in the Australian landscape and were as much an act of the colonial imagination as were the pastoral runs themselves. British colonialism in Australia was, at heart, an urban project which required an imposed rubric of towns and cities to articulate the administrative, cultural, economic, political and social discourses of authority on which it relied.

Accordingly, nineteenth-century Australian towns, including Belfast (Port Fairy), Kiama, Kilmore and Stawell, were sites where the white colonial self found expression through agency, memory and identity. But, as we have argued, this selfhood was never unitary, never unchallenged. Rather, it was multi-vocal, always changing and always contingent on circumstance. White – invariably male – hegemonies existed, certainly, and found effective expression either through formal institutions like the Road Boards and Borough Councils which gradually shaped municipal life from mid-century, or informally via various associational groups such as Mechanics' Institutes, Caledonian Societies, or Hibernian Associations. Most of these hegemonies found opportunities to imprint their own particular values on some aspect of the material spaces of the towns, whether by the construction of civic or other buildings, or by the periodic appropriation of public urban space for parades and processions. But none of the material and performative spaces so created supported single meanings. As William Wall's diaries demonstrate, even that most functionalist of civic spaces, the Shire Auditor's office, might become a site of resistance to British Imperialism. Similarly, the erection of civic amenities and celebrations of modernity and civic virtue were also susceptible to contested inflections of memory, as the municipal projects at Stawell in the 1860s demonstrated. Bridges and hospitals could be sites of conflict as well as of civic achievement. Even that most culturally authentic of all urban spectacles, the St Patrick's Day parade, can be found, on close inspection, to have become thoroughly hybridised, for a time at least, towards the end of the nineteenth century.

In short, although ethnic consciousness played a part in constructing the semiotics of urban experience for Scottish and Irish settlers, its effects were modified by circumstance and considerations of gender, social status and wealth. Moreover, each of these interactions was subjectively constructed and intensely personal in its outcome and meaning. Consequently, the narratives of urban place performed in Belfast, Kiama, Kilmore and Stawell were as varied as the people themselves. Each of these material places embodied a kaleidoscope of human experience in which the individual's sense of belonging, whether to their remembered past, their colonial present, or, in truly diasporic fashion, to both, was a question of proactive consciousness. Within these fragmented, multi-faceted urban worlds, national labels hide as much as they reveal. The colonial experiences of William Wall, John Grey and Mary Honan could hardly have been more different. They were all Irish, but of different ethno-cultural traditions and class. What impact had religion on these already complex performances of identity and place?

Notes

1   *Kilmore Free Press*, 20 March, 1873.
2   'Obituary of Thomas Brown', newspaper article dated 18 August 1925 by Frank McCaffery (no title of paper), UOWA, D92.
3   *Kilmore Free Press*, 4 May, 1865.
4   Anthony Trollope, *New South Wales and Queensland* (London, 1874), cited in D. N. Jeans, *An Historical Geography of New South Wales to 1901* (Sydney, 1972), pp. 309–10.
5   L. Proudfoot and D. Hall, 'Memory and Identity in "Irish" Australia: Constructing Alterity in Belfast (Port Fairy), c. 1857–1873', in M. McCarthy (ed.), *Ireland's Heritages. Critical Perspectives on Memory and Identity* (Aldershot, 2005), pp. 89–104.
6   Notably, Alick Osborne, who conducted a speaking and recruiting tour in Ulster and especially in his home parish of Dromore, County Tyrone, in the late 1830s. See I. C. Young, 'The Armstrong story', *Khanterintee*, No. 32 (1998), pp. 3–7.
7   For context see R. Murray and K. White, *The Golden Years of Stawell* (Stawell, 1983), pp. 36–44. For a discussion of similarly cosmopolitan gold-rush towns in New Zealand, see L. Fraser, *Castles of Gold. A History of New Zealand's West Coast Irish* (Dunedin, 2007).
8   D. Dickson, 'The Place of Dublin in the Eighteenth-century Irish Economy', in T. M. Devine and D. Dickson (eds), *Ireland and Scotland 1600–1850* (Edinburgh, 1983), pp. 177–92; D. Dickson (ed.), *The Gorgeous Mask. Dublin 1700–1850* (Dublin, 1987).
9   J. Perkins and J. Thompson, 'The Stockman, the Shepherd and the Creation of an Australian National Identity in the 19th Century', in D. Day (ed.), *Australian Identities* (Melbourne, 1998), pp. 15–25; A. Curthoys, 'History and Identity', in W. Hudson and G. Bolton (eds), *Creating Australia. Changing Australian History* (St Leonards, 1997), pp. 23–38.
10 S. Macintyre, *A Concise History of Australia* (2nd edn, Cambridge, 2004), pp. 108–9.
11 J. M. Powell, *An Historical Geography of Modern Australia. The Restive Fringe* (Cambridge, 1991), pp. 21–9.
12 T. Dingle, *The Victorians. Settling* (Sydney, 1984), pp. 152–60; J. Jupp and B. York, *Birthplaces of the Australian People. Colonial and Commonwealth Censuses, 1828–1991* (Canberra, 1995), pp. 4, 33.
13 Jeans, *Historical Geography of New South Wales*, pp. 127, 295–7.
14 H. Carter, *An Introduction to Urban Historical Geography* (London, 1983), p. 112.
15 Jeans, *Historical Geography of New South Wales*, pp. 298 ff.
16 P. Stratham (ed.), *The Origins of Australia's Capital Cities* (Sydney, 1990), pp. 1–36; Dickson, *Gorgeous Mask, passim.*
17 W. E. Vaughan and A. J. Fitzpatrick (eds), *Irish Historical Statistics Population 1821–1971* (Dublin, 1978), pp. 28–9, 32–3, 36–7; S. A. Royle, 'Industrialisation, Urbanisation and Urban Society in Post-famine Ireland, c.1850–1921', in B. J.

Graham and L. J. Proudfoot (eds), *An Historical Geography of Ireland* (London, 1993, pp. 258–92.

18 Jeans, *Historical Geography of New South Wales*, pp. 302–7.

19 For a study of the processes of boom and bust in an individual gold town, see Alan Mayne's exemplary, *Hill End. A Historic Australian Goldfields Landscape* (Melbourne, 2003).

20 Jeans, *Historical Geography of New South Wales*, pp. 105–12.

21 R. L. Heathcote, *Australia* (2nd edn, Harlow, 1994), pp. 170–1.

22 R. Wright, *The Bureaucrats' Domain. Space and the Public Interest in Victoria, 1836–84* (Melbourne, 1989), pp. 25–40.

23 Cited in Heathcote, *Australia*, p. 169.

24 *Ibid.*, pp. 165–7.

25 Jeans, *Historical Geography of New South Wales*, pp. 127–8. Among numerous local urban histories detailing this process, two of more than usual merit are D. Garden, *Hamilton. A Western District History* (Melbourne, 1994), and T. Barker, *A History of Bathurst* (2 vols, Bathurst, 1992–98).

26 Jeans, *Historical Geography of New South Wales*, p. 112; M. Williams, *The Making of the South Australian Landscape. A Study in the Historical Geography of Australia* (London, 1974), pp. 354–8.

27 S. J. Tazewell, *Grand Goulburn* (Goulburn, 1991), pp. 7–9.

28 Cited in Jeans, *Historical Geography of New South Wales*, pp. 111–12.

29 Paul Carter's *The Road to Botany Bay. An Essay in Spatial History* (London, 1987), explores the complexities of understanding traveller and settler spaces through naming and map making.

30 Margaret Moore, Elizabeth D'Arcy and Bridget Hodges (all née Levy) were born in County Longford and went on to marry and live in Stawell. See: 'Copies of Church of England marriage certificates' held by the Stawell Historical Society for the marriages of Margaret and Bridget and for Elizabeth. See also 'Copy of Stawell Cemetery Register' and Inquest VPRS 24/p/0000/350 1876/103.

31 M. V. Tucker, *Kilmore on the Sydney Road* (Kilmore, 1988), p. 36, citing Rutledge descendant information.

32 Obituary of Martin Doyle, *Stawell News*, 30 April 1880.

33 These and other mines were run as organised companies with directors and shareholders; as such their activities were reported regularly in the press. See, for example, *PCN*, 7 August 1869.

34 *PCN*, 10, 12, August 1869.

35 *APCA*, 20 March 1868. For more information about David Scallan and his circle see D. Hall and L. Proudfoot, 'Irish Identities, Family Lives and the Pleasant Creek Gold Fields', in C. Fahey and A. Mayne (eds), *Tailings: Forgotten Histories of Family and Community on the Central Victorian Goldfields* (Melbourne, forthcoming).

36 Analysis of the Stawell rate book shows that the Irish-born did not congregate in any particular area, nor did they avoid others.

37 *APCA*, 3 January 1868.

38 McCaffery papers, UOWA, D92. Indexed copies in Kiama Family History centre, 9/84.

39 J. Hirst, 'Local Government', in G. Davison, J. Hirst and S. Macintyre (eds), *The Oxford Companion to Australian History* (rev. edn, Oxford, 2001), pp. 399–400; Government of New South Wales Education website: http://.curriculumsupport. education.nsw.gov.au.

40 S. Priestley, *The Victorians. Making Their Mark* (Sydney, 1984), p. 51.

41 Public Record Office of Victoria, Agency VA 2467, Metcalfe, www.access.prov.vic. gov.au.

42 Public Record Office of Victoria, Group VRG 12, Municipalities, www.access.prov. vic.gov.au; Public Record Office of Victoria, Agency VA 2803, Central Roads Board, www.access.prov.vic.gov.au.

43 *PCN*, 7 October 1886.

44 Murray and White, *Golden Years of Stawell*, pp. 30, 36, 46.
45 *Ibid.*, pp. 56–61.
46 Tucker, *Kilmore*, pp. 36–9; J. W. Powling, *Port Fairy. The First Fifty Years* (Melbourne, 1980), pp. 140–52, 207–16.
47 C. E. Sayers (ed.), *Earle's Port Fairy, A History by William Earle* (Olinda, 1973), pp. 24, 35–6.
48 As the frequently lively and often acrimonious meetings of the Belfast Borough and Shire councils demonstrated. See Powling, *Port Fairy, passim*. For a similar narrative in Stawell, see R. Kingston, *Good Country for a Grant. A History of the Stawell Shire* (Stawell, 1989), pp. 75–92.
49 William J. Wall, 1859–1899, Diaries (Manuscript) 1878–1898, SLV, Ms 12444, Box 3295/1–12, entries for 1, 18 May, 6 June 1878; 26 March 1879; 12 March, 27 August 1880; 16 July 1881; 13 July, 22 October 1883; 3 October 1884; 25 January 1887; 3 April 1890.
50 Wall, Diaries, entries for September 1883 and August and September 1884, *passim*. See also Powling, *Port Fairy*, pp. 290–1.
51 Wall, Diaries, entries for 1, 18 May, 6 June 1878; 26 March 1879; 12 March, 27 August 1880; 16 July 1881; 13 July, 22 October 1883; 3 October 1884; 25 January 1887; 3 April 1890.
52 Wall, Diaries, entries for 26 March, 10 November, 3 December 1879; 9 August 1883; 24 May 1884; 21 June 1887.
53 Wall, Diaries, entries for 1–31 July 1880, *passim*; 1–28 February 1883, *passim*; 9, 12, 13 March 1889; 16, 18, 19, 20 April 1892; 1–30 September 1894, *passim*; 1–31 October 1897, *passim*.
54 Wall, Diaries, entries for 24 May, 4, 14, 21 June 1887.
55 Wall, Diaries, entry for 8 August 1889.
56 *PCN*, 23 November 1863.
57 George had arrived in Sydney at the age of 19 and had travelled extensively around the colonies before settling in Stawell in his late thirties in 1859. Obituary, *Stawell News*, 3 September 1897.
58 Y. J. Collins, 'The Provision of Hospital Care in Country Victoria 1840s to 1940s' (unpublished PhD thesis, Department of History and Philosophy of Science, University of Melbourne, 1999).
59 Victorian Heritage Database, http://vhd.heritage.vic.gov.au/places/heritage11 3169.
60 C. E. Sayers, *Shepherd's Gold. The Story of Stawell* (Melbourne, 1966), p. 64. Patrick D'Arcy was a miner and hotel owner, born in Carlow. See 'Stawell Cemetery Register'; Sayers, *Shepherd's Gold*, p. 32–3; Hall and Proudfoot, 'Irish Identities' (forthcoming).
61 *APCA*, 28 December 1860.
62 *APCA*, 1 January 1861.
63 *APCA*, 4 January 1861.
64 *APCA*, 3 September 1863.
65 Cited in Tucker, *Kilmore*, p. 67.
66 Caleb Collyer, Reminiscences, RHSV Box 6/6a and 6*, pp. 77–8.
67 Caleb Collyer, Reminiscences, p. 82.
68 M. Cronin and Daryl Adair, *The Wearing of the Green. A History of St Patrick's Day* (London, 2002), *passim*.
69 *The Argus*, 1 December, 1884; 17 March 1885.
70 *APCA*, 22 March 1863.
71 *The Argus*, 18 March 1885.
72 *The Argus*, 18 March 1895.
73 *The Melbourne Age*, 18 March 1900.
74 *APCA*, 4 January 1860; C. M. Williams, 'Collective Memory and Identity in Melbourne's St Patrick's Day Celebrations, 1900–1939', in T. Foley and F. Bateman (eds), *Irish Australian Studies. Papers Delivered at the Ninth Irish-Australian Conference Galway, April 1997* (Sydney, 2000), pp. 273–85.

75   *The Argus*, 1 December 1884.
76   Sayers, *Shepherd's Gold*, p. 36.
77   *APCA*, 5 January 1862.
78   *APCA*, 5 January 1863, 5 January 1869; *PCN*, 3 September 1869.
79   P. O'Farrell, *The Irish in Australia 1788 to the Present* (3rd edn, Sydney, 2000), pp. 102–3.
80   For a summary, see K. S. Inglis, *Australian Colonists: An Exploration of Social History, 1788–1870* (Melbourne, 1993), pp. 102–8.
81   N. Jenson, 'Unlawful Assemblies and Party Processions: "Orange" and "Green" Violent Confrontations Revisited in Mid-nineteenth Century Melbourne' (MA thesis, University of Melbourne, 1999), p. 18, citing *The Port Phillip Patriot*, 30 June 1842.
82   *The Argus*, 14 and 24 July 1846.
83   *The Argus*, 14 July 1846.
84   Inglis, *Australian Colonists*, p. 109.
85   Cronin and Adair, *The Wearing of the Green*, p. 91; *The Argus*, 18 March 1875.
86   *Kilmore Free Press*, 24 March 1870.
87   *Kilmore Free Press*, 23 March 1871.
88   *The Argus*, 18 March 1875.
89   *PCN*, 29 September 1868.
90   'St Patrick's Church Building Committee Minutes', manuscript copy held by the Stawell Historical Society, Stawell.
91   *APCA*, 5 January 1863. There were several McGregor families settled in and around Stawell, most of whom were related. J. Kinsella won the putting the stone. There were at least two J. Kinsellas resident in Stawell at the time: John, from Dunamore, Wexford and John from Carlow, who married Isabella Gillies in 1873. See (respectively) Dorothy King, 'Stawell (Pleasant Creek) Cemetery Register', Stawell Historical Society; and Index, Registry of Births Deaths and Marriages.
92   *Kilmore Free Press*, 2 March 1870.
93   *The Melbourne Age*, 18 March 1900.
94   UOWA D92, 'Frank McCaffery collection'.
95   UOWA, D92, 'Frank McCaffery collection'.
96   For the Orange Order in Australia in general see O'Farrell, *The Irish in Australia*, pp. 101–5; and for South Australia, David Fitzpatrick, 'Exporting Brotherhood: Orangeism in South Australia', *Immigrants and Minorities*, Vol. 23, Nos 2–3 (2005), pp. 277–310.
97   For a description of the assassination attempt and its aftermath, see O'Farrell, *The Irish in Australia*, pp. 209–11.
98   *Kiama Independent*, 30 April 30 1868; *Sydney Morning Herald*, 30 April 1868.
99   Grey family history is drawn from Lynn Rawson, *Illawarra Greys* (Melbourne, n.d.), and *Illawarra Pioneers: Pre 1900* (Wollongong: The Group, 1988), p. 76. Frank McCaffery thought that the threatening letters either were jokes or were written by Orangemen to fan the flames of hatred, UOWA, D92, 'Frank McCaffery collection'; Kiama Family History Centre, 'Indexed copy of Frank McCaffery collection'.
100 This was the belief expressed by Frank McCaffery, based on the angle of the bullet in the pommel of the saddle.
101 A lack of resources beset many Orange Lodges in diaspora. For a discussion of the local organisational difficulties that befell Orange Lodges in the north of England, see D. MacRaild, *Faith, Fraternity and Fighting: the Orange Order and Irish Migrants in Northern England, c. 1850–1920* (Liverpool, 2005).
102 R. Anthill, *Settlement in the South: A Record of the Discovery, Exploration and Settlement of the Shoalhaven River Basin, 1803–1982* (Kiama, 1982), p. 123.
103 *PCN*, 12 July and 6 November 1880.
104 *PCN*, 12 July 1882.
105 For Walter Swan's marriage to Mary Ellen O'Brien, see *APCA*, 27 November 1863; for his career as a writer, see H. Heseltine, 'Introduction,' *Luke Miver's Harvest by N. Walter Swan* (Sydney, 1991).

106 *APCA*, 22 March 1863.
107 C. McDannell, 'Going to the Ladies' Fair: Irish Catholics in New York City, 1870–1900', in R. H. Bayor and T. J. Meagher (eds), *The New York Irish* (Baltimore, 1996); E. O'Donnell, 'How the Irish Became Urban', *Journal of Urban History*, Vol. 25 (1999), p. 271.
108 The trophy is in the family collection. See Rawson, *Illawarra Greys*, pp. 96–8.
109 *PCN*, 15 September 1868.
110 *Kilmore Free Press*, 20 March 1884.
111 'John O'Brien' [Patrick Joseph Hartigan], *Around the Boree Log and Other Verses* (Sydney, 1921).
112 Frank McCaffery, *Kiama Reporter*, 5 August 1931, clipping in McCaffery collection, UOWA, D92.
113 P. Hamilton, 'Domestic Dilemmas: Representations of Servants and Employers in the Popular Press,' in S. Margery *et al.* (eds), *Debutante Nation: Feminism Contests the 1890* (Sydney, 1993), pp. 71–90.
114 *APCA*, 12 and 19 May 1863. For further analysis of this incident, see D. Hall, 'Irishness, Gender and "An Up-country township"', in L. Proudfoot and M. Roche (eds) *(Dis)placing Empire: Renegotiating British Colonial Geographies* (Aldershot, 2005), pp. 81–98.
115 *APCA*, 14, 17 and 18 July 1863, for the initial reports of the incident. For the subsequent trial see *APCA*, 12 February 1864.
116 *APCA*, 9 February 1864.

CHAPTER 8

Sites of faith and memory

I wish my descendents to know and *feel* that though Australian by birth and fealty, they are Irish in blood and have not a drop of English blood in their veins. I wish them also to be unflinching in their fidelity to the Catholic faith. (Nicholas O'Donnell, Melbourne, 1908[1])

Rev. Mr Baily brought into the church at Jamberoo a thing he called a desk, others called it by different names, but we, regarding it as a ritual-istc innovation, called it St Patrick . . . As we went up to the sacramental table we removed his saintship out of the way, which kindled the wrath of Mr Baily not a little. (*Kiama Independent*, 1872[2])

Throughout the nineteenth century, emigrant religious practice played an important role in shaping the narratives of place performed in Australia's colonial landscapes. Unlike most colonies, however, those in eastern Australia were soon characterised by large numbers of Catholic settlers, almost all of whom were of Irish descent. This cir-cumstance quickly gave rise to an easy elision between nationality and religion in the eyes of contemporary (and later) observers, which in turn had profound consequences for religious discourse in the country. During the latter part of the nineteenth century and beyond, Australia's main Christian denominations were assumed to be broadly synony-mous with different ethno-national elements in the British and Irish migration stream. The Catholic Church had St Patrick's Day celebra-tions and a seemingly continuous stream of priests with Irish accents; the Presbyterians were generally Scots, while the Church of England, Methodists and various other Nonconformist denominations provided for those of English and Welsh or Cornish heritage.

As Nicholas O'Donnell's comment suggests, behind such easy stere-otyping lay a certain truth. Religion did play a formative role in the construction and representation of ethnic identity. Yet, as the report in the *Kiama Independent* makes clear, the narratives of place produced by the assumed elision between ethnicity and religion did not remain uncontested. Within every ethno-religious tradition there were both hegemonic and subaltern voices. Moreover, to the extent that each denomination was seen as other to someone else's self, the places they created might be contested by those who felt their identity or sense of belonging in Australia to be challenged by them. Consequently, the narratives of place constructed by Irish and Scottish religious memory and practice were, like all others, multi-vocal. Despite their formative role in the replication of ethnic identity, they did not sustain single, essentialist meanings. They were also discursively framed: in the case of Catholicism, by the ultramontane Hibernicising project of the Cullenite Church, and among Presbyterians by the consequences of the 'Disruption' of 1843. Both discourses operated within, but were not necessarily conformable to, the discursive practices of British imperialism at large.

In this chapter we endeavour to recover something of the workings of these various processes and influences as they contrived to form diverse religious narratives of place in and around our sample towns, Kiama, Kilmore, Stawell and Belfast (Port Fairy). We explore various ways in which notions of religious self and other were constructed and represented as part of these narratives, and pay particular attention to the local emplacement of cultural memories transferred and transformed through the emigration experience. The churches and other buildings that materialised these narratives possessed their own histories, which elided with memories of religious practice in Ireland or Scotland. We examine instances of this as evidence of the diasporic character of these place narratives. We begin, however, by examining some of the discursive networks that framed these varied constructions of religious place.

Diasporic churches and empire

From the outset of penal settlement in New South Wales, religion was perceived to be a marker of ethnicity and nationality and, crucially, to refract notions of civility and social order. The forthright Anglican minister, Rev. Samuel Marsden, argued in 1807 that 'if the catholic religion was ever allowed to be celebrated . . . the colony would be lost to the British empire in less than one year', because it was practised by Irish of the 'lowest class, wild, ignorant and savage'.[3] He proposed to ban the Catholicism of these suspect Irish convicts and to impose his own brand of Anglicanism on the diverse prison population in a bid to civilise them all. Attitudes like these had some measure of success in the colony's early years. Only occasional officially sanctioned Catholic services were held during the first thirty years of its existence, and

Catholic convicts were required to attend Anglican services.[4] As white settlement began to expand beyond the Limits of Location, so the pastoral needs of the increasing and predominantly Irish Catholic minority became more acute, and were recognised as such by the British colonial administration, the papacy and the Catholic hierarchy in Dublin. At around the same time as Catholic Emancipation removed the last structural barriers to Catholicism in Britain and its Empire in 1829, Governor Richard Burke set about ensuring that all denominations would be fairly provided for in Australia. He legislated against the establishment of the Church of England and ensured that government money was available to all denominations for stipends and church building in proportion to the sizes of their congregations.[5]

During the first half of the nineteenth century, the Catholic hierarchy in Australia was English, not Irish, and the Vicar-Apostolic in Britain liaised with Rome concerning Catholic affairs in the Australian colonies. In the early 1830s, in response to pleas from Sydney and pressure from Rome, and with the agreement of the British government, William Morris, the Benedictine Vicar-Apostolic in London, appointed two English monks from his order to take charge of the nascent Australian Church. William Ullathorne was appointed Vicar-General of New South Wales in 1832 and his mentor, John Bede Polding, was appointed Bishop of Sydney and Vicar-Apostolic of New Holland and Van Diemen's Land two years later. Both men were to lead the small band of Irish priests who were already in New South Wales, and who included John McEncroe, Philip Connolly and John Therry.[6] All were faced with the task of establishing churches and schools to serve the widely scattered Catholic communities.

Although Polding retained his dream of a Benedictine-led Australian Church, Ullathorne and McEncroe recognised that Catholicism would flourish only as an Irish Church led by Irish clergy. Attempts to recruit English priests for Australia had failed, while the number of Irish among the laity continued to increase. Ullathorne, in particular, recognised that this combination of Irish priests and Irish laity 'Hibernicised our Mission', concluding that the colony would become an 'Irish mission'.[7] This tendency was symbolised at the consecration of Sydney's second church, St Patrick's Church Hill, in 1840.[8] According to Ullathorne, the foundation ceremony was one of the first demonstrations of Irish 'national feeling' in the colony. There were plans to turn the event into vehemently Irish performative space with the use of banners, scarves and various symbols of Irishness.[9] These plans were seen as a provocative political act by a suspicious government, nervous of Orange counter-demonstrations, and Ullathorne persuaded the committee to tone down the Irishness of the occasion.

This 'Irishing' of the colonial Catholic Church gathered pace by mid-century and was deeply influenced by the personal and theological ties between Irish appointees to Australian bishoprics and the ultramontane Archbishop of Dublin, Cardinal Cullen.[10] Ever since his arrival as chaplain to the Catholics of New South Wales in 1832, John McEncroe had urged the need for Irish priests to minister to the Irish laity and the associated need for Irish bishops to lead them, citing increasing difficulties with the English Polding.[11] His efforts bore fruit in the 1860s with the arrival of six Irish bishops direct from Ireland, all friends or relatives of Cardinal Cullen.[12] McEncroe had been supported by the first Catholic bishop of Melbourne, James Goold, in advocating the need for Irish clergy to Rome. Goold was appointed to Melbourne in 1847 and maintained his preference for Irish clergy throughout his episcopate. In 1873, citing the fact that the vast majority of Australian Catholics were Irish, he argued that Irish bishops and priests were required because 'to successfully govern a people, even in spiritual matters, it is expedient to be acquainted with their disposition, their inclinations, their habits, their customs and their language and especially to secure their affection'.[13] Throughout the 1870s and 1880s, complaints continued about the lack of priests and the unwillingness of Irish clergy to serve under Polding and his successor, fellow Englishman Roger Bede Vaughan.[14] The triumph of the Irish faction culminated in the appointment in 1884 of Cardinal Cullen's nephew and private secretary, Patrick Moran, as Archbishop of Sydney to lead what he termed the 'Irish spiritual empire'.[15] His strongly voiced attachment to Ireland and Rome, and his political activities within the Australian colonies, were seen as emblematic of Catholic disloyalty to Australia and the British Empire.

The policy of fostering Irish clericalism within the Catholic Church in Australia constituted one discursive network linking Australia and Ireland with other parts of the Empire. Cardinal Cullen's network of relatives and friends extended to Irish diasporic communities as far afield as South Africa and New Zealand.[16] While this helped to unite the Church as an Irish Church, it was as the Cullenite, Roman Irish Church rather than one that had links to earlier nineteenth-century Irish Church practices. Consequently, as the Catholic Church grew in the latter half of the nineteenth century in Australia, its developing parochial structures and massive building expansion created Catholic religious spaces that were inflected with an Irishness that was unlikely to be familiar to many laity who had left Ireland in the earlier part of the century.[17] Moreover, Irish clergy and laity familiar with the extensive, intimate and localised parochial system in Ireland arrived in the colonies to be greeted with settings that appeared both foreign and bereft of religious meaning. The vast Australian distances, large Protestant population and increasingly secularised laity, used to only intermittent contact with priests, ensured that Catholicism could never be expressed in exactly the same way in Australia as it had been in Ireland. All of these factors contributed to the discontent over church building programmes that occurred in New South Wales and Victoria.

While English bishops and Scots laity were present within the Catholic churches in Australia, Protestant commentators could only ever see Irishness, and a version of Irishness that they found intimidating and alarming. The most vocal opponent of Catholicism in nineteenth-century Australia was the redoubtable campaigner John Dunmore Lang. He used his missionary zeal to promote migration schemes to Australia designed to attract Scots and Irish Protestants in order to counteract what he perceived as the 'Catholic threat' to the colonies.[18] For Lang, the Catholic Church was a 'monstrous perversion of everything like honesty and justice'.[19] While Lang's opinions were not representative of all Protestants, he was a vocal and prolific critic of Catholicism. He wanted to build Australia as a Protestant and, preferably, Presbyterian society. Although he succeeded in attracting significant numbers of Presbyterian clergy and other migrants to Australia in the 1830s, his dogmatic and abrasive personality contributed significantly to the dissension that characterised the Presbyterian Church in Australia thereafter.

Foremost among these divisions was the 'Disruption' of 1843, which divided the Presbyterian Church world-wide. In Australia, its effects were exacerbated by personality clashes among the leading clergy (including Lang) and by the problems inherent in ministering to widely scattered congregations. The causes of the Disruption were complex, but a major area of contention in both Scotland and the colonies was the issue of State Aid to Churches, and the implications this had for government interference in clerical appointments. In Australia this was of immediate import in Governor Burke's provision of government money for buildings and clerical stipends. The upshot for Presbyterianism was that the Free Church of Australia Felix aligned itself with the Free Church of Scotland in refusing all government monies, thus remaining unconnected with the state. The Presbyterian Synod of Australia voted to remain in communion with the Established Church in Scotland and so receive government assistance. Further divisions continued until the late 1850s, when successful moves towards union between a majority of the Free Church and the Presbyterian Synod of Victoria created the Presbyterian Church of Victoria. A minority of the Free Church dissented and continued as the Free Church of Victoria until 1913, when they joined other Free Presbyterians to form the Free Presbyterian Church of Australia. In New South Wales similar dissension over State Aid occurred, with union between previously opposed factions also taking place in the 1860s.[20]

Memory, place and religion

While questions of disloyalty and disruption were widely reported throughout the colonies, daily religious life centred on local issues that circulated through circumscribed networks. In scattered rural communities, emerging regional centres and metropolitan areas alike, people came together to build churches of all denominations. In doing so, they brought not only theological meaning but also the comforts of familiar rituals and events to unfamiliar landscapes. Their success was considerable. By the latter half of the nineteenth century most communities had access to churches, or were at least visited periodically by clergy of the main denominations. The presence of a church in even the smallest colonial township offered a material reflection of the metropolitan heart of empire and memories of home. Each church's design and dedication, as well as the decoration and iconography within its walls, had the capacity to invoke the emigrants' memories of their past life in places that had held particular meaning for them in Scotland, Ireland or England.

Churches were thus among the most important of all focal points for communities. In many rural areas, attendance at Sunday church services or other festivals was the only recreation time available, ensuring that churches possessed multiple meanings as places of religious practice and social intercourse. When local committees got together to raise funds to build churches and host clergy, they actively worked towards a number of different objectives. In part they were engaged in the process of community building, the ongoing colonial project of establishing British legal, economic, cultural and social structures in the seemingly uncivilised wilderness of the untamed Australian landscape. Thus, in 1851 the wife of a newly arrived Presbyterian minister in Queensland wrote of her reception in her new home:

> All is in the rough here save with a few yet they are earnest that their minister should be respectable and comfortable. It will be a splendid and populous district in a brief period . . . [21]

In transforming the 'rough' to the 'respectable' these groups of colonists availed themselves of land and financial grants that were assigned for the purpose by the church and colonial authorities. These were equally eager that the benefits of European civilisation and modernity should be emplaced in the bush.[22] Within this broadly and – undoubtedly implicit – imperial frame, other objectives included the explicit aim of ensuring access to religious services and the provision of recreational space. Such recreation was based on the shared values of the denomination in question, and was thus inextricably entwined with cultural memories of 'home'.

Efforts at church, school, manse and presbytery building were invariably communal, particularly in terms of their financing, but also sometimes in the provision of labour and materials. Normally, local committees were formed to oversee the work, and their membership usually reflected the settlers' diverse regional origins in the British Isles. For both Catholic and Presbyterian laity these committee meetings were often occasions when they were able to express their ethnic identity and memory most clearly. But despite this, in working towards a common goal, these committees also effectively merged their varied membership into a single diasporic group. The history of the building process thus itself became part of the semiotic meanings of place that were encoded into these religious sites. Often these were added to stories remembered and handed down from the early settlers' own histories in Ireland or Scotland.

In the early years of colonial settlement, before the churches were able to establish a formal presence in many areas, squatters frequently hosted clergy and provided informal venues for services. One area of early settlement to the south of Sydney, the Illawarra, was regularly visited by Irish Catholic priests from the 1830s. The first recorded mass was celebrated there by Father Therry in 1833, and from 1838 Father John Rigney, one of Ullathorne's initial recruits from Ireland, travelled through the region conducting mass at private houses. These informal sites became known locally as mass stations, in a cultural reference to places in rural Ireland where mass was conducted during the Penal Era.[23] Similarly, among the rapidly shifting population of the Victorian goldfields, Father Barrett reported in 1858 that as well as holding mass in tents on the Ararat and Pleasant Creek diggings he had also established three mass stations in the outlying areas of Horsham, Raglan and Avoca, with varying attendance.[24]

If the churches established an informal presence in the shifting spaces of the expanding frontier, in settled areas more formal processes of church foundation quickly assigned religious meanings to place in other ways. In areas that were surveyed for settlement, land was usually granted by government to each of the major denominations, although in some cases landowners donated money, land and buildings. Thus Moses Brennan, a prosperous former convict transported for his involvement in the 1798 United Irishmen's Rebellion, gave the land for the first Catholic church at Jamberoo.[25] Some landowners and pastoralists were particularly praised for providing money or land to build churches to which they personally did not belong. James Atkinson, proprietor of the Belfast Special Survey, gave land and money for a Catholic church in Port Fairy in 1847 and again, for its larger replacement, ten years later.[26] Martin Shanahan, an Irish Catholic pastoralist, is locally reputed to have given money towards the building of the Presbyterian church near his property at Marnoo, at much the same time as he accommodated the itinerant Catholic priests who held mass in his homestead.[27]

During the early years of settlement clergymen of all denominations travelled long distances to visit members of their flock. These travels generated origin narratives that became part of the histories of the new communities. Thus, when Father Barrett, the abrasive Catholic priest based at Ararat, was travelling in remote country and sought shelter from one McDonald, a staunch Scottish Calvinist, the unexpectedly convivial evening spent by the pair entered into local memory as the cause of the Scotsman's subsequent benign toleration of Irish Catholics. These different origin narratives enabled emerging congregations to ground their experience as emigrants, their roots and routes, in the immediate locality. By providing them with localised memories of place that connected to their previous lives, these stories helped to create a diasporic sense of belonging in two worlds: the there and then of memory and the here and now of the colonial present. In this way the rebel background of Moses Brennan, the 'typical' Scottish attitudes of McDonald transformed by the affable Irish priest and the generosity of Irish pastoralists towards local churches of other denominations, all blurred the essentialist ethnic and sectarian certainties of the past in the uncertain and changing terrain of the colonial present.

Placing the church

These elisions of past and present were intensely personal, as were the meanings of place that individuals ascribed to the newly built churches and other buildings. In 1869 an English traveller, Thomas Sharpe, encountered the newly built Anglican church in the small village of Jamberoo:

> I was very much gratified by seeing in this lonely spot such a building. It is a complete church and must gladden the eyes of all good churchmen to see it in such a specimen of correct church architecture . . . On a Sunday the young men and young women come trooping down on horseback to attend the services of the Church you see horses every where round the fencing of the ground . . . This says a good deal of the people of these lonely dales and hills. They are well dressed and conduct themselves with the greatest decorum in the house of God . . . I know of no church in the

colony to be compared for neatness, chaste design and beauty of structure as the little church ... at Jamberoo.[28]

For Sharpe, the church's 'completeness' and 'correctness' signalled its civilising role in the process of colonisation. As a material manifestation, in so remote a spot, of English social norms and Anglican doctrine it provided reassuring evidence of their discursive authority in this particular part of Empire. All of this, of course, was duly authenticated in the mind of the writer by his own memories of Anglican Church life in the parishes of England.

It is salutary, therefore, to realise that the calm and normality evoked by this idyllic description masked significant divisions within the Anglican community at Jamberoo over religious practice. These originated in the different Anglican traditions which members of the congregation brought with them from England and Ireland. The tensions had given rise to very public expressions of disapproval by different sections of the congregation only a few years before Sharpe's visit, and these still simmered under the surface in 1869. The 'specimen of correct architecture' which he so admired represented, in fact, an uneasy compromise between the English-born minister, who favoured a more English style of church decoration, and his predominately Fermanagh-born congregation. The latter were adamant that they wished to worship in surroundings untainted by any hint of a decorative style they associated with Catholicism.

The church's original design was very plain, but the minister in charge at the time of its completion in 1866, the Reverend Mr Baily, wanted more decoration and arranged for the addition of a Norman-style doorway and crosses. Each time an addition was made to the new church, harsh words were spoken within the congregation. The *Kiama Reporter* noted that 'every attempt at decoration is jealously watched by some who regard any external symbol as belonging only to a communion which they seem to regard it as the highest proof of piety to hate'.[29] Eventually three stone crosses that had been placed on the church by Mr Baily were removed during the night. He replaced one cross, but the following year this too was taken down and destroyed. In May 1867 the minister finally acceded to his congregation's wishes and removed the wooden replacement cross. His congregation immediately increased substantially.

Undeterred, the beleaguered Mr Baily subsequently tried to introduce a desk as a piece of altar furniture. His parishioners immediately assigned decidedly negative ethno-religious meaning to this. Naming it 'St Patrick', they either refused to attend services while it was present or else pointedly moved it aside during communion, to the indignation of the minister. Local gossip held the extended Grey family and their associates – all Fermanagh-born members of the Church of Ireland – to be responsible for orchestrating this opposition. Whoever was responsible for these acts of resistance, they provide an apt reminder of the importance of religious place in the construction of diasporic identity. This was perhaps especially true among emigrants for whom religion had always been an important marker of their sense of self and belonging overall, as had been the case in the contested landscapes of nineteenth-century Ulster. Seemingly, such people formed a signifi- cant element among the Church of England congregation at Jamberoo. Consequently, their actions in ensuring that the religious spaces in which they had invested such meaning were performed in ways that were amenable to them were both determined and sustained.

The putative Irishness of the Catholic Church in Victoria was signalled early in its history by the foundation stone laid in 1841 for its first church, St Francis, Melbourne. This recorded that Patrick Bonaventure Geoghegan was 'an Irish priest, O.S.F, the first who offered the sacrifice in Australia Felix'.[30] Six years later, when James Goold, the Irish-born first Catholic Bishop of Melbourne arrived, little had changed. He found a primitive organisation, with St Francis as the only church and six priests in residence. Goold was eventually appointed Archbishop and died in 1886. He spent the rest of his episcopate cre- ating a network of parishes and supporting diocesan structures, and promoting the construction of churches, schools and presbyteries.[31] He was a firm believer in the benefits of strong, centralised Episcopal authority, especially regarding the financial and administrative man- agement of the building works in the new parishes. Nevertheless, as we have suggested, the involvement of laity in the local management of these projects and in raising funds for them itself created spaces for individual and group identity formation. At Stawell, the committee formed to raise money for the new Catholic church (Figure 8.1) con- sisted of thirty-three prominent Irish Catholic men, with a working cadre of about ten who attended fortnightly meetings and organised the collection of donations. Additional fund-raising activities were also organised, such as the bazaar in May 1872, when women held five stalls and raised £730.[32]

Management of the financial aid provided by the colonial govern- ment provoked fierce disagreements between the Catholic laity and Church hierarchy, particularly in Victoria during Goold's episcopate, and also in New South Wales at the same period.[33] Goold interpreted these objections as evidence of disloyalty to the (Irish) Catholic Church. Writing to Dean Fitzpatrick while on a visit to Dublin in 1859, he concluded:

8.1 Stawell Roman Catholic church

Their want of truth and their usual vicious attempts to secularise the administration of the Church together with the treacherous praise of the Orange and Protestant press of the colonies will draw down upon them contempt and pity.[34]

Some lay parishioners and Irish priests interpreted Goold's demand for unilateral control over funds raised by the laity for church building as evidence both of the Church's failure to adapt to colonial conditions and of the poor quality of its Irish clergy.[35] Michael O'Reilly, the fire-brand editor of *The Banner of Belfast*, was as strident a critic of Bishop Goold as he was of Belfast's founder, James Atkinson, and Irish land-lordism.[36] His criticism of what he saw as Goold's misappropriation of money donated for church building revealed fault lines in the body of the Catholic Church and led to the suspension of the local priest, Father Dunne.[37] Dunne's relationship with Goold had been tense for a number of years. He had previously had difficulties over plans for a new church at Geelong that were first halted and then changed by Goold.[38]

Dunne's attempts to explain and justify his parishioners' discontent with reference to custom in Ireland further exacerbated the situation. Dean Fitzpatrick admonished him: 'Anyone reading your note would think that you wished to encourage the lay people to interfere in church matters against the Bishop.'[39]

What was in evidence here were the disruptive intersections between Goold's authoritarianism, on the one hand, and the Irish settlers' experience of living 'unchurched' in the colony and their memories of the relatively liberal pre-Cullenite Catholic Church in Ireland, on the other. Goold's actions were informed by his own tenacious belief, born of his own memories of Ireland and his education at Rome, in the prerogative of the episcopacy to make decisions on behalf of the laity. These conflicting perspectives were heightened by the mutually antagonistic personalities of Goold, Dunne and O'Reilly. Their disagreement about diocesan financial management escalated into a major conflict over the issue of clerical and lay rights in the Church. This spread beyond Victoria to involve the other Australian colonies, Rome and Ireland, and ultimately required Vatican intervention to settle it (in Goold's favour).[40]

One reason why conflicts over finances reached such levels was the importance the Irish Catholic laity attached to investing in churches and other buildings. Their generosity resulted in the donation of many small amounts of cash, goods in kind and labour to ensure both that they had buildings in which to worship and educate their children, and that these buildings enhanced their status claims within the community. Architecturally imposing churches proclaimed their identity as a sometimes surprisingly prosperous Irish Catholic minority within the hegemonic English and Protestant spaces of many towns.[41] Dr Ullathorne expressed this principle in 1838 in a sermon preached at the laying of the foundation stone of the Parramatta church: 'All our public acts of religion are performed with ceremonies expressive of their nature.'[42] These performances underwrote the presence of Irish Catholics in these localities as an ethnic group that could not be ignored.

Clearly, the size and design of churches depended, in the first instance, as much on the congregations' resources as on the availability of government aid. In many communities the earliest churches were small and makeshift, and often built without formal design. Many of these buildings have not survived, usually because their communities swiftly outgrew them. A rare example of a late survival is the log cabin-style Presbyterian church at Dimboola, with its plain design and rough-cut features.[43] The Presbyterian churches that replaced these earliest structures were also relatively austere. Barn-like in shape, they

8.2   St Andrew's Presbyterian church, Belfast (Port Fairy)

reflected the importance attached to preaching rather than to liturgical practice. St Andrew's church at Belfast (Port Fairy) provides a case in point (Figure 8.2). The first Presbyterian church in the township was a slab-and-sapling affair, and was completed in 1843. In 1849, James Atkinson gave a two-acre site for a more permanent structure. After four years of fund raising, the foundation stone of the new building was laid in November 1853 by Charles MacKnight, the Providentially minded Scots squatter discussed in chapter 6. Built in the 'Classical Revival' style, the church's design is thought to reflect in particular the Northern Irish influence of the then incumbent minister, the Rev. Thomas Craig.[44]

After the reunion of previously divided Presbyterian factions in Victoria and New South Wales in the 1860s, the increasing wealth of their congregations led to many churches being built in more ornate Gothic styles.[45] St Matthew's Presbyterian church, Stawell, is one example (Figure 8.3). Designed by the successful church architect Robert Love, it was built in 1868–69 in late Gothic style, with a spire and a broad nave.[46] Newspapers in Stawell were fulsome in their praise. The *Pleasant Creek News* commented: 'The graceful appearance bestowed by both drapery and lights now stamps it as one of the most beautiful structures for public worship outside of Melbourne.'[47] Civic

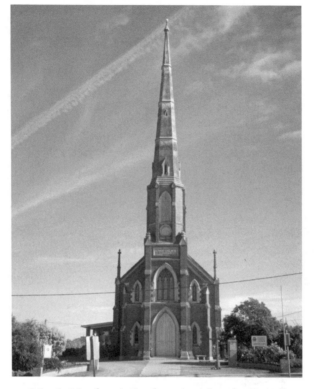

8.3   St Matthew's Presbyterian church, Stawell

pride is clearly evident here, and is a reminder of the importance many citizens assigned to church buildings of all denominations as formative elements in the imagined places of their everyday urban lives.

Most Catholic churches, particularly in Victoria, were also built in the Gothic style. Irish bishops would have been aware of the ecclesiological debates in Britain and Ireland over the most 'correct' style of church architecture, in which A. W. Pugin's High Gothic designs were particularly influential. Bishop Goold favoured the Gothic style of Catholic convert W. W. Wardell and Henry Caselli, the latter a disciple of one of Pugin's English followers, Charles Hansom.[48] Their work is exemplified at Belfast (Port Fairy), where St Patrick's church was built in controversial circumstances in 1857–59 to a design of Charles Hansom's (Figure 8.4).[49] This church was much bigger than the one originally planned by Patrick Dunne and his lay committee, and its enlargement was typical of Bishop Goold's plans for large and imposing parish churches throughout Victoria. Goold kept tight control

[219]

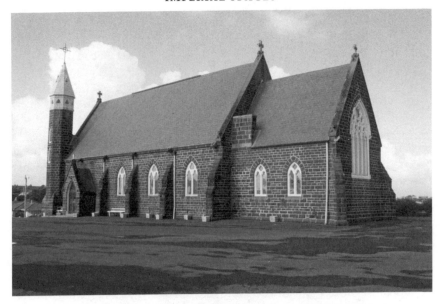

8.4 St Patrick's Roman Catholic church, Belfast (Port Fairy)

over the plans for churches and altered the architects' plans to suit his vision for the various communities. In 1857 he wrote from Rome to his Vicar-General with details of the plans to be used: 'the plan of Kilmore church would be the one for St Augustine's site – whilst the one you will receive from Dublin – I mean the large one – would answer for St Mary's. Mr Wardell will be able to give you one for Collingwood.'[50]

In the Wimmera region of north-west Victoria, Irish-born architect Michael Ryan designed several small Catholic churches, including those at Dimboola, Jerparit, Goroke and Willaura. These were all similar in design and employed simplified Gothic features, including roundel stained-glass windows, porches, and paired lancet windows in the nave.[51] As in many other Catholic churches, no overt Irish or Celtic ornamentation was included. This suggests that if ethnic memory was invoked by these buildings, it was through the social and cultural performances within them rather than their architecture. Ryan was also involved in the design of the new Catholic church at Stawell. Here, the needs of the Catholic congregation quickly outstripped both the tent initially put up for service by Father Barrett and the modest weatherboard building that replaced it. In 1869, a local committee comprised of prominent Irish Catholic miners and professional men under the leadership of Father Barrett decided to replace the old building with a much bigger and grander church. They initially engaged Michael Ryan to submit designs for a church in the early Decorated Gothic style, with a capacity to seat 500. The plans were then submitted to Archbishop Goold for approval. According to the *Pleasant Creek News*, the design included a tower and spire, and the church was to have been built of brick, faced with cement.[52] At about the same time, relations between the parishioners and Father Barrett broke down, and the laity refused to hand over money collected for the Catholic Association while he remained associated with Pleasant Creek.[53] In a situation that echoed events at Belfast (Port Fairy) twelve years earlier, Goold refused his approval and the architect, Caselli of Ballarat, was commissioned to design a much larger church. This opened in 1873 with accommodation for 700 people, although it was never completed in its entirety, due to lack of funds.[54]

Just as church dedications to St Patrick might denote an active Irish consciousness on the part of the clergy or laity, so too the architectural design and iconography of the church's interior decoration could be culturally inflected. In Catholic churches, much of the decoration was fairly standardised and reflected a metropolitan focus that looked more to England and Rome than to Australia or Ireland. Many Catholic churches were supplied with furnishings by the Birmingham firm John Hardman and Co. It had been founded by A. W. Pugin, and supplied plate and metal fittings, as well as stained glass, in the Puginist Gothic Revival style.[55] Although the Catholic church at Stawell was dedicated to St Patrick, the most notable additions to its religious decoration sustained typically nuanced readings. These were the carved Stations of the Cross donated by Irish-born Jane Kinsella (née Jennings) in 1899 and the statue of St Joseph given by her Australian-born niece Emilie in 1909.[56] The Kinsella/Jennings families were local supporters of Irish causes and adopted Irish symbols on their own grave-stones. However, in publicly expressing their identity within the shared spaces of the church, they opted for another persona, that of wealthy local miners and colonial landowners. Their donations of gold nuggets to the Pope were noted with pride and some awe in the local newspapers.[57] Each of these gifts signalled the complexity of the Kinsella/Jennings families' sense of selfhood, and consequently the multi-vocal character of the places they helped to perform.

The much larger Irish Catholic community at Kilmore worshipped in another church dedicated to St Patrick, where statues to St Patrick and St Brigit dominated the nave. Carved bosses at the west end of the nave depicted the Virgin Mary, Jesus Christ, Saints Patrick and Brigit, and Daniel O'Connell and Brian Boru.[58] This amalgam of religious, cultural and political symbolism speaks to the same truth as the Kinsella/Jennings monuments at Stawell. As place, St Patrick's (Kilmore) supported multiple meanings for its congregation and others, which were capable of varied interpretation according to individual circumstance and experience. The community at Kilmore also had access to impressively large schools and convents that, by the end of the nineteenth century, dominated the hills around the town. In Victoria the 1872 Education Act withdrew government support from all Church schools in favour of secular state education.[59] The aim of the Act was explained to the people of Kilmore in a speech given at the opening of the local state school in 1875. The school would be not 'English, Scottish or Irish, but Victorian'.[60] Catholics, led by Bishop Goold, were not convinced, and argued that their specific educational needs could not be met within a secular system. Eventually, the Act led to the establishment of a system of Catholic schools throughout the Australian colonies, and these survived without government financial support until the late twentieth century. Following the 1872 Education Act, in a pattern that was repeated throughout the colonies, the Kilmore Sisters of Mercy opened a school for Catholic girls in 1875, while a Marist Brothers College for boys was opened in 1893.[61]

For all denominations, the erection of substantial churches within the shared spaces of the towns and villages of Victoria and elsewhere helped to underscore these groups' presence within the changing narratives of place enacted there. The meanings assigned to the buildings varied, among both their congregations and outsiders. Arguably, the subaltern status allegedly assigned at different times to the predominantly Irish Catholic community as a suspect 'other' may have ensured that for them, their buildings were particularly important as symbols of material success and cohesive communal identity. But as events at Kilmore, Stawell and Belfast (Port Fairy) demonstrated, this unanimity might be more apparent that real. Whatever their denomination, all churches had the capacity to become sites of resistance where, as at Jamberoo, subaltern voices within the faith community might challenge the prevailing religious hegemony. In short, churches and other buildings, like all material expressions of place, attracted meanings that continuously changed according to time and circumstance. Ethnicity and memory played their part in this, but in subjectively constructed ways which ensured that these religious spaces were never essentialist in meaning.

Soundscapes

Establishing religious spaces was not just about financing and constructing buildings, but also involved creating familiar organisational structures and styles of worship. While church iconography and styles of architecture offered tangible expressions of identity, non-material performative markers of ethnicity were also highly significant for many church communities in colonial Australia. The most obvious of these were the sounds of the voices and music used in services. The soundscape of churches resonated with memory and meaning as much as ethnically inflected decorations on the walls. In the new communities people meeting in religiously demarcated space brought with them divergent ideas, memories and expectations. As these personal religious meanings were negotiated in and through the spaces of the church, so they took on an increasingly diasporic character as they became informed by the mundane practices of colonial life.

The extent to which English was spoken by the earliest Irish convicts is not known, although such evidence as exists suggests that a high proportion were Irish speakers, some of whom may have arrived as monoglots.[62] The significance of language in demarcating ethnically defined religious space is clear from the early complaints about the use of Irish at mass, as well as from the clearly expressed preference of the early Irish priests for reinforcements who could speak Irish.[63] The Irish laity obviously appreciated such priests. Anecdotes of spoken Irish being used within the early Church were repeated in Archbishop Moran's *History of the Catholic Church in Australasia* written in 1894, and through this became incorporated into the received Irish history of Australian Catholicism.[64] In one alleged instance which subsequently became a well known part of this public history, Father Connolly in Tasmania is reputed to have written down the confession of a condemned man in Irish, so as to thwart the interest of Governor Arthur in the statements.[65]

While it is to be expected that some early convicts spoke Irish, it is also noteworthy that the migrants who crowded the streets of Melbourne and the rural towns at mid-century also included Irish speakers. The presence of these Irish-speaking laity and priests allowed the spaces of Catholicism to be reinforced with particular ethnic meaning. The use of Irish at mass excluded all but a certain sort of Irishman (or woman). In 1853, the newly arrived Father Francis Moore was introduced to a Melbourne Catholic Association meeting as a man who could speak 'both in the Queen's language and in the fine old Irish tongue'.[66] On the Bendigo goldfields, Father Maurice Stack used a humorous and personalised Irish/English language poem during a sermon to name and praise those who had contributed money and gold to a collection in his church.[67] Stack's use of Irish in this fashion enhanced communal identity in ways which invoked memories of home and added layers of diasporic meaning. The congregation's new found wealth was part of their expatriate present,

[223]

undreamt of in Ireland. Their liberality with it was authenticated in terms which reconnected them to the values of their past. The sermon and the poem also reaffirmed the congregation's communal identity in the face of threats from Protestant troublemakers who had attacked the priest and prompted the outpouring of support. But this particular linguistic space was also hybrid. The poem employed alternate Irish/ English lines. Although this was a common Irish poetic device of the time, it meant that non-Irish speakers in the congregation could share in the sense of belonging and performed Irishness. That this performance took place within a Catholic church merely emphasised the connection between this denomination and Gaelic Irish ethnicity within the polyglot and multicultural spaces of this particular part of colonial Victoria.

The mutually reinforcing connections between language, cultural memory and religious practice were also felt by the numerically smaller but still cohesive Scots Catholic migrant stream. The needs of some of the smaller Scots Gaelic communities in Western Victoria were recognised in 1855, when the Bishop of Glasgow agreed that Father Ranald Rankin of Badenoch and Moidart could emigrate to minister to many of his former parishioners who had settled near Belfast (Port Fairy).[68] In Scots Presbyterian communities the use of Gaelic by ministers and lay preachers was considered normal wherever there were sufficient Gaelic speakers.[69] This practice continued throughout the nineteenth century. For example in the Wimmera region, Calum mór McInnes, who migrated from the Isle of Skye in the 1850s, continued to preach in both Gaelic and English well into the 1890s.[70] However when the needs of English and Gaelic speakers had to be accommodated within the same church there was potential for conflict. In the 1860s tensions arose between Lowland and Highland Scots in the Grafton area of New South Wales, where a significant group of Gaelic-speaking Highlanders had settled south of the Clarence River. Their support for Gaelic-speaking preachers in direct opposition to the official and English-speaking Presbyterian minister, Mr Gordon, raised doubts over the congregation's ability to support a permanent minister.[71] In this case at least, ethnic commonality outweighed religious feeling.

Similar rifts over the use of language and music were also evident in the divided Presbyterian congregations at Kilmore. The first Presbyterian services were conducted in Gaelic from 1843 in the woolshed of Joseph Sutherland's station, Moranding.[72] As the population grew the need for a resident minister became evident and finally, in 1850, John Hume was appointed directly from Scotland, and the Kilmore church was formed under the principles of the Free Church of Victoria.[73] Under Hume's stewardship, a Gaelic speaking teacher,

Charles McKay, was appointed to the denominational school after the previous teacher had left to try his luck on the goldfields. Tension centred around McKay at the time of Hume's death in 1855, and when the English-speaking minister Andrew Maxwell accepted the call to preach in Kilmore the crisis came to a head. McKay resigned after much animosity and most of the Gaelic speakers withdrew from Maxwell's congregation.[74] Under instruction from the Free Church Synod, Maxwell and the elders attempted to resolve the differences between the two groups by appointing a Gaelic-speaking elder, Roderick McLeod, to liaise with the Highlanders. These overtures were resisted, however, and the latter were 'unanimous in declaring that they would have nothing to do with Mr Maxwell or the English speaking congregation, that they would not accept the services of Mr McLeod as they had already as good (Mr McInnes) to conduct their services'.[75] The dedications of the two churches – St Andrews for the Gaelic speaking Highland Church and St George for the predominately English speaking Church where the northern Irish as well as Lowland Scots worshipped – signalled to the wider community of Kilmore the Presbyterians' very real ethno-religious disagreements. The Highlanders continued to conduct their own services in Gaelic at St Andrew's until the early 1870s, when a carefully constructed reintegration of the two groups was initiated.[76]

Language was only one method of marking ethnically inflected religious space, music was also important. Archbishop Polding urged Catholic congregations to sing as a devotional exercise. Arguing that singing hymns was another form of prayer, he encouraged the faithful to sing to familiar music as this would enable them to join with a wider community of worshippers.[77] Using familiar music ensured continuity with past practice as well as enhancing contemporary communal identity. One of the popular hymns sanctioned for use in Catholic churches was 'Hail, Glorious St Patrick!' which closes with the lines that evoked a strong diasporic sense of Irishness: 'And our hearts shall yet burn, wheresoever we roam/For God and St Patrick and our native home.'[78]

Music and singing formed another site of resistance within many Presbyterian churches in colonial Australia.[79] The Presbyterian communities at Stawell and Kilmore both found that church music was divisive rather than inclusive. In 1867 at St Matthew's Presbyterian church in Stawell, an organ was introduced in the face of sustained and vocal opposition.[80] At Kilmore the issue was even more heated. Both St Andrew's and St George's had followed the Scots tradition of using unaccompanied metrical psalms led by a lay precentor.[81] While the Presbyterian Church of Victoria had begun moves to introduce hymns using a specially commissioned hymnbook as early as 1861, in

Kilmore there was deeply felt resistance to the idea. The congregation at St George was originally part of the Free Church, and only considered the issue of using hymns after they had joined the Presbyterian Church of Victoria in the late 1860s.[82] The issue was put to a vote in 1871 and defeated. The following year another vote was taken which was passed at St George's but not at St Andrew's.[83] The use of music was one of the areas of contention which remained unresolved when the two churches were eventually united in 1878.[84]

In their deeply felt disagreement over the devotional value of language and music, the Presbyterian churches at Kilmore appealed to atavistic identities that were rooted in their members' Scottish and Irish experience. This was always individual, always subjectively constructed. So divergent were these Presbyterian identities that for thirty years they could not be reconciled within one community. When a form of unity was finally achieved, it was only as a result of a generational shift in the congregations' membership. Once first generation emigrants with their deeply personal memories of Scottish or Irish practice had passed away, compromises over music and language were achieved which created a new form of liturgical Presbyterian space rooted as much in the colonial present as in the remembered past.

Sites of remembrance

Besides the church buildings, schools and halls where they practiced their religion in life, like all settlers, the Scots and Irish also inscribed their religious affiliation on the gravestones erected for many of them in death. Layered in meaning, these mirrored the wider functions performed by cemeteries within the community. In semiotic terms, they were primarily places where religious and ethnic individualism could be expressed within socially acceptable constraints. Personal grief and religious sentiment might be materialised using a well understood symbolic language in which the religious element was subject to regulation. Catholic priests and prominent laity in particular were urged to exercise 'discreet censorship over inscriptions' in order to ensure that they 'suggest[ed] salutary thoughts'.[85] Yet despite this, many of the bereaved chose to mark grave stones with commemorative symbols of the deceased's individuality in the colonies and origins in Scotland or Ireland.

During the mid-nineteenth century, church graveyards were increasingly supplemented by the use of community cemeteries in Britain and Ireland and elsewhere.[86] This shift coincided with the advent of mass migration to Australia, which in turn meant that there was only a short tradition of church graveyards there. By the second half of the century, the vast majority of cemeteries in Australia were public sites and administered by secular committees rather than by Churches. Cemeteries were divided into separate sections for each denomination, and distinguished not only between Catholic and Protestant, but also between Methodist, Presbyterian and Anglican, as well as between Chinese, Jews and Aborigines.[87] Since denominational affiliation can be assumed from each grave's location, a religious association can be assigned to indications of place of birth or ethnic markers. Cross cutting these religious associations was a well-understood symbolic language of floral and other designs which was widely used by all denominations.[88]

In the four towns analysed here, the Irish-born were much more likely than the English or Scots-born to indicate place of birth on gravestones, even though they were less likely to have a gravestone over their grave. As in colonial cemeteries in North America, the dominant forms of iconography used to signal identity varied between localities.[89] These localised differences in style reflected the varying skills and availability of stonemasons in each area as well as, to an extent, differences in the communal identity displayed by the Irish- and Scots-born and their descendants over time. In any case, erecting a headstone was a luxury only the comparatively wealthy could afford. For example, only 25 per cent of the 7,000 burials made before 1920 in the Stawell cemetery were marked with a headstone.[90] Among those graves with a headstone 114 commemorated Irish-born and 127 Scots-born emigrants. Some 30 per cent of the former indicated the Irishness of their dead through a combination of place of birth inscriptions and symbols such as shamrocks, harps or Celtic crosses (Figure 8.5). The use of Irish symbols increased over time at Stawell. More were used on gravestones that were erected in the later nineteenth century, presumably influenced by the widespread availability of Irish iconography made fashionable by the Gaelic Revival.

Irish symbols also occurred on earlier gravestones, such as the stone commemorating Elizabeth Broughton, née Kelly, who died in 1865 aged 37. Her gravestone was made from marble by a local stonemason, Francis Watkins, an Irish Protestant, and has an incised cross decorated by three small shamrocks at the base. At Stawell, Protestant Irish settlers were less likely to inscribe headstones with place of birth: only five out of thirty-three (15 per cent) did so. Moreover, none of the Irish Protestants buried in the Stawell cemetery were commemorated by any sort of 'authentic' Irish symbolism. For example, when Samuel Hamilton – a stalwart of the local Presbyterian church – died in 1901 his large marble headstone recorded his place of birth in Ballygawley, County Tyrone, but was decorated with a typical nineteenth-century mourning iconography of roses and passion flowers. By comparison,

8.5   Irish tombstone iconography

54 per cent of the headstones at Stawell which commemorated Irish Catholics also had some sort of Irish marker, either in the form of a inscription of place of birth or shamrocks, harps or other symbols.

Scots settlers in Stawell did not use symbols of ethnic origin in the same way: only three of their headstones there carry any sort of recognisably Scottish emblem. Rather, as the McAllister family graves exemplify, there were other, nuanced, ways to give material expression to diasporic identity on a head stone. When Keith and Christy McAllister died in 1887 and 1890, they had achieved much since they set out from the Isle of Skye in the 1850s with their six children. Arriving in Geelong under an assisted immigration scheme and speaking only Gaelic, the family worked their way to become substantial land owners. By the time of Keith's death they owned or leased nearly 4,000 acres of land in the Marnoo district about fifty miles north of Stawell. To commemorate Keith's death and those subsequently of other family members, a group of substantial marble headstones was erected on a rise in the Stawell cemetery.[91] Apart from the family names, there is no indication

that the McAllisters were Scottish and there is no emblematic signifi-
cation of their migrant identity. The family's success is indicted solely
by the number and size of their gravestones. In commemorating their
colonial lives, the family's identity as migrants was not as important
to them as their subsequent success as substantial landholders. The
prominence of their graves signalled their success in their chosen new
world, and perhaps also their eagerness to erase their humble origins
as illiterate crofters. Seemingly, for the McAllisters, the presentism of
their diasporic existence may have been more important to them than
the remembered places of their past.

Of the three cemeteries in the Kiama area, those serving the villages with largest Irish-Catholic populations in the nineteenth century
– Jamberoo and Gerringong – also have the largest number of graves
displaying Irish markers. One is inscribed 'God Save Ireland', and com-
memorates a former Irish convict transported to Western Australia
in 1867.[92] At Kiama, symbols such as shamrocks and Celtic crosses
are comparatively rare.[93] This cemetery served a population with an
unusually high proportion of Irish Protestants, among whom a comparatively large number chose to record the deceased's place of birth
in Ireland. The gravestone of Margaret and James Walker exemplifies
this tendency. A plain white marble stone topped with an urn, it is
inscribed with the couples' names as well as their counties of birth –
Monaghan and Tyrone. There are no explicitly Irish symbols. Rather,
the iconography and design are typical of late nineteenth-century
Anglican gravestones throughout the colonies. Consequently it is from
the birth-place inscription, the tomb's position in the Anglican section
of the cemetery, and its Anglican iconography, that we may infer the
couple's origins as members of the Church of Ireland. Once again, these
signifiers speak of the nuanced ways in which religious and other identities might be expressed in the colonial spaces of Australia, and the
inevitable 'silences' which these expressions leave unfilled.

Arguably, in towns like Kiama where the voice of the hegemonic
(and in this case, Protestant) community was relatively powerful, there
was little felt need among the majority to make overt statements of
ethnicised religious affiliation in death – or in life. At Kilmore, where
despite its dominant Irish-Catholic population there was a strong
undercurrent of sectarian division, it is possible that more people felt
it necessary to assert their ethnic origins in the more evenly divided
spaces of the town. Certainly, the cemetery there has many more Irish
symbols on the gravestones than at Kiama. Surveys of the extant gravestones show that over 40 per cent of those in the Catholic churchyard
and in the Catholic section of the general cemetery display either
Irish iconography, or place of birth, or both. Although this is slightly

less than in Stawell, it includes a significantly larger number of Irish markers on gravestones of second-generation Irish. The higher levels of sectarian tension in the town – higher certainly than at Stawell – may have been one reason for this. These divisions were expressed in other ways as well. The self-assertive Irish Catholic population had their own newspaper, *The Kilmore Free Press,* that ran articles on Irish history, politics and cultural affairs and promoted the interests of Irish-born Catholic local politicians. This newspaper vehemently opposed its Protestant run rival, the *Kilmore Advertiser,* which supported the Protestant, primarily Scots and English population in aggressive disagreement with the *Free Press.*[94] Conceivably, there was much more at stake in claiming an Irish identity in Kilmore than there was in Stawell, which was founded later and with a more mobile and cosmopolitan population of miners. Kilmore, by contrast, was founded in the 1840s and from the start numbered a much larger proportion of Irish men and women in its population. Here, the ethno-religious certainties of their remembered past may have been more easily transcribed into their colonial present.

Summary

The narratives of place performed by Irish and Scottish settlers in Victoria and New South Wales included the re-creation of religious spaces that consciously evoked remembered religious sites and practice in Ireland and Scotland. For Catholics and Presbyterians alike, this colonial engagement occurred at much the same time as momentous changes in religious discourse in both Ireland and Scotland. The Irish Catholic Church's transformation under the leadership of Cardinal Cullen privileged explicit missionary enterprise, which meant that the Church hierarchy in New South Wales developed in tandem with the Church in Ireland. Despite initial attempts to create an English Benedictine hierarchy and leadership for the colonial Catholic Church, an explicit agenda of Hibernicisation resulted in the recruitment of mainly Irish clergy by the 1880s, exemplified by the appointment of Cardinal Moran, Cardinal Cullen's nephew and secretary, as Archbishop and Metropolitan of Sydney. Moran viewed his appointment as a means of building the Irish Catholic Church anew in a colonial landscape. At local levels this was achieved by strong Episcopal control over building programmes, iconography and liturgy. Although there was opposition from Irish laity based on their perception of lay/ clerical relations in Ireland and their more recent experience in the colonies, the physical spaces of the Catholic Church in Victoria and New South Wales became inflected with a clerical Irishness. This, however, was tightly controlled and liturgically speaking, looked more to Rome than to native Irish memory or culture.

Presbyterian and Anglican settlers from Ulster and Scotland also brought with them determined ideas about the sorts of architecture and decorative spaces, as well as soundscapes, they wanted for their churches. Periods of conflict, such as those between Low Church Ulster Anglicans and their more High Church minister in Jamberoo, and the disputes over language and music in the Presbyterian churches in Kilmore, brought these memories and ideologies into the open. The neat stone or wooden churches that dotted the rural landscapes of colonial Victoria and New South Wales were material expressions of the ways in which cultural memory elided with the quotidian experience of colonial life to create truly diasporic religious place meanings in the settlers' new Australian world. These meanings were contingent – they depended on the experience and circumstances of the reader; inchoate – they changed with time and circumstance; and multiple – different people read them simultaneously in different ways. Thus whatever the authorial intentions of people like Archbishop Goold, Father Dunne, James Atkinson, or the Rev. Mr Bailey, neither the Catholic iconography and practice at churches such as St Patrick's, Belfast (Port Fairy) nor its Anglican equivalent at Jamberoo, sustained single, authentic, essentialist meanings. As a component in the construction of ethnic identity, religious practice was subjectively constructed and as varied as the places to which it gave rise.

Religious sites of the sort described here thus constituted an important part of the ever changing mosaic of semiotic meaning inscribed as place in the Australian landscape by hegemonic and subaltern groups in the white migration stream. In life as in death, they connected individual men, women and children to broader discursive networks that linked them – in this world – to other places at the metropolitan heart of Empire and elsewhere, and to a fervently hoped-for future in the next. For this reason, cemeteries were, and remain, as potent in their meaning as place as the sometimes more contested spaces of the churches themselves. As sites of memory they were (and are) particularly personal, and redolent of the particular understanding families had of the deceased. Yet even these meanings were multivocal and partial. Inscriptions of place of birth in Scotland or Ireland even when embedded in a well-understood iconography of Irish or Scottish ethnic symbolism, tell us remarkably little about who these people really were, and of how they performed their lives in the unfamiliar spaces of colonial Australia. Rather, these monuments tell us something about the way in which these long dead emigrants and their families were represented by and within the communities of which they formed part.

[231]

As such, they provide one more piece in the complex jigsaw of identity, memory and performance that placed Irish and Scottish settlers in the landscapes of colonial Australia.Notes

Notes

1   Nicholas O'Donnell, 'My Autobiography', NLA, Brennan Papers, MS mfm G 7703–7704.
2   Letter in the *Kiama Independent*, 1872, cited in *Church of the Resurrection, Church of England, Jamberoo, 1867–1967*, Weston collection, UOWA, D103/19/24.
3   Samuel Marsden, 'A few observations on the toleration of the Catholic Religion in New South Wales', reprinted in P. O'Farrell (ed.), *Documents in Australian Catholic History 1788–1884*, 2 vols, vol. 1 (London, Dublin and Melbourne, 1969), p. 73.
4   A. M. Whitaker, 'The Convict Priests: Irish Catholicism in Early Colonial New South Wales', in P. O'Sullivan (ed.), *The Irish World Wide. Volume 5 Religion and Identity* (London and New York, 1996), pp. 25–42.
5   I. Breward, *A History of the Churches in Australasia* (Oxford, 2001), p. 68; K. Inglis, *Australian Colonists: An Exploration of Social History 1788–1870* (Melbourne, 1993), p. 90. This State Aid was progressively withdrawn in the different colonies in the second half of the nineteenth century.
6   W. Ullathorne, *The Catholic Mission to Australasia* (Liverpool, 2nd edition 1837), pp. 10–15.
7   Cited in P. O'Farrell, *The Catholic Church in Australia: A Short History 1788–1967* (Melbourne, 1968), p. 43.
8   J. Waldersee, 'Father Therry and the Financing of Old St Mary's', in P. O'Farrell (ed.), *St Mary's Cathedral Sydney, 1821–1871* (Sydney, 1971), p. 24.
9   Cited in O'Farrell, *The Catholic Church in Australia*, p. 51.
10   K. T. Livingston, *Emergence of an Australian Catholic Priesthood* (Sydney, 1977), pp. 58–64; O'Farrell, *The Catholic Church in Australia*, p. 93.
11   O'Farrell, *The Catholic Church in Australia*, pp. 78–9; C. Barr, 'Imperium in Imperio: Irish Episcopal Imperialism in the Nineteenth Century', *English Historical Review*, Vol. 123, No. 503 (2008), pp. 627–30; F. O'Donoghue, *The Bishop of Botany Bay: The Life of John Bede Polding, Australia's First Catholic Archbishop* (London and Sydney, 1982).
12   Barr, pp. 627–30. They were James Quinn – Brisbane, 1859; his brother Matthew – Bathurst, 1866; their cousin James Murray – Maitland, 1866; another cousin, Timothy O'Mahony – Armidale, 1871; William Lanigan – Goulburn, 1867; Daniel Murphy – Hobart, 1866. H. J. Gibbney, 'Quinn, James (1819–1881)', *Australian Dictionary of Biography*, Vol. 5 (Melbourne, 1974), pp. 465–6; B. J. Sweeney, 'Quinn, Matthew (1821–1885)', in *ibid.*, pp. 466–7; W. G. McMinn, 'Murray, James (1828–1909)' in *ibid.*, pp. 320–1.
13   Cited in Patrick Francis Cardinal Moran, *History of the Catholic Church in Australia from Authentic Sources* (Sydney, 1894), pp. 786–7.
14   The long and detailed disagreements between the Irish clergy and their archbishops are explored in A. Cunningham, *The Rome Connection: Australia, Ireland and the Empire, 1865–1885* (Sydney, 2002).
15   A. E. Cahill, 'Moran, Patrick Francis (1830–1911)', *Australian Dictionary of Biography*, Vol. 10 (Melbourne, 1986), pp. 577–81; O'Farrell, *The Catholic Church in Australia*, pp. 136–95.
16   Barr, 'Imperium in Imperio', *passim*.
17   E. Larkin, *The Pastoral role of the Roman Catholic Church in Pre-famine Ireland 1750–1850* (Dublin, 2006).
18   D. W. A. Baker, *Days of Wrath: A Life of John Dunmore Lang* (Melbourne, 1985).
19   D. W. A. Baker (ed.), John Dunmore Lang, *Reminiscences of My Life and Times* (Melbourne, 1972), p. 197.

20 The effects of the Disruption in Australia are discussed in histories of the Presbyterian church in Australia. See: Baker, *Days of Wrath: A Life of John Dunmore Lang*, pp. 143–54, 219–22; R. Hamilton, *A Jubilee History of the Presbyterian Church in Victoria* (Melbourne, 1888), pp. 36–7 ff; R. S. Ward, 'Spiritual Movements in Scottish Gaelic Communities in Australia, 1837–1870', in R. S. Ward (ed.), *A Witness for Christ: The Presbyterian Church in Eastern Australia, 1846–1996* (Wantirna, 1996), p. 85; Idem., *The Bush still Burns: The Presbyterian and Reformed Faith in Australia, 1788–1988* (Watirna, 1989), pp. 58–78.

21 NLA, JAF 158/206, Amy Carter to Mrs Lang, 12.2.1851.

22 Breward, *A History of the Churches in Australasia*, pp. 72–83.

23 P. J. Faherty and M. A. O'Keefe, *The Catholic Church in the Illawarra, 150 Years 1838–1988* (Wollongong, 1989). The list of stations at Wollongong, Dapto, Jamberoo and Shoalhaven is given in the *Australian Catholic Directory of the Year 1841* . . . (Sydney, 1841), reprinted in O'Farrell (ed.), *Documents in Australian Catholic History 1788–1884*, pp. 299–300.

24 Melbourne Diocesan Historical Commission, 'Diocese of Melbourne Returns for Missions 1858', p. 345.

25 Faherty and O'Keefe, *The Catholic Church in the Illawarra*, p. 60.

26 W. Ebsworth, *Pioneer Catholic Victoria* (Melbourne, 1973), p. 78.

27 Webb/Campbell notes, RHSV, MS 000255, Box 90/2; C. E. Sayers, *Shepherd's Gold: The Story of Stawell* (Melbourne, 1966), p. 81.

28 State Library of New South Wales, MS A1502, 'Papers of Rev. Thomas Sharpe, 1826–1869: Journal for 1869', p. 210.

29 Cited in *Church of the Resurrection, Church of England, Jamberoo, 1867–1967*, Weston collection, UOWA, D103/19/24.

30 The inscription is cited in Fathers of the Blessed Sacrament, *Saint Francis' Church 1851–1941: A Century of Spiritual Endeavour* (Melbourne, 1941), p. 18.

31 A scholarly biography of Goold remains to be written. A parish-based history of the Catholic Church of Victoria can be found in Ebsworth, *Pioneer Catholic Victoria*. See also F. O'Kane, *A Path Is Set. The Catholic Church in the Port Phillip District and Victoria 1839–1862* (Melbourne, 1976); and O'Farrell, *The Catholic Church in Australia*.

32 'Minutes of the building committee, St Patrick's Church, Pleasant Creek', typescript, Stawell Historical Society, p. 21.

33 O'Farrell, *The Catholic Church in Australia*, pp. 84–100.

34 James Alipius Goold at Dublin to John Fitzpatrick at Melbourne, Feast of Pentecost 1859. SLV, MS8899 MSB 442.

35 M. Pawsey, *The Demon of Discord: Tensions in the Catholic Church in Victoria, 1853–1864* (Melbourne, 1982).

36 Chapter 5. See also L. Proudfoot and D. Hall, 'Memory and Identity in "Irish" Australia: Constructing Alterity in Belfast (Port Fairy), c. 1857–1873', in M. McCarthy (ed.), *Ireland's Heritages Critical Perspectives on Memory and Identity* (Aldershot, 2005), pp. 89–104.

37 The conflict centred around Archbishop Goold's decision to postpone building of the church at Belfast and to use some of the monies collected to pay a debt to the previous parish priest, Fr Shinnick. This led to very public disagreements between Goold and Dunne and eventually Dunne went to Rome to put his case. Details are outlined in Pawsey, *The Demon of Discord*, pp. 7–10, 22–4, 27–9; and O'Kane, *A Path Is Set*, pp. 94–105. See also: Proudfoot and Hall, 'Memory and Identity in "Irish" Australia', pp. 89–104.

38 O'Kane, *A Path Is Set*, p. 95.

39 John Fitzpatrick to Patrick Dunne, 6 May 1856, letter published in *Copy of a statement addressed by the Rev. P. Dunne, late of the diocese of Melbourne to the Most Rev. Dr. Polding, Archbishop of Sydney and Metropolitan of Australia* (Dublin, 1859), p. 4.

40 Pawsey, *The Demon of Discord*, pp. 75–6.

41   P. O'Farrell, *The Catholic Church and Community. An Australian History* (Sydney, 3rd edition, 1992), p. 183.
42   W. Ullathorne, *Sermons with prefaces* (London, 1842), p. 219, reprinted in O'Farrell (ed.), *Documents in Australian Catholic History 1788–1884*, p. 109.
43   SLV, Postcard of Dimboola Presbyterian Church, 1930s, PCV PCA 88.
44   M. A. Syme, *Seeds of a Settlement. Buildings and Inhabitants of Belfast Port Fairy in the Nineteenth Century* (Melbourne, 1991), pp. 102–3.
45   W. Philips, 'The Denominations', in M. Lewis (ed.), *Victorian Churches: Their Origins, Their Story and Their Architecture* (Melbourne, 1991), p. 10.
46   M. Butcher, *Robert Alexander Love: Goldfields Architect, 1814–1876* (Strathdale, 2000); M. Lewis (ed.), *Victorian Churches*, p. 149.
47   *Pleasant Creek News*, 2 October 1869.
48   Philips, 'The Denominations', in Lewis (ed.), *Victorian Churches*, p. 8; M. Lewis, 'Church Architecture', in Lewis (ed.), *ibid.*, p. 22.
49   *Ibid.*, p. 141.
50   James Alipius Goold, Rome, to John Fitzpatrick, 26 December 1858, SLV MS 8899.
51   Michael Ryan plans, University of Melbourne Archives, drawings 6; 12; 7; 17 (1–3) 85/160.
52   *PCN*, 4 November 1869. The design does not survive among Michael Ryan's papers in the University of Melbourne Archives, 85/160.
53   Letter from Rev. Moore to John Fitzpatrick dated 31 August 1870 (synopsis), Melbourne Diocesean Historical Archives, Linane's Priests files B11. Barrett had a history of bad-tempered exchanges with parishioners in all the parishes with which he was associated. Pawsey, *The Demon of Discord*, pp. 60–1.
54   The minutes for the building committee for 1870 have not survived. By the time the minutes resume in 1871, Caselli's plans had been adopted. See 'St Patrick's Church Pleasant Creek, Building Committee Minutes', typescript, Stawell Historical Society. The opening of the church was reported in *PCN*, 1 April 1873.
55   J. O'Callaghan, *Treasures from Australian Churches* (Melbourne, 1985), p. 11.
56   *Stawell News*, 17 January 1899 and 8 August 1909.
57   *SN*, 16 May 1899.
58   'St Patrick's Church, Kilmore', unpublished typescript, Kilmore Mechanics Institute Library, now housed at the Kilmore Historical Society.
59   O'Farrell, *The Catholic Church in Australia: A Short History 1788–1967*, pp. 100–32.
60   M. V. Tucker, *Kilmore on the Sydney Road* (Kilmore, 1988), p. 137.
61   Ebsworth, *Pioneer Catholic Victoria*, pp. 111–15; Tucker, *Kilmore on the Sydney Road*, pp. 137–8.
62   The history of the Irish language in Australia remains under-researched. See D. Lonergan, *Sounds Irish: The Irish Language in Australia* (Adelaide, 2004). P. O'Farrell, *The Irish in Australia* (1st edn, Sydney, 1986), p. 25, argues that monoglots acquired English as soon as possible and lost their Irish. See V. Noone, 'Facing Cultural Chasms: Irish Speakers in Southeast Australia', unpublished paper delivered at the *Thirteenth Irish Australian Conference, University of Melbourne, 2004*. Noone argues that there were far more Irish speakers in the first half of the nineteenth century than O'Farrell recognised. Our thanks to Val Noone for making his unpublished papers available.
63   Rev. P. Conolly to Rev. Dr Poynter, 12 June 1824, reprinted in O'Farrell (ed.), *Documents in Australian Catholic History 1788–1884*, p. 10.
64   Moran, *History of the Catholic Church in Australia, passim.*
65   *Ibid.*, p. 243.
66   Ebsworth, *Pioneer Catholic Victoria*, p. 125.
67   Noone, 'Facing Cultural Chasms', quoting T. Culhane, 'Irish in an Australian Goldfield', *Journal of the Kerry Archaeological and Historical Society*, No. 4 (1971), p. 165.
68   Ward, 'Spiritual Movements', pp. 69–70.

69 Hamilton, *A Jubilee History of the Presbyterian Church in Victoria*, pp. 85–6.

70 'Reminiscences' by his grandson, Malcolm McInnes, cited in C. Morey, *History of the Presbytery of Wimmera to 1868* (unpublished typescript, 1968), University of Melbourne Archives, p. 104.

71 William Fairweather, North Grafton, to John Dunmore Lang, Sydney, 10 February 1866, NLA, JAF 158/610; Alexander Cameron, Rockymouth, Clarence River, to John Dunmore Lang, Sydney, 9th March 1866, NLA, JAF 158/615.

72 C. A. Fraser, *Historical Sketch of the Presbyterian Church of Kilmore* (Melbourne, 1927), p. 5.

73 Ward, *The Bush Still Burns*; Hamilton, *A Jubilee History of the Presbyterian Church in Victoria*, p. 42.

74 Details are in the Presbyterian Church Archive, Melbourne. See 'Minute Book of the Deacon's Court of the Free Protesting Church of Kilmore', and 'Minute Book of the Session of the Free Protesting Church of Kilmore'. The exact nature of the argument was not recorded in the minutes of the church, however, although it was clearly associated with the choice of language for instruction and services.

75 'Minute book of the Session of the Free Protesting Church of Kilmore'. See also Elizabeth Quinn, 'Roderick Mcleod: No Godless Goat of Wallan', *Kilmore Connections*, June (2002), p. 7.

76 Fraser, *Historical Sketch*, p. 14.

77 Archbishop Polding, Letter July 1856, originally published in the *Catholic Almanac*, reprinted in O'Farrell (ed.), *Documents in Australian Catholic History 1788–1884*, p. 118.

78 *Manual for the Use of the Holy Family* (Sydney, 1884), reprinted in O'Farrell (ed.), *Documents in Australian Catholic History 1788–1884*, p. 340.

79 L. Moore and D. Gome, 'The Not So Dour Scots and Their Hymnody in Victoria 1859–67', *Australian Studies*, Vol. 18, No. 1 (2005), pp. 5–40.

80 Morey, *History of the Presbytery of Wimmera*, p. 104.

81 Moore and Gome, 'The Not So Dour Scots', pp. 5–40.

82 There was further dissension between St George's Kilmore and the Free Presbyterian Church over the proposed Union with other branches of Presbyterians. This led to Andrew Maxwell and Roderick McLeod of Kilmore being expelled from the Free Church in 1857. Ward, *The Bush Still Burns*, p. 190; Quinn, 'Roderick Mcleod: No Godless Goat of Wallan', p. 8.

83 Tucker, *Kilmore on the Sydney Road*, pp. 78–9. The initial vote was introduced on 17 July 1871. The elders did not support the introduction of hymns. See 'Minute book of the Session of the Free Presbyterian church of Kilmore'. Fraser (*Historical Sketch*, p. 33) records that they did. See also R. S. Ward, 'Spiritual Movements', p. 72, on the fact that St George's Church left the Synod in 1857 and did not rejoin until 1867.

84 Fraser, *Historical Sketch*, p. 33; *Kilmore Free Press*, 11 July 1878.

85 Archbishop Polding, 'The pastoral monition of John Bede Polding . . . to the . . . Clergy of the Archdiocese, 1861', reprinted in O'Farrell (ed.), *Documents in Australian Catholic History 1788–1884*, p. 126.

86 D. Hall and L. Proudfoot, 'Memory and Identity among Irish Migrants in Nineteenth-Century Stawell', *Australasian Journal of Irish Studies*, 7 (2007/8), pp. 67–83; B. Linden-Ward, '"Strange but Genteel Pleasure Grounds": Tourist and Leisure Uses of Nineteenth-Century Rural Cemeteries', in R. Meyer (ed.), *Cemeteries and Gravemarkers* (Ann Arbor, 1989), pp. 293–328; H. Mytum, 'Popular Attitudes to Memory, the Body, and Social Identity: The Rise of External Commemoration in Britain, Ireland and New England', *Post-Medieval Archaeology*, Vol. 40, No. 1 (2006), pp. 103–9.

87 C. McConville, 'Cities of the Dead: The New Cemeteries of the Nineteenth Century', *Urban Futures*, Vol. 22, June (1997), pp. 41–5.

88 *Ibid.*, p. 44. Monumental masons published catalogues with different standard designs of gravestones as well as the meanings of carvings. See Morgan Jageurs Monumental Sculptors Catalogue, c. 1896–1900 (Private Collection). Our thanks to Dr Pamela O'Neill for access to this catalogue.

89 F. J. E. Gorman and M. DiBlasi, 'Gravestone Iconography and Mortuary Ideology', *Ethnohistory*, Vol. 28, No. 1 (1981), pp. 79–98.

90 Comparison of graves with extant grave stones was possible for the Stawell/Pleasant Creek cemetery where the cemetery register survives. Field study of the cemetery was then compared with the register and supplemented with vital registration data to determine the place of birth of each person buried in the cemetery. Originals of the cemetery registers are held by the Stawell City Council. 'Stawell (Pleasant Creek) Cemetery Register and Headstones 1858–1983, transcribed by Dorothy King', Stawell Historical Society.

91 C. Campbell, *Emigrants from Sky: Family Saga 1852–1979* (Marnoo, 1979).

92 J. Graham, *A Gerringong Fenian: The Story of John O'Neil Goulding and the 1867 Kerry Rising* (Gerringong Historical Society, n.d.).

93 None of the cemeteries in the Kiama area have extant registers of burials. This analysis is based on field surveys of the Kiama, Jamberoo and Gerringong cemeteries. There is therefore no way of measuring the proportion of burials that either have a headstone or whose headstones record a place of birth.

94 Tucker, *Kilmore on the Sydney Road*, pp. 144–8.

CHAPTER 9

Conclusion

Come in the name of god to a land of freedom and plenty, even though subject to the Saxon yoke . . . Oh may the vengeance of heaven fall upon that bloody government and may we live to witness the dismemberment of her empire, and England sink in the seas by which she is surrounded. (Michael D'Arcy, Adelaide, 1848.[1])

Irishmen prize the freedom and access to equal opportunity which obtain in Australia, and they have never allowed their political power to be warped or dictated by considerations alien to the true interests of this community. (Cardinal Moran, Sydney, 1907.[2])

A stranger on arriving in the colonies is inclined at first to vote the 'Australian' fast, forward and self-opinionative . . . the younger race do not attempt to conceal their dislike to anything and everything English. They forget they are an English speaking race extracted from Britain . . . their motto being 'Australia for the Australians' . . . Long may Australia remain a British possession. Long may Britain remain Queen of the Earth. And long may all the present British subjects sing with zest 'God save our gracious Queen'. (W. J. Douglas, Ballarat, 1892.[3])

Three voices, three spatial narratives, three encounters with Australia and Empire. Michael D'Arcy, disillusioned editor of the radical Irish *Morning Chronicle* in Sydney in the 1840s; Patrick Francis Moran, polemicist and Cullenite prince of the Catholic Church in Australia by the turn of the century; and the perceptive provincial Scottish druggist, W. F. Douglas, each encountered a personal Australia that was as much a subjective construction of their own imagination as an objective material reality. So too did every other Irish and Scottish emigrant who, like their descendants, formed part of the white settler presence on this southern continent during the nineteenth century. That presence was both hegemonic and dialectical. Legitimised and empowered by British imperial discourse, it was contested not merely by the indigenous peoples whom it subordinated and othered, and sometimes brought within its own cautious embrace, but also internally by white groups and individuals who occupied subaltern positions within it. Moreover, as D'Arcy, Moran and Douglas's comments testify, this settler presence also evinced a thorough-going spatial consciousness. It could hardly be otherwise. Each settler's encounter with their chosen new world was the outcome of a long process of geographical translation. Conveyed through real and imagined time-space from the material and perceived worlds of their past, Irish, Scottish and other settlers eventually arrived in a colonial environment which until then had only existed for them as an act of the imagination.

In offering a place-centred analysis of this settler experience we have critiqued the ethnic essentialism that has characterised much settler history in general and Irish-Australian historiography in particular. In doing so, we have argued for increased recognition of the ways in which the complex 'local worlds' construed from place by settlers gave meaning to their experience and understanding of empire. Taking as our premise the inherent spatiality of human existence, we have exemplified the ways in which settlers created and consumed different forms of valorised or semiotic space in pursuit of their everyday lives. This valorisation involved individuals assigning, on the basis of experience and aspiration, specific social, cultural, ethnic, economic and sometimes political significance to the mundane behaviour they themselves engaged in and encountered in others, and to its materialisation in the landscape. These 'sites of meaning' or places were inevitably multivocal and contested, since different people brought different understandings to encounters they shared in particular material locations. Thus Patrick Coady Buckley's engagement with the 'blacks' on the beach at Coadyvale in 1845 held very different meanings for him and the man he dragged through the surf on a rein. For Buckley, the beach apparently became a site of retributive justice; for the Aborigine, a place of near fatal entrapment. Moreover, since the significance people assigned to others' behaviour depended on their own changing experience, so too meanings of place also changed for them. Hence William Wall's increased antipathy towards successive public performances of imperial loyalism at Belfast (Port Fairy) as his sympathies for radical Irish politics deepened during the 1880s.

By adopting this place-centred approach we have, moreover, been able to accommodate the divergent tropes which have characterised recent studies of emigrant experience as diaspora, and which are germane to Irish and Scottish experience within the Empire and beyond. By emphasising the non-essentialist though materialised character of place as a contingent site of agency, memory and meaning, we

[238]

can resolve the tension between understandings of diasporic consciousness as grounded, re-located identity on the one hand, and de-territorialised transnational becoming on the other. In representing place as an imagined *site* of becoming, of inchoate practice and meaning, we recognise the necessarily locatedness of agency and the possibility of it giving rise to material – though possibly quite transient – landscape imprints. In short, in our conceptualisation, place was central to Irish and Scottish diasporic experience as it was to all others', whether in Australia, North America, or elsewhere.

For all of these reasons, we argue that narratives of the British Empire which fail to recognise the complex and contingent localism of British and Irish immigrant experience, or its subjective construction as place, provide an at best partial account of these settlers' experience. This is not to deny the importance of the Empire's great discursive themes – emigration and the expansion of 'Greater Britain', the encounter with the cultural and environmental other, and metropolitan and colonial relations – in framing the local lives enacted through place that we have privileged here. Although we have shown how white settler experience of empire was primarily an encounter with the quotidian and local, we have also demonstrated the extent to which these broader discursive issues obtained purchase on local political and cultural consciousness. But the importance of these discursive contexts lay in their local and immediate effects. For settlers and their descendants, it was the experience of the colonial present, inflected no doubt by these discourses but framed by the immediate horizons of their daily lives, that constituted the 'empire'.

Settler responses to colonial land legislation exemplify the point. Grounded in the materiality of their colonial existence, squatters like Charles MacKnight at Dunmore, William Moodie at Wando Dale, or Robert Scott at Mount Boninyong, performed their narratives of place, their 'local worlds', in the spaces created by sometimes conflicting discourses of modernity and improvement, indigeneity and environmental understanding. In turn, all of these were mediated by colonial land laws that formed part of a wider imperial discourse of land allocation. This underwrote settler experience in the peripheral colonies of white settlement as it had done, historically, in the 'internal colonies' of the metropolitan core – Ireland and Scotland. In effect, therefore, for individual squatters the discursive environmental, economic and cultural spaces of pastoralism in Australia were shaped by the imperatives of the wider imperial political economy. Yet for these individuals, the Fetherstonhaughs, Learmonths and MacKnights of pastoral Australia, this wider imperial purpose (and the conflicts of interest between the colonial and metropolitan authorities which it engendered) only had instrumental significance insofar as it impinged on their daily life. Thus the primary concern for most squatters under the Selection Acts of the 1860s was the preservation of their property, not calculations of the wider social good of the sort that drove Duffy's Land Act in Victoria in 1862.

Nevertheless, as Michael O'Reilly's strictures on squatting as editor of *The Banner of Belfast* testify, for some settlers these discursively framed local worlds were also inflected by the past. Accordingly, as we have emphasised throughout our discussion, they raise issues concerning colonial identity construction and the importance to this of memory and origins. For O'Reilly, the unusual pattern of landownership on the Belfast and Farnham Special Surveys and the hegemonic presence there of landlords of protestant Irish origin provided more than sufficient grounds for a comparison with landlordism in Ireland. Initially, O'Reilly drew these comparisons in an entirely negative and hostile fashion. Appealing to claimed collective memories of landlord oppression in Ireland, he highlighted what for him was the danger of this reappearing in Australia under the guise of squatting. At this point, in the early 1850s, his comparisons were stark, implicitly sectarian, and essentialist, and adopted the same bitter rhetoric of alienation and exclusion that Michael D'Arcy had used in Sydney a few years earlier. With the passage of time, however, as the allegedly negative imprints of landlordism around Belfast (Port Fairy) faded under the relentless impact of changing colonial circumstance, so O'Reilly's essentialism gave way to a wider social vision which placed less emphasis on the remembered ills of the past. In short, O'Reilly's performance of Belfast as place altered as radically as William Wall's was to do twenty years later. But whereas Wall, an Australian native, responded to the cultural prompting of his Irish-born parents' generation by privileging and radicalising the Irish dimension to his identity, O'Reilly's representations became increasingly inclusive of other, non-Irish, marginalised groups. For O'Reilly, the essentialism of ethno-national memory gave way to a broader grounding in the colonial present. For Wall, acquired memory served to heighten the exclusiveness of his understanding of the past and harden its effect on his performance of place in the present.

These differences in the way memory acted to inform the behaviour of two members of the Irish diaspora, whose lives briefly overlapped in the material spaces of Belfast, remind us once again of the individualism as well as the localism of settler experience. But they also point to the ambiguous part played by ethnic consciousness in the narrations of place performed by Irish, Scots and other settlers as part of their imagined local worlds in Australia. Our argument has been that the ethnic diversity of the nineteenth-century British and Irish migration stream to Australia added hitherto under-regarded cultural complexity to the hegemonic white presence on that continent. On the one hand, most postcolonial analyses of empire have been written 'from the margins', privileging indigenous experience and the complex and ambiguous ways in which the subaltern non-white self-responded to the European other. Few studies in this genre have explored the ethnic and racial diversity of white emigration to the colonies of settlement as an end in itself, or examined the implications of this for the experience of empire for indigenes and settlers alike. On the other hand, most empiricist representations of Irish emigration in general and Irish settlement in Australia in particular have tended towards ethno-national essential-ism, privileging in a frequently un-reflexive way only the Gaelic/Catholic version of 'Irishness' as truly authentic. To be Irish was to be Catholic and a Gael.

In rejecting this sort of primordialism we have argued for a different understanding of ethnicity that stresses its performative and contin-gent nature. Claims to ethnicity arise out of individual performances of the self that express a particular cultural consciousness shared with a wider solidarity. This sense of common cultural selfhood may invoke religion and language, almost certainly a sense of shared history, and possibly regional affiliation. Despite this, ethnicity is not a synonym for either nationality or race: different imagined nations may contain numerous ethnic groups or traditions, as we have argued to be the case in Ireland. Thus the Irish migration stream (i.e. the flow of people from Ireland) contained various ethnic traditions claiming descent from dif-ferent periods in the country's history in a complex mix of religion, culture, language and genetics. Gaels, Vikings, Huguenots, Lowland Scots, Welsh, Flemings, Southern English, Dissenters, Anglicans, Presbyterians, Catholics, monoglot Irish and Lallans speakers, all either once had, or in the nineteenth century still continued to contribute to its ethnic diversity.

It is this sort of anciently rooted but still vital ethnic complexity that essentialist representations of Irish and, for that matter, Scots settlement in Australia have obscured. More than this, because ethnic consciousness derives from the active assertion of claims to a particu-lar cultural identity, it has to be actively maintained. Consequently it is capable of either diminishing or strengthening over time and space. The evidence we have presented here highlights this, and suggests that although ethnic consciousness informed many aspects of Irish and Scottish settler life, it was invariably mediated by other factors such as social status, economic and political circumstance, and the strength and nature of existing associational networks. Accordingly, expres-sions of Scottish and Irish ethnicity in narratives of place were rarely clear cut, but instead formed part of a continuing process of identity negotiation which connected the settler's colonial present with their diasporic past in various ways.

The ambiguity of these ethnic imprints and the sometimes muted expressions of cultural memory associated with them have constituted a recurrent theme throughout this book. On the ships that carried the Scots, Irish and others from their known past to their imagined future, the cramped social terrain reified boundaries of all kinds, but for cabin passengers a least, rarely in an explicitly ethnicised way. Only among the government-assisted emigrants occupying the more egalitarian spaces of the lower decks do overt collective expressions of ethnicity appear to have been common. And, save for the eternally 'othered' Catholics, even these appear to have been as much a function of the ships' surveillance regime as the emigrants' own cultural consciousness. Once ashore, the vast distances and 'timeless' spaces of the Australian landscape appear to have elicited various performances of place by Scottish and Irish squatters. Once again, these speak to the individualism of their experience. Many if not most of their material imprints in the colonial landscape were innocent of cultural memory and ethnic meaning, although Scottish and Irish toponyms, and more rarely, architectural forms, occasionally spoke of the remembered past. But if these material spaces of Irish and Scottish colonial pastoralism were largely presentist in character, they might still be enacted as place through lives which imbued them with ethnic meaning through the maintenance of familial and other cultural networks. Thus Acheson Ffrench at Monivae and the Scotts at Mount Boninyong celebrated their Irish and Scottish origins in various performative and non-material ways. At Ercildoune, on the other hand, the Learmonths – also for their own reasons – memorialised their Scottish upbringing in stone.

But if Scots and Irish ethnic consciousness found private and variable expression in the exclusive cabin accommodation of the poop deck and the intimate domestic spaces of pastoral stations, we have demonstrated that in other narratives of place its imprint could be overt, collective and contested. Anglican, Catholic and Presbyterian churches all provided material space in which hegemonic and subaltern understandings of particular denominational truths could be negotiated, and their consequences for the new lives being led by the faithful in Australia worked out. These negotiations were as thoroughly discursively framed as the colonial land legislation and equally robustly contested. Moreover, the elision for many people between religious affiliation, cultural memory and consciousness, and regional if not national origins, ensured that these discursive and contested local negotiations possessed a distinctly ethnic flavour. Churches of all denominations became, in short,

[242]

places where diasporic identities were continuously redefined. First, in response to the continuing claims to customary social, cultural and moral authority being made by the newly translated colonial Church on the one hand; and second, to attempts by the laity to locate themselves within the relatively liberal social spaces of the colonies on the other. Consequently, local churches supported multiple narratives of place that could be subversive of the very clerical authority they were commonly thought to embody. Such was the case during Archbishop Goold's celebrated attempts to exert his authority over local Catholic church building in Victoria in the 1850s, or when Ulster-born members of the congregation expressed their dislike of Patrician symbols in the Anglican church at Jamberoo in the 1870s.

It appears, therefore, that in the colonial Churches providing for the needs of Irish and Scottish settlers, shared ethnic consciousness was no guarantee of uniformly essentialist narratives of place. This was also true of the performative spaces periodically created in colonial towns by annual ethno-national commemorations and associational events, such as St Patrick's Day and the Loyal Orange Order's celebrations of the Twelfth of July. Despite their reputation as celebrations of particularly atavistic (and thoroughly opposed) cultural values grounded in different moments in Irish history, the Australian evidence indicates not only that these events were frequently culturally hybrid but also that their performance, and the transient semiotic spaces this created in the streets of Melbourne and other towns, was thoroughly contingent on wider imperial events. Thus after 1868, performances of Irish loyalism on the streets of Australian towns continued to be this and more, as they caught the wider colonial mood and gave expression to an imperial loyalism revivified by O'Farrell's attempt to assassinate the Duke of Edinburgh. Equally, towards the end of the nineteenth century, St Patrick's Day Parades in Melbourne became increasingly hybrid affairs as different ethno-national groups participated in the spectacle in ways which subverted any essentialist meaning it may once have had. Tellingly, however, the demands of the Church and the discursive effects of Irish Nationalism ensured that this brief period of increasing cultural hybridity was more or less over by 1911.

This reminder of the performative character, cultural ambiguity, and time-space contingency of these most 'authentic' of Irish events in Australia draws us back to our fundamental argument, and provides an apt point on which to conclude. The narratives of place imagined and enacted by Irish and Scottish settlers and their children in Australia formed part of inchoate and polyvocal cartographies that bore witness to the ethnic diversity and quotidian spatiality of the European presence on that continent. As in other parts of the empire, colonial settlement in Victoria and New South Wales was the outcome of individual and collective understanding and aspiration informed by memory and experience. None of this was essentialist; none of it primordial. As experience and understanding grew, so the significance of memory altered and constructions of the self changed. So too did the ascriptions of place that constituted part of this. Mutually formative, self and place provided a continuously changing rubric for the construction of the local worlds that gave the settlers' existence meaning in Australia.

It is difficult, accordingly, to continue to feel comfortable with representations of the Irish and Scots in colonial Australia that privilege a primordial understanding of ethnicity as the main driver of their behaviour. Understandable though the felt need to do this may be in the case of Ireland, given that country's troubled and contested modern history, such essentialism merely perpetuates division and ensures that our future is held hostage to our past. Much the same might be said of Scotland. Despite its less contentious political history, it continues to occupy an equally subordinate place within the United Kingdom, and has witnessed the emergence of an times cautious, but at others, strident, Scottish nationalism. Above all, the dangers and limitations of such binary essentialism should be evident to Australia's historians. 'Black armband' history speaks not merely of the country's racialised past, but also of the ways its chooses to represent itself *to itself* in the present. The places we have explored here suggest that a more nuanced accommodation is possible.

Notes

1   Michael D'Arcy, Adelaide, to David D'Arcy, Ireland, 23 September 1848, D'Arcy family letters, 1841–1851, to family in Ireland, NLA Ms 5368.
2   'Notes: Speech at St Patrick's Day, Sydney, 1907, Cardinal Moran presiding', Hugh Mahon Papers, NLA Ms 937
3   W. J. Douglas, 'Illustrated journal containing pasted-in lithograph newspaper illustrations, dried leaves and flowers of native flora, and excerpts from local newspapers', W. J. Douglas Diary and Letters, 1891–1894, NLA Ms 1629/1.

INDEX